PASTORAL FORMS AND ATTITUDES

PASTORAL
Forms and Attitudes

HAROLD E. TOLIVER

UNIVERSITY OF CALIFORNIA PRESS
BERKELEY   LOS ANGELES   LONDON   1971

University of California Press
Berkeley and Los Angeles, California
University of California Press, Ltd.
London, England
Copyright © 1971 by The Regents of the University of California
ISBN: 0-520-01896-6
Library of Congress Catalog Card Number: 74-142747

Designed by W. H. Snyder
Printed in the United States of America

To Brooks and Tricia

Preface

So variable a form as pastoral, with its capacity to devour elegies, lyrics, plays, fairy tales, masques, odes, and even to gnaw ambitiously at romances, epics, and novels, is especially challenging and likely to have different kinds of implication for practical criticism. Whether or not the texts examined here need all be considered "pastorals" is not as important finally as our discovering something in them through this lens that would be less noticeable through another. Thus in attempting not to deprive the idea of the genre of its potential usefulness, I have extended the principles of the old shepherd poem freely to literature that abandons many of its conventions while illustrating its theme and attitudes. Most critics who have dealt with pastoral theoretically since Empson's *Some Versions of Pastoral* have done the same, among them Renato Poggioli, Leo Marx, and John Lynen. Though the conventions of pastoral that are first identifiable in the idylls and eclogues of Theocritus and Virgil are obviously important to a theory of pastoral, too many themes and strategies converge even in earlier texts to make conventions the dominant interest of the form; and when we add the equally important themes that Ovid contributes to the tradition, the possibilities of the form increase several fold. Fairy tale marvels, romance journeys, the domestic trials of fishermen and housewives, the immanence of gods capable of granting or taking away paradise, the seasons and biological life that are the context of pastoral games and activities, the collision of social attitudes, the incongruity of certain intruders in Arcadia's idyllic place, the tension between naturalness and artifice, and metamorphosis are a few of pastoral's recurrent concerns. Moreover, literary forms do not develop in a vacuum but respond continuously to pressures of a complex kind, from social history to discoveries in science to the impact of individual poets who have reconceived inherited conventions in the light of their own experience. The historical vagaries of pastoral require that we practice sociological as well as generic criticism at times. Conventions and inventiveness, creation and imitation, established form and changing social contexts wage such an indecisive battle in the history of pastoral that neither formalistic nor sociological criticism can deal with it satisfactorily unless they learn to keep channels open to each other.

In order not to place too many initial barriers between the reader and the main texts to be examined, I have consigned some largely thematic and formalistic matters to appendixes, one of which considers the Ovidian elements in the pastoral tradition and should be read primarily in conjunction with the essays on Sidney, Spenser, and Shakespeare.

Because studies of the main figures considered here, Sidney, Spenser, Shakespeare, Herbert, Marvell, Milton, Pope, Wordsworth, Keats, Hardy, Bellow, Stevens, and Frost, have proliferated in the six years during which this book has been in the making, I have not been able to engage relevant criticism as often as I would have liked. With a few exceptions, I have not added citations of articles and books appearing after 1965. I am especially indebted to those who have written about pastoral in a theoretical way, and those whom I have used for particular purposes are mentioned in appropriate places. My general debt to Kenneth Burke and William Empson will be obvious; I have disagreed with Renato Poggioli's article "The Oaten Flute" freely, as one does only with interesting and useful criticism. I am grateful to the John Simon Guggenheim Memorial Foundation for providing an unencumbered year in 1963–64 and to several readers since then whose criticism has caused the main outlines to emerge more clearly than in early drafts. One section of chapter eight concerning Pope has been published previously, in *Concerning Poetry* (1968).

Contents

ONE

Pastoral Contrasts

The specific critical tasks that follow may come into focus more easily if we begin with some of the broadest implications of the idyllic element of pastoral—usually imaged as a paradisal place where *"Sei piace, ei lice,"* or where "if you like it you may have it"—which habitually calls forth an opposite and promotes a variety of "perspective by incongruity." Whether the scene is an explicit Arcadian society or some place of enclosed quiet, it is likely to be exposed to such things as industrialism, death, unrequited love, unjust property division, or merely an opposing idea of perfection.[1] D. H. Law-

[1] Virgil's eclogues, for instance, employ the following dialectical pairings. In the first eclogue, Meliboeus and Tityrus, having fallen into entirely opposite fortunes, "match" them in dialogue. In the second, Corydon burns for love of Alexis and without much hope tries to win him; the eclogue is in effect a rhetorical match between them, though Corydon is technically alone when he speaks, one coaxing, the other resisting. In the third, Menalcas and Damoetus, two scoundrels at odds with their society, fall into a singing contest somewhat rougher than usual. In the fourth, the Golden Age is described in terms of a crowning transformation of the present, implicitly an iron age. The urgency of the poem is increased by the rhetorical appeal of the poet to the child to begin the new age soon and by his own proposed ascendancy over Pan as the poet of that age. In the fifth, Menalcas encounters Mopsus, and their songs compose the tragicomic movement of the elegy, first dirge and then rejoicing, interlaced with references to other kinds of competition. In the sixth, after a general reference to competition among poets with respect to the weight of their undertakings, the speaker presents the songs of old Silenus, who has been in sporting competition with two boys. He now sings to them to free himself from their bonds. The songs themselves are concerned with marvelous transformations of Apollo, and they rise to the stars, the imagery generally being of constriction transcended through poetry. In the seventh, a contest between Corydon

rence touches upon a typical pastoral contrast when he remarks that "a conquered universe, a dead Pan, leaves us nothing to live with. . . . And whether we are a store-clerk or a bus-conductor, we can still choose between the living universe of

and Thrysis is contained in an outer narrative of Meliboeus, whose "work" is countered by their "pastime." In the eighth, a previous contest between Damon and Alphesiboeus is recited and reveals two inner matches between lovers, one that has dissolved in nos-talgia as the lover is thought to be about to die unrequited and the other having led to an attempt to enchant a reluctant lover through magic. In the ninth, Moeris has been turned off his farm as politics and war invade the normal peace of Arcadia. The tenth concerns the anguish of Gallus over hapless love.

Love in these poems is treated as a yearning for what one can-not possess, not as the unrestricted erotic indulgence of softer and less anguished Arcadias; it underlies many of the artificial pastoral devices of ornamental lament, beseeching, and melancholy resigna-tion that characterize the songs of shepherds in the tradition. (The songs themselves offer some consolation for its woes and contribute to its passivity.)

William Empson in *Some Versions of Pastoral* (London: Chatto and Windus, 1935) and Renato Poggioli in "The Oaten Flute," *Harvard Library Bulletin*, 11 (1957), 147–184, stress aspects of pastoral quite different from these strategic contrasts. Poggioli writes: "The function of pastoral poetry is to translate to the plane of imagination man's sentimental reaction against compulsory labor, social obligations, and ethical bonds; yet, while doing so, it acts as the catharsis of its own inner pathos, and sublimates the instinctual impulses to which it gives outlet. It therefore performs with especial intensity the role that Freud assigns to art in gen-eral: that of acting as vicarious compensation for the renunciations imposed by the social order on its individual members, and of rec-onciling men to the sacrifices they have made in civilization's behalf" (p. 174). Though quite valid in itself, this view leads to a puzzling generic notion: "The poetic of the pastoral fully reveals that its subgenres must be reduced to the common denominator of the lyric mode. The *epyllion* is not epic; the pastoral romance is not narrative; pastoral drama is not dramatic." While most idyllic moments are lyric, "pastorals" as distinct from idyllic passages are often dramatic, and even relatively pure idyllic moments fit well into epic and dramatic modes such as *Paradise Lost* and *As You Like It*. We can avoid some basic difficulties by not arbitrarily ex-cluding prosaic and dramatic elements from pastoral and by ob-serving closely the ways in which even "vicarious compensations" encounter reality indirectly as they seem to dodge it.

Pan, and the mechanical conquered universe of modern humanity" ("Pan in America," *Phoenix*). Traditionally, such contrasts not only vary a good deal from one period to another but tend to elicit different potentials from the pastoral setting according to how it is opposed. When "society" and "nature" are juxtaposed, for instance, such characteristics as the following emerge:

NATURE	SOCIETY
freedom	constriction
organicism	mechanical formality
democracy	hierarchy
plainness and honesty	masked artificiality
innocence, simplicity	experience, complexity
barbaric violence	cultured order

When opposed to art, nature becomes something quite different:

NATURE	ART
rough, inchoate	ordered, ornate
open, indefinite	timeless, permanent, enclosed
existential, immediate	artificial, imitative

Divided against itself, it becomes:

IDYLLIC NATURE	ANTIPASTORAL NATURE
vernal or cyclical	wintry
humanized	indifferent or cruel
place of love and renewal	place of unrequited love, age

Or finally, if divided into levels:

NATURE	CELESTIAL PARADISE
temporal garden or Golden Age	apocalyptic sacred place
lesser gods (Venus, Pan, Cupid)	Hebraic or Christian God
shepherds and rustics	angels
mechanical or botanical nature	sublime nature

Such contrasts permeate the pastoral tradition from Theocritus to the eighteenth century and create similar tensive structures in pastorals with less definite conventions thereafter.

Not all pastoral makes explicit or full use of them, however. At one extreme, in the pure idyll, the poet leaves it largely to the reader to remember whatever contrasts the normative world affords—as Marlowe's passionate shepherd ignores the harsher realities that occur to Raleigh, Donne, and C. Day Lewis in their answers to him. At the opposite extreme, forms of realism and naturalism concentrate on what *is* rather than what *might be* or what *ought to be,* even when the setting seems designed to capitalize on pastoral contrasts. Robinson Crusoe on his semiparadisal island, for instance, is absorbed almost completely in material goods that can be arranged, labeled, traded for other goods, consumed, or wielded against those who would subtract from the total—with provender and produce, with seeds, slaves, goats, waterholes, linens, and other aspects of a pragmatic life. His basic impulses are closer to georgic than to pastoral in that he watches over the processes of fertility and renewal by which nature, through timely and efficient labor, is coaxed from a dormant period, brought to fruition, and prepared for harvest. Pastoral nature is more ceremonial than useful; it has no need of planting, cultivation, or harvest, and its periodic renewal is less economic than symbolic or miraculous. Crusoe begins where the pastoral phase of Milton's Adam ends, as he is exiled to a landscape that requires management and contains dangers. Crusoe progresses from that primitive georgic occupation to the more complex economy of the marketplace and toward the social relations of the more typical documentary novel whose society belongs to the drawing room and city.

Such enterprising programs of accretion as Crusoe's assume the importance of possession and property distinctions—which as a French anarchist once insisted, cause one to be inspected, directed, docketed, indoctrinated, assessed, taxed, valued, admonished, extorted, squeezed, hoaxed, and betrayed, among other things unknown to Adam. A pastoral society, in contrast, is noncompetitive or else converts a limited competition into such games and ceremonies as the friendly exchanges of rival singers. To the winner, the society of shepherds offers humble gifts more ornamental than practical. A pastoralist writing in this tradition might not have given Crusoe's island greater abundance than Defoe does, but the scene would have yielded its gifts much more easily, and if capital expansion had proved unavoidable, every increase would have brought a corresponding loss in simplicity and quiet. That Defoe is not concerned with such pastoral devices and themes is of course no criticism of *Robinson Crusoe* as a novel: the point here is a limited one, that where the potential contrasts between a golden age and the normative world are not exploited, we do not have the dialectical, tensive structure characteristic of all worthwhile pastoral.

Such a structure is not in itself difficult to isolate as an abiding feature of pastoral, but it operates on many levels and changes significantly in the evolution of pastoral forms. One of the tasks of a theory of pastoral is to explain the interaction of these levels and to use them to gauge the influence of the social and intellectual context on variations of pastoral form. Obviously lyrics, odes, elegies, romances, and novels and epics with pastoral elements handle that tension quite differently, and every period interprets and reconstitutes them in its own ways.

LEVELS OF PASTORAL

When we consider the images of the golden age that the classical and Christian tradition bequeathed to the Renaissance, it becomes clear that they tend to arrange themselves not as equals but as elements of a dynamic, vertical spectrum. A given shepherd may pass from one of these levels to another, undergoing a metamorphosis from a rustic figure to a devotional celebrator of the gods, for instance, as the poem transposes from one style to another. Marvell's shepherdess Clorinda does something like this, as she begins by trying to entice Damon into simple rustic pleasures and then joins him in a hymn to great Pan or Christ. The following shepherd's song from the renaissance collection *England's Helicon* is typical in putting its combination of levels in terms of musical styles, one level based on the humble literary shepherd of the tradition,

the other on a vision he has of the shepherd's possible elevation:

> Sweete Musique, sweeter farre
> Then any Song is sweete:
> Sweete Musique heavenly rare,
> Mine eares (O peeres) dooth greete.
> You gentle flocks, whose fleeces pearl'd with dewe,
> Resemble heaven, whom golden drops make bright:
> Listen, O listen, now, O not to you
> Our pipes make sport to shorten wearie night,
> But voyces most divine
> Make blisfull Harmonie:
> Voyces that seem to shine,
> For what else cleares the skie?
> Tunes can we heare, but not the Singers see:
> The tunes divine, and so the Singers be.
> . . . .
> For loe the worlds great Sheepheard now is borne
> A blessed Babe, an Infant full of power:
> After long night, up-risen is the morne,
> Renowning *Bethlem* in the Saviour.
> Sprung is the perfect day,
> By Prophets seen a farre:
> Sprung is the mirthfull May,
> Which Winter cannot marre,
> In *Davids* Cittie dooth this Sunne appeare:
> Clouded in flesh, yet Sheepheards sit we here.
> ["The Sheepheards Song," E. B., *England's Helicon*]

The pagan shepherd who provides the starting point for such
transformations from sportive pipes to "blisfull Harmonie"
Renato Poggioli describes as one who

by picking berries and gathering straw . . . may fill his bowl
and build a roof over his head. This redeems him from the
curse of work, which is part of man's estate, and the specific
lot of the peasant, who earns his daily bread by the sweat of his
brow. It is this triumph of the "days" over the "works," rather
than the mere replacement of a rural with a pastoral setting
that marks the difference between the bucolic and the georgic.
. . . The shepherd of fiction is likewise neither a pioneer nor
a settler, but rather a homesteader, or better, a stay-at-home;
he is never a nomad, as real shepherds are often forced to be.

He lives a sedentary life even in the open, since he prefers to linger in a grove's shade rather than to wander in the woods. He never confronts the true wild, and this is why he never becomes even a part time hunter.[2]

This traditional literary shepherd is so lowly and unambitious that he requires a miraculous change to become a citizen of David's city.

Even in Theocritus and Virgil, however, he occasionally reaches surprising heights. We find the rustic and the sacred mixed almost from the outset in the pastoral tradition. In Virgil's fourth eclogue, for instance, Arcadia is newly exalted by the consulate of "Pollio," which some commentators in the Renaissance read allegorically as the coming of the Christian reign:

> Muses of Sicily, sing we a somewhat ampler strain: not all men's delight is in coppices and lowly tamarisks: if we sing of the woods, let them be woods worthy of a Consul.
> Now is come the last age of the Cumaean prophecy: the great cycle of periods is born anew. . . . In thy consulate, in thine, O Pollio, shall this glorious age enter. . . . He shall grow in the life of gods, and shall see gods and heroes mingled.[3]

The romantics, too, contrast the "intimations of immortality" that nature makes possible to the common men who are most available to receive them. Wordsworth's pastoral manifesto in the *Preface to the Lyrical Ballads* calls for a new marriage between the lowly and the exalted; Keats's mortal shepherd Endymion seeks the love of a high goddess; and Shelley's Adonais is translated from the realm of physical nature to a quite different realm of Platonist verities. Modern figures such as Bellow's Henderson and Frost's rural speakers are "rustic" and yet capable of commerce with higher powers.[4]

---

[2] Poggioli, "The Oaten Flute," p. 152.

[3] Fourth Eclogue, from *Virgil's Works,* trans. J. W. Mackail (New York: Random House, 1950).

[4] In slightly lower ranges, pastoral's ampler strain has a kinship with folklore and fairy myth, the happy reversals and marvelous

Though the central figure in these levels is no longer a shepherd after the classical conventions of pastoral disappear, patterns of contrast and transformation are repeated in unexpected places in modern texts. Since our concern later will be not only traditional forms of pastoral but also their metamorphosed modern equivalents, I will pause long enough on an example here to suggest ways in which recurrent pastoral attitudes have assumed new forms. One of the more striking examples of transformation and the dialectical conflict of levels is G. K. Chesterton's novel *The Man Who Was Thursday*. Chesterton initially contrasts simply anarchists and lovers of order, but these unmask and turn into one another in a strange comic pantomime of opposites reminiscent of riot and order in the old pastoral masque and antimasque. Chesterton eventually translates his "masquers" into somewhat startled and awed archetypes of the divine creator's peace and the devil's chaos, and looking backward from that conclusion we realize that various episodes have foreshadowed the pageant of the six days' creation. The "wood of witchery," for instance, gives us a glimpse of the cosmic dimensions of the contest:

The sun on the grass was dry and hot. So in plunging into the wood they had a cool shock of shadow, as of divers who plunge into a dim pool. The inside of the wood was full of shattered sunlight and shaken shadows. They made a sort of shuddering veil, almost recalling the dizziness of a cinematograph. Even the solid figures walking with him Syme could hardly see for the patterns of sun and shade that danced upon them. Now a man's head was lit as with a light of Rembrandt, leaving all else obliterated; now again he had a strong and

---

transformations of which Tolkien describes as an "eucatastrophe" in which we see "in a brief vision . . . a far-off gleam or echo of *evangelium*." Whereas in explicit pastoral, such an *evangelium* is grafted onto clear reminders of Virgil's prophetic eclogue or the Christian equivalent, in the fairy tale it is a miraculous reversal of unspecified origin. A sacred cause reveals itself behind the apparently capricious and cruel surface of nature, and lowly people are given a sense of *Gloria* higher than anything they could have imagined. See *The Tolkien Reader* (New York: Ballantine Books, 1966), p. 74.

staring white hands with the face of a negro. . . . Was anyone wearing a mask? Was anyone hiding anything? This
wood of witchery, in which men's faces turned black and
white by turns, in which their figures first swelled into sunlight
and then faded into formless night, this mere chaos of chiar-
oscuro (after the clear daylight outside) seemed to Syme a perfect symbol of the world in which he had been moving for
three days, this world where men took off their beards and
their spectacles and their noses, and turned into other people.
. . . He found the thing which the modern people call Im-
pressionism, which is another name for that final scepticism
which can find no floor to the universe.[5]

But Chesterton quickly removes the figures in the chase from
the forest, where these opposites shatter and shake each other
by a succession that leads toward "final scepticism"; he sets
them securely in the sunlight of the comedy, where sinister
plots can be easily converted into the farcical plotting of God's
cops and robbers. There the people of the seven days are transformable into the "works of nature during the creation" presided over by Sabbath, the "peace of God . . . contentment,
optimism . . . and ultimate reconciliation," which links the
daily cycles to their archetypal source. These seven days become aspects of the divine being entering a temporal phase
where it unfolds as veiled or masked becoming. The transformational goal of the book might be described as the saving
of the idyllic feeling by a conversion of sinister elements into
lighthearted playthings, all mobsters becoming picnickers, and
so on up the scale to Eden's creation and the devil's ineffectual
resistance.

Such transformations, spells of magic, and unmaskings of
obscure divine and demonic forces, are recurrent themes of
pastoral romances and masques. But the presence of higher
levels of idyllic peace may also be a source of nostalgic longing
or despair if the "shepherd" is unable to find the key to transformation. In the elegy, the shepherd's lament is often left
unresolved, or the poet may simply look backward from a
distance toward a time when gods and goddesses appeared to

[5] G. K. Chesterton, *The Man Who Was Thursday* (London,
1937), pp. 127–128.

lowly shepherds and made possible miraculous changes from wintry blight to vernal renewal.

The paradisal archetype is useful to gain perspective on such situations beyond cure, and it too crops up in a variety of modern texts. In Strindberg's *Miss Julie*, for instance, the main characters (Miss Julie and Jean the valet) are tempted to think that they can put aside class differences and other barriers between them and recapture the freedom of a classless society. But their positions prove incompatible with that hope: those below on the social scale cannot avoid the need to advance, and those on top cannot escape their own suicidal impulse to leap down. The dream of transcending property and station recoils upon them destructively. Moreover, the dream itself is plagued by hierarchy:

Julie. . . . . Life, human beings, everything, just scum drifting about on the water until it sinks—down and down. That reminds me of a dream I sometimes have, in which I'm on top of a pillar and can't see any way of getting down. When I look down I'm dizzy; I have to get down but I haven't the courage to jump. I can't stay there and I long to fall, but I don't fall. There's no respite. There can't be any peace at all for me until I'm down, right down on the ground. And if I did get to the ground I'd want to be under the ground. . . . Have you ever felt like that?
Jean. No. In my dream I'm lying under a great tree in a dark wood. I want to get up, up to the top of it, and look out over the bright landscape where the sun is shining and rob that high nest of its golden eggs. And I climb and climb, but the trunk is so thick and smooth and it's so far to the first branch.[6]

Jean's paradise is hemmed around with the same guilt and fear that infect all hierarchy: "If it's true that a thief can get to heaven and be with angels, it's pretty strange that a labourer's child here on God's earth mayn't come in the park and play with the Count's daughter." The park of the Count is a "Garden of Eden," but it is also "guarded by many terrible angels with flaming swords"; it contains the tree of life but also the forbidden apple. After the daughter has been in fact

[6] August Strindberg, *Miss Julie,* trans. Elizabeth Sprigge (London: Constable, 1955), pp. 83–84.

"played with," Jean confesses that even when he watched her among the roses from his onion patch "I had the same dirty thoughts as all boys." "Infernal" realities break through the dreams, which collapse into the minimal realities of biology and common sinfulness. The only course remaining for Julie is to seek "peace" underground, and for Jean to resume the empty life of the servant. As to transformation: the magical power of the Midsummer Eve festival allows Jean to play with the new identity he imagines for himself and encourages Julie to "come down," because only if they "sleep in nine midsummer flowers" will their "dreams . . . come true." The awakening finds them beyond the reach of pastoral's benevolent atmosphere.

Both Chesterton's novel of fantasy and Strindberg's play illustrate modern versions of pastoral's fluid exchange of identities and the vicarious participation of levels and classes in each other. In the elegy, the shepherd mourners sometimes awake to a sacred influence beyond nature's ordinary surface and discover death redefined as transfiguration; in the old pastoral masque, courtiers pretending for an evening to be shepherds discover ancient powers in nature that have been concealed from them in their more rigidly costumed moments; in pastoral romance, a knightly wanderer stumbles upon a pastoral realm where his heroic pursuits are held in abeyance while he shares in a shepherd life that, though below him and foreign to him, is possessed of a natural simplicity and magical atmosphere. The interpenetration of levels in these variations of pastoral is not merely the wooing of hierarchical social elements that Empson finds central to pastoral but also a discovery of unfamiliar dimensions of nature and a common sacred ground in the landscape, the mysteries and primitive symbols of which are so basic that all participants in them are "leveled" upward.

THE POEM AS PASTORAL ENCLOSURE

A related theme in many pastorals is the contrast between reality and the poem itself, as a fictional construction—as its own kind of transforming locality capable of reshaping nature

in art (to make "poetic" is in part to "pastoralize"), and one of
the important threads in the evolution of pastoral is the shift-
ing relationship between the poetic enclosure and the exterior
world. Poggioli writes of the conventional shepherd figure that
he "represents man neither as *homo sapiens* nor as *homo faber,*
but only as *homo artifex:* or more simply, as a musician and a
poet." [7] This association of the poet with the shepherd and of
the poem with Arcadia comes about partly because when
shepherds retreat to an enclosed and harbored world of song
they are in a privileged position to indicate the nature of
aesthetic distance and poetic transformations of reality. The
force of the analogy between the poem and paradise is evident
when whole books of verse in the Renaissance are taken to be
bowers of bliss in which a reader can browse for idyllic or
erotic pleasure.

An Arcadian retreat is not necessarily a lyric sublimation of
unpleasantries, however (as Poggioli suggests); it is an image
of nature so clearly artful as to suggest openly the poet's inevitable improvements on it. (If the poet assumes that reality is
badly arranged or scattered, he may imagine its possible recon-
struction in the order of words as perhaps the only reconstruc-
tion it is likely to receive.) The analogy between a poem and
a perfect landscape holds to some extent even when the poet
makes no explicit claim for it. Consider Emily Dickinson's
description of a storm:

> The leaves unhooked themselves from trees
> And started all abroad;
> The dust did scoop itself like hands
> And threw away the road.

The storm is scarcely gentle, but the stanza cannot help tam-
ing its violence and suggesting a *locus amoenus* or pleasant
place in spite of itself. It humanizes the leaves and the dust
and appeases our desire to find correspondences between the
human and the natural world. (The two sentences develop in
units of eight and six syllables in almost identical metrical
arrangements, syntax, and grammar: the twenty-eight syllables

---

[7] Poggioli, "The Oaten Flute," p. 167.

move in exact formation, commanding the event to take part in their poetic ritual.) Though these elements do not make the stanza explicitly pastoral, they do in a sense quiet discord and produce a pastoral harmony and transformation. With its "rhyme" of daily and seasonal recurrence, its songs, and its graciously integral harmony, paradise often converges aesthetic ideal and scene in this way. That literary shepherds should spend more time singing than tending sheep is entirely in keeping with the impulse that a pastoral place indulges to celebrate nature rather than improve it with the georgic arts of the gardener or the home economist.

Rather than imposing a total harmony on nature, however, pastoralists in the main tradition usually suggest that paradise is beyond the reach even of poetry. It stands apart as the poet tries to imagine it, so that his description of it becomes a self-conscious artifice. Arcadia's dreamlike quality is especially marked from the romantics onward, as poets find it difficult to reconcile the harbored bowers of pastoral with a world given over increasingly to industry and social strife. The poet must come forth from his dreams, Moneta tells the Keatsian dreamer in "The Fall of Hyperion," and speak directly to the social problems of the times: he must put his pastoral vision to use as social therapy. At the same time, the poet cannot claim too much for whatever therapy poetry and its idyllic dreams may work on its subject or on the minds it touches, since it is after all merely verbal. "Every good poem is very nearly a Utopia," W. H. Auden writes, an idyllic "community of substances forced to yield their disagreements for the sake of the poem," and therefore "an attempt to present an analogy to that paradisal state in which Freedom and Law, System and Order are united in harmony." [8] But its harmony "is possible and verbal only." When it issues forth to do its work in society it may accomplish very little, and it may itself be changed in the minds of hearers—the only place where it really exists. The words "of a dead man [Yeats specifically] are modified in the guts of the living." Ireland's madness and her weather remain

[8] W. H. Auden, *The Dyer's Hand* (New York: Random House, 1962), p. 71.

as they always have been, her madness as far beyond cure as
her thunderstorms:

> Poetry makes nothing happen: it survives
> In the valley of its saying where executives
> Would never want to tamper; it flows south
> From ranches of isolation and the busy griefs,
> Raw towns that we believe and die in; it survives
> A way of happening, a mouth.
> ["In Memory of W. B. Yeats"] [9]

Since poems cannot pull the real world all the way into their
paradisal orders, "Ariel," the spirit of beauty, must learn to live
with "Prospero," who demands exacting truth:

The effect [of a poem's] beauty . . . is good to the degree
that, through its analogies, the goodness of created existence,
the historical fall into unfreedom and disorder, and the possibility of regaining paradise through repentance and forgiveness
are recognized. Its effect is evil to the degree that beauty is
taken, not as analogous to, but identical with goodness, so
that the artist regards himself or is regarded by others as God,
the pleasure of beauty taken for the joy of Paradise, and the
conclusion drawn that, since all is well in the work of art, all
is well in history. But all is not well there. [*The Dyer's Hand,*
p. 71]

Thus modern versions of pastoral often suggest that the
distance between fictional idylls and the daily world precludes
any geniune transformation of reality except an imagined
one. Aware of pastoral's artifice and of the contrast between
fiction and reality, the modern pastoralist is likely to take a
skeptical view of the pastoral tradition and use it primarily as
a device for gaining perspective on the nature of the imagination itself.

HISTORICAL CONTEXT

This shift in emphasis constitutes one of the main lines of
pastoral's evolution. Although images of idyllic places, dialec-

[9] Auden, *The Collected Poetry* (New York: Random House,
1945).

tical contrasts, and levels of pastoral ideality remain constant ingredients in the texts to be considered, each period does what it needs to with them, and it is part of our critical task to gauge the interplay between established conventions and the special social and intellectual topics of given periods. Any recapitulation of that interplay will inevitably oversimplify it, but it may be useful to anticipate here the sequential arrangement of what follows and its bearing upon the problems of form.

In Sidney and Spenser, nature and society are represented by and large by rustics and knights respectively. Both poets examine the stratification of feudal society from the perspective that a semidemocratic Arcadia assumes on the problems of social class, and they stress the difficulty of any permanent social transformation: the "classes" entertain each other only momentarily in the atmosphere of Arcadia before the world of social realities reasserts itself. Spenser's contrast between knight errantry and shepherdom in the sixth book of *The Faerie Queene* is complicated somewhat by his use of the shepherd Colin Clout as a proponent of a simple and elegant poetry free of moral considerations of the kind that Spenser's own didactic romance involves. Thus Arcadia harbors not only an ideally simple society but also an ideal aesthetic principle. It is dangerously attractive both to the hero, who should not abandon his quest when he discovers it, and to the poet, who should remember that he is an apologist for a set of courtly values and an imitator of moral and social realities. Neither Spenser nor Sidney can imagine an Arcadia that manages to stay intact; both work within a Christian framework that seeks a satisfactory "good place" only beyond the temporal world and fully expect the harbored places of the world to be ransacked. A poet who would remain true both to his idyllic vision and to the normative world of social strife and moral conflict may endorse feudal society as the best conceivable social arrangement, but he casts a longing eye on the simple life of Arcadia and the higher paradise that Arcadia at times seems to foreshadow.

Shakespeare, too, contrasts court and pastoral societies, but whereas a Calidore or a Musidorus undergoes no real change in his exposure to Arcadia, when Shakespeare exposes heroes and heroines to the green world they are significantly changed. In *A Midsummer Night's Dream, As You Like It, The Winter's Tale,* and *The Tempest,* he identifies the magical influence of nature with the powers of the imagination and implies that the capacity to change people which the forest's fairy citizenry (or simply its atmosphere) exercises is similar to the poet's power to work upon the mind. His poets, fairies, and magicians are in such complete command that they prevent the separation of idyllic wish and realizable social change: when they have finished working upon those who fall under their spells, the spirit of romantic pastoral reigns throughout the society, as it has not in Spenser and Sidney and will not in subsequent pastoral.

Despite a large flock of pastoral poems, plays, and romances in the first three decades of the seventeenth century, later poets tend to abandon social and political pastoral as the Puritan revolution approaches. For Herbert, Milton, Traherne, Vaughan, and Marvell, the social world is not compatible with the *locus amoenus,* not because of some inherent clash between "courtly" and "shepherd" cultures but because of more complex metaphysical and psychological reasons. To them the pleasant place is not a fiction or a metaphoric locality for the artist's own magic but an example of divine creativity standing apart from the social order. The idyllic imagination in each of these poets therefore rejects, in its own way, the evaluation of courtly culture that Sidney, Spenser, and Shakespeare sustain in their pastorals. For the later Milton, for instance, Adam and Eve are above artifice and adornment, and paradise, once lost, becomes internal—until it can once again be realized in a rediscovery of God's image in the wilderness.

Paradise Lost and *Paradise Regained* were in a sense anachronisms even when they were written, and the pastorals of Herbert, Marvell, Traherne, and Vaughan, too, obviously belong to a productive but short-lived phase of pastoral. Post-Restoration pastoral takes a quite different direction. On one hand, it revives the conventions and artifices of the old shepherd play, the court masque, and the eclogue, and the bulk of the pastorals written during the hundred years after the publication of *Paradise Lost* are uninspired reapplications of new makeup to an aging countenance. On the other hand, going a step beyond this formalist concern with conventions, Pope, Swift, and Gay explore the relationship between artifice and nature and undermine the uncritical faith in formulas that most pastoralists of the period maintain. And beyond this mannerist self-consciousness about the mode are two other concerns—how in fact to construct enclosed good places by uniting the best of nature and art in an ideal compromise, and how to escape enclosed pastoral places altogether in an expansive, romantic vision of all nature as somehow sacred and spiritual. In one, some of the old inventories of the *locus amoenus* still prove useful; in the other, the poet seeks a sublimity beyond fixed forms and enumeration, beyond the garden.

The romantics, especially Wordsworth in his praise of simplicity and distrust of urban life, reconceive the tension between society and nature and between levels of nature itself, and they abandon the man-made bower as a suitable idyllic place. It follows that they would also abandon the artifice of the old shepherd poem and look to different exemplars of the idyllic life. Under their influence pastoral takes a divided road, one branch exploring the implications of the idealizing imagination and leading eventually to Frost and Stevens, and the other taking up social themes and abandoning the notion of a pastoral place except as a perspective on provincial towns or urban life, as in the novels of Hardy and such modern figures as Faulkner, Bellow, and Ken Kesey. The separation itself tells much of the historical drift of pastoral after the dissolving of public concepts of Eden or Arcadia. Hardy returns to an older, almost Shakespearean, interplay between rustic and sophisticated cultures, but confidence in the upper hierarchy is shaken, romantic magic has disappeared from nature, and "marriage" no longer serves either as a sign of the union of nature and society or as a promise of renewal. *Henderson the Rain King* brings the traditional theme of civilized men in retreat up to date and suggests that psychological terms have altered our sense of primitivism and what it has to offer modern men. (Several other recent novels would serve as well to illustrate the modern collision of nature and society, Peter Matthiessen's *At Play in the Fields of the Lord* and Ken Kesey's *Sometimes a Great Notion,* for instance.)

For theoretical matters, the path that leads to Frost and Stevens is more interesting because it explores poetry's harboring of pastoral visions and the imagination's capacity to conceive of new "supreme fictions." It is clear to Frost and Stevens, as to the later Keats, that much that was once considered real must be treated as invention and that once poets have ceased to assume the possible accuracy of the large pastoral fables of Western culture—the golden age, Eden, Arcadia, and various futuristic paradises—they necessarily become more concerned with the kind of reality that their own constructions have. Keats's contact with "heaven's bourne"—where mortal sensuousness and immortal permanence fuse as they once did in the golden age—is approximately the same as that of the beholder's contact with a work of art: the marble urn in "Ode on a Grecian Urn" exists on a different plane, as does any ideal the poet might imagine. For Stevens and Frost, however, the contrast between reality and poetic invention (the order of words and the disorder of things) is no longer destructive or disillusioning. Frost characteristically encloses places against the "dark and doubt" that surround him and speaks of the poet's momentary stays against confusion, which are triumphs of form. Stevens probes nearly every conceivable relationship between art and nature, society and art, imagination and reality, nature as it is and celestial perfection as one might seek to give it "poetic" reality.

I anticipate these thematic topics in a broad way now to indicate the impact of historical moments upon the recurrent patterns of pastoral and to suggest that pastoral provides a convenient way of talking about some aspects of literary history and theory: its renewed inspection of the nature of artifice and fictions makes it frequently an index of poetry's continuously revised relationship to its external world. For instance, the versions of renaissance pastoral and the several figures to which we will now turn are the product of an interaction of traditional pastoral devices and certain feudal, Platonist, and Christian values. In nearly all English pastoralists from Spenser to Marvell, that interaction produces a mannerist consideration of the nature of poetry itself and an abundance of new forms—based on classical models of the shepherd poem but taking their own direction. We will begin far enough back to consider some of the social uses (and perhaps causes) of courtly pastoral in Italian pastoral drama and then consider the difficulties these uses encounter in a mode so hospitable to naturalism and uncourtly rusticity. By taking that route I hope to suggest some reasons for Spenser's introduction of the poet himself as a participant in the "class" problem in *The Shepheardes Calender* and for Shakespeare's discovery of common ground between the green world retreat and the theater of illusions that the playwright manipulates in the interests of social harmony.

TWO

Pastoral Hierarchy
and Entelechy

Renaissance pastorals represent two separate but parallel and often mixed ideals in the landscape of Arcadia: social grace, usually courtly even though located in shepherdom, and a Christian or Platonist "grace" that prefigures an ultimate paradise beyond normal Arcadian nature. Both Guarini and Sidney reinforce the semifeudal order of Arcadia with oracular messages suggesting the interest of the gods in the social order, and shades of divinity and miracle hover around Shakespeare's pastoral romance societies at times. A hero who participates in two such radically different pastoral ideals, social and religious or mythic, is required to make difficult adjustments between them. Later renaissance poets such as Vaughan, Herbert, and Milton separate the two areas and suggest that if the poet is committed to the idea of a higher paradise, he must put aside competing social motives. Even in *As You Like It,* where a general benevolence pervades the forest of Arden, those who are seriously concerned with divine purpose, such as Jaques and the usurping Duke, leave the court group to seek the wisdom of hermits and holy men. Marvell in "The Coronet," though expecting at first merely to convert the decorative flowers of courtly pastoral into religious ornament, finds that he must sacrifice the old pastoral altogether. Rather than putting together a worthy offering for Christ, he has merely replaced the old conventions with a new verbal nest for satanic ambition:

> Alas I find the serpent old
> That, twining in his speckled breast,
> About the flow'rs disguis'd does fold,
> With wreaths of Fame and Interest.

All pretty adornment and courtly rhetoric prove to be self-advertising. For the Puritan, too, all courtly elegance is discredited by comparison to the personal vision of paradise available to him.

The earlier renaissance tradition, however, especially Italian pastoral plays and masques, is more likely to find social elegance analogous to and compatible with divine perfection. Though populated with satyrs and rustics and given to erotic indolence, Arcadia is also graced with set pieces of courtly rhetoric and oracles which guarantee the destiny of certain "royal" shepherds. Beginning with that analogy, we can approach the uneasy compromise between courtly and religious elements in the Arcadias of Spenser and Sidney, and then from another direction, the dissociation of social themes and paradise in Herbert, Marvell, and Milton.

ARCADIAN COURTSHIP AND THE PLATONIST LADDER

The faithful shepherd of Italian plays and masques often takes for his emblem some variation of "i'amo; i'ardo; io moriro" ("I'm in love; I'm burning; I'll surely die"), languishing in a Petrarchan manner and expecting imminently to perish—though not before stylizing his suffering in complaints elaborately balanced in cadence and syntax, delicate and self-sacrificing in sentiment, and highly adorned in conceit. His suffering is puzzling because the life portrayed in the play is scarcely unpleasant, and oracles have usually suggested that everything will work out for the better if he only has patience. In many cases his predicament is a translation into pastoral attitudes of Platonized hierarchy and styles of courtship as elaborated in the books of manners of the times. What is demanded of him primarily is a purification of his love through self-denial, and thus his transformation from one level of love to another.

The analogy between courtly manners and Platonist spiritualization is clear when we put together social and philosophical aspects of the courtly love as discussed at various courts during the sixteenth century. Kenneth Burke's comment on *The Book of the Courtier* suggests the ease with which comments on courtly love could be "mysteriously" reinforced by religious motives:

In making "beauty" both courtly and religious, *The Book of the Courtier* makes religion courtly, thereby "mystically" fusing social and religious "reverence." "Even as in the firmament the sun and the moon and the other stars show to the world (as it were) in a glass, a certain likeness of God: So upon the earth a much more liker image of God are those good Princes that love and worship him, and show unto the people the clear light of justice." And by being so explicit in its way of advancing from a worldly to a celestial hierarchy, it gives us insight into situations where the "mystery of divinity" inspirits relations, that, on their face, call for purely mundane motives.[1]

What Cardinal Bembo's oration does to make this association between spiritual and social values in *The Book of the Courtier,* many *tratatti d'amore* do less explicitly. "Emulation" whether of the prince or of the pure lady is regarded as a means of transcending the "body" (roughly translatable as "the unreclaimable part that desires possession"). Transformation is therefore primarily etherealization and self-denial and is reserved for classes who have risen above the lower appetites of the body politic.

A similar equation operates in English pastorals but with certain complications that we can postpone examining until later, when both religious and social motives are connected with the Platonist ladder. In Jonson's masque *Oberon the Faery Prince,* for instance, that identification of social grace and cosmic hierarchy is partly concealed by the introduction of fairies (as it is also in Spenser's use of fairyland for a setting). After quieting the rude rout of satyrs, Sylvane and Silenus command the knights who surround the prince (Prince Henry) to "relinquish":

> and all their glories lay
> At's feet, and tender to this only great

[1] Kenneth Burke, *A Grammar of Motives and A Rhetoric of Motives* (Cleveland and New York: Meridian Books, 1962), p. 756.

True majesty, restored in this seat:
To whose sole power, and magic they do give
The honor of their being; that they live
Sustained in form, fame, and felicity,
From rage of fortune, or the fear to die.
                    Silenus

. . . .

His meditations, to his height, are even:
And all their issue is a kin to heaven.

. . . .

'Tis he, that stays the time from turning old,
And keeps the age up in a head of gold.
That in his own true circle, still doth run;
And holds his course, as certain as the sun.
He makes it ever day, and ever spring
Where he doth shine, and quickens every thing
Like a new nature: so, that true to call
Him, by his title, is to say, he's all.

As an equivalent to Pan, Henry exercises the functions of divine surrogate—a circular model keeping all nature just. For this function, the metaphor "Oberon the fairy prince" is appropriate because the mode of his reception of divine authority is inexplicable except as a magic vaguely associated with nature. The emulation of princes replaces love as the means by which a noble model influences the social body.

Platonic love and social and political models of elevation and excellence have in common just such a concept of ritual sacrifice in Italian books of manners and treatises on love. Ficino defines love as a seeking for "beauty," by which he means partly courtliness as well as spiritual luminosity: beauty of soul is a splendor born of "moeurs" or customs.[2] This connection between love and station is reinforced in Pseudo-Denys by the notion that love is not merely a union of equals but a happy "death" of a lower self and rebirth in a higher. When two people die to themselves and are reborn in each other, they lose one life to find another, and so much the better when one

[2] Marsilio Ficino, *In Convivium Platonis sive de Amore,* ed. Raymond Marcel (Paris, 1956), p. 159.

who is below is reborn in love for a higher social and spiritual being. When cavaliers speak of love—divine, angelic, spiritual, or natural—they mean basically the innate attraction that those who are superior exercise over inferiors, who, Ficino says, "turn toward those who are better and more noble" (p. 161). "Substance" in a philosophical sense (Jonson's "being" and "form") is thus identified with substance as property and position (Jonson's "titles" and "honors"). Cardinal Bembo reinforces that association in *The Book of the Courtier* in re-examining what others have said regarding social grace under the general quest for divine grace. Emulation of one's prince extracts social and spiritual potentials that have lain concealed in crudeness and rusticity until the prince releases them. Once one is redirected toward love of a princely model, he becomes a "true lover" and "may unite with divine beauty in a per-petual and most sweet bond." [3]

The point with respect to pastoral tragicomedies—tragedy-averted forms in which miraculous reversals are often fore-told by oracles—is that acts of self-denial and reluctant pursuit may represent both social and religious attitudes. In the coterie plays popular at the *corte d'estense* in Ferrara and at similar courts in Venice and Florence, Platonist theories of love, hav-ing been translated already into terms applicable to the social ladder, were further converted into the plots of the *pastor fido* and *fida ninfa,* and Arcadia was used for purposes never dreamed of in Theocritus or Virgil. Ordinarily in these plays, Venus rewards faithfulness to temperance and courtly codes by setting right a previous fall that has destroyed the Golden Age (often restored in masques by a prince allegorically situ-ated at the center of the pageantry, as in Milton's *Arcadia*). In the heroic figures the vulgar or acquisitional self dies and a

---

[3] Baldesar Castiglione, *The Book of the Courtier,* trans. Charles S. Singleton (New York: Doubleday, 1959), p. 357. Bonarelli's philosophical defense of *Filli di Sciro* suggests that whoever loves earth will become earthy; whoever loves God becomes godlike: "Ecco la trasformazione, per forze della quale dicesi: *Moritur quisquis amat.* Onde il Petrarca, invocando Amore, 'O viva morte, o dilettoso male.'" Guidubaldo Bonarelli, *Filli di Sciro, discorsi e appendice,* ed. Giovanni Gambarin (Bari, 1941), p. 177.

new social-spiritual self replaces it, loyal to the values of the aristocratic caste. The shepherd lover thus undergoes a series of ordeals to demonstrate his observance of the *vita cavelleresca,* represented in its most ethereal trophy, the cold nymph; for sexual we may often read social abstinence and for marriage, union with the princely model. Or a discovery of proper fortune may accompany marriage, as in *As You Like It,* in which various pretenders to position are reformed and each lover finds at one and the same time his appropriate marital arrangement and his appropriate status. Stylized courtship and reluctance in pursuit are often the credentials for success, while aggression (especially in fauns and satyrs, who represent the natural beast) is cause for exile from the final, purged society. The governing force in the "subplot" of the fauns and their disorder is the sensuality of Cupid while the main plot falls under the jurisdiction of the oracles and a higher Eros.[4]

As *The Book of the Courtier* further suggests, making the royal shepherd—however stylized and aristocratic his behavior—appear *natural* is one of the functions of the pastoral masquerade. His superiority is all the more convincing for being so obvious when everyone supposes him to be an ordinary shepherd. Ottaviano remarks concerning nature's sanction

[4] The real as opposed to the "mystified" meaning of oracles in court plays is revealed in Allan Ramsay's late version, *The Gentle Shepherd,* an eighteenth-century royalist play in which one Sir William Worthy pretends to fall into a trance and predict a rich future for the "gentle" shepherd, his son. The oracle thus promises lineal inheritance, made possible in this case, as Ramsay indicates, by the restoration of Charles II to the throne and the return of stolen property to its rightful owners. Fanshawe's 1647 translation of *Il Pastor Fido* echoes similar sentiments in an accompanying treatise.

The hero of Giovanmaria Guicciardi's *Il Sogno* (1601), on the other hand, receives his destiny through a dream that reinforces the mystifying power of that destiny. Florindo shoots an arrow and follows it to his "fate," discovering that it has struck Jove's sacred oak and that Silvia, who happens to be hiding inside, has been wounded by it. Thus the arrow of "desire" is also the arrow of fortune-seeking and "death." Having violated sacred law by presuming to pursue his object too actively, the hero is condemned

of hierarchy that only the rule of a good prince can restore the Golden Age, the most natural of all times: "I should always prefer the rule of a good prince [to a republic] because such a rule is more according to nature, and . . . more like that of God who single and alone governs the universe. . . . So too in our body, where all the members do their work and fulfill their functions at the command of the heart." Nature teaches "obedience as a very salutary thing." [5] Thus the prince's likeness to God, the naturalness of his government, and a basic analogy between discipline of the body and political discipline reinforce the shepherd's obedience, chastity, and faithfulness—

---

under law. At the last minute, after his loyalty proves unquestionable, he is redeemed by grace. In James Shirley's later imitation of Italian drama, *Death and Cupid* (1653), death and love have interchangeable functions, Death's arrow causing an old couple to love and Cupid, a rebellious force of individualism in this case, causing a young man to sink into age and death. But Mercury descends and prevents permanent disruption: performing his Jungian functions, he awakens Nature, banishes Cupid, and establishes the happy destiny of the chastised knights and ladies:

> Cupid, the gods do banish thee
> From every palace; thou must be
> Confin'd to cottages, to poor
> And humble cells. Love must no more
> Appear in princes' courts: their heart,
> Impenetrable by thy dart,
> And from softer influence free,
> By their own wills must guided be.

Death is allowed to rage on but he too must not "engage / On persons, in whose breasts divine / Marks of art or honour shine." With that, the grand masquers (the nobles of the court) appear in Elysium, and the formerly slain lovers are seated in "glorious habit." The implication is that the real ravages of love and death are for the humble, their transformed powers for the educated.

[5] Castiglione, *Book of the Courtier,* p. 303. As Ottaviano points out, the prince becomes the legislator of manners through the law of idealistic archetypes: rising above the masses, he is automatically the "source" of what "emanates" from him. If the "prince is good . . . his people are good, because the life of the prince is a norm and guide for the citizens, and all behavior must needs depend on his" (p. 307).

all alien to the contrasting and more prevalent concept of Arcadia as a place of erotic freedom and equality. In defining the ideal courtier, Messer Federico indicates that pastoral entertainments are a calculated strategy designed to reveal the cavalier in the most favorable light. Though in his own person the knight may not with propriety dance or wrestle with peasants (to lose would be humiliating and to win would yield no honor), in a masquerade he can freely enact his natural grace:

indeed, there is no better way of showing oneself in such things, at public spectacles . . . because masquerading carries with it a certain freedom and license, which among other things enables one to choose the role in which he feels most able . . . and to show a certain nonchalance in what does not matter: all of which adds much charm; as for a youth to dress as an old man, yet in loose attire so as to be able to show his vigor; or for a cavalier to dress as a rustic shepherd, or in some other costume, but astride a perfect horse and gracefully attired in character.[6]

Federico's emphasis falls upon "show" because the function of the knight-as-shepherd is to model excellence, not to slay dragons. The strategy might be described as a variation of "descendentalism," to borrow an apt word from Carlyle's Professor Teufelsdröckh, an unclothing that reveals the inner man and hence his normal right to dress in elegance. (An unidealized descent would be something like Lear's "unaccommodated man," stripped of all the magic and accoutrements of royalty—a king become a beggar. For as Lear says of a naturalism quite different from this, "Take physic, pomp; / Expose thyself to feel what wretches feel" (3.4.33-34). "Thou wert better in a grave than to answer with thy uncover'd body this extremity of the skies. Is man no more than this? Consider him well. Thou ow'st the worm no silk, the beast no hide, the sheep no wool, the cat no perfume. Ha! here's three on's are sophisticated. Thou art the thing itself; unaccommodated man is no more but such a poor, bare, forked animal as thou art. Off, off, you lendings! Come, unbutton here.") [3.4.103-112]

[6] *Ibid.*, p. 103.

If the comparison of primitive and cavalier is to work, the disguise must be transparent. When

the prince puts off his identity as prince, and mingles with his inferiors as an equal (yet so that he can be recognized) then, in rejecting his own, he attains to a higher greatness, which is to seek to surpass others not by authority but by ability, and to show his own worth is not the greater merely because he is a prince.[7]

His greatness is all the more obvious for the rustic surroundings of the forest or meadow.

Despite these attempts to use pastoral conventions to set off the qualities of the prince or cavalier, however, the Arcadian scene tends to exert pressure in a quite different direction at times: it levels all social elements to an Arcadian democracy and brings into question the value of honor and fame when the simple pleasures of shepherdom are so readily available. Giason De Nores's *Discorso intorno a que' principii, cause, et accrescimenti, che la comedia, la tragedia, et il poema heroico recevono dalla philosophia morale, & civile, & de' governatori della republiche* (1586), written in reaction to Guarini's *Il Pastor Fido,* is quite right in its own terms to accuse Guarini of bad form in bringing rustics and nobles together so freely. Peasants have too little to offer cultivated urban dwellers by way of edifying example and too much to offer that detracts from honor and grace. Mixed pastoral forms are stylistically confusing; Horace wisely advised the distinct separation of categories:

when woodland Fauns are brought on to the stage, they should be careful not to languish in love-verses, like city exquisites, nor rap out filthy and shameful jests. For those who possess horse, father, or estate take offence; nor do they receive with favor or award a crown to everything that the purchaser of fried peas and chestnuts may approve.[8]

[7] *Ibid.,* pp. 103–104.

[8] Horace, *Ars Poetica,* trans. Edward Henry Blakeney (New York, 1936), p. 405. Cf. G. A. Timermani's edition of *Il pastor fido, con l'annotazioni alla medisima dell'autore,* II (Verona, 1737), 278 ff.

De Nores's distrust is justified insofar as much of the energy and force of such plays, especially Guarini's, falls to satyrlike naturalists. The usual strategy is to counteract their vigor by anticipating from the outset a reassertion of propriety: the oracles make the rewards for languishing faithfulness seem inevitable as well as divinely sanctioned. Crude force is thus negated by the "mysteries" of higher Arcadian courtship, guided by the gods to prevent marriages across class lines. In addition, one of the potential noble lovers often begins as a naturalist scoffer at love, intent on pursuing his own game. In the course of the play he is struck by Cupid's arrows and becomes a converted "seeker," honoring courtly love with the same passivity and self-torture as the faithful shepherd. So long as satyrs remain semiallegorical tempters, the point is easily made. But when the playwright allows them more persuasive arguments, as in Tasso's *L'Aminta* and Cintio's *Egle*, the contrast tends to work in their favor. In Guarini's play, Corisca, whose false hair is torn off in an undignified scuffle with Satiro, is typically crude in her "unnatural" lust (which, as Platonic orthodoxy specifies, turns quickly to enterprising hate); yet the vigorous comic scenes between her and Satiro also expose the lifeless posing of Amarillis and Mirtillo in the highly ornate style of their Platonist courtship.

Then, too, most of those who wrote pastoral plays were aware of the cardboard stiffness of the masquerade. (Guarini complains of it in his letters.) Inevitably, a certain amount of regret over the loss of simplicity creeps into the portrait of the shepherd as a man elaborately hedged in by the codes of the renaissance drawing room even in Arcadia (*et in Arcadia ego,* Honor says to him). With typical love of symmetry, Guarini attempts to circumvent the difficulty raised by the contrast of sensuous and ethereal love by separating the lovers into three groups of ascending value, Corisca and Satiro representing love perverted by lust into hate, Dorinda and Silvio representing pure nature without notable social graces or fraud but needing to be softened, and Amarillis and Mirtillo representing love purged both of the acquisitive instinct and of cruelty.[9] Guarini defended this mixture of classes against De Nores's attack on the grounds that it reflects the government of a mixed republic, between democracy and an absolute *tyrannos,* and that it contains elements both of tragedy, with its imitation of the *persona grande,* and of comedy, with its imitation of lower social levels. Tragicomedy he thus regarded as a harmonious combination of the two, designed to demonstrate the proper place of each: "E perchè de' pastori altri son nobili, e altri no, questi fanno la Comica, quelli la Tragica, ed ambo insieme la Tragicomica pastorale."[10] But, unfortunately, mixing these three kinds of pursuit demonstrates not so much the superiority of Amarillis and Mirtillo as the deficiencies of each group taken separately. Silvio's reform from truancy is unbelievable, and Mirtillo himself comes off badly as an exponent of fatalistic patience—or so it seems to a modern, and one imagines that it must have seemed so to some of Guarini's contemporaries as well:

[9] According to Guarini's gloss, Amarillis represents pure soul and divine felicity and Mirtillo the magnanimous man governed by faith and the light of reason. Cf. Bembo's *Gli Asolani,* ed. Carlo Dionisotti-Casalone (Torinto, 1932), p. 112. From the first hour of genuine (ethereal) love, a transformation comes over the lover: he sheds his "prime rustichezze" and learns the customs of gentility and whatever is becoming to "cittadinesca vita," much as Orpheus charmed the crudeness from primitive nature by teaching it Platonic love. Likewise, Tullia D'Aragona, in stressing the "infinitá di amore," separates the dishonorable, the uncultured, and the sensual from rational lovers: "lo amore è di due ragioni: l'uno chiameremo 'vulgare' overo disonesto, e l'altro 'onesto' overo virtuoso. Il disonesto, che non è se non degli uomini volgari e plebei, cioè di quelli che hanno l'animo basso e vile e che sono senze virtú o gentilezza. . . . L'amore onesto, il quale è proprio degli uomini nobili, cioè che hanno l'animo gentile e virtuoso . . . non è generato nel desiderio, come l'altro, ma dalla ragione; ed ha per so fine principale il trasformarsi nella cosa amata con disiderio che ella si trasformi in lui." *Dialogo della Signora Tullia D'Aragona della Infinitá di Amore,* from *Trattati D'Amore del Cinquecento,* ed. Giuseppe Zonta (Bari, 1912), pp. 222–223.

[10] Timermani, *Il pastor fido,* III, 264.

I have tane the height
Of my unhappy Star, my sullen fate
Made me for fuell onely, born to smother
In fires I cannot kindle in another.
Yet since Fate's pleas'd I should affect death more
Then life, at least I'ld have her know before,
That shee's beholding to me for my death
And deigne when I sigh out my latest breath
To cast her fair eyes on me, and say, *Dye.*

[*Il Pastor Fido,* I.2]

Nor does the last minute reform of the sensualists succeed in demonstrating the appeal of a "pure" love affair. Hence, though the ostensible magical elements of the play are fewer than those of Cintio's *Egle,* Epicuro de' Marsi's *Mirzia,* or Beccari's *Il Sacrifizio*—all earlier and clumsier plays resolved by marvelous metamorphoses—the force that keeps the hero and heroine in ascendancy is no less mystifying. In their symbolic "suicidal" attitudinizing, the faithful shepherds offer themselves up to a merely social code taken to be a power of spiritual metamorphosis.

CIRCE AND NOBLE SAVAGES AMONG THE HUMANISTS

The form of attitudinizing that Guarini's noble shepherds illustrate may seem minor in the total spectrum of renaissance pastorals; certainly these plays are ineffectual by comparison with Shakespeare's romance comedies, both as works of art and as comments on the relationship between art and nature, "shepherds" and "courtiers." But the historical point is useful because the cavalier-shepherd of Italian pastorals represents one extreme in the translation of feudal institutions into pastoral form, an extreme that concerns pastoral through the eighteenth century. Unlikely as it seems today, the controversy over tragicomedy was one of the lively critical issues of the times; and beyond that, Guarini's concept of the idyllic state is related to the general dispute as to whether or not nature could be captured by the aristocratic life and transformed by Platonist etherealizing. As might be expected, the main challenge to the courtly view of the *vita cavelleresca* and its system of analogies between the social and the natural-divine order came from naturalists who did not believe in the capacity of the courtly seeker to change either his bodily or his spiritual nature by "emulation" of Platonized models. Three examples will suffice to illustrate the point, Giovanni Battista Gelli, Tasso, and Montaigne.

Gelli's *Circe*

Like Machiavelli, Gelli undermines the institutions of the courtier by stressing common sense, daily experience, and man's wolfish, disease-ridden impulses on all levels from passion to intellect. He suggests in *Circe* (written in the turbulent period after Platonism had reached the height of its influence in the Medici court in Florence) that the closer to primitivism one moves the more natural he becomes and that the Platonist view of perfection as transcendence and self-mortification is incompatible with the laws of biology and the social order. His view of Circe is indicative. Whereas other renaissance descendants of this magician—various sirens and satyrs like Milton's Comus—metamorphose incontinent and intemperate people into beasts, Gelli's Circe makes them merely contented. By contrast, "spiritualization" seems an illusory invention prompted by self-deceit, like Ulysses' humanism, which she finds little more than sophistry. Circe herself remains delightfully objective about those whom she has tempted to become animals, confident that none of them will want to be human again. Though they have come from several ranks, to all of them being human means living in poverty, fear, and pain. They prefer humble comfort to imitations of a perfection they cannot achieve.

Her argument goes beyond an attack on courtly idealism from the standpoint of naturalism, however. She and her metamorphosed animals also find serious flaws in nature itself, which is anything but a model for the human order. Their main criticism of humanistic and courtly institutions is not that they are artificial but that they offer insufficient protection against daily evils, even for those in relatively high and insulated positions. For all the beasts except the elephant, man is not a separable body and soul but a unity put together for the most excruciating of miseries. The primitivism of Circe's island is therefore a retrenchment, a redefining of goals in the interest of what is possible in a generally bad world. Human society only aggravates an already unpalatable misery, and unlike human biology, as the hare points out, lacks sanction in the natural order:

Let this suffice, Ulysses, to show you how sharp and bitter a thorn poverty is that to escape it men actually become servants one to another which is so base a practice that among us beasts there is none so vile but would rather suffer death than voluntarily condescend to serve another of his own species, in return for maintaining him in necessaries. Nature, however, has been more indulgent to us than to you, for thanks to her we have nothing of this infamous servitude among us. On the contrary, she has endowed each of us with the ability to govern himself.[11]

Though a mere rabbit says it, it is a surprisingly frank statement against the system of privilege, more solidly entrenched than ever during the postrepublican reaction against semipopular rule in Florence. The deer reinforces the complaint against injustice, especially the courtly view of womanhood, which masks a reality that faithful shepherds never confront:

you men make mere slaves and servants out of us, whereas we were originally designed for your assistants and associates, and that's what by rights we should be; and your degrading us is so impious, and so much against the rule of nature, that no animal but man ever even attempts it . . . man assumes to himself a tyrannical power and prerogative, styling himself lord and master of the whole species, and domineers and insults over her whom he ought to cherish and succor, only because her constitution is not so hardy as his. [P. 85]

Courtly idolatry, the deer implies, has little to do with the real women of the renaissance household.

Hence Ulysses finds himself, among other things, an antifeminist, hypocritically pretending to hold a spiritualized view

---

[11] Gelli, *Circe,* trans. Thomas Brown with corrections by R. M. Adams (Ithaca: Cornell University Press, 1963), p. 20.

of women. "Confronted by these assaults on the concept of transcendence through love and emulation, he loses his courtly bearing and is reduced to stiff formality, his arguments stripped of apparent dignity and logic, his class-consciousness sinking into mere authoritarian assertion:

I could hardly have happened upon a worse fellow to persuade than this. I suppose he was some ignorant wretch in his time; and his trade sufficiently shows it, for men who pursue fish or birds are all low fellows, of feeble understandings. . . . Well, then let me . . . try to reason with the mole. . . . I will walk up to him and accost him without more ceremony. [P. 20]

That nature grants a better life to a few is Circe's rather than Ulysses' point, and it is the realist who enjoys it, while the Platonist aspirant continues to seek the unattainable:

Oh, Ulysses, I thought that during the little time you remained with me here you would enjoy all the delights in which this beautiful island of mine abounds. And if nothing else could move you, yet the perpetual springtime which this climate enjoys might have raised your delight—especially if you considered that security and delight which the different beasts take one with the other, sporting about all day long in the green and pleasant woods, after the manner of those early happy times called the Age of Gold, and so often celebrated by the poets, when discord and hatred had got no footing in the world. [Pp. 110–111]

In sum, virtually everything that must have seemed uncultured and unnatural to his Florentine intellectual friends the shoemaker makes out to be true "pastoralism"; what they valued as culture and bearing he finds thinly veiled snobbery. Had he stopped here, his island paradise might have made an effective argument for liberalizing the social order. As it is, however, Ulysses is given a last-minute escape. Confirmed in his belief that the multitude is as "fickle, ignorant, mutable" as ever, he demonstrates the superiority of intellectual pursuits to the satisfaction at least of the elephant, and together they decide that one *can* achieve a high degree of tranquillity through "art and reason": "How beautiful the light seems to

him that has always lived in darkness. . . . Sordid and unhappy wretches, who for a little sensual pleasure are resolved
to live like brutes! I thank you, Ulysses, with all my heart, for
showing me the truth, and by the power of your eloquence
drawing me to it" (p. 176). But then, as R. M. Adams aptly
observes, Aglaphemus (the elephant) "does not accept full
humanity . . . and Gelli leaves open the wry possibility that
he was a rather stupid elephant to begin with, whom Ulysses
soft-talked back into humanity against his real interests" (p.
xxx).

Actually, the form of Gelli's serial dialogues between the
courtly man and the common, biological man presupposes that
the area of compromise is small and that neither can "accept
full humanity." The most illuminating clash would have been
between the elephant as intellect (a representative of hierarchy
and order) and another animal as a representative of natural
instinct and physical being. Instead, the animals say "no" and
"yes" separately without staging the central confrontation that
their positions seem to demand. We can only speculate that as
a shoemaker Gelli disliked the snobbery and optimism that
Platonism was called upon to reinforce and yet, as a self-
educated philosopher, valued intellectual coherence and some
form of hierarchical knowledge. He found no way to separate the two. But his very failure to accommodate the extremes represented by the elephant and the other animals
makes him valuable as an index to the fundamental tension
between an anarchic self that finds the relaxed freedom of
Arcadia so appealing and the restrictive institutions of courtly
society. His ambivalence toward animalism and the civilized
arts is a forerunner of mixed feelings in later renaissance pastorals toward noble-ignoble savages and toward a shepherdom,
that allows courtly wayfarers to realize their private dreams
but also leads them away from duty and courtly values.

Tasso's *Aminta*

Like Cintio's *Egle* before it, *Aminta* makes no attempt to
disguise the advantages of uncurbed instinct: one *should*
pursue his native bent. Thirsis finds immediate possession

better than waiting for fate to work itself out; and Daphne considers resistance against, rather than yielding to, sensual love "rustic and savage." Tasso, however, like Gelli is not fully committed to unrestricted impulse. The one most obviously in accord with Thirsis's advice and the Chorus's praise of liberty is not Aminta or Daphne but a grasping satyr who tries to perform in fact what Aminta only considers. Moreover, Thirsis's trip to court has revealed to him a magnificent and noble house of art, and his oaten pipe has since become "more loud and sonorous," more heroic.

The popularity of Tasso's play undoubtedly derived in part from this ambivalence toward nature and life at court: the audience could indulge in a dream of free eroticism and yet not be asked to believe unconditionally in it. In the fourth act, the usual machinery of the *tragedia di lieto fin* brings about a pious reaffirmation of ethereal love—and thus implicitly of the courtly manner associated with it:

> Truly the law, with which love governs eternally,
> Is neither hard nor unjust, and his works,
> Full of providence and mystery,
> Others condemn wrongly. O with what art,
> And along what unknown roads
> He leads man to his happiness,
> And among the joys of his amorous paradise places him
> Just when he most believes himself in the depths of evil.
>
> [5.1]

Yet despite this turn toward conventional reverence, the final chorus allows worldliness one last aside to the court:

> I do not know whether or not the bitterness
> Which this servant has tested by loving,
> Weeping, and despairing,
> Can be sweetened enough
> With present pleasure;
> But if good becomes more dear
> And tastes better after evil,
> I do not ask you, Love,
> This greater happiness—
> Bless others in that way:

Let my nymph receive me
After short entreaty and brief service.

The shepherdess has been brusquely knocked from her high
pedestal—and with her the elaborate modes of courtship that
divide courtiers from peasants. What separates the tutored
from the untutored is worldly wisdom.

Montaigne's Noble Savagery

The essays of Montaigne concerning cannibalism and social
customs represent another, much more radical and less ambivalent, attitude toward naturalism. Like Gelli, Montaigne
finds a connection between Platonism and social position and
believes that to destroy Platonist universals is in effect to destroy the foundations of caste. "To know," to Montaigne, does
not mean to "rise to pure intellect," but to descend into one's
biological self, into the smells, tastes, habits, and tactile sensations of the moment. Hence the primitivism that Gelli only
halfway endorses, Montaigne makes into a new measure of
"nobility," the nobility of the candid primitive man. All arts
designed to set man above nature he finds merely distortions
of nature. He complains that everyone gives the title of "barbarism to everything that is not according to his usage" when
"we ought rather to call those wild whose natures we have
changed by our artifice and diverted from the common order.
. . . It is not reasonable that art should gain the point of honor
over our great and powerful mother, Nature": [12]

For it seems to me that what we now see by experience of
those nations (i.e., savage nations) does not only surpass all
the images with which the poets have adorned the golden age
and all their inventions in imagining a happy state of man,
but also the conception and even the desire of philosophy.
They were incapable of imagining so pure and so simple an
innocence as we by experience see it; nor were they capable of
believing that human society can be maintained with so little
human artifice and solder. [P. 79]

[12] Montaigne, "Of Cannibals," trans. Charles Cotton-W. Hazlitt;
ed. Blanchard Bates (New York: Random House, 1949).

Even what passes for public service and spiritual betterment is little more than self-aggrandizement:

> let us boldly appeal to those who are in the midst of the dance; and let them cudgel their conscience and say whether . . . the titles, the offices, and the hurly-burly of the world are not rather sought out to gain a private profit from the public. ["Of Solitude," p. 90]

Montaigne's criticism of the usual hierarchies is that all biological and personal experiences are essentially equal: only the costumes change. Though men have preferences and consider some experiences more important than others, such predilections illustrate "habit" rather than rational selectivity. Having set aside hierarchies of value, however, he must also make all moments more or less equal and deny any kind of programmatic development. Indeed, if we lived by schedules of value, the inconsistencies of both common and great men would not reveal, as they do, that

> we are all made up of fragments, so shapeless and strangely assembled that every moment, every piece plays its own game. And there is as much difference between us and ourselves as between us and others. ["The Inconsistency of Our Actions," p. 114]

Hence though we may assume an elevated style for specific reasons, we cannot be *essentially* high: one who sits down honestly before himself in the solitude of his own chamber must submit to the primitive man behind the disguise.

THE POET AS HIS OWN BESTOWER

Out of what, then, is art shaped? It is clear to Spenser, Sidney, and Shakespeare that to subscribe to an extreme naturalism that sacrifices social order and art to unrestricted, momentary impulses is to shatter all form and allow the barbarity of the Blatant Beast, lawless rustics, and Edmunds to destroy enduring monuments and governing institutions. In the name of honesty Montaigne undermines many of the renaissance stays against confusion: the divine models of creative form, artifice, and Platonist idealism. He returns to nature with a vengeance that Lear's unaccommodated man would have understood, but also feared to the roots of his unsheltered being. That pastoral's compromise between art and nature, rusticity and courtliness, nature and grace might provide an answer is a possibility that nearly all varieties of pastoral romance explore. But the conflicting accounts of the arts of the courtier that we get from Guarini, Gelli, Tasso, and Montaigne are complicated by two other matters in most English pastorals concerned with the courtier and the shepherd: an evaluation of art that gives it credit for its own special kind of existence (as well as for its service to the social order), and a concept of grace that reevaluates both art and nature. Though we cannot expect simple critical maxims to emerge where so many strands come together, it is legitimate to say that the very ambiguity of poetry as a demonstration of social style on one hand and as an appeal to divine power on the other was sometimes useful to the poet, who could claim to have invented fairyland or Arcadia where, under the magic of his imagination, nature and art live harmoniously together. That is, it is his own imaginative enclosure that provides the ground on which discordant values could be reconciled: where else but in *The Faerie Queene* are destiny, holiness, and politics so much in agreement? Where outside Shakespearean comedy, with its Forests of Arden and its magical therapy, are the diverse levels of Elizabethan society so content and so well in accord with nature?

Even beyond this serviceability of poetry in making peace between otherwise irreconcilable values, Sidney, Spenser, Shakespeare, Herbert, and Milton each gives poetry its own scale of values at times and allows the poet either to bestow gifts of grace or to appeal for them beyond the directives of his society. In the sonnets, for instance, Shakespeare substitutes the high worth of poetry for several other kinds of value; when live models of beauty and manners perish, the poet's words live on. The argument is unassailable by those who would defend "idealization" on general principles since the most refined of cavaliers is as nothing above gross nature compared with the transcendence of poetry over mere "things":

> When I consider everything that grows
> Holds in perfection but a little moment,
> That this huge stage presenteth nought but shows
> Whereon the stars in secret influence comment;
> When I perceive that men as plants increase,
> Cheered and check'd even by the self-same sky,
> Vaunt in their youthful sap, at height decrease,
> And wear their brave state out of memory;
> Then the conceit of this inconstant stay
> Sets you most rich in youth before my sight,
> Where wasteful Time debateth with Decay
> To change your day of youth to sullied night;
>   And all in war with Time for love of you,
>   As he takes from you, I engraft you new.
>
> [Sonnet XV]

The argument rests on the equality of men considered as vegetation, which makes manners and bearing ("shows") mere food for decay. All physical existence is "cheered and check'd" by the same natural law, but what time and nature take away, sonnets may restore. In poems the perfection of nature is possible; poetry alone has the godlike power to restore paradise, and what holds true for the preservation of the historical "you" of the sonnet presumably holds for all things of state, nature, and self that the poet might choose to engraft.[13]

The obvious rejoinder is that, whatever the poet may gain in permanence by making verbal monuments, he loses in physical and psychological particularity—that "engraft" really means "substitute words for," which might not seem an impressive immortality to one who preferred living in the flesh. Shakespeare tentatively explores that argument in the sonnet that follows "When I Consider." Whereas breeding an

---

[13] Castiglione's ideal courtier takes art more lightly. "Let the courtier turn to music as a pastime, as though forced, and not in the presence of persons of low birth or where there is a crowd. And although he may know and understand what he does, in this also I would have him dissimulate the care and effort that is required in doing anything well." Castiglione, *Book of the Courtier*, p. 104.

heir would defeat time by incarnating the father's image anew, mere enshrinement in rhyme, by itself, is barren. At the least a poet requires real objects to refer to and to engraft—a child if not the original beauty of the father. Poems cannot create something out of nothing. Yet even so, renewed generations only provide more food for the "keen teeth" in time's "fierce tiger's jaw"; eventually one must fall back upon verbal monuments to beauty to offer whatever images and models of perfection, once visible in particular faces and manners, that he can.

The association between poetry and pastoral enclosures where ideal harmony reigns timelessly is common in the period from 1579 to about 1610 and again in Marvell and Herbert. Collections of lyrics such as *Brittons Bowre of Delights, The Arbor of Amorous Devices,* and *England's Helicon* suggest that the poem is its own bower where time is suspended, a land of miracle like the one Marlowe's shepherd describes to the reluctant nymph. As Raleigh's answer points out, such a world exists nowhere but in the poet's "lies"; yet shepherd singers of "sweet ditties" like Richard Barnfield's in "The Shepherd's Content" can nonetheless be satisfied with it. The shepherd-poet's rare pleasures can thrive only in this place set apart from contention, where one can sing about the pleasures of song itself if about nothing else:

O let that time a thousand months endure,
Which brings from heaven the sweet silver showers,
And joys the earth (of comfort late deprived)
　　With grass and leaves, fine buds, and painted flowers.
　　Echo, return unto the woods obscure.
　　Ring forth the shepherd's songs in love contrived.
　　　Let old loves be revived,
　　Which angry winter buried but of late
　　　And that in such a state
　　My soul may have the full accomplishment
　　　Of joy and sweet content.
　　　　　　　　　　　　　[*England's Helicon*]

If society enters here, it must leave strife behind and come prepared to dance in rings.

But the pastoralist's impulse to withdraw into the world of

his own ornamental song is checked in most pastoralists by an
equally strong urge either to spread the dream abroad, as a
socially relevant ideal, or to project it as a final reality, a greater
paradise, into which one may eventually move, where "sweet
Societies / . . . sing, and singing in their glory move" without
end. These two impulses, to apply the vision of a golden age
to the world of politics and history and to withdraw totally
into it, are recurrent in the tradition. They dominate Marvell
and are prominent in Keats and again in Frost and Stevens.
In the Renaissance, each pastoralist finds his own way to
reconcile them. Guarini suggests that in the pastoral retreat we
discover the basic naturalness of the hierarchical social pattern
and particularly the inherent superiority of the royal "shepherd," which makes the pastoral retreat a strategic image of
social interests. In Sidney and Spenser, the peaceful life of
shepherds and the militant life of knights are too basically
opposed to be reconciled: the pastoral ideal and the singing
shepherds stand apart from any conceivable social organization. To this tension between the idyllic landscape as a place
of truant escape and as a strategic reinforcement of the courtier's inherent superiority, the Christian pastoralist adds a dimension that completely redefines both the active and contemplative lives. Milton insists that we return to Eden, in
imagination, in order to reestablish the divine plan at the heart
of the only activity that matters, the moral regeneration of
the fallen Adam in us, and eventually the restoration of paradise, other kinds of reform being useful only insofar as they
keep the idyllic vision always before us. Paradise is both an
ultimate object of contemplation and the most effective imaginable standard by which we measure contemporary civil and
religious institutions. Moreover, the poem as its enshrinement
and as a sign of grace finds a new status beyond other social
functions and lesser graces. Supported by the sacred muse, the
poet rediscovers for us our archetypal source and reinforces
scriptural truths in monuments to timeless beauty and form
undreamed of even in Shakespeare's poetic "engrafting." For
Herbert and Milton both, the poem houses aspects of divine
being itself. In his recapturing of images of the sacred creation,

the poet may use classical pastoral as a stage toward their realization, but the tendency among Christian pastoralists is to find the tradition somewhat pretty and fragile and sometimes dangerously erotic. It becomes merely a stage to be discarded and transcended, as, in "Lycidas," an original bucolic society, described primarily in Theocritean and Virgilian terms, is disrupted by death and injustice and eventually replaced by a pastoral ideal based mainly on scriptural sources. This final transcendence enables the pastoralist to cope with nature's fall and with death: rather than closing off ornate pastoral bowers from these realities, the pastoralist can let them have their way with the classical Arcadia or the doomed Eden, confident that a subsequent stage in the dialectic will lead through the wilderness to a paradise that can be sealed off permanently from them.

The courtly elements of the Italian Arcadias are the first to be disputed and abandoned by this later renaissance use of the tradition. Whereas Montaigne levels social ranks by making every moment and every part of nature of approximately equal value, Christian pastoral tends to level them by making all temporal distinctions negligible before the idea of paradise. The courtly shepherd thus proves to be vulnerable from two sides, to the democratic spirit of naturalism and to the vision of a higher paradise constantly before the Christian poet and more than peripheral to him. For Milton, the "landscape" that a poem seeks to imitate is ultimately the entire manifest plan for the universe; nothing less is of permanent interest to him. This concept of paradise inscribed in the poet's imagination and in the poem, in Milton's view, exposes the vanity of cavalier shepherds and nymphs in their fictitious and artificial Arcadias and yet manages to salvage classical pastoral motifs and conventions by redefining them. They become tarnished versions of paradise, restored in its purity by a sacred poetry whose images from nature foreshadow paradise.

But this view of Eden lost and paradise restored is a long time in finding what to do with the classical tradition and quick to disappear as a major element in pastoral after *Paradise Regained*. The problems of social class and artifice that oc-

cupy the pastorals of the earlier Renaissance reappear again in
the Augustan compromise between nature and art—before the
reaction of romanticism once again conceives of landscapes
capable of expressing spiritual powers that favor men unused
to social or poetic artifice.

THREE

Sidney's Knights
and Shepherds

Time ever old, and young is still revolved
　　Within itself, and never taketh end:
　　But mankind is for aye to nought resolved. . . .

Justice, justice is now (alas) oppressed:
　　Bountifulness hath made his last conclusion:
　　Goodness for best attire in dust is dressed.
Shepherds bewail your uttermost confusion;
　　And see by this picture to you presented,
　　Death is our home, life is but a delusion.

　　　　　　　　　　　　　　—DICUS

I

Gentle sorrow is a pervasive mood in the songs of Sidney's
Arcadia because perfection, though foremost in expectation, is
for various reasons unattainable. Elegiac yearning makes for
formal inconclusiveness because whether the shepherds face
backward toward a golden age or forward toward a better
but distant time they find their present condition incurable
and "drawn out." Ceremonies of resignation often bring about
a kind of peace-in-progress as passivity undermines desire for
minor adjustments ("I joy in grief, and do detest all joys,"
Sidney's Strephon sings almost comfortably); but songs alone
cannot lay their longing to rest. They sit not quite anesthetized
on hard rock:

　　No, no, forever gone is all our pleasure;
　　Forever wandring from all good direction;
　　Forever blinded of our clearest light;
　　Forever lamed of our surest might;

Forever banished from well placed affection;
Forever robbed of our royal treasure.

Let tears for him therefore be all our treasure,
And in our wailful naming him our pleasure:
Let hating of ourselves be our affection,
And unto death bend still our thoughts' direction.
Let us against ourselves employ our might,
And putting out our eyes seek we our light.

While shepherds never actually do employ might against themselves, they compile statements toward an infinity of "plaining."

For questing knights, too, the enemies that Arcadia offers are often too intangible or too entrenched in the nature of things to be defeated. No given act can modify significantly a sorrow as diffused through nature as the sorrow Strephon illustrates. Hence a pastoral-heroic mode is likely to bring together styles of action and kinds of hopelessness in a strange reciprocity. In Sidney's *Arcadia* that reciprocity is reflected in a double plot having contemplation and humble shepherdom on one level and chivalric manners and action on the other.

Sidney turns the combination of these pastoral and romance elements in several ways. Shepherdom encompasses not only the contemplative life and the ceremonial assuagements of poetry but also low comedy, rusticity, and the disorder of ungovernable mobs. Besides the pastoral games at the end of each section that emphasize the polite artificiality and the conventions of traditional pastoral, Arcadia contains ambitious butchers and ridiculous country lovers. When associated with the eroticism and femininity that Basilius and Pyrocles illustrate in their surrender of reason to passion, it suggests an abdication of social structure and government; but, when equated with the contemplative life, it models purity, intellect, and simplicity. The inactive rustics of Sidney's *Arcadia* are obsessed with the Golden Age as a distant and unreachable ideal, while active rustics try illegitimately to seize control of the government. (Rustics also perform the arts and crafts of Arcadia and are the vital producers in its economy.) Knights have perhaps even more variations. When active and disciplined, they model styles of honor and courage, but again, when surrendering to "feminine" passion they represent perverted, sensual corruption. A genuinely contemplative prince may participate in the shepherd's life of simple honesty, but in order to do so he must abandon his heroic pursuits, and lawlessness is likely to break loose while he sits idle.

This spectrum of contrasts between the heroic and pastoral elements of the *Arcadia* is complicated with each new incident and causes the prose of the work to bristle with elaborate comparisons and contrasts. The episodic structure that romance encourages allows Sidney to create an abundance of parallel incidents and emblem or tapestry-like panels. It is a penalty of the iron age that even the best of princes must choose a limited combination from the total possibilities of the tapestry, and putting the deficiencies of his choice in focus is one function of the shepherd life that is so unavailable, finally, to him.

II

First, the matter of structure and the reciprocity of the romance and pastoral elements. As originally conceived, the *Arcadia* was composed of five acts plotted tragicomically, the two princes Musidorus and Pyrocles heading toward apparent disaster and being saved at the last moment when it is discovered that they have not in fact actually slain king Basilius. The instability of the Arcadian government in the old version is corrected by a rereading of the oracle and by the demonstrated faithfulness and virtue of the unmasked lovers. All told, the outcome reinforces the positive virtues of the cavalier while suggesting that he gains very little from his exposure to shepherdom except a chance to prove his immunity to it. In the revised (1590) version, Sidney reshapes this dramatic structure, interlacing elaborate narrative flashbacks and weaving together more meaningfully the exploits of knight errantry and the quieter life of shepherds. He lessens the paralyzing effect of the pastoral retreat and makes the pastoral games and eclogues (the skirmish of reason and passion in the second eclogues, for instance) reflect the romance plot more directly. The compendium of model situations in which the knights demonstrate their various virtues and failings is enlarged and infused with the dreamlike atmosphere of Arcadia.

The first incident in the revised version sets the tension between romance and pastoral as Pyrocles falls among rebels and Musidorus arrives at the estate of Kalander on the periphery of Arcadia and sees the "delightful prospect" of Arcadian scenery as an outsider:

There were hills which garnished their proud heights with stately trees: humble valleys, whose base estate seemed comforted with refreshing of silver rivers: meadows, enameled with all sorts of eye-pleasing flowers: thickets, which being lined with most pleasant shade, were witnessed so to by the cheerful disposition of many well-tuned birds: each pasture stored with sheep feeding with sober security, while the pretty lambs with bleating oratory craved the dam's comfort: here a shepherd's boy piping, as though he should never be old: there a young shepherdess knitting, and withal singing, and it seemed that her voice comforted her hands to work and her hands kept time to her voice's music. As for the houses of the country . . . they were all scattered, no two being one by th'other, and yet not so far off as that it barred mutual succour: a show, as it were, of an accompanable solitariness, and of civil wildness.[1]

The controlling order of the passage is a multilayered harmony of contrasts which amounts to an implicit defense of the separation of noble and rustic elements, yet a recognition of their mutual need. The pleasures of each degree are set off and heightened by the contrasts, as humble valleys by hills, whose "base estates" are in turn comforted by elegant "silver" rivers. The shepherdess's work is governed by her singing, which regulates it and gives it the tempo of joy. The separation and mutual aid among classes is also suggested by the stationing of

[1] *The Prose Works of Sir Philip Sidney,* ed. Albert Feuillerat (Cambridge, 1962), pp. 13–14. Quotations are from vol. 1 unless otherwise indicated. I have modernized spelling where rhythm allows.

the houses and by the final two oxymoronic flourishes of the passage ("Accompanable solitariness" and "civil wildness").

The balance is carefully maintained with respect to mood as well. Musidorus' guides are the mournful Claius and Strephon, who have lost Urania (universal harmony), and Musidorus himself experiences the scene as solace, after a shipwreck has separated him from Pyrocles. The shepherd's boy pipes as though he should never be old, the conditional mood quietly admitting a sense of regret even while the pleasantness of the scene collaborates with it to convert it into a pleasing elegy. The apparent perfection is left hanging in doubt by the repetition of "seems": we are too far away to know precisely the state of mind of these people. Likewise, economically, the comfort of the scene is set against its wildness and solitude. The plenty of the pastures stored with sheep is conditioned by a certain Puritan sobriety, just as the hunger of the lambs is keen enough to give their bleating oratory a sharp edge.

Hence the discipline of the landscape as a whole suggests both that disturbances may intrude into Arcadia and that ideally they can be contained there by good management. Unlike the setting of satiric Utopias (such as Gulliver's) this harmonious scene is not created merely to be exploded by a closer look—say, at the absurdities that men live by while pretending to dignity. Rather, it is allowed to stand as an ideal model, Sidney's point being not that men are like this but that they ought to be and perhaps could be. The institutional order (the life of politics and active virtue) and the Arcadian mood are comfortably adjusted to each other.

Kalander's house, a model of domestic economy, is similarly ordered as contrastive harmony. Its elegance is balanced by a severe functionalism that bespeaks the discipline necessary to an iron age:

The lights, doors and stairs, rather directed to the use of the guest, than to the eye of the artificer: and yet as the one chiefly heeded, so the other not neglected; each place handsome without curiosity, and homely without loathsomeness: not so dainty as not to be trod on, nor yet slubbered up with good fellowship: all more lasting than beautiful, but that the consideration of the exceeding lastingness made the eye believe it was exceeding beautiful. The servants not so many in number, as cleanly in apparel, serviceable in behavior, testifying even in their countenances, that their master took as well care to be served, as of them that did serve. [P. 15]

Since poorer shepherds live in strict humility, it would not be proper for Kalander to display his superiority by superfluity. On the other hand, the only justification for a larger house is that Kalander has inherited a sense of grace and beauty missing in his subjects. And so the beauty of his house is made a quality of its usefulness, as a model of nobility, good taste, and modest wealth, and is later set against extremes of poverty and sensual luxuriance. (The Aristotelian mean embodied in the husbandry of the estate is not an argument for an equality of all ranks between luxury and poverty, but an acknowledgment of the need in each order to seek its own appropriate moderation.) It is revealing, too, that though Kalander claims in Strephon's presence that he asks nothing concerning "men's pedigrees" so long as he knows their virtues (p. 15), he "more respectfully" entertains Musidorus after seeing his chest of jewels.

Sidney gives the passage a stylistic elegance and dignity to suggest the even pace and rational discipline of the household. Each aspect of the total icon is filled out with pictorial exactness as each idyll is carefully stretched onto the framework of the long paragraphs and eventually fitted into the whole narrative. Antithesis and measured cadence suggest a masculine order without excessive ornamentation—nothing indeed being "slubbered up with good fellowship." The negatives of the model have the effect of disciplined understatement and controlled reason rather than enthusiasm. It is obviously a stoic version of Arcadia. Like Kalander's doors and stairs, the style is "directed for the use of the guest" rather than for the eye of the artificer; and yet as the one is chiefly heeded, the other is not neglected.

Kalander's disciplined household, then, is one way, the princely way, of dealing with the iron age; Strephon and

Claius, as I suggested, have another, the contemplative way. (The opening paradigm cannot be taken as quite a full model because these two styles are not fully integrated.) They establish no compensatory institutions to replace the lost Urania. Rather, when the "earth begins to put on her new apparel against the approach of her lover," their hopelessness becomes most poignant; "remembrance, remembrance, restless remembrance" is an incurable ache beyond whatever palliatives an ideal prince might devise. Urania in fact is never found in the old version of the *Arcadia,* though the shepherds receive messages from her; the last sentence recalls the fruitless quest for her that sets the new version in motion. Their lack of graceful action sometimes renders them all the more obviously "rustic" (Claius has nearly dropped her in helping her down from her horse), and as they dwell upon her transcendent beauty, they become aware of their own clownishness:

Hath not the only love of her made us (being silly ignorant shepherds) raise up our thoughts above the ordinary level of the world, so as great clerks do not disdain our conference? Hath not the desire to seem worthy in her eyes made us when others were sleeping, to sit viewing the course of heavens? . . . Hath not she thrown reason upon our desires, and, as it were given eyes unto Cupid? Hath in any, but in her, love-fellowship maintained friendship between rivals, and beauty taught the beholders charity? [Pp. 7–8]

To shepherds as contemplative outsiders, then, realization through action—which is a form of possession—is denied.

A third element in the opening set of situations is the Laconian Wasteland where the rebel Helots have destroyed all levels of idyllic existence and good government, and where because the peasants have taken it upon themselves to act against tyranny, all roles are reversed. As Musidorus joins Kalander's household, Pyrocles, the more warlike of the two, helps to organize and control the rebels. In place of the companionable solitariness that characterizes Kalander's estate, the Helots have fallen into general fear and distrust. They observe no ceremonies, and civil war has disfigured "the face of nature" in the economy outside their gates.

In these three model situations, the active virtues and the contemplative life of Arcadia are established as opposites both to rebellion and to each other. To the heroes as knights, the dangers of strife call for majesty in danger, fairness in victory, reasonableness in statesmanship, proper condescension toward inferiors. For the subordinate classes as subjects, the threat of strife, inner and outer, requires proper recognition of authority, simple dignity, skill in execution of duties, sobriety, and loyalty to the hierarchical order. For those shepherds like Strephon and Claius whose desire fastens on something out of reach, politics holds little interest.

III

The episodes that follow in the later version of the *Arcadia* explore the imperfections of nobility and rusticity and their relations, in various combinations of broken form. I will cite only a few salient and useful examples of these, without attempting to establish their places in the text. On the highest level, Basilius illustrates the effects of passion on the kingship; Musidorus and Pyrocles illustrate the dangers of the courtier in love; and on the level of rusticity, the subjects of Arcadia represent several subsidiary dangers as they depart from their natural functions and become clowns or chaotic rabble. Perversions of nobility and rusticity naturally vary in thoroughness. The rebellious mobs, for instance, illustrate humbleness become seriously prideful, while Mopsa and Damaetas represent a merely farcical ambition. The interaction of these elements results in a series of social transvaluations or changes of costume and station but in no genuine changes in character. One either fulfills the potential inherent in his birth and station or perverts it: he cannot metamorphose himself into another class. Thus as we are shown knighthood as shepherds practice it and eclogues as knights sing them, it is clear that each is and will remain basically foreign to the other.

Conceit, burlesque, and wit generally—modes that cause us to see one thing in terms of something else—bring these opposites together incongruously. The immediate effect of the contrasts is to sharpen social distinctions and fixed categories despite Arcadia's normal tendency to remove barriers between classes. The tone of the satire derives from Sidney's sense of the fixed manner or decorum associated with each state. The antiromance battles of Arcadia, for instance, are narrated with a mixture of aristocratic disdain, irony, and grotesque realism which makes the mob, when it intrudes in the realm of knighthood, a monstrous joke. The realism is an implicit answer to naturalists such as Montaigne who would destroy distinctions of rank on the basis of men's mutual animalism as though a touch of nature made all men kin. The comedy not only assigns a place to shepherds but offers the princes opportunities for exhibitions of graceful bearing. A knight wields comfortably and ceremonially objects that trip up those enviously reaching for new possessions:

Yet among the rebels there was a dapper fellow, a tailor by occupation, who fetching his courage only from their going back, began to bow his knees, and very fencer-like to draw near to Zelmane. But as he came within her distance, turning his sword very nicely about his crown, Basilius, with a side blow, struck off his nose. He (being a suiter to a seamster's daughter, and therefore not a little grieved for such a disgrace) stooped down, because he had heard, that if it were fresh put to, it would cleave on again. But as his hand was on the ground to bring his nose to his head, Zelmane with a blow, sent his head to his nose. That saw a butcher, a butcherly chuff indeed . . . and lifted up a great leaver, calling Zelmane all the vile names of a butcherly eloquence. But she (letting slip the blow of the leaver) hit him so surely on the side of his face, that she left nothing but the nether jaw, where the tongue still wagged, as willing to say more, if his master's remembrance had served. O (said a miller that was half drunk) see the luck of a good fellow, and with that word, ran with a pitchfork at Dorus: but the nimbleness of the wine carried his head so fast, that it made it overrun his feet, so that he fell withal just between the legs of Dorus; who setting his foot on his neck (though he offered two milch kine, and four fat hogs for his life) thrust his sword quite through, from one ear to the other; which took it very unkindly, to feel such news before they heard of them, instead of hearing, to be put to such feeling. [Pp. 312–313]

Dorus then cuts the hands off a painter and divides another miller in two at the waist, the miller's soul issuing forth "in wine and blood."

The same devices of syntactical balance and antithesis that characterize the description of Kalander's house Sidney here uses to reinforce the ironic comedy. The description is conceived as a series of nicely turned phrases that reduce physical violence to farce. By emphasizing occupations and the vulgarity of the mob, Sidney exposes its sensual preferences—the tailor's for his nose (only a nose, Tristram Shandy would insist), the miller's for his property, and the painter's for the excessive realism of the counterfeit battle he intends to paint. By pinning all their hopes on certain absurd fragments of things as property or as symbols of their independence and worth, they have in effect already lost the soul's mastery of its housing. The butcher's blasphemous tongue continues to wag, though separated from memory and soul. The miller's head and feet go at different paces toward Dorus, and his soul, rather than flying ethereally to heaven, is materialized and spills away.[2] Insofar as the *Arcadia* is a book of instructions in war as well as a book of manners, this grotesqueness prepares the young prince for treating rebellious subjects as things, their parts forming humorous symbols for the passions that have carried them off. They are no more than limbs of the state already lost. The discrepancy between the expectations of the subjects and their just punishment forestalls our sympathy for them; and that they would have been doomed anyway by further strife among themselves—whether or not the knights were there to administer punishment—is revealed later when the mob divides into factions that begin killing each other for

[2] The dying of members of the mob suggests that the townsmen share the materialism of Lucretius, which makes the independence of limbs evidence of the material nature of the vital spirit: "Another, who has lost a leg, does his best to stand up, while on the ground at his side the dying foot twitches its toes. A head hewn from the still warm and living trunk retains on the ground its lively features and open eyes." Lucretius, *The Nature of the Universe,* trans. R. E. Latham (London: Penguin Books, 1951), p. 115.

lack of a common goal. Once the closely balanced classes are allowed to pull apart, nothing can prevent their flying at each other's throats.

This is merely one of many panels in the total tapestry of lowborn self-interest and the double conceit of "mobster-government," "humble-courtliness." As the shift to irony and farce illustrates, the style of Arcadian knighthoood varies according to the anti-idyllic element the prince has to contend with. The contrast between comic reality and "romantic" or knightly pretension is further developed in the riotous tournament of rustic warriors. The shepherd Damaetas, of course, fails in his imitation of the knightly manner:

Then the trumpets sounding, Damaetas-his horse . . . when he thought least of the matter, started out so lustily that Damaetas was jogged back with head, and body, and pulling withal his bridle hand, the horse (that was tender of mouth) made half a stop and fell to bounding, so that Damaetas threw away his lance, and with both hands held by the pummel: the horse, half running, half leaping, till he met with Clinias: who fearing he should miss his rest, had put his staff therein before he began his career: neither would he then have begun, but that at the trumpet's warning, one (that stood behind) struck on his horse, who running swiftly, the wind took such hold of his staff, that it crossed quite over his breast, and in that sort gave a flat bastonado to Damaetas: who, half out of his saddle, went near to his old occupation of digging the earth, but with the crest of his helmet. . . . Damaetas, when he saw him come with his sword drawn, nothing conceiving of any such intent [as Clinias surrendering to him] went back as fast as his back and heels would lead him. But as Clinias found that, he began to think a possibility on the victory, and therefore followed with the cruel haste of a prevailing coward; laying upon Damaetas, who did nothing but cry out to him to hold his hand: sometimes that he was dead, sometimes that he would complain to Basilius. [Pp. 432–433]

Though similar in some ways to Chaucer's dressing a middle-class bumpkin in knightly paraphernalia, Sidney's anti-pageant is no reflection upon knightly codes and ceremonies themselves, which appear all the stronger for the incapacity of rustics to enact them. Though the ostensible sin of Damaetas

and Clinias is cowardice, Sidney's main delight is obviously
in their deficiency of style, as, after accidentally gaining victory,
Damaetas intends to slaughter Clinias as he would an animal:
"Therefore he thought best to kneel down upon him, and with
a great whittle he had (having disarmed his head) to cut his
throat, which he had used so with calves, as he had no small
dexterity in it" (p. 434). And so on with the other burlesques
of romance in the *Arcadia:* Mopsa in the tree mistaking
Damaetas for Apollo, come, she thinks, to make her a queen
as queens are made as in fairy tales; Damaetas digging furiously for gold that is to transform him into a propertied citizen; village orators hatching plans for a new civil order;
Mopsa as an object of exalted love and subject of sonnets:

Like great god Saturn fair, and like vair Venus chaste:
As smooth as Pan, as Juno mild, like goddess Iris fast.
With Cupid she foresees, and goes god Vulcan's pace:
And for a taste of all these gifts, she steals god Momus grace.

IV

If Sidney's rustics err in assuming the power and ceremonies of
nobility, nobles are equally out of propriety in costuming themselves as lovers and rustics and abandoning their proper stations. Basilius unfortunately has the virtues appropriate to a
feminine nature, meekness, courtesy, mercifulness, liberality,
and his wife Gynecia has the princely virtues of strength and
greatness. His misplaced kindness causes him to transform
Damaetas's rustic qualities into integrity, and "beastly ignorance" into virtuous simplicity (p. 22). Whereas this "descent"
of Basilius has primarily social and political importance, that
of the two princes is predominantly psychological, a descent of
reason into passion. In each case, the defection from just and
proper standards results in a destructive if temporary metamorphosis, symbolized in Basilius by his mistaken and unrea-
soning pursuit of the wrong sex and in the princes by their
transvestitism:

Transformed in show, but more transformed in mind,
I cease to strive with double conquest foiled:

For (woe is me) my powers all I find
With outward force, and inward treason spoiled.

[P. 76]

Yet at the same time, such degradation provides an experience of the lower orders (passion, shepherdom) that ultimately serves to strengthen the romance heroes. It is on the basis of this unpredictable benefit that a tragicomic reversal of their fates is sanctioned. Sidney implies that whatever the need for Evarchus's intervention to save the princes from their own miscalculations, they can make use of the lessons of Arcadia; they have done no serious damage and are predestined by the oracle to win the ladies. Rusticity and nobility may participate to some extent in their opposites: though a king cannot step outside his office and become an admirer of Damaetas without risking the health of the kingdom, the princes are free adventurers. The question that confronts them is not so much whether or not to participate in all the activities of the shepherds as how reciprocity between them and shepherd life is to be kept from becoming debilitating. The goal of their education is to discover a manner of engaging rusticity while remaining separate from it and essentially untransformed.

Their participation is made easier by shepherdom's own function as a model of ideal friendship, an unambitious and simple marriage of true minds. Strephon and Claius, as we have seen, counterbalance Musidorus and Pyrocles initially, and subsequently they represent a relatively high form of contemplative pursuit. The difference between the two pairs is similar to that between true simplicity and the complexities of court in Sidney's poem "Dispraise of a Courtly Life." The best of friendships is found "in poor shepherds' base degree":

Nay, what need the art to those,
To whom we our love disclose?
It is to be used then,
When we do but flatter men:
Friendship true in heart assured,
Is by nature's gifts procured.

Therefore shepherds wanting skill,
Can Love's duties best fulfill:

> Since they know not how to fain,
> Nor with Love to cloak disdain,
> Like the wiser sort, whose learning,
> Hides their inward will of harming.

The pursuit of a hopeless love enables Strephon and Claius to claim "love-fellowship" and "charity." In accordance with the Platonist concept that love can metamorphose one for the better as well as for the worse (it "doth transform the very essence of the lover into the thing loved, uniting, as it were incorporating it with a secret and inward working"), they are transformed spiritually by their love for Urania: "For . . . love of heaven makes one heavenly, the love of vertue, vertuous" (p. 78). At the same time, in a social sense, they remain merely the rustics Strephon and Claius.

The equilibrium required of a shepherd situated low and reaching high is perhaps as difficult as that demanded of knights who find themselves embroiled in confusing plots and forced by love to surrender their habitual dignity and join the activities of shepherdom. Musidorus and Pyrocles are by and large successful in these activities but in danger unless they can find ways to demonstrate their courtly status in them. In the first eclogue contests, for instance, Musidorus pauses to consider love's torments as though from outside himself, as Lalus beckons to him:

> Come Dorus, come, let songs thy sorrows signify:
> And if for want of use thy mind ashamed is,
> That very shame with Love's high title dignify.
>   No style is held for base, where Love well named is:
> Each ear sucks up the words, a true love scattereth,
> And plain speech oft, than quaint phrase, better framed is.

Songs "signify" sorrow in the sense of rendering its significance, which is one task of art, and they dignify love by giving it "high title" in plain speech. The ravages of passion, degrading in "real" life, thus become strength in art. Though Dorus resists putting high love in shepherd terms ("Nor true love loves those loves with others' mingled be"), Lalus answers that in the games of Arcadia, all may be equal:

If thou wilt not be seen, thy face go hide away,
Be none of us, or else maintain our fashion:
Who frowns at others' feasts, doth better bide away.

Thus Dorus is forced to accept the challenge, and both he and
Lalus attitudinize at length, Dorus having the better of it, as
Ringler points out.[3] The result is a new respect for the arts:

Of singing take to thee the reputation
New friends of mine; I yield to thy hability:
My soul doth seek another estimation.

But Dorus then turns, as the active life encourages, from the
pleasures of song for its own sake to the usefulness of song as
a means of winning the lady, to the achieving of another
"estimation" from that of the rustic singer.

But ah my Muse I would thou hadst agility,
To work my Goddess so by thy invention,
On me to cast those eyes, where shine nobility.
    Seen, and unknown; heard, but without attention.

If the highest art is both useful and beautiful, the art of the
ideal prince should carry him one step farther than art as pure
ceremony: when he sings he would be heard where it counts;
he would be seen by "those eyes, where shine nobility."

For shepherds, however, art is at its highest when it removes
the need for action. In moments of highest yearning for perfection, Strephon and Claius move farthest away from the
princely attitude toward the iron age. In *Seven Types of
Ambiguity,* Empson has pointed out the ambiguity of the dirge
"You Goatherd Gods," in which disappointment over the lost
Urania is elevated to universal sorrow so broadly conceived
that it precludes all except ceremonial strategies for dealing
with it. "Plaining music" becomes an "ideal state" of mourning, a pleasing lament that defies action:

Yee Gote-heard Gods, that love the grassie mountaines,
Yee Nimphes that haunt the springs in pleasant vallies,

[3] See *The Poems of Sir Philip Sidney,* ed. William A. Ringler,
Jr. (Oxford, 1962), pp. 385-386.

You Satyrs joyde with free and quiet forrests,
Vouchsafe your silent eares to playning musique,
Which to my woes gives still an early morning:
And drawes the dolor on till very evening.

Claius

O *Mercurie,* foregoer to the evening,
O heavenlie huntresse of the savage mountaines,
O lovelie starre, entitled of the morning,
While that my voice doth fill these wofull vallies,
Vouchsafe your silent eares to plaining musique,
Which oft hath Echo tir'd in secrete forests.

So pervasive is sorrow that stately mountains "transforme
themselves" to "lowe dejected vallies"; nightingales' songs become the music of owls. Though the nearly exact formal dupli-
cation of the stanza in each singer suggests dialectical statement and response, the "reply" is amplification only: it becomes clear that the result of their exchange is gray uniformity.
The shepherds threaten to go "mad with music," as they are
mad with worship of her "whose parts maintainde a perfect
musique, / Whose beautie shin'de more than the blushing
morning."

v

Whatever the mutual benefits of their exposure to each other,
the active and contemplative lives must eventually separate.
The emphasis in the last group of eclogues (as Sidney's original editors arranged them) is upon dissolution of the bonds
between the knights and the shepherds. While Pyrocles and
Musidorus become totally involved in maneuvers and repercussions, the "shepherds, finding no place for them in these
garboyles, to which their quiet hearts (whose highest ambition was in keeping themselves up in goodness) had at all no
aptness," retire "from among the clamorous multitude." Their
achievement is the art of lamentation itself, "austerely maintained sorrowfulness," distilled, elegiac, contemplative. Though
they reflect upon the immediate action of the romance plot,

their "universal complaint" is concerned with a "universal mischief" in contrast with which the events of Arcadia are only a passing affair.

Even so, their retreat helps to set the romance plot in focus by revealing the limitations of heroic achievement. The tragicomic ending is shaded all round with ambivalence.[4] The suggestion of rebirth and miraculous transformation in Basilius's revival is offset by a hopeless denial of rebirth in Dicus's lament:

> The filthy snake her aged coat can mend,
>   And getting youth again, in youth doth flourish:
>   But unto man, age ever death doth send.

The final interplay of eclogue and narrative thus has Virgilian effects in suggesting joy enacted in a diffused atmosphere of deprivation. Though "Princes" may be metamorphosed symbolically into flowers, flowers weep forever:

> And you, O flowers, which sometimes Princes were,
>   Till these strange alterings you did hap to try,
>   Of Prince's loss yourselves for tokens rear,
> Lilly in mourning black thy whiteness dye:
>   Of Hyacinth let AI be on thee still.
>   Your doleful tunes sweet Muses now apply.

In terms of the politics of Arcadia, this view suggests that, since princes cannot magically transform the iron into the Golden Age, the mind that reaches out to the distant vistas of a Strephon or a Claius must withhold a little of itself from the temporal order. Whatever new harmony one might imagine for the eclogues had Sidney finished revising the *Arcadia,* the contemplative shepherd would have to participate in it symbolically or ritualistically, as the order of knights continues its noble pageantry and its pursuit of achievement. As

[4] Cf. Walter R. Davis, *A Map of Arcadia* in *Sidney's Arcadia* (New Haven: Yale University Press, 1965), pp. 59–113, and David Kalstone, *Sidney's Poetry* (Cambridge, Mass.: Harvard University Press, 1965), pp. 9–101. These studies of the *Arcadia* appeared too late to benefit my own, which is much slighter, but they confirm several points and complement others.

it is, high-minded shepherds continue to lament "justice, justice is now (alas) oppressed / . . . . Goodness for best attire in dust is dressed," and rustic shepherds no doubt continue dreaming vainly of favors from Apollo. The two realms, though Sidney has them engage each other as thoroughly as any pastoral romance manages, drift apart. It is left for Shakespeare to imagine a more far-reaching transformation of the courtly group when it is exposed to shepherdom or the land of faery, and left for Milton to conceive of a paradise that demands one's total absorption. For Sidney, the landscape of the idealizing imagination and probably the making of poems, too, are momentary if irresistible diversions from an active political and social life that calls one to arduous duties.

FOUR

Spenser: The Queen and
the Court Singer

I

Hans Christian Andersen's anecdote of the nightingale and the emperor illustrates the difficulties of more than one poet in the service of kings. In the distant parts of an enormous garden surrounding a Chinese palace of precious porcelain, a nightingale sings unheard except for a fisherman and now and then a few travelers, all rustic by comparison with the elegant people of the court. The emperor at length hears about it and summons it, and when it sings it is a smashing success. Unfortunately, the king then has it caged and tied with a silk ribbon to be held by twelve servants when it goes abroad. Besides that, an artificial diamond-studded-imitation-nightingale soon arrives in the mail from another emperor and sings rather more to the pleasure of the court. And so the live bird is banished—until one day much later Death comes to the emperor's chamber and the now ailing machine bird proves to be of no help in getting rid of the unwanted visitor. The live singer returns and charms Death back to the graveyard; the emperor recovers and promises never again to put his singer in a cage.

But he is an unusually wise emperor to appreciate the real as opposed to the decorative value of the poet. Spenser was never so securely situated. Though the Elizabethan court acknowledged the worth of poetry, it tended also to insist in subtle ways upon the cage and the ribbon. The ambivalent feelings in pastoral toward the humble poet-shepherd, together with the indirections of allegory, allowed him to lodge protests and make pleas, and at the same time explore the relative value of social advancement and artistic achievement. The implication of Calidore's intrusion upon Colin Clout's vision of the graces on Mt. Acidale is that, compared with the poet's pure version of the graces, the best of the court's representative knights, the Knight of Courtesy—at least in his present stage of development—is crude and unseeing. This representative of the court, rather than ordinary intruders in Arcadia such as untamed nature, love, death, or animalism, is responsible for Colin's loss.

Looked at in retrospect with that encounter in mind, Spenser's pastoral works from 1579 to the early 1590s leave the impression that the poet's relationship with the court was never easy. His shepherds are nearly always neglected singers and social critics. In *The Shepheardes Calender,* the poet-shepherd suffers from both the torments of unrequited love and the ache of unfulfilled ambition. Since the hapless shepherd adopts similar tactics of forlorn "courtship" in each case, and Colin's feeling about Rosalind (whom McLane identifies with Queen Elizabeth) [1] can be equated roughly with Spenser's attitude toward bettering his fortune, Colin's and Spenser's conditions may be taken as analogous to each other. The poem's apparatus reinforces that connection. The analogy accounts for the odd tactics of the poem as a strong complaint against a current lack of regard for poetry and yet a deferential and apologetic acknowledgment of the poet's humble place: for the poet must write humbly, in the realism of plain speaking, old-fashioned shepherds, and at the same time elegantly, in an assortment of nicely turned rhetorical figures which reveal his gifts. All the eclogues except the sportive exercises deal with one or another aspect of the ambition-humility complex and its mixed style, but to extract a precise complaint out of them directly from Spenser is impossible. Every twist in the succession of attitudes and varied modes is serpentine, doubling back upon some other.

The brash young climber of the February eclogue, for in-

[1] Paul E. McLane, *Spenser's Shepheardes Calender: A Study in Elizabethan Allegory* (Notre Dame, Ind.: University of Notre Dame Press, 1961), pp. 27 ff.

stance, causes the destruction of a sacred institution, the royal oak:

> For it had bene an auncient tree,
> Sacred with many a mysteree,
> And often crost with the priestes crewe,
> And often halowed with holy water dewe.
>
> [207–210]

Besides undermining a peaceful reign, the briar's ambition torments the climber himself, which suggests that the poet realizes clearly the dangers of pushing too hard. And yet Colin has already been shown to be perishing from lack of acknowledgment from Rosalind and has smashed his pipe in despair (though the motto of the poem is "still hope"!). And the implication of the April eclogue is that he is potentially the best poet to celebrate "fayre Eliza, queen of shepheardes all" even though so pitifully outcast that his friends (including Gabriel Harvey as Hobbinoll) must deliver his song for him.

Thomalin in the March eclogue actively pursues the god Cupid but soon becomes the hunter hunted. His festering wound is the product of an innocent aggressiveness. It is clearly better to avoid the hunt, but then one is struck by "love" (as the assertion of the desire to possess) before he realizes it. The May eclogue concerns ambition in religious circles and implies that the proper business of the pastor is merely to attend his flock:

> *Piers.* But tract of time, and long prosperitie,
> (That nource of vice, this of insolencie,)
> Lulled the shepheards in such securitie,
> That not content with loyall obeysaunce,
> Some gan to gape for greedie governaunce,
> And match them selfe with mighty potentates,
> Lovers of lordship and troublers of states.
>
> [117–123]

Spenser suggests that ordained ministers should recognize the necessity for loyal obedience: in religious orders as well as in those on the outside, respect for "mighty potentates" must

come foremost. But the difference between poet and pastor is
that the religious establishment is in a position to promote
itself while the poet has no organization and presents no danger. Palinode replies angrily to Piers's notion of obedience,
giving the other side of the argument:

> who can counsell a thirstie soule,
> With patience to forebeare the offred bowle? . . .
> Thou raylest on right withouten reason,
> And blamest hem much, for small encheason.
> How shoulden shepheardes live, if not so?
> What! should they pynen in payne and woe?
> Nay saye I thereto, by my deare borrowe,
> If I may rest, I nill live in sorrowe.
>
> [138–139, 146–151]

The answer that Piers makes is cast as a story of the kid and
the fox. But since it is relevant only to the Catholic-Protestant
level of the conflict and does not dispose of Palinode's objections concerning humility in general, Palinode suggests
that they carry it to Sir John in the local church: he, too, a
lover of idle fiction, is habitually beside the point—which is
a bold statement, but after all, again, it is only Palinode who
makes it. The allegorical veil and the old-fashioned language
make the quarrel seem relatively harmless.

The June eclogue compresses this ambivalence toward ambition into a single two-pronged poem. While denying his
ambition, Colin claims Tityrus (Chaucer) for a teacher and
hopes that—though he pipes only to please himself and even
that badly—his complaints might serve as "messengers of all
my painfull plight." Humility leaves the door open for Rosalind to change her mind, but the grievance is strongly urged.
The July, September, and October eclogues condemn the
scramble for recognition even more bluntly, partly by associating it with Rome; but Spenser insists that the values of poetry
are distinct from those of society generally. Predicting Colin's
outburst on Mt. Acidale, Piers comments on the present state
of poets:

> O pierlesse Poesye, where is then thy place?
> If nor in princes pallace thou doe sitt.

(And yet is princes pallace the most fitt)
Ne brest of baser birth doth thee embrace.
Then make thee winges of thine aspyring wit,
And, whence thou camst, flye backe to heaven apace.

[October, 79–84]

Though poetry "flies" only in the service of some noble truth, it cannot survive in a cultural vacuum and requires princes' palaces, its most fit habitation. Scorning "such famous flight" as Piers describes, Colin is clearly blighted; yet love when purified, as Piers remarks, is the very force that teaches him to "climbe . . . hie." It

lyftes him up out of the loathsome myre:
Such immortall mirrhor as he doth admire
Would rayse ones mynd above the starry skie,
And cause a caytive corage to aspire;
For lofty love doth loath a lowly eye.

[92–96]

But then again Cuddie answers that

The vaunted verse a vacant head demaundes,
Ne wont with crabbed Care the Muses dwell:
Unwisely weaves, that takes two webbes in hand,

and associates even "pure" poetry with the cruder free-inspiration of wine, admitting that it fails him. Hence better to be humble after all:

But ah! my corage cooles ere it be warme;
Forthy content us in thys humble shade,
Where no such troublous tydes han us assayde.
Here we our slender pipes may safely charme.

[115–118]

And so the argument goes, ambition and humility, the desire to be immune from the scramble and the dubious inspiration of love counterbalancing each other, suggesting that the poet's value does not lie merely in his capacity to provide entertainment and that poetry should receive social recognition even for its nonsocial flights.

The problem of relating the order of nature and the order

of grace crosses this theme of ambition on a bias. Because ambition under the Christian scheme is ill-advised, divine grace
offers little temporal hope in the poet's attempt to reconcile
politics and poetry.[2] Theology associates the blighting of the
poet's hopes with the inevitable disappointments of temporal
life. Thus the elegiac lament of the November eclogue finds
"Dido," like Colin, an unfulfilled victim of destiny, destroyed
by the "trustlesse state of earthly things":

> and slipper hope
> Of mortal men, that swincke and sweate for nought,
> And shooting wide, doe misse the marked scope:
> Now have I learnd, (a lesson derely bought)
> That nys on earth assuraunce to be sought.
>
> [153–157]

But

> maugre Death, and dreaded sisters deadly spight,
> And gates of Hel, and fyrie furies forse,
> She hath the bonds broke of eternall night,
> Her soule unbodied of the burdenous corpse.
>
> [163–166]

The problem of preferment is thus brought into focus as
part of the universal pattern of mortal disappointment, to give
way eventually to another kind of reward (as in "Lycidas,"
"fame" is no plant that grows in mortal soil). The Christian
paradox of dying to achieve life transcends but does not dis-

----

[2] Following the lead of A. S. P. Woodhouse, a number of
critics emphasize the conflict between the order of nature and the
order of grace. See A. C. Hamilton, "The Argument of Spenser's
Shepeardes Calender," *ELH,* 23 (1956), 171–182; Robert Allen
Durr, "Spenser's Calendar of Christian Time," *ELH* 24 (1957),
269–295. Closer to the central concern of the poem is Hallet
Smith's excellent account of pastoralism as a "rejection of the
aspiring mind" and of the tradition of dispraise of court life in
preceding pastorals, *Elizabethan Poetry* (Cambridge, Mass.: Har-
vard University Press, 1952), p. 11. See also Muriel Bradbrook,
"No Room at the Top: Spenser's Pursuit of Fame," in *Elizabethan
Poetry, Stratford Upon Avon Studies,* 2 (1960), 91–109; John F.
Danby, *Poets on Fortune's Hill* (London, 1952), p. 35.

place the poet's paradox of annihilating oneself in humility, ritually killing off hope (*"Gia speme spenta"*), in order to fulfill highest ambition.

From Colin's viewpoint, the mood of that final permutation is mixed. While Dido "lives . . . with the blessed gods in blisse," the poet himself moves toward a final December blight. But the Spenser who adds the apparatus of the poem is not identical with Colin, of course; the change he would supposedly suggest for the poet is neither the "death" of Colin nor the resurrected life of Dido, but merely a suitable recognition of the court singer. The dedicatory poem and the concluding poem are integral parts of the poem's tactics, halfway between the fictive masks and allegorical figures of the eclogues and the "real" Spenser. With these appendages, *The Shepheardes Calender* as a whole becomes an indirect form of beseeching, addressed to various powers in the Sidney-Leicester group as well as to the queen (including "Maister Philip Sidney" and an unnamed "gentlewoman of no meane house"). For the apparatus, like the text, adopts a humble pose and at the same time suggests what might be said for the poet:

> But if that any aske thy name,
> Say thou wert base begot with blame:
> Forthy thereof thou takes shame.
> And when thou art past jeopardee,
> Come tell me what was sayd of mee:
> And I will send more after thee.
> > Immerito.

The "exterior" poet points out that poems, not princes, last forever: *vivitur ingenio: caetera mortis erunt* ("talent lives; all else perishes"):

Loe! I have made a Calender for every yeare,
That steele in strength, and time in durance, shall outweare:
And if I marked well that starres revolution,
It shall continewe till the worlds dissolution.

The awkward poet, "base begot," appears to imitate base speech, and yet his "rough and harsh termes enlumine and make more clearly to appeare the brightnesse of brave and glorious words" as E. K. says. The "lyttle Calender" is thus sent forth as a "free paseport"; by disposing of Colin so piti-lessly, Colin's creator opens doors for the poet, who still lives and may be rescued from oblivion by the court.

II

Calidore's pastoral interlude in the sixth book of *The Faerie Queene* has analogies not only with *The Shepheardes Calender* and interim works such as "Virgil's Gnat" and "Prosopopoia" but also with the encounters of various knights in earlier books with untutored crudity, intuitive goodness, corrupted sophisti-cation, perverse nobility, and the like. All told, these encounters make clear that the correction of man's wolfish nature de-mands more from poetry than images of ideal form and beauty. For as an allegorical, didactic romance itself testifies, poetry has a corrective, ethical function. When the social in-stitutions defended in Calidore's heroic quest encounter "po-etry" (Colin's vision), the mandate of Queen Gloriana takes preference.

The implications of their competition will perhaps be clearer if we consider Milton's pastoral-heroic combination, which retains the corrective, panegyric, and satiric functions of poetry but jettisons the "furniture," as Milton calls it, of chivalric contests, the "emblazon'd Shields, / Impreses quaint, Caparisons and Steeds: / Bases and Tinsel Trappings, gor-geous Knights." He substitutes for these the doings of a wife and husband who regard dignity as a matter not of feudal service but of divine propriety, deriving from their cosmic situation. Like the man who asked "When Adam delved and Eve span, / Who was then the gentleman?" Milton wields the myth as a kind of swordlike Puritan weapon, retracting his early admiration for Spenserian romance. Eden rather than the queen's fairy court becomes the achetypal center to which the idyllic imagination refers; and unlike the land of Pas-torella, it remains relevant as a model of heroic dignity to those in historical duress. As both a foreshadowing of Paradise regained and as a model of ideal divine-human, man-wife relations, it offers a higher standard than chivalric lovers do.

In Spenser's queen-centered model, the idyllic life is not a standard but a fragile rival order, comparable to the imagination's truancy from feudal service in "pure" poetic vision. Rather than icons of Eden (hieroglyphs of the divine presence in nature), Spenser's pastoral bowers and paradisal love represent a step downward in the scale of courtship, which in its highest form carries the hero upward from "nature" through the formal institutions of church and state. Plain, unadorned man does not have the requisite decorative abundance or ceremony that a fully instituted pursuit demands, nor does he have the discipline. To abandon courtly institutions for idyllic love is therefore to allow the Blatant Beast to run wild:

> Who now does follow the foule Blatant Beast,
> Whilest Calidore does follow that faire mayd,
> Unmyndfull of his vow, and high beheast
> Which by the Faery Queene was on him layd?
> [6.10.1]

The function of a poetry of paradisal icons is correspondingly different in Spenser than in Milton. The first Poet in Milton is Adam himself, from whom hymns issue almost by instinct and rise to God's ear without intermediaries. Even in postlapsarian life, when nature has grown hostile and needs correction, the poet requires only rigorous spiritual discipline, scripture, and inner light. To Spenser, the artist who neglects standards of elegance and refinement for Arcadian pleasures is as guilty of truancy as the knight-hero. Since uneducated nature is little more than barbaric instinct, it is impossible to unite nature and art ideally except through courtly refinement. But as the Bower of Bliss illustrates, art when less than ideal can be as great a danger as false eroticism (the two are related). While the Garden of Adonis is "nature, fecundity, life," as C. S. Lewis writes in *The Allegory of Love,* the Bower is "artifice, sterility, death" (p. 326). Its gatekeeper, Genius, maintains governance through "guilefull semblance" and protean illusion, which suggests a corruption of nature by art; the Bower itself is extravagantly lavish:

Mantled with greene, and goodly beautifide
With all the ornaments of Floraes pride,
Wherewith her mother Art, as half in scorne
Of niggard Nature, like a pompous bride
Did decke her, and too lavishly adorne,
When forth from virgin bowre she comes in th' early morne.
[11.12.50]

"Mother Art" and "niggard Nature" are sinuously intertwined and yet choking each other rather than bringing forth their mutual best. The failure to observe the inclinations of simple nature leads to an erotic daydream that falls more properly to Sir Guyon's correction than to a knight of courtesy. Hence, left entirely to itself, nature becomes artlessly savage. But sophisticated evil is equally dangerous. Given the lover's and the poet's tendency to lapse into sensuality, Spenser clearly prefers the dignity that is the product of training to adamic "native dignity" with its implicitly egalitarian faith in right reason. As an enactment of degree in manners, courtesy is necessary to both Arcadian love (Pastorella) and to the highest art (Colin's vision): degree applied to style is decorum; applied to love, graceful courtship.

   In book six of *The Faerie Queene,* having already ranged Love, Chastity, Justice, and other virtues on a scale from mundane to divine (with Queen Gloriana at the peak of earthly virtue together with Arthur), Spenser associates Courtesy with appropriate speech and just conduct:

What vertue is so fitting for a knight,
Or for a ladie whom a knight should love,
As curtesie, to beare themselves aright
To all of each degree, as doth behove?
[6.2.1]

Not only does the ideal chivalric knight conduct himself toward each according to the place of each, but is himself immediately recognizable by manner:

> True is, that whilome that good poet sayd,
> The gentle minde by gentle deeds is knowne:
> For a man by nothing is so well bewrayd
> As by his manners, in which plaine is showne
> Of what degree and what race he is growne.
>
> [6.3.1]

Given this emphasis upon degree, it is not surprising that one of the social-political duties of the knight is to defend titles; decorum involves not only the display of proper manners but also the official recognition of position, and the Blatant Beast is not so much a natural savage as a backbiting gossiper who disregards the proper and acquired names of rank. For defaming is a way of transferring substance by leveling "character." The knight of courtesy, serving as a corrective function in a world of gossip, must be as quick to chastise a Crudor as to reward a Tristram. The wounds of his battles are metaphoric stings of infamy. Rituals of greeting and other ways of observing station occupy the first part of book six, in which Spenser defines the differences between those of noble birth such as Briana and Crudor (who contrast to the "low" courtesy and hospitality of the shepherds later); those of noble birth only half trained but basically good such as Tristram; nobles totally untrained such as the savage man; ignoble savages such as the cannibals and brigands; and finally perverted nobles who steal and slander until made to stop.

That training as well as instinct underlies courtesy is clear in Tristram, who is of high birth but untutored as a knight, and in the savage man, who takes pity upon Calepine and Serena. The latter is eventually found to be of noble blood, which induces him to honor Serena's royal beauty:

> But the wyld man, contrarie to her feare,
> Came to her creeping like a fawning hound,
> And by rude tokens made to her appeare
> His deepe compassion of her dolefull stound,
> Kissing his hands, and crouching to the ground;
> For other language had he none, nor speach,
> But soft murmure, and confused sound
> Of senselesse words, which Nature did him teach.
>
> [6.4.11]

But the wild man, lacking Adam's immediate instinct for language and articulate courtesy, is the lowest of good people. As we soon learn, Serena could as readily have been torn apart and eaten as fawned upon. Obviously, mere natural love of this kind, without ceremonies of courtesy, leaves one little better than a spaniel. The implication is that, rather than an unnecessary intrusion upon the plain and virtuous man, training in the manners of knighthood provides a ladder by which one often advances toward "grace": grace first social, then divine. The incident of savage man is revealing because of the images of courtship or approach in book six (the arrivals at castles, the welcome to shepherd land, the challenges at crossings, the hailing of knights in the open plain, the intrusions upon knights and ladies in their private bowers, and so forth), it alone brings together the extremes of the scale.

But the savage's immediate recognition of high birth is also part of old shepherd's tales stressing the "natural" superiority of nobility, and this lesson the Pastorella episode illustrates also. For Calidore's falling in love with Pastorella is not an adamic impulse for union with some universal good but a matching of exactly appropriate levels of courtesy and bearing. Pastorella is symbolically seated "higher than the rest" and the swains receive her—as Milton's Eve in moments of weakness, would have herself received—"as if some miracle of heavenly hew / Were downe to them descended in that earthly vew." And unlike the wild man or his more advanced brother Coridon, Calidore knows the proper manner to approach such a "miracle."

Yet despite his natural grace and acquired manner, the knight of courtesy falters badly in confronting the shepherd-poet. Knowing how to dispose of various forms of barbarity does him little good in dealing with the disinterested beauty of Colin Clout's vision. Cantos nine and ten present his progressive approach toward that center: first a reduction to the severely plain life of Melibee's society (with a flashback narrative of Melibee's own retreat from the social scramble), and then a conversion of Calidore's knightly games into Arcadian equivalents:

from henceforth he meanes no more to sew
His former quest, so full of toile and paine;
Another quest, another game in vew
He hath, the guerdon of his love to gaine:
With whome he myndes for ever to remaine,
And set his rest amongst the rusticke sort,
Rather than hunt still after shadowes vaine
Of courtly favour, fed with light report
Of every blaste, and sayling alwaies in the port.

[6.10.2]

The last step of the withdrawal, from lowland pastoral to the highest level of the idyllic life, puts him off balance. His hailing of the enraptured poet is discourteous because it fails to regard the poet's "kind." For clearly Colin's rapture does not represent the kind of licentious indulgence that Calidore is equipped to handle, nor does it fall under the other categories of social types that he encounters. The poet is in a class by himself.

Spenser carefully prepares the place of Colin's vision to suggest its purity and elevation and therefore the reverence with which Calidore should approach it. Unlike the Bower of Bliss, Mt. Acidale is not overpopulated; one reaches the peak only by discipline and chastity. Though it is symbolically elevated, high and low merge gradually: "the hill with equall hight / Did seeme to overlooke the lowly vale." Though "clowns" are barred, the vision does not require social elevation:

It was an hill plaste in an open plaine,
That round about was bordered with a wood
Of matchlesse hight, that seem'd th' earth to disdaine;
In which all trees of honour stately stood,
And did all winter as in sommer bud,
Spredding pavilions for the birds to bowre,
Which in their lower braunches sung aloud;
And in their tops the soring hauke did towre,
Sitting like king of fowles in majesty and powre.

And at the foote thereof, a gentle flud
His silver waves did softly tumble downe,
Unmard with ragged mosse or filthy mud;
Ne mote wylde beastes, ne mote the ruder clowne

Thereto approch, ne filth mote therein drowne:
But nymphes and faeries by the bancks did sit,
In the woods shade, which did the waters crowne,
Keeping all noysome things away from it,
And to the waters fall tuning their accents fit.

[6.10.67]

The lower rung of the arts is more fanciful than the vision of
the top, but it is equally in keeping with nature (with the
"waters fall") and equally protected from beasts and "filthy
mud." The vision of the graces itself, the climax of the shepherd's calling, is tangible without being sensual, symbolic without requiring a gloss:

All they without were raunged in a ring,
And daunced round; but in the midst of them
Three other ladies did both daunce and sing,
The whilest the rest them round about did hemme,
And like a girlond did in compasse stemme:
And in the middest of those same three was placed
Another damzell, as a precious gemme
Amidst a ring most richly well enchaced,
That with her goodly presence all the rest much graced.

.   .   .   .

She was, to weete, that jolly shepherds lasse,
Which piped there unto that merry rout;
That jolly shepheard which there piped was
Poore Colin Clout (who knowes not Colin Clout?)
He pypt apace, whilest they him daunst about.
Pype, jolly shepheard, pype thou now apace
Unto thy love, that made thee low to lout.

[6.10.12, 16]

By contrast to this peaceful image of ideal beauty, the
knight's conventional greeting is imperceptive and maladroit—
even comic, in the mode of the country lad who stumbles into
objects while staring at new sights:

'Haile, jolly shepheard, which thy joyous dayes
Here leadest in this goodly merry make. . . .
Tell me, what mote these dainty damzels be,
Which here with thee doe make their pleasant playes?

> Right happy thou, that mayst them freely see:
> But why, when I them saw, fled they away from me?'
>   [6.10.19]

Though the blunder is partly excused by his mystification, his
vacant cheerfulness is annoying to Colin. The sly implications
of "freely"—as though to imply "it's a good thing you've got
going; how does one get in on it?"—reduces courtesy to the
dealings of a man among men and reminds us that Calidore
has been somewhat quick to abandon the pursuit of the beast
in order to pursue Pastorella. His subsequent apology fares
little better:

> 'Right sory I,' saide then Sir Calidore,
> 'That my ill fortune did them hence displace.
> But since things passed none may now restore,
> Tell me, what were they all, whose lacke thee grieves so sore.'

Which is to treat another man's passions rather lightly.

Still, if we are correct in assuming that Spenser took the
didactic function of art seriously, an intrusion of some kind
is inevitable. As William Nestrick points out, the "conflict
between poetic discipline and freedom parallels a conflict in the
conception of the virtue courtesy."[3] The militant discipline

---

[3] William Nestrick, "The Virtuous and Gentle Discipline of
Gentlemen and Poets," *ELH*, 29 (1962), 364. Cf. William Nelson,
The Poetry of Edmund Spenser (New York, 1963), pp. 293 ff.
Donald Cheney in *Spenser's Image of Nature: Wild Man and
Shepherd in "The Faerie Queene"* (New Haven: Yale University
Press, 1966), suggests that fairyland can be equated with pastoralism, which is diffused throughout the poem and realized explicitly
in the sixth book with the emergence of Colin Clout. The ideal
history of the Faerie Queene and the natural, historical world of
Elizabeth outside the poem tug at each other. They are to converge in an ideal Elizabethan court. But lines so nearly parallel
converge only in the distance: the subjunctive land of the imagination and the indicative historical world can fuse only in the future (or, in nostalgic pastoral, in the distant past). Hence, Calidore's sojourn in the land of Pastorella serves finally to emphasize
the gap between them. Poetry, fairyland, and pastoral form one
end of a polarity whose opposite end is politics, the active life, and

appropriate to Calidore has its counterpart in the didacticism
of the poem, which interferes with whatever vision of pure delight a poet might conjure with his pipe. The maladroitness
of the encounter is caused not so much by the mutual guilt of
Colin and Calidore as by an inevitable internal fissure in the
nature of poetry when the criterion of meaning and usefulness
is admitted. A breakdown of discipline results sooner or later
in the unleashing of the brigand elements and the scramble of
self-gain. And just so, whether specifically encouraged by the
queen or simply holding himself answerable to the correction
of the world's imperfections, the poet cannot forget his own
mandate as a "commissioned" poet constructing a composite
image of virtuous and gentle discipline. He cannot forget that
a poem faces outward to its society as well as inward, in maintaining its own laws of consistent form.

I do not mean to overemphasize the division between poetry
as formal beauty and poetry as a useful social instrument because they clearly reinforce each other at times—in resisting
levity, maliciousness, unrestrained indulgence, and untutored
crudity, for instance. Yet the "discipline" of pure form, for
art's sake, the iconology of Mt. Acidale suggests, results in a
circular dance; discipline for the sake of the civil order and
social welfare results in hot pursuit of the beast. And as the
Red Cross Knight and Calidore both reveal, in Spenser's court-
oriented fairyland the hero must be gotten down from hills of
high vision as well as up: unlike the Maid on Scrabble Hill,
neither saint nor poet can continue growing into the sky. The

---

history; neither can become the other, though each can provide a
way of seeing the other. In Cheney's words, "the very concept of
Fairyland is a 'pastoral' projection of human motives into a sim-
plified world where they can be challenged and anatomized while
escaping temporarily some of the confusion and murkiness of our
own fallen natures. By repeatedly insisting on the differences between Faery and Briton—their modes of perception, their roles in
time and history, their relation to Providence—Spenser maintains
a double awareness of human desire and limit. . . . The emergence of the narrator in the form of Colin Clout at the end of
Book VI, and the concurrent emergence of explicit, literal pastoral, may be felt to bring into focus a perspective which has been
more dimly felt throughout the poem" (p. 4).

Red Cross Knight's unfavorable comparison of Cleopolis with the New Jerusalem is answered by his guide:

> "Yet is Cleopolis, for earthly frame,
> The fairest peece that eie beholden can
> And well beseemes all knights of noble name,
> That covett in the' immortall booke of fame
> To be eternized, that same to haunt,
> And doen their service to that soveraigne dame,
> That glory does to them for guerdon graunt:
> For she is hevenly borne, and heaven may justly vaunt."
>
> [1.10.59]

At the same time, neither can the knights of holiness and courtesy be brought immediately down from their heights, as though their respective mountains were mere courtly tourist curiosities; Spenser has Calidore and Colin return to society gradually. The patching up of their relationship begins when Colin explains the vision to Calidore and acknowledges his duty to "great Gloriana": he should not, he confesses, have suggested that a "poor handmayd" could excel a queen. (This apology implicitly prepares Calidore for the resumption of his own quest.) Colin's translation of his high vision into historical allegory is a way of collapsing its ideal grace and mythic dimensions into specific referential statement, as *The Faerie Queene* is both a model of ideal forms and a historical reflection of Elizabethan politics. And whereas all men of vision may be equal in mythic dreams (as in their share in the story of Adam and Eve), they become handmaids or servants or courtiers in the stories of real history: poets of high archetypes become chroniclers of feudal lords. The poem remains a romance and Queen Elizabeth a fairy queen, but the poet includes the court panegyrist as well as the visionary.

But perhaps more convincing than Colin's retraction, as an argument against the pursuit of private idylls, is the subsequent destruction of shepherdom. (Spenser may or may not have intended Calidore's two opponents, the Beast and Shepherdom to be taken as metaphors for the same reality—the lower orders as opposed to courtesy on a high level. But Calidore must nonetheless resist them both equally because to "lower" himself is equivalent to destroying decorum, which is in turn equivalent to turning loose the uncourtly beast. Colin, too, would be Calidore's enemy if he did not apologize and come down from the high hill with him.) Thus in keeping with the collapse of the visionary poet into the realist and satirist, the ideal pastoral society, too, metamorphoses into a scene of pitched battle. The pastoral enclosure is broken open to the ravages of the exterior world as Pastorella proves vulnerable to the forces Calidore has been neglecting:

> Like as sort of hungry dogs, ymet
> About some carcase by the common way,
> Doe fall together, stryving each to get
> The greatest portion of the greedie pray;
> All on confused heapes themselves assay,
> And snatch, and byte, and rend, and tug, and teare,
> That who them sees would wonder at their fray,
> And who sees not would be affrayd to heare:
> Such was the conflict of those cruell Brigants there.
> [6.11.17]

In terms of the tension between the contemplative and active lives, as brutality forces its way into a life that has seemed self-sufficient and idyllic, the order of the detached mind gives way to the lesser (but effective) order of the commonwealth.

Insofar as it is Spenser's dilemma that Calidore and Colin represent, he maintains the ambivalence with which he originally set out in *The Shepheardes Calender*. The difficulties nightingales have with kings prove basically unsolvable—until the poet and his society set aside "emblazon'd Shields, / Impreses quaint, Caparisons and Steeds," which the emperor is not likely to do on his own. Poetry as service to the secular order is necessarily at odds with poetry as an image of idealized (pastoralized) beauty. Having decided to begin with a rejection of secular models of "grace," Milton will be free to reintegrate duty and poetic praise, to castigate the historical world and to celebrate the divine order. Thus the man of holiness (not a knight) and the poet become the same person, bent on paradise and scornful of Satan's feudal "glory." But for Spenser, the exchange of courtesies between Colin and

Calidore is not an adequate means of negotiating between the poet's best vision and his necessary service. And like the poet, Pastorella, to be worthy of the knight of courtesy, must find a respectable parentage and abandon Arcadia for a chamber near the queen.

FIVE

Shakespeare's Inner Plays
and the Social Contract

When Romeo and Juliet declare their love in the balcony scene, at the meeting place of the parent dominated household and the freer world of moonlit nature, they are making one of Shakespeare's first associations between love, nature, and the imagination. In many of the comedies, Shakespeare adds to that association a master controller, such as Oberon, Rosalind, or Prospero, who cooperates with nature in changing the minds of those who for one reason or another stand in the way of new and harmonious societies that love tries to bring forth. I would like to examine the effects that their masterful good sense and the magic of the atmospheric place apart from society—the forest, the island, the pastoral scene—have upon the social raw materials that come under their influence. I select *A Midsummer Night's Dream, As You Like It,* and *The Tempest* because they are especially typical of renaissance pastoral themes in their exposure of nobles to rustics and in their concern with contrasts between art and nature. Yet, these are also quite different plays, and together with *The Winter's Tale* they illustrate the complexity and ingenuity with which Shakespeare reworked his own as well as traditional materials.

Since many of the concerns of *A Midsummer Night's Dream* are refracted through a pervasive lunar glow, readers could do worse than heed Bottom's admonition, "Find out moonshine, find out moonshine!" [1] Clearly a play so bristling

---

[1] Cf. Sheldon Zitner's comment that the play contains a large, airy universe including temporal powers, various social levels, and the world of fairies, all suffused with "a bright, though waning moon," "The Worlds of *A Midsummer Night's Dream*," *South Atlantic Quarterly,* 59 (1960), 398.

with antitheses—court and forest, nature and art, imagination and reason, to name but a few—can use an alembical power to support the normal marriage plot that Shakespearean comedy employs to subdue its conflicting forces. We can credit moonlight in part for extending a single initial marriage proposal between Theseus and Hippolyta into a rash of marriages and for spreading a pervasive natural harmony through a society whose rigid order is initially not inclined to heed the promptings of the heart. But moonlight is also a strange sort of elixir, mixed with fairy concoctions, marital quarrels, shape-changing, and plays within plays. It collects a number of transformational powers that threaten to dissolve the civil order altogether. Perhaps the key to all its operations is the epistemological problem of what constitutes true seeing. Are the lovers deceiving themselves when they give their oaths first to one and then to another true love? What kind of reality do the fairies have? What is the relationship between the moon's influence and the stage moon of the Pyramus play, and what kind of reality does the inner play itself have? Whose leg is Puck pulling?

The initial comments of Theseus and Hippolyta about the moon, together with their subsequent differences concerning the imagination, suggest that the moon may work in either of two ways—to strengthen the bonds of love by revealing the heart's deepest bonds, or to disrupt rational vision and provoke fickleness. Either way it influences the mind's construing of what we see and want. Theseus and Hippolyta resolve their initial difference in favor of Hippolyta's dreamy moon—which as Theseus acknowledges, will heal in the "everlasting bonds of fellowship" the injuries he has committed against her state with the sword. (Theseus, too, has undergone a radical metamorphosis, from enemy to lover.) Then Egeus suggests that the immediate effect of moonlit love is to scramble all conventions by which the generations are ruled and fathers define their children's choices. To him Lysander is a magician who has "bewitched" his daughter with verses of feigned passion, which makes moonlight equivalent to false seeing, disharmony, and encouragement of "crazed titles" to the rights of others under law. Moon dreams are thus a first step toward anarchy. In either version, moonlight helps the cause of romance and makes the imagination function; it causes lovers to think that they love and fathers to think them mad, as it causes poets to imagine wonderful things and critics to laugh at them. The two scenes of the play, forest and court, extend the tension between authority and moonlight, the forest being obviously moon-dominated and the court, father-dominated. Yet both scenes have counterchecks. The silliness of love and bizarre products of lunacy like Bottom's transformation supply the Egeuses of the city with evidence to indite lovers and poets, yet they themselves do not fare well without it; and though the fathers' concern for property and propriety hinders the forming of a more profoundly human social contract in Athens, the forest, too, has its difficulties with these things.

As we first see Titania and Oberon, the combined difficulties of love and authority have divided them as severely as they have Athens, and fairy "charms," one branch of the Department of Moonshine, soon prove capable of intensifying strife. Certainly love charms and moonlight are not to be loosed indiscriminately on everyone. Before entering the forest Hermia is lost in the irrationality of desire and if allowed to pursue her course would lead a barren, ascetic life, chanting "faint hymns to the cold fruitless moon." But after experiencing the full spell of the moon and Oberon's magic, she is even worse off, and Helena eventually wants to escape the forest altogether (3.2.314–317). Beyond these dangers inherent in the irrationality of love are elements of disorder that no magic can cure:

> *Lys.* Or, if there were a sympathy in choice,
> War, death, or sickness did lay siege to it,
> Making it momentany as a sound,
> Swift as a shadow, short as any dream,
> Brief as the lightning in the collied night,
> That, in a spleen, unfolds both heaven and earth,
> And ere a man hath power to say "Behold!"
> The jaws of darkness do devour it up:
> So quick bright things come to confusion.
>   *Her.* If then true lovers have been ever cross'd,
> It stands as an edict in destiny.
>
>   [1.1.141–151]

The peaceful alembic of moonlight changes in Lysander's imagery to lightning flickering over confusion in the "collied night," and the "sympathy in choice" it prompts may only tantalize one with what he most wants before time and decay take it from him. This confusion is reflected in the forest's fluidity of shapes and identities, its tendency to create monsters, and its mishaps, all of which give it a decidedly nightmarish cast.

Athens is even more vulnerable to self-division. The social contract, as the fathers would have it, excludes nonfilial love, which establishes unpredictable "contracts" and disturbs the continuity of authority:

> To you your father should be as a god,
> One that compos'd your beauties, yea, and one
> To whom you are but as a form in wax
> By him imprinted, and within his power
> To leave the figure or disfigure it.
>
> [1.1.47–51]

It is inconceivable to Egeus that the allegiance of those whom he holds in trust could be won away by anything less than black magic. Yet the "ancient privilege" that he defends offers no genuine social bond, only protection for vested interest. Thinking of the marital contract as an exchange of property, he would allow his property only to him "I love": "she is mine, and all my right of her / I do estate unto Demetrius." Even Lysander pleads "rank," possession, and the rights of private property. But the fathers' claims to original, definitive power as creators of social form is undermined by prior claims, and love proves in time to be more profoundly formative. As Helena remarks, "Things base and vile holding no quantity, / Love can transpose to form and dignity" (1.1.232–233), which, though offered by a spokesman somewhat less than authoritative, is an accurate account of what the play demonstrates. If there is to be a general social harmony, it must come from levels of the mind where basic alliances are formed without regard to rational choice, levels open only to the poet's and lover's subrational delvings.

Despite their seeming incompatability, however, authority

and love can learn to negotiate. The forest's dream-therapy is eventually effective in healing wounds opened by these initial contests for "property," and the daylight clarity of Athens in turn rids moonlight of some of its monstrosities. Oberon promises that when the lovers awake,

> All this derision
> Shall seem a dream and fruitless visions;
> And back to Athens shall the lovers wend
> With league whose date till death shall never end.
> [3.2.370–373]

As the "fierce vexations of dreams" end in three different awakenings in act four, a gentle concord pervades the forest and results in betrothals based on reconstituted true identities—henceforth unchanging enough, Theseus suggests, to knit the couples "eternally." Demetrius says of his own several changes of mind:

> all the faith, the virtue of my heart,
> The object and the pleasure of mine eye,
> Is only Helena. To her, my lord,
> Was I betroth'd ere I saw Hermia:
> But, like in sickness, did I loathe this food;
> But, as in health, come to my natural taste,
> Now I do wish it, love it, long for it,
> And will for evermore be true to it.
> [4.1.173–180]

Hippolyta testifies not only to the marvelous transfiguration of troubled minds from dream states to "natural taste" but also to the great "constancy" that strange and admirable events have brought about.

The testimony from all observers therefore emphasizes the conjunction of civil order and natural inclinations or "fancy" (meaning what one "loves" and what one "imagines"). The daylight world witnesses and endorses what fancy's images have brought forth from nightmare and made available to awakened vision:

> But all the story of the night told over,
> And all their minds transfigured so together,

> More witnesseth than fancy's images,
> And grows to something of great constancy;
> But, howsoever, strange and admirable.
>
> [5.1.23–27]

The fact of the transformation and the direct influence of dreams and love potions in bringing it about are both clear, then.

But exactly how the world of shadows communicates with daylight reality remains problematic. Taking Puck's clue, we can assume that one means is the representation of real things in shadowy form, as the several enacted pageants within the total "story of the night" offer images of love taking shape and seeking its proper contract. At the same time, certain discrepancies between acting or role playing and inner truth keep us skeptical of what we have seen and aware of the false alliances of bad dreams. In the Saturnalian mixup of the four lovers and the Bottom-Titania farce, it becomes obvious that no means of expression, even the most intimate and strongly felt language of the heart, is completely trustworthy. Language as well as the social order will disintegrate if headstrong lovers and fairyland have their way. Betrayed lovers are stunned into disbelief at what they see and hear, and they attack one another scornfully as actors in a pageant designed to deceive and humiliate them. "Counterfeit sad looks / Make mouths upon me when I turn my back," Helena instructs Hermia (3.2.237): "You counterfeit, you puppet" (3.2.288). Together with the interior play's problem with representation and falsely theatrical speech, this confusion forces a society to seek some authority for its bonds and oaths besides the impulses of the forest; it must ask what social agreement can verify reality against the "fierce vexation of a dream," as the various awakenings, by restoring what people are wont to see, reiterate a customary sense of reality safely beyond the trauma of momentary visions and the foggy night. The melodious harmony that descends upon the lovers as they emerge from the forest seems to them to put things in distinct focus; united in meaningful connections, what they see and hear seems more real than unconnected or blurred objects. With the coming of dawn, then, all nature returns to a self-testifying form that matches the perceiver's precondition for reality, and visions of love assume the authority of reason and may be approved by Theseus, the symbol of authority joined to love.

The contest between authority and love, dream and awakening, however, includes more than lovers and fathers, and the Shakespearean social agreement includes more than the tightly knit group of the courtly romance. By introducing Bottom, Quince, Snug, Flute, Snout, and Starveling into the forest and the court, Shakespeare paradoxically both extends the range of moon therapy and increases our skepticism about it. He allows humorous or rustic "pastoral" to jostle the romantic business of love and dreams and thus offers a perspective from outside on courtly style—so full of posturing and melodrama. The rustic player's involvement in the dream world of the moon is twofold: in the forest their play is brought under the power of moonlight and Bottom plays an unexpected and "real" part; at court moonlight becomes a mere stage prop in their play, having approximately the reality of Wall and Lion. (This cross-reference matches that of the lovers and fairies who enter each other's realms.) Whereas in the forest, changes of identity such as Hermia's into Helena and Titania's into the lover of the clown are genuine (though incongruous and temporary), in the "inside" Pyramus play, Bottom's bush and moon are a tacky staging of staging. The forest might be said to represent the real workings of imagination on receptive minds until they believe in the roles they play, and the Pyramus and Thisbe play to represent the inadequate machinery by which the imagination's images are put into production. Oberon and Robin (whose "scene" is the entire planet) and Bottom the actor (whose scene is a limited stage) are thus two sides of the same emergence of the imagination into gesture, act, and overt deed where reason can confirm it or deny it.

The influence of natural moonlight on the Athenian elements that enter it is perhaps best measured in the scenes between Titania and Bottom, which bring together the most radical levels of the play, fairy-poetry and low comedy—one discredited at court because it is shadowy and the other because it is crude. These scenes are prepared for by the discussion among the Pyramus players (six characters in search of a style) of the problem of acting and putting on alien identities. After that discussion, Bottom is translated into Oberon's play, where, under the spell of the master-reveler, Titania supposes dream to be truth and radically mistakes its nature—which makes her in turn not less poetic but certainly more exposed to "impurities" than fairy-poets normally are. Since to her transforming ear Bottom's singing sounds like an angel's, she might be said to "pastoralize" discordant reality into celestial harmony, a hairy beast into a romantic lover:

> I pray thee, gentle mortal, sing again.
> Mine ear is much enamour'd of thy note;
> So is mine eye enthralled to thy shape;
> And thy fair virtue's force perforce doth move me
> On the first view to say, to swear, I love thee.
>
> [3.1.140–144]

Because it is based on a mistaken identity, such a bond-creating oath obviously cannot have the objective validity of the betrothal of a Theseus and Hippolyta.

But we discover later that others of more reputable standing make similar mistakes, without the aid of love potions. Theseus himself has a transforming ear: his love of "the musical confusion / Of hounds and echo in conjunction" is much like Titania's for Bottom's song, as echoed in her poetic rewriting. Fairyland imagination in one and nature's return of dog voices in the other not only reduplicate nature's "original" (art as "imitation") but also transform its confusion (art as reformation). Such a harmony draws even Hippolyta into the ranks of those who live among the antinomies of art and nature; and the voices of the hounds seem to her, too, to tune all nature:

> Never did I hear
> Such gallant chiding; for, besides the groves,
> The skies, the fountains, every region near
> Seem'd all one mutual cry: I never heard
> So musical a discord, such sweet thunder.
>
> [4.1.118–121]

Though these voices individually could not be much better than Bottom's and are certainly worse as a chorus, to Theseus and Hippolyta they are "more tuneable" than a symphony. Might not a playwright argue, then, that what a play seems when inadequately performed is not necessarily what a sympathetic imagination should make of it?[2] And if that is true of plays, might not harmony also be made of many other discordant things and bring a "gentle concord" among offended fathers and their daughters, weavers and dukes who begin the play arguing in discordant voices?

Partly because of this general concord and the tolerance of incongruities that moonlight fosters, and partly because of Titania's genuine verbal charm, we cannot quite dismiss her scenes with Bottom as total foolery. Her response to Bottom's song may be in one sense further evidence against those who fail to distinguish between dreams and reality: the potion gives her the reflexes of the mad poet, who, seeing something hairy, gives it a face of beauty and addresses it in pretty words, themselves a little strained ("force perforce," for instance). Name and referent are obviously not well paired, and no oath can sustain itself unless word matches identity—unless words do not create, but echo, what exists outside them. But the pageant of Titania and Bottom does not make quite the same criticism of the imagination and verbal mismatching as the Pyramus play does and should not be confused with it. If the daylight, untransformable reality of the "rude mechanicals" were meant to shatter the frail effects of Titania's imagination, Bottom would crash through its artifice like a bull through cobwebs. As it is, he is drawn willy-nilly into the spirit of moonshine until he finds it difficult to resist it or forget it. The crude physical beast is modified by the encompassing romance, as Titania verbally converts the grossness of Bottom's onion-watering eyes into moonlit imagery: "The moon methinks

[2] Paul N. Siegel notes that the play was performed at a wedding and that Shakespeare's references to the play itself reflect his awareness that the audience would need to assist the staging with their imaginations. See *"A Midsummer Night's Dream* and the Wedding Guests," *SQ* 4 (1953), 139–144.

looks with a wat'ry eye; / And when she weeps, weeps every little flower" (3.1.203–204).

As we step back to situate the fairy-workingman's courtship into the play's total combination of antitheses, it is this union of the poetic and the monstrous that stands out as most incongruous. All of Bottom's roles, but especially this one, emphasize the grossness of the lower orders; here he performs as we suspect that he has always wanted to be. The exhibitionism of his language and the fervor of his acting derive from a buried desire to play a better social role than weaving gives him. It is gratifying indeed to have a queen say:

> And I do love thee; therefore, go with me.
> I'll give thee faries to attend on thee,
> And they shall fetch thee jewels from the deep,
> And sing while thou on pressed flowers dost sleep.
> And I will purge thy mortal grossness so
> That thou shalt like an airy spirit go.
>
> [3.1.159–164]

Throwing a layer of dreaminess over the absurd, Bottom, like all poets, thinks of making his romance public, as part of a performance the Duke should not miss:

> I have had a most rare vision. I have had a dream, past the wit of man to say what dream it was . . . the ear of man hath not seen, man's hand is not able to taste, his tongue to conceive, nor his heart to report, what my dream was. I will get Peter Quince to write a ballad of this dream. It shall be called "Bottom's Dream," because it hath no bottom; and I will sing it in the latter end of a play, before the Duke. [4.1.209]

Bottom in fairyland thus results in a double association: the bungling farce of production and its inadequate poetic language with the romance of the imagination that demands showing; and commoners (workers and stagers of plays) with the fairy queen. In his bizarre way, he manages to suggest a possible adjustment of crude nature to disparate levels of the social order and even to the mythopoeic imagination.

A similar set of incongruities is evident in fairyland itself. As the names Peaseblossom, Cobweb, Moth, and Mustardseed suggest, the fairy court has not only its own light and airy poetry but its common, earthy flavor, which as Dover Wilson and Elizabeth Sewell point out, fuses the worlds of nature, fancy, and trade. The ensemble of workers and fairies who surround the incongruous romance of the weaver and the queen suggests natural materials and various means of putting them to human use, in utilitarian as well as poetic production: "Bottom" means a "core of the skein" upon which the weaver's yarn is wound as well as a "foundation" and part of the anatomy; "quine" or quoins are blocks of wood used for building, "quince" is a fruit, "Snout" refers to muzzles, nozzles, or sprouts, "Flute" to a bellows-mender, "Robin Starveling" to the bird and the proverbial leanness of tailors—an odds-and-ends assortment of tools, fruits, weeds, and seeds. Together they imply "the great unity of natural history, plants and trees, animals, man as body and mind, the arts. . . . They have struggled up out of the vegetable and animal into the human condition." [3]

If fairyland with Bottom in it unites layers of nature, society, and the imagination under moonlight, the world of playacting with Bottom at its center brings about a rapport of a kind between players and noble critics under stagelights. This rapport is already implicit in Theseus's receptiveness to a music as crude as the baying of dogs and his willingness to overlook incongruities or make them a source of amusement. Though the play's exaggerations of the high style (an inversion in a sense of the strategy of Italian tragicomedies in which rustic life is staged transparently by nobles) may suggest that nobility itself is a pretense, actors such as these will clearly never master the art: even the title sounds to Theseus like the kind of intriguing nonsense that reassures one of his own good sense and noble bearing. Hence though he wonders how to "find the concord" of this romantical-tedious-brief-wondrous-strange-farcical-tragedy, when Hippolyta calls it "the silliest stuff that I ever heard," he is quick to respond: "The best in this kind are but shadows; and the worst are no worse, if imagination amend them" (5.1.212).

[3] See Elizabeth Sewell, *The Orphic Voice: Poetry and Natural History* (New Haven: Yale University Press, 1960), pp. 130, 133.

His estimate is probably intended to encompass more than Bottom's performance: as Robin Goodfellow suggests in the epilogue, the imagination should have its way with the audience of *A Midsummer Night's Dream,* too. Those who prefer "cool reason" to airiness can, if they wish, dismiss what they have seen and no one will gainsay them, but while reason has slept, the subterranean powers of the mind may have worked upon them. In addition to the awakening of the fairy queen, the four lovers, and Bottom, we thus have the return to consciousness of those who have "slumber'd here, / While these visions did appear." In any case, awake or dreaming, we will have been beckoned into the play's moonlight and exposed to its magic without sacrificing our awareness of the "rusticity" of the performance. Our attitude toward it remains double, in the manner of sophisticated visitors to Arcadias populated with wonders and "hard-handed men . . . Which never labor'd in their minds till now." Having participated imaginatively in the strange ways of the play's several realms, the audience is ready to accept with tolerance and amusement the motley and varied crowd that jostles toward the exit. Shakespeare has inserted the play's contrasts into the transforming alembic of the imagination, put the noble next to the rustic to allow comment to pass both ways between them, and then brought the benefits of the forest to court as the fairies apply their potions and carry their blessings to the wedding night. In so doing, he has prepared for the audience's exit by making it critically aware both of its dreams and its own possible social bond.

In contrast to Oberon's brews, which do no permanent damage even when they inadvertently scramble things, *Macbeth's* mixtures of magic and supernatural charms "Cancel and tear to pieces that great bond / Which keeps us pale" (3.3.49). Witch-conjuring not only fires the imagination against the social order but also turns everything in nature wrong-side out and cuts it loose from its proper place:

> Fillet of fenny snake,
> In the cauldron boil and bake;
> Eye of newt and toe of frog

> Wool of bat and tongue of dog,
> Adder's fork and blind-worm's sting,
> Lizard's leg and howlet's wing,
> For a charm of pow'rful trouble,
> Like a bell-broth boil and bubble.
>
> [4.1.12–19]

The element most lacking in this version of the "fairy" charm is the magic of Venus and the therapy of the "goodfellow's" potions, which cause one to desire what basically he should. Its nightmare quality and the ambition it stimulates cancel the benefits of sleep and dream associated with the proper (or humorous) alignment of desire and its object in *A Midsummer Night's Dream*. Part of the difference between the early comedies and later plays lies in this deepening of discord and in the consequent need to impose a stronger discipline upon the imagination.

The simulated storms of *The Tempest* are counteractions against the trouble fomenting in usurpers and potential murderers of the king. The range of evils on Prospero's island requires a *preemptive* use of magic. Having in the past been "transported / And rapt in secret studies" and therefore unconcerned with government, Prospero has allowed Antonio to create "new forms and creatures." "In my false brother / Awak'd an evil nature," he explains to Miranda, so that, henceforth, in the presence of sleeping kings, Antonio's first thought is to dispose of them. Likewise, Caliban, Trinculo, and even Ariel—who would remain indifferent to human affairs but for the threat of being transfixed in a tree—have a strong instinct for rebellion. It is clearly not advisable for the master to slumber: as Caliban remarks with only slight exaggeration, all his creatures "do hate him . . . rootedly." "For every trifle are they set upon me," Caliban complains of his torturers:

> Sometime like apes that mow and chatter at me
> And after bite me, then like hedgehogs which
> Lie tumbling in my barefoot way and mount
> Their pricks at my footfall; sometime am I
> All wound with adders who with cloven tongues
> Do hiss me into madness.
>
> [2.2.8–14]

More eager to worship wastrels as celestial demons than to obey Prospero, he would offer them his services without receiving even the pay he now receives if he were not continually disciplined. He is slavishly impressed by the "divine drunkards":

> I prithee, let me bring thee where crabs grow;
> And I with my long nails will dig thee pig-nuts;
> Show thee a jay's nest, and instruct thee how
> To snare the numble marmoset; I'll bring thee
> To clustering filberts, and sometimes I'll get thee
> Young scamels from the rock.
>
> [2.2.166–172]

Given this animal-like nature of the clown group, Ariel's stings and pricks are as necessary as Prospero's. Whereas the hope of curing the strife of Athens lies in an escape from "ancient privilege" in a magical application of imagination to the social bond, the therapy of *The Tempest* consists largely of a reimposing of reason and discipline in all areas of social activity. With a control that is "fascist" in the sense of "bundling in" all elements, Prospero works in the manner of a supreme plotter at the still center of the action to "chase the ignorant fumes that mantle" the "clearer reason" of the usurpers. No part of the island escapes his intelligence system. The sailors of the king's ship are imprisoned in sleep below decks; all parties are spied upon and manipulated, or cajoled, pricked, beaten, cramped, forced into labor, or set upon by harpies. They are led on, put off, and generally thrashed into changing themselves willy-nilly into what a healthy social order demands that they be. The force of Prospero's voice thus shatters as well as commands ceremonies. Ferdinand and Miranda would be as Adam and Eve but for his interception of their courtship. He breaks off the harvest ritual of Ceres, remembering the conspiracy that is brewing and the responsibilities of government. He makes a wage-laborer of Ariel (in Ariel's view of it) and a serf of Caliban (a Marxist critic once suggested), and he does not always bother to distinguish the guilty from the innocent since the innocent, too, can benefit from discipline. If he has no compelling reason to interfere with

the natural course of things, he invents reasons. "They are both
in either's power," he notices about Miranda and Ferdinand,
and so pretending to be a suspicious father he makes their too
swift business uneasy,

> lest too light winning
> Make the prize light. [*To Ferd*] One word more; I charge thee
> That thou attend me. Thou dost here usurp
> The name thou ow'st not; and hast put thyself
> Upon this island as a spy, to win it
> From me, the lord on't.
>
> [1.2.450–456]

The hospitality of Arcadia thus gives way to a regimentation
as severe in its way as that of Sidney's ideal prince.

In contrast with Prospero's rigorous government, Gonzalo
would let each go as he chooses despite the obvious inappropriateness of softer versions of the idyllic life to the island of
Sycorax and Caliban:

> no kind of traffic
> Would I admit; no name of magistrate;
> Letters should not be known; riches, poverty,
> And use of service, none; contract, succession,
> Bourn, bound of land, tilth, vineyard, none;
> No use of metal, corn, or wine, or oil;
> No occupation; all men idle, all;
> And women, too, but innocent and pure;
> No sovereignty . . .
> All things in common nature should produce
> Without sweat or endeavor. . . .
> I would with such perfection govern sir,
> T'excell the golden age.
>
> [2.1.148–168]

Antonio, who should know, tells him that, living under those
conditions, they should all become knaves and whores. But
Prospero too, of course, inclines toward a softer pastoral at
times—not by relaxing discipline but by distilling beauty from
nature in poetry and pageants. He reforms not merely by
moral lecture and punitive force but by enticements of song;
Caliban's bestial nature is sung to as well as pinched. Ariel

was himself once much more severely vexed than he is under
Prospero, whose art has set him free from a cloven pine:

> it was mine Art,
> When I arriv'd and heard thee, that made gape
> The pine, and let thee out.
>
> [1.2.291–293]

By means of a music that soothes disarranged emotions, Ariel's
music and pageantry in turn mellow the wills and transform
the minds of those who watch and listen, as Ferdinand's passions are allayed by a "sweet air" that transforms death itself
into beauty:

> Full fathom five thy father lies;
>   Of his bones are coral made;
> Those are pearls that were his eyes;
>   Nothing of him that doth fade
> But doth suffer a sea-change
> Into something rich and strange.
>
> [1.2.396–401]

Prospero describes the successful rejuvenation of society in
terms of a gentle melting of mists and fogs:

> The charm dissolves a pace,
> And as the morning steals upon the night,
> Melting darkness, so their rising senses
> Begin to chase the ignorant fumes that mantle
> Their clearer reason.
>
> [5.1.64–68]

This clarity brings a new harmony to the various classes as
well as to the imagination and reason: Gonzalo is reconciled to
the Boatswain, whom he had found impudent and eminently
suitable for hanging. Seeing the folly of making kings and
gods of vulgarians, Caliban decides to "be wise hereafter / And
seek for grace." Having rebelliously chanted "Flout 'em and
scout 'em / And scout 'em and flout 'em; / Thought is free"
(3.2.130–132) and called for the overthrow of all authority
("Monster, I will kill this man. His daughter and I will be

king and queen,—save our Graces!—and Trinculo and thyself
shall be viceroys," [3.2.114]), Antonio, Trinculo, and Stephano
are finally brought into line. Ariel's tabor and pipe bring
therapeutic dreams to them and set even Caliban thinking
of visions beyond Stephano's free marriage between clowns
and queens:

> This isle is full of noises,
> Sounds and sweet airs, that give delight and hurt not.
> Sometimes a thousand twangling instruments
> Will hum about mine ears, and sometimes voices
> That, if I then had wak'd after long sleep,
> Will make me sleep again; and then, in dreaming,
> The clouds methought would open and show riches
> Ready to drop upon me, that, when I wak'd,
> I cried to dream again.
>
> [3.2.143-51]

Though Stephano thinks of the added value such free music
will give his future kingdom ("This will prove a brave kingdom to me, where I shall have my music for nothing"), none
of the schemers and rebels will pose a serious threat hereafter.

But despite these pleasantries, art also has to be rough to
counteract the blistering, unwholesome, howling nature of the
island and elements of black magic that would frustrate the
artist's good intentions. Despite the effectiveness of Prospero's
cure, there are clear limits to his magic and a suggestion of
continued need of authority among the new generation. Beyond that, *The Tempest* looks forward to an all-encompassing
dissolution of the pageant that no magic can prevent. The
mood is elegiac as well as "wonderful"; the conventional comic
order established out of the purged elements of the old society
is projected against a vision of its eventual dispersal. Distinctions between nature and art and between rusticity and nobility
will be removed permanently by the dissolution of the world's
greater pageant. Behind the various roles that we play and
visions that we see is the insubstantial stuff of dreams:

> Our revels now are ended. These our actors,
> As I foretold you, were all spirits, and

Are melted into air, into thin air;
And, like the baseless fabric of this vision,
The cloud-capp'd towers, the gorgeous palaces,
The solemn temples, the great globe itself,
Yea, all which it inherit, shall dissolve
And, like this insubstantial pageant faded,
Leave not a rack behind. We are such stuff
As dreams are made on.

[4.1.148–157]

The realization that life is ultimately "such stuff" as fictions
and illusions undermines the conventional finality of the
happy ending. Yet in another sense, it also "pastoralizes" all
contrasts of order and disorder, authority and soft golden
visions. As Prospero abandons his role of divine stager in a
withering away of government, nature prepares to resume
control:

Ye elves of hills, brooks, standing lakes, and groves,
And ye that on the sands with printless foot
Do chase the ebbing Neptune, and do fly him
When he comes back; you demi-puppets that
By moonshine do the green and sour ringlets make,
Whereof the ewe not bites . . .
    by whose aid,
Weak masters though ye be, I have bedimm'd
The noontide sun, call'd forth the mutinous winds . . .
    To the dread rattling thunder
Have I given fire, and rifted Jove's stout oak
With his own bolt . . .
By my so potent art. But this rough magic
I here abjure, and, when I have requir'd
Some heavenly music, which even now I do,
To work mine end upon their senses that
This airy charm is for, I'll break my staff,
Bury it certain fathoms in the earth,
And deeper than did ever plummet sound
I'll drown my book.

[5.1.33–57]

As a final leveling, the dissolution is a melancholy prospect, but
it also softens Prospero's rigid demands with a pleasant Virgilian dissonance. Like Sidney's happily married knights in the

proximity of Arcadia's mourning shepherds, the play's brave new society must balance its satisfaction against an intangible vista of waste.

Having situated all art and politics in that framework, the play shrinks back into the world of continental dukedoms. Returning to the mainland as a retired Milanese man of responsibility (a kind of sixty-year-old smiling public man), Prospero will leave behind not only his book and staff but also Ariel and Caliban. Life on the magic island remains distinct from life among Europeans. The ambivalence of the ending is increased by the prospect of Ariel wandering freely but useless to humans while Caliban prowls among roots and beetles in a nature returning to primitivism. Another "playwright" like Prospero, capable of putting together a compromise between nature and art, romance and authority, clowns and their masters, may not appear in the island-theater for a long time.

As You Like It: FROM DUEL TO DANCE

By bringing two roles together in one character, the use of disguises works a transvaluation of what each role separately implies. Even without the alembic of moonlit forests and magic potions, such playacting may bring about unexpected associations of values and social levels and hence negotiations between them—especially if in addition to wearing disguises, given characters are transported into an alien scene such as the Forest of Arden. What they ordinarily are is then inserted into its opposite as into a new "plot": the noble into the rustic, the sophisticated into the idealized, true romance into its false variations. The effects of these juxtapositions are broadened if onlookers witness the marital bargaining of others, which converts their private negotiations into public pageantry. In *As You Like It,* conditions beyond their control force members of the exiled court to act and react differently from their custom and to participate in their opposites. The emphasis falls eventually upon separate and appropriate fortunes for each lover as he likes it; but even then the unmasking arranged by Rosalind reveals primarily cooperative natures, whose sociability has been prepared for by the dialectical processes of the forest's social mixture.

In "pure" romance, the investigation that precedes the discovery of marriageable entities is comparatively uncomplicated. As Rosalind tells Orlando concerning the dissolving of barriers between Celia and Oliver—once a sinner against the social bond—"Your brother and my sister no sooner met but they look'd; no sooner look'd but they lov'd; no sooner lov'd but they sigh'd; no sooner sigh'd but they ask'd one another the reason; no sooner knew the reason but they sought the remedy; and in these degrees they have made a pair of stairs to marriage. . . . They are in the very wrath of love and they will together" (5.2.34). Thus the discovery of true identities, once the masks are off, immediately stimulates a desire for courtship; that desire issues in a language of love and brings about an exchange of "goods." In terms of pastoral dialectic, the lovers transcend their former egoistic natures that set brother against brother and discover a kind of oppositional harmony ("wrath of love"). Though Touchstone and Corin, the courtly and natural realists of the play, may not arrive at a comparable agreement and no one succeeds in removing the self-isolating pessimism of Jaques from the play, this is the pattern of "wooing" by which those who can cooperate soon learn to do so.

But *As You Like It,* for all its miraculous conversions and dreamy atmosphere, is not pure romance. Though Rosalind, too, for instance, takes a relatively quick trip to marital cooperation, enroute she talks mostly in ironic disparagement of love's insanity and plays her own opposite. She assumes that love deserves "as well a dark house and a whip as madmen do." Testing Orlando's wrath of love, she claims (in the disguise of Ganymede) to have set a would-be lover every day to woo her, at which time, she says, "would I, being but a moonish youth, grieve, be effeminate, changeable, longing and liking, proud, fantastical, apish, shallow, inconstant, full of smiles" (3.2.427). Though these tactics are avowedly designed to set the lover on the path toward the monastery in a "humor of madness," Rosalind's real aim is to make the patient con-

sider love with a certain amount of social and self awareness—
to realize that he is in fact choosing a role to act, though
Jaques finds our roles assigned to us. The cure for excessively
literary postures in love is much the same: an awareness of
where acquired manner begins and nature ends, and how best
to put them together.

Whereas the rough edges of social disorder are smoothed
primarily by magic and authority in *The Tempest* and dissolved in the imagination's dream in *A Midsummer Night's
Dream,* then, they are filed by satire, irony, and masked participation in opposites in *As You Like It.* The difference between Rosalind's ironic wooing and ordinary romantic wooing is that irony brings into the social contract an awareness
of its total environment and touches on a variety of social
levels, without which love would remain merely personal, the
beloved a piece of property (as Audrey is to Touchstone).
Jaques's will to each pair sums up the play's attitude toward
this variety in an appropriate manner, giving "honor" to the
restored Duke, "love that your true faith doth merit" to Orlando, "land, and love, and great allies" to Oliver, a "long and
well-deserved bed" to Silvius (who has been put off too long),
but only "wrangling" to Touchstone, whose "loving voyage /
Is but for two months victualed" (5.4.196). What each deserves is approximately what he wants and has "produced"
himself in love's labors in the forest.

Because the play is about the society of lovers as well as the
romance of individual pairs, its final order, in contrast with
court pastorals of the Italian tradition that assign blessings
only to cavalier-shepherds, is all encompassing. It balances the
various sets of values in a series of challenges, responses, and
matchings of people both honored in themselves and "evened"
in temperament by their encounters. Even "nature's natural"
serves, as Celia remarks, to sharpen the wits of his superiors
(Touchstone as whetstone): "Perceiving our natural wits too
dull to reason of such goddesses, [Nature] hath sent this
natural for our whetstone; for always the dullness of the fool
is the whetstone of the wits" (1.2.54). (Touchstone further
tests the principle of testing itself by burlesquing it in his

description of the Quip Modest, Reply Churlish, Reproof Valiant, and Countercheck, in which the combatants, rather than sharpening each other's wits and arriving at an agreement to shoot each other, merely edge further apart, agreeing to disagree in peace.) It is out of such encounters—dull rustic of witty sophisticate, court of forest, literary and naturalistic love—that each discovers what is fit for his particular nature and fortune.

Love is a matching of one's instinctive nature, marriage of one's nature and fortune. Both are in one sense a reward and in another sense the basis of the social contract and first assignment of property under oath. Fortune and love must be submitted to social approval before marriage can seal the instinctive union of the lovers.[4] Initially, the discrepancies between fortune and nature are pointed up by the contrast of settings, forest and court—fortune reigning (or misruling) in the civil world and nature in the forest. At court the caprices of fortune have upset lawful inheritance and assigned its gifts to those who lack both manners and any desire for an enduring contract. The Forest of Arden, conversely, is wintry and crude but has a perfect society singing and feasting in mutual respect around a "natural" Duke. The labor demanded by the forest is disciplinary and purgative; it renders each his due. "Sir, I am a true labourer," Corin, its lowliest inhabitant, says; "I earn that I eat, get that I wear, owe no man hate, envy no man's happiness, glad of other men's good, content with my harm, and the greatest of my pride is to see my ewes graze and my lambs suck" (3.2.77).

While Corin's is a natural state for him, however, the forest

---

[4] Variations of the word "nature" occur over twenty times in the play, some dozen times in the first two scenes, which establish both the distinction between fortune and nature and the possibility of reaffirming natural bonds between servant and master, brother and brother, duke and subjects. See John Shaw, "Fortune and Nature in *As You Like It*," *SQ*, 6 (1955), 45–50; R. P. Draper, "Shakespeare's Pastoral Comedy," *Études Anglaises*, 11 (1958), 1–17; Harold Jenkins, *"As You Like It," Shakespeare Survey*, 8 (1955), 40–51; C. L. Barber, *Shakespeare's Festive Comedy* (Princeton: Princeton University Press, 1959), pp. 222–239.

is undeniably too savage for others. Its austere economy forces
nobles as well as the shepherds' "natural philosopher" to be
aware that "the property of rain is to wet and fire to burn,"
that ewes are greasy. The problem lies in the disjunction of
court and forest, whose incompatibility is illustrated in its
most obvious form in the encounter of Touchstone and Corin.
It is difficult to imagine a natural court under these circumstances and impossible to create a less severe nature. The alternative to proper fortune for each is a translation of "the
stubbornness of fortune" into a quiet and "sweet style"
(1.2.20), which the Duke has managed well and others less
well. Touchstone indicates that for the realistic courtier, no
amount of stylization and imaginative avoidance will change
the basic reality of nature:

> *Cor.* And how like you this shepherd's life, Master Touch-
> stone?
> *Touch.* Truly shepherd, in respect of itself, it is a good life;
> but in respect that it is a shepherd's life, it is naught. In respect
> that it is solitary, I like it very well; but in respect that it is
> private, it is a very vile life. Now, in respect it is in the fields,
> it pleaseth me well; but in respect it is not in the Court, it is
> tedious. [3.2.11–19]

In other words, if your perspective is limited enough or if you
can manage double-talk well enough, it will do; otherwise
you want better company.

At court initially, these contrasts are revealed in the debate
between Orlando and Oliver, then in the wrestling match between Orlando and Charles, and finally in the match between
Orlando and Rosalind, which predicts the direction of the play
as a whole from crude wrestling over property to marital cooperation. Oliver intends the wrestling match to be an assas-
sination masked as sport, a brutal struggle designed to reinforce a would-be monopoly of family property. In ironic
counterpart to this unexpected brutality, Orlando will discover
genuine civility in the rude forest. For the present, he rebels
against being confined "rustically" at home in a manner no
different from "the stalling of an ox." Oliver, he complains,

"lets me feed with his hinds, bars me the place of a brother, and, as much as in him lies, mines my gentility with my education . . . and the spirit of my father, which I think is within me, begins to mutiny against this servitude" (1.1.19):

> *Orl.* Shall I keep your hogs and eat husks with them? What prodigal portion have I spent, that I should come to such penury?
> *Oli.* Know you where you are, sir?
> *Orl.* O, sir, very well; here in your orchard.
> *Oli.* Know you before whom, sir?
> *Orl.* Ay, better than him I am before knows me. I know you are my eldest brother; and, in the gentle condition of blood, you should so know me. The courtesy of nations allows you my better, in that you are the first-born; but the same tradition takes not away my blood. . . .
> *Oli.* What, boy!
> *Orl.* Come, come, elder brother, you are too young in this.
> *Oli.* Wilt thou lay hands on me, villain?
> *Orl.* I am no villain; I am the youngest son of Sir Roland de Roys. [1.1.40–60]

As manners break down, it becomes clear that the propertied eldest son has mistaken fortune for nature, whereas for Orlando, his father's noble spirit is true nature warring within him. Orlando's relatively easy victory over Charles, an extension of the wrangle in the orchard, suggests that boorishness can be overcome partly by a demonstration of strength. But his final wrestling match against the Arden lion indicates that genuine brotherhood results from spiritual conversions.[5] Only under the influence of the forest does Oliver transform bestiality into sweetly tasting identity:

[5] The ancient oak under which Oliver lies as the serpent and lion approach suggests the iconological tree under which Damaetas digs furiously for gold in Sidney's *Arcadia* and the unproductive oak of medieval encyclopedias (such as Hildegard's, J. P. Migne's *Latin Patrology,* 197:1234 ff.). The lion, too, is unproductive, "with udders all drawn dry." Cf. Perceval's vision of the lion and serpent and the "good man's interpretation" in *The Works of Sir Thomas Malory,* ed. Eugene Vinaver (London, 1954), pp. 664 ff.; Erwin Panofsky, *Meaning in the Visual Arts* (New York: Doubleday, 1957), figs. 52 and 53; Edward I. Watkin, *Catholic Art and Culture* (New York, 1944), appendix.

Cel. Are you his brother?
Ros.   Was't you he rescu'd?
Cel. Was't you that did so oft contrive to kill him?
Oli. 'Twas I; but 'tis not I. I do not shame
To tell you what I was, since my conversion
So sweetly tastes, being the thing I am.

[4.3.134–138]

In contrast, Orlando and Rosalind are spiritually well-matched to begin with but are confronted with the problem of displacement, and upon entering the forest both encounter questions of basic sustenance that echo their difficulty at court. Challenging the duke at sword point and demanding goods for survival, Orlando is admitted to a highly civil gathering of miscellaneous unequals. Freed of the false court's material interests, the forest-court has managed to refine the wilderness and transform conflict into social cooperation:

Orl.   But whate'er you are
That in this desert inaccessible
Under the shade of melancholy boughs
Lose and neglect the creeping hours of time;
If ever you have look'd on better days,
If ever been where bells have knowll'd to church,
If ever sat at any good man's feast,
If ever from your eyelids wip'd a tear
And know what 'tis to pity and be pitied,
Let gentleness my strong enforcement be;
In the which hope I blush, and hide my sword.
  Duke S. True is it that we have seen better days,
And have with holy bell been knowll'd to church,
And sat at good men's feasts, and wip'd our eyes
Of drops that sacred pity hath engend'red;
And therefore sit you down in gentleness.

[2.7.109–124]

In response to Orlando's rhetorically balanced challenge, the duke's quasi-ritualistic answer implies the interdependence of gentility and religious grace, both based on compassion. But the society surrounding him derives partly from somewhere else and has indeed seen "better days": it is not the product of an "inaccessible desert." Its very excess of ceremony serves as an ironic reminder of what nature ought to be where the social order functions normally. As Jaques indicates, the forest and its new inhabitants are ill-adapted to each other. The deer are the only "native burghers of this desert city" (3.1.23): and though Jaques's sullenness in brooding on their intrusion is ridiculed, he is undoubtedly meant to be correct in maintaining that nobles "are mere usurpers, tyrants" who "fright the animals" and "kill them up / In their assign'd and native dwelling-place" (2.1.61). For one's natural place is indeed "assign'd and native," part of the blood.

Jaques tries to cleanse the "foul body of th' infected world" by satiric sharpness, assuming that human nature is warped too seriously for civil remedies. It is largely because of him that we do not accept at face value the claims that the exiled court "fleet the time carelessly, as they did in the golden world." He considers ceremony mere acting and all life a disillusioning play: its democracy is an equality of deprivation, everyone alike ending in nature and fortune without teeth, eyes, taste (3.7.166). His play's final unmasking is a discovery of nothingness at the end of time's ripening and rotting. Hence Orlando's contest against Jaques is crucial to the "socializing" of love, which needs to be rescued from naturalistic and primitive as well as social perversions. His first answer is made implicitly when he bears the old Adam to the duke's feast and thereby demonstrates that at least one old man is not without care and veneration. But primarily Orlando and Adam form a potential social cooperation of young and aged, servant and master, that hearkens back not to Eden but to "the constant service of the antique world" (2.3.56). If in modern times "none will sweat but for promotion / And having that do choke their service up / Even with the having" (2.3.60), they, at least, are willing to go halves and settle upon some "low content."

But then Adam as a servant does not expect a better fortune "than to die well," and "low" or rustic stabling is precisely what Orlando set out to avoid when his father's spirit moved in him. As other layers of the forest's economy unfold, having it as you like it appears increasingly difficult. Neither Orlando nor the play provides a final answer to Jaques, who remains sufficiently out of tune with the new order to abandon it.

The wit contest between Orlando and Jaques in the third act points up not only Jaques's position as an outsider but also the limits of the idyllic order. Their contest is sandwiched between others that have to do with an assortment of lovers and pastoral attitudes arranged as mirrors around the central contrast between the court and nature, first the falling out of Duke Frederick and Oliver, now having their barbaric difficulties, and then a debate between Corin and Touchstone on the relative merits of civilized and shepherd lives. Each of these exchanges has its relevance to Orlando's concern with the search for a social place suitable to his given nature. Insofar as the excesses that they illustrate are purged by the encounters and bring about a recognition of "kindness, nobler ever than revenge, / And nature stronger than . . . just occasion," the spirit of the romance is allowed to triumph. But Orlando cannot rid himself of Jaques's pessimism so easily. If the dramatic movement in the contests as a whole is from enmity and dialectical encounter to cooperative venture, Orlando's reaction to Jaques exposes a lack of the very civility that he seeks as a gentleman:

Jaq. . . . Will you sit down with me? and we two will rail against our mistress the world, and all our misery.
Orl. I will chide no breather in the world but myself, against whom I know most faults.
Jaq. The worst fault you have is to be in love.
Orl. 'Tis a fault I will not change for your best virtue. I am weary of you.
Jaq. By my troth, I was seeking for a fool when I found you.
Orl. He is drown'd in the brook. Look but in, and you shall see him. . . .
Jaq. I'll tarry no longer with you. Farewell, good Signior Love.
Orl. I am glad of your departure. Adieu, good Monsieur Melancholy. [3.2.294–302, 310–311]

His apparent victory is the result partly of superior self-awareness (Jaques is less keen on his own faults than those of others) and partly of the power of love, which even in his

imperfect grasp is greater than that of melancholy, though obviously of no help in communicating with Jaques. Though
they discover in their probing the proper labels for each other—
Signior Love (the romantic hero) and Monsieur Melancholy
(the sad realist)—neither is prepared as yet to tolerate the
other at a wedding banquet. The mutual exclusiveness of
romance and realism, the source of their rudeness, prevents
cooperation until a higher perspective can be found that incorporates both.

As we have seen, the check or counterforce to the romantic
spirit of the play is dispersed among several characters, notably
Touchstone, who vulgarizes romance but nonetheless illustrates its power; Jaques, his opposite, on whom it is wasted;
and of course those who resist it but are reformed and eventually share it. The most important combination is found in
Rosalind, who embodies both the forward spirit of love and
its countercheck in their most intelligent forms. It is she, the
central manipulator, who is given the task of reconciling the
widest range of opposites in an adequate formula of social
harmony. Though to begin with she is herself disinherited,
Celia offers to share her own property with Rosalind:

> *Ros.* Well, I will forget the condition of my estate, to rejoice
> in yours.
> *Cel.* You know my father hath no child but I . . . and, truly,
> when he dies, thou shalt be his heir; for what he hath taken
> away from thy father perforce, I will render thee again in af-
> fection. [1.2.16]

"Affection" as opposed to "force" is the best of nature, the basis
of friendship as well as love, and it can find rustic as well as
courtly means of operating. Upon entering the forest, Celia
and Rosalind "buy in" and set about correcting some of its
imbalances, especially its rustic crudeness and incivility and
the artificialities of pastoral courtship. Some of these aberra-
tions Rosalind encounters internally as personal problems as
well as externally in those whom Shakespeare brings before
her for cures. (She recognizes herself even in Silvius's Petrarchan poses, for instance: "Alas, poor shepherd! searching of

thy wound, / I have by hard adventure found mine own.")
She oversees Silvius and Phebe's sacrifice of natural desire to
stultified convention, working against the perversities of a
code that draws out the courtship even more unnaturally than
Touchstone hurries it. Her advice to Phebe is to trade goods
immediately, without trying on the stylized manner of another
set whom it fits better:

> Sell when you can; you are not for all markets.
> Cry the man mercy; love him; take his offer.
> Foul is most foul, being foul to be a scoffer.
>
> [3.5.60–62]

Since her contest with Phebe is not really genuine, only a
game of mistaken identities, it is possible for the exposure of
the game to restore nature.

In Touchstone's case, wit and poetry are quasi-courtliness
put to the service of seduction, becoming not an articulation
of love but mere stages that civilized lovers pass through on
their way to sensual gratification. Even the rites of marriage,
performed by a vicar of doubtful credentials, are used as an
instrument of legal possession, for as Touchstone says, "We
must be married, or we must live in bawdry" (3.3.99). The
best guarantee of keeping one's property is not the sacred vow
itself but the choice of a mate so plain that no one else wants
her: "I press in here, sir, amongst the rest of the country
copulatives," Touchstone explains with his customary bluntness, "to swear and to forswear, according as marriage binds
and blood breaks. A poor virgin, sir, an ill-favour'd thing,
sir, but mine own. A poor humor of mine, sir, to take that no
man else will" (5.4.57). He is the only one of the lovers with
a rival to run off and he disposes of him boorishly. Though
the ranking of love affairs makes it clear that some are higher
on the scale than others, the play's concept of permissible contract is moved aside to make room for Touchstone's opinion.

Rosalind has very little to do with that opinion beyond predicting with Jaques, "You'll be rotten ere you be half ripe"
(3.2.125). Her most ambitious therapy is saved for Orlando
and herself. Without losing sight of the goal of courtship, her

cure delays that goal until Orlando can be teased out of affectation. All told, their courtship manages to have it both ways:
its sonnets and courtly poses distinguish it from the Touch-
stone-Audrey level of natural necessity, and yet its ironies and
its genuine romance distinguish it from arid pastoral stylization. As a paradigm of courtship both ironic and romantic, it
might be said to combine nature and art in just proportion
in the context of those who fail to do so; it marries social
grace to natural grace.

Despite the differences among the four marriages, then, each
of Rosalind's final pairings is obviously appropriate in its way
and improved by her manipulation of it. The contest between
court and forest; the inverted and unnatural relations of
lovers and brothers, duke and subject; and the rudeness and
incivility are overcome by the marriage rite and its implicitly
multilayered social contract:

> Then is there mirth in heaven,
> When earthly things made even
> Atone together.
>
> [5.4.114–116]

As event and fortune match desire, all things are "evened"
out, as heaven desires and Rosalind foresees. Each has achieved
his proper possession, much in the spirit of Corin's community
of good will.

But the marriage union in Shakespeare is not a confusion
of levels, of course. As Lavatche remarks in *All's Well,* the
differences between the way of glory and the way of humility
cannot be altogether disregarded:

I am a woodland fellow, sir, that always loved a great fire, and
the master I speak of ever keeps a good fire; but sure he is the
prince of the world; let his nobility remain in's court, I am for
the house with the narrow gate, which I take to be too little
for pomp to enter; some that humble themselves may, but the
many will be too chill and tender, and they'll be for the flow'ry
way that leads to the broad gate and the great fire. [4.5.44 ff.]

Even as he says it and the audience recognizes its accuracy,

a kind of sympathy is struck all around. The separation of
levels arouses some nostalgia for the particular "fire" one is
denied—in the humble house or the great mansion—but the
social accord implied by the clown's merely saying it so clearly
and with such fatalism brings about resignation to the inevitable. The broad and the narrow gate, the great fire and
the chill, are fixed—and therefore leave us in peace.

Such an arrangement is obviously not quite "paradisal" in
the sense that each receives everything, but in the last exchanges of *As You Like It,* the language becomes more ritual-
istic than responsive, more idyllic than challenging:

> *Ros.* [To the Duke] To you I give myself, for I am yours.
>   [To Orlando] To you I give myself, for I am yours.
> *Duke S.* If there be truth in sight, you are my daughter.
> *Orl.* If there be truth in sight, you are my Rosalind . . .
> *Ros.* I'll have no father, if you be not he;
>   I'll have no husband, if you be not he.
>
>   [5.4.122–129]

These declarations of identity and acknowledgment of "property" Shakespeare places between the songs of Hymen. Re-
stating as fact the promises that Rosalind has extracted from
the lovers in preparation for the unmasking, they have the
ring of vows kept, of time anticipated and fulfilled. The duke
promises a proportionate sharing of "returned fortune / According to the measure of their states" and is happy to leave
the forest; but as a final acknowledgment of the rustic, semidemocratic spirit of the forest, he encourages them for the moment to forget together "this new-fall'n dignity / And fall
into . . . rustic revelry" (5.4.182). The antagonistic battles of
wit and muscle with which the play begins give way to dance
measures that, with Jaques's blessing, enact a comprehensive
harmony of opposites.

Shakespeare's romance comedies usually regroup in this
manner momentarily divided societies that have discovered a
rustic common denominator. The idyllic feeling in these
communal choruses suggests that despite the breaking up of
the feudal order, heroes may still appear from among the old

faction-ridden hierarchy whose values can be the center of a new society. The prince still seems dignified, perhaps hopefully young, idealistic, and promising, and his displacement seems a cultural tragedy. The plays we have examined bring to bear sufficient resources of imagination and social courtship to cure the loosening of the social bond—the rebellion of youth against fathers in *A Midsummer Night's Dream* and the usurping of proper inheritance and dukedoms in *As You Like It* and *The Tempest*.

In narrative forms based on the same sense of the feudal hierarchy such as the *Arcadia* and Calidore's venture into pastoral society, the hero undergoes an essentially lone journey. His visit to shepherdom represents a self-conscious social descent, often a kind of initiatory rite, and at the same time a momentary freedom from the burdens of class and a discovery of nature's potential for peacefulness. Though Arcadia offers him more than vegetable comfort, he is sooner or later expected to return to a courtly society that has not changed as he has: the two realms, roughly romance and pastoral, inevitably separate. In contrast, in Shakespeare's pastoral comedies, the journey is not an individual or "heroic" education but a group exile that transports an entire society into the forest where it undergoes therapy. Its return is to a new integration of its components after exposure to the depths of imagination, primitiveness, or moonlit exchanges of identity. Yet these plays also rest their compromise upon the centralizing authority of the dukedom or kingship and upon aristocratic marriages, with their implications of lineal renewal, continuity, and legality. Though natural setting and spontaneous manners assist the establishing of the bond (which curiously excludes tradesmen and shopkeepers), full institution of a new culture requires constitutional monarchy and primogeniture.

I have attempted in each case to define the combination of transformational forces that cures the initial sickness of the society and then to relate them to the theater's effect on the audience's own emphatic "journey" beyond its habitual stratification. Love, the operation of magic and authority, and the playing of roles dissolve an initial set of antinomies and create a bond that fathers and sons, nobles and shepherds, can subscribe to without sacrificing their particular "fortunes." Though Shakespeare concedes a good deal to the marvelous effect of dreamscapes in making these rites work, the therapy of the green world and the therapy of poetry overlap as means of promoting a meeting of minds. The stage proposes to work miracles as wonderful as those of the Forest of Arden or Prospero's island upon the people who fall under its sway. Both forest and theater represent somewhat closed and harbored places; but the audience beckoned into them is eventually educated in how to leave them and to carry the experience of the sojourn with them as they exit.

In sum: the pastoralism of Sidney, Spenser, and Shakespeare is similar in putting class difficulties in the context of a view beyond them in the leveling powers of nature and imagination. The difficulty in such Arcadias is to apply the visions of the harbored pastoral place to the divisive and leaden realities of the social hierarchy. Each poet proposes his own solutions. Of the three, Sidney seems most bent upon living with the tension between the courtly life and shepherdom, which give us perspectives on each other but remain basically irreconcilable. Spenser forced himself to discipline the imagination and its love of ideal Arcadian graces in the interests of service to chivalry: the writing of a didactic romance as ambitious as *The Faerie Queene* is evidence of his commitment to aristocratic values, and at the same time the disappointment of Colin over Calidore's intrusion is evidence of the ambivalence he felt toward that commitment. Shakespeare sought to change the deepest levels of awareness in each social class by revealing each to the others in the context of mutual dreams and basic elements of nature, and yet to make their imaginative and spiritual marriage merely a new condition of their old order, now revitalized and enlightened. Upon both of these conditions—the marriage of minds and social differentiation—the social contract depends. The poet's function, while he has everyone seated in the theater, is to make them see the nature of the play itself as the vehicle of their imaginative association. Only if the therapy that works onstage also works upon them in the theater can it spread into the world outside.

I plan now to turn to the second stage of renaissance pastoral in which views of Paradise are juxtaposed with the wilderness. These Platonist and Christian perspectives on the mode do not require that we stay within the boundaries of the poem to discover perfect harmony, because whatever a poem may create verbally by way of a *locus amoenus* the cosmos will eventually surpass in reality. The vision of a paradise to be regained, however, is always qualified by the remembrance of a lost paradise and by the need for a significant transformation of the fallen world, whose remaking is a fearful cataclysm as well as a promise. The idea of a perfect society itself grows so exalted in Milton that it requires a violent overthrow both of the old courtly compromise and the gentler pastoral of Arcadia. Both Herbert and Milton pass beyond political and social pastoral in the usual sense. Though their concepts of a divine power of transformation capable of regenerating a fallen world is by no means irrelevant to social questions, as *Paradise Regained* in particular illustrates, it was left to Marvell's political poems to try to reconcile transcendent and social versions of pastoral.

Poetry as Sacred Conveyance
in Herbert and Marvell

When all perfections as but one appeare,
That those thy form doth show,
The very dust, where thou dost tread and go,
Make beauties here.

Where are my lines then? my approaches? views?
Where are my window-songs?
—"DULNESSE"

The poet, the stony-hearted sinner, and the priest in Herbert's *The Temple* approach communion in separate ways—through words, cleansing of the heart, and sacraments—but their methods often overlap and reinforce one another. Each of the three seeks conveyances to bring the mind to Christ and Christ into visible form where his Real Presence may be experienced. As Malcolm Ross points out, the bread and wine of the sacrament may serve as "signs," [1] encroaching upon the domain of poetry, and poems in turn may be treated as sacred chalices or instruments of instruction for the sinner. In turn, the heart contains both "ink" and "blood," which require miraculous transubstantiations to become the Word and the Presence that Herbert seeks:

Since blood is fittest, Lord, to write
Thy sorrows in, and bloudie fight;

[1] Malcolm M. Ross describes the meeting place of substance and spirit in Herbert as a kind of "pretty Cartesian porch" reserved for dispatches, where all the world of sense that proves untranslatable is, "cut off cleanly from the world of spirit." *Poetry and Dogma* (New Brunswick, N.J.: Rutgers University Press, 1954), p. 180.

> My heart hath store, write there, where in
> One box doth lie both ink and sinne.
>
> ["Good Friday"]

The temple itself is threefold, a house of sacraments and sacred objects, the poet's book of verse, and the inner self of the sinner; and the altar, the first object that greets us across the threshold, is the heart, a poetic artifact, and the place of the priest's reenactment of the sacrifice. On certain occasions and in certain poems, the three strands join, as in devotional songs or antiphons that call for nature to join their full-voiced concert:

> VERS. The Heav'ns are not too high
>   His praise may thither flie:
>   The earth is not too low,
>   His praises there may grow.
> CHO. Let all the world in ev'ry corner sing,
>   *My God and King.*
>
> ["Antiphon I"]

At those moments, poems become effective mediating devices between the raw materials of nature and the object of praise.

Unfortunately, not all words sing as simply and as purely as the last four of "Antiphon I," nor can "all the world" always be trusted to join in. Neither hearts nor words have anything inherently sacramental about them. As they are given to a poet by his culture, words refer to a multitude of unconnected things that may rebel against form; they spread ring upon ring of association, link alien things through rhyme and puns, and entangle the poet in emotional and social complexities that cloud his mind and wit. Though the poet-priest-sinner would like to use them to pull the world into the "antiphon," they can just as readily enable the world to pull him into it. Likewise, the traditional and sometimes derelict genres with which the poet works, unlike the priest's sacraments, are ill suited to his purpose. He must transform the secular courtship of the sonneteers, for instance, into processes of mortification and divine appeal before he can expect Christ to "tread and go" in the march of his rhyme and meter; and in a poem like

"Dulnesse" that transformation requires more than a substitution of "Lord" for "Lady": it requires the reconceiving of social distance as a gulf between planes of existence. The poet's
petition is therefore an "inspiriting" similar to that which en-
livened Adam's clay, the "quickness" of which is not merely
inventive wit but a new life uniting divine being to human
dust:

> Why do I languish thus, drooping and dull,
>   As if I were all earth?
> O give me quicknesse, that I may with mirth
>   Praise thee brim-full!

Discovery of an appropriate mode of praise depends upon the
poem's receptivity to renewal; as for the sinner, capacity to
render praise depends upon the heart's preparation for sanc-
tification and for the priest, upon the validity of the rites he
administers. When each of these conveyances succeeds, Christ,
the original of paradise, is rejoined to nature in them:

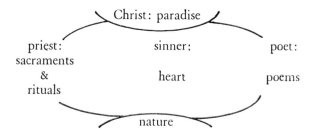

In order to make that reunion of Christ and nature possible
in the poem, Herbert must rehabilitate not only such modes
as the song and sonnet but also pastoral. Rather than merely
repeating conventional purling streams and the artifices of Arcadian courtship, he must draw them into the precincts of the
temple's symbolism and make them an aspect of the incarnation, a habitation of the Word. In the temple it is possible to
re-create such an emblematic universe of symbols that look
backward toward Eden and forward to paradise restored. By
reconstituting these in the poetic enclosure of *The Temple,*
Herbert seeks to find God again making "one place ev'ry

where." The heart, the temple, and the poem, the symbolic objects, views, "window-songs," and ritual patterns that the priest and the poet arrange for the reader may then become an epitome of a greater creation, a single organic and harmonic order.

In examining the means by which Herbert makes poetry an enclosed epitome of the world and an incarnation of paradise, we may regard *The Temple* as in many ways typical of seventeenth-century experiments with a Christian poetic. I plan accordingly to suggest certain parallels with Marvell's attempt to find in drops of dew and other objects similar vestiges of paradise and to use both poets to estimate the range of theoretical and practical matters that a concept of sacred poetic and pastoral enclosures involves.

I

Unlike the guilt-free shepherd of traditional pastoral who dwells in an accomplished Arcadia where one may give reign to natural desire, Herbert's sinner requires a preliminary cleansing before he can return to paradise. In the initial poems of *The Temple,* the poet therefore prepares for the priest's central ceremony, the "mystical repast" that will be consummated in "Love III," by purgative rites in which he cooperates with the priest. Homiletic genres, for instance, begin the process of cleansing by admonishing those who approach the temple to remember their duty and to attend to verse as to a sermon:

> Thou, whose sweet youth and early hopes inhance
> Thy rate and price, and mark thee for a treasure,
> Hearken unto a Verser, who may chance
> Rhyme thee to good, and make a bait of pleasure,
>   A verse may finde him, who a sermon flies,
>   And turn delight into a sacrifice.
>   ["The Church-porch"]

A poet who would celebrate God must first join with the sinner in his confession and with the priest in his sacrifice. In either verse or sermons the sweet bait is intended to lead sin-

ners to the "altar," where verse and heart become sacrificial
offerings ("The Altar"). The poet begins by flattering the
sweet youth who steps through the entry but quickly directs
the praise elsewhere and draws him toward the tasting of the
sacrificial lamb:

> Thou, whom the former precepts have
> Sprinkled and taught, how to behave
> Thy self in church; approach, and taste
> The churches mysticall repast.
> ["Superliminare"]

Within *The Temple* proper, the purgative functions of verse
accomplish more than the moral redirection of the youthful
reader. As an imitation of Christ, a poem offers an image of
original beauty; as personal expression and confession, it clears
the way for the poet's own union with God; as rhetoric, it
negotiates between the poet and God and between the poet
and his audience; as narrative, it recapitulates history and discovers in the temporal progression of the Old and New Testa-
ments an anagogic reality that continually prefigures paradise;
and as description, it discovers recurrent signs of paradise in
the seasons and in nature's potentially emblematic objects.[2] The
structure of *The Temple* through the first sequence of poems
(to "Easter-wings") is a complex overlaying of these functions
of poetry and of several modes of progression: the poet's and
the reader's initial entry into the "temple"; the historical events
of Christ's life that set the pattern for the church's liturgical
offices, sacrifice, death and rebirth, and all symbolic passages

---

[2] Concerning parallels between the poet's re-creation and original
divine authorship, see Joseph Summers, "The Conception of
Form" and "The Proper Language" in *George Herbert* (London:
Chatto and Windus, 1954), pp. 73–119: "The ideas of God as the
Great Artificer and as Absolute Beauty were theological concep-
tions with inevitable aesthetic corollaries, and the work of art
could be valued exactly because it reflected the divine pattern," pp.
76–77. See also Rosalie L. Colie, *Paradoxia Epidemica* (Princeton,
N.J.: Princeton University Press, 1966), pp. 170–215. Miss Colie
stresses the "paradoxes of being" that grow out of the poet's imitations of the creator.

from the old to the new dispensation ("The Sacrifice," "Good Friday," "Redemption," "Sepulchre," "Easter"); the poet's search for an appropriate medium ("The Altar," "The Thanksgiving," "Good Friday," "Easter," "Easter-wings"); and the sinner's handling of the barriers that sin erects against the mystical repast ("The Reprisal," "The Agonie," "The Sinner," "Redemption"). These modes of progress are recapitulated in "Easter-wings," which sorts them out and clarifies them, in a preliminary way, before they become the substance of subsequent detailed explorations of the three "temples"—heart, poem, church—and their epitomizing of patterns dispersed in nature and in scriptural chronicles.

The poet both initially and recurrently seeks to estimate correctly the materials with which he works and the inadequacy of his specific talent. In "The Thanksgiving," for instance, he tries to imagine ways of approaching the sacrifice and is forced to reject several inappropriate styles:

> Oh King of grief! (a title strange, yet true,
>   To thee of all kings onely due)
> Oh King of wounds! how shall I grieve for thee,
>   Who in all grief preventest me?
> Shall I weep bloud? why, thou hast wept such store
>   That all thy body was one doore.
> Shall I be scourged, flouted, boxed, sold?
>   'Tis but to tell the tale is told.
> *My God, my God, why dost thou part from me?*
>   Was such a grief as cannot be.
> Shall I then sing, skipping thy dolefull storie,
>   And side with thy triumphant glorie?
> Shall thy strokes be my stroking? thorns, my flower?
>   Thy rod, my posie? crosse, my bower?

Seeking to answer Christ's example, the poet cannot imagine a mode that will serve. If he conceives of the poem as an imitation, all alternatives seem equally futile because the sacrifice, as history and deed, speaks more fully than words can. Perhaps, then, Herbert suggests, one can be God's fool and acknowledge, in antic skipping, the clownishness of poems: the flogging that Christ underwent he will convert into the stroking rhythm of the lines; thorns he will make into flowers; rods into posies; crosses into pastoral bowers. He can at least provide the kind of ironic entertainment that openly confesses its own incongruity.

But poetry must try to do something more than mock itself. It might, for instance, sum up the "one God" in an amassing harmony:

> My musick shall finde thee, and ev'ry string
>   Shall have his attribute to sing;
> Then all together may accord in thee,
>   And prove one God, one harmonie.
> If thou shalt give me wit, it shall appeare,
>   If thou hast giv'n it me, 'tis here.
> Nay, I will reade thy book, and never move
>   Till I have found therein thy love,
> Thy art of love, which I'le turn back on thee.

Thus a poet may arrive at a heavenly music by concentrating on one divine attribute at a time, trusting that, when examined closely, all attributes together will prove to be analogues of a single reality. Or he may canvas scripture for appropriate ways to render praise and then imitate them. ("Holy Scriptures II" suggests that God's integral harmony is revealed there as well, in the connectives and recurrent images, as the Form behind all substances.) The moment of conversion from separate attributes to one harmony would presumably be the completion of a true hymn, a kind of *summa theologia* in rhyme in which the title "God" stands over a realized aesthetic order. Rather than offering an accomplished example, however, the poet uses the poem in this case merely as a preparatory rite and confesses that the passion precludes further speech: "Then for thy passion—I will do for that—/ Alas, my God, I know not what."

"The Thanksgiving" suggests adequate reasons why Herbert treats the act of poetic composition ironically and frequently devalues its currency before arriving at such plain-style assertions as, "There is in love a sweetness readie penn'd: / Copie out onely that, and save expense," or "nor let them punish me with losse of rime, / Who plainly say *'My God, My King!'* " The difficulty is that the Christian poet cannot really say even this much without a considerable expense of wit preceding:

only in the context of his agitated path to peaceful conclusions do such substantives as "Love" and "God" become meaningful. The stages of realization that so often carry the poet through false ideas of style and displays of temper are a concession to his need to take very devious and indirect ways to basic truths. Love is a positive and unquestioned reality between the speaker and God, yet is usually enacted in a context that forestalls it. In "Love I" and "Love II" it is certified genuine by contrast to another kind of love, the misdevotion of Petrarchans whose manner and whose sonnet forms the poet feels called upon to examine before he can define the real thing. He must repair what sonneteers have wrought in misnaming the courtly game of scarfs and gloves "love." Having done so, he asks the "author of this great frame" to descend into the poem and consume lesser love-fires in his greater fire. The poet promises to lay poetic invention at love's altar. In secular love, "Wit fancies beautie, beautie raiseth wit: / The world is theirs; they two play out the game"; in divine love the scattered wits find a beauty that instills new life in its dust-blown inventions.

It is evident from these and other poems that poetry for Herbert is on the same footing as other conveyances requiring regeneration; the cleansing of old modes follows the pattern of personal redemption and the pattern of nature's death and resurrection. The poet divines the same messages in his own perishing "poesies" as he does in nature's flowers, and he himself blooms, wears garlands, and eventually withers. The body of words, like the dust of nature, requires the renewal of the Word, which makes Paradise where there was decay. A merely natural or unredeemed poesie would be incapable of sustaining life against the pressure of time:

> I made a posie, while the day ran by:
> Here will I smell my remnant out, and tie
>   My life within this band.
> But Time did beckon the flowers, and they
> By noon most cunningly did steal away,
>   And wither'd in my hand.

The blight carries up the speaker's arm to the heart, and he finds in the admonition a sugared suspicion of his own "fatall

day." Properly interpreted, the scent of flowers is medicinal as well as sweet because it hints at something imperish-
able beyond flowers, if only by contrast. But a second posie-
poem concludes, with respect to its own devices:

> Invention rest;
> Comparisons, go play; wit use thy will;
>   Less then the least
> Of all God's mercies is my posie still.

Such a poem exists only to point out its own sacrificial death
and direct the mind to the afterdeath, "for cures."

As the poem called "The Flower" indicates, however, God
is present in some sense even in the destructive cycles of nature in which the poet practices dying. The present moment
of the poem, a moment of green rebirth, is held in check by
the poet's awareness of the divine purpose behind these temporal cycles. He petitions for a place where flowers always
bloom and authors "shoot up fair," but the vision of such a
place serves, for the moment, only to make it clearer that the
poet is to read the divine purpose only in flowers—and is himself merely a flower:

> O that I once past changing were,
> Fast in thy Paradise, where no flower can wither!
>   Many a spring I shoot up fair,
> Offring at heav'n, growing and groning thither:
>   Nor doth my flower
>   Want a spring-showre,
>   My sinnes and I joining together.
>
>   But while I grow in a straight line,
> Still upwards bent, as if heav'n were mine own,
>   Thy anger comes, and I decline.

Meanwhile he must abide until he can make a "chiming of a
passing-bell"—a happy marriage tune of the suffering of his
"shrivel'd heart." [3] He must live with the complex awareness
that not this or that—not for instance a spring or a winter, a

---

[3] Cf. Donne's Sermon no. 36 in *LXXX Sermons:* that heaven
is glory and joy "makes a Tolle an Ave, a Vae an Euge, a Cruci-
fige an Hosanna; It makes my death-bed, a marriage-bed, And my
Passing-Bell, an Epithalamion."

growing or a dying—is real in any final terms; only God's word is. Yet this or that in alternation is precisely what he is given and what nature's metaphors reveal to him. The full Word provides no image for itself, only a name:

> These are thy wonders, Lord of power,
> Killing and quickning, bringing down to hell
>   And up to heaven in an houre;
> Making a chiming of a passing-bell.
>   We say amisse,
>   This or that is:
> Thy word is all, if we could spell.

Thus though in recurrent creative moments the poet can "once more smell the dew and rain, / And relish versing," as merely a flower he can never do more than "offer" at heaven. Ultimate poems and the poet ultimately-to-be are drowned in tears of "groaning" and tormented pains of "growing," sins and tears being soil and water to this cyclical poetic crop.

Conceived against the final killing and quickening of dooms-day, this creation is very little, but usually Herbert is not content to think of poetry as limited to the same possibilities as flowers: a poem is embedded in nature but may also transcend it in some respects. Often, in fact, it annihilates one world in order to re-create its own, beyond the world's materials—as Christ destroys the world at doomsday and gathers the scattered dust into a new harmonious order. The pattern of a truly divine music of praise is thus not the pattern of Eden, where creation issues from divine commandments and returns its hymn of thanksgiving, but the pattern of sacrifice and ultimately of apocalyptic destruction, followed by a totally new music:

> Man is out of order hurl'd,
> Parcel'd out to all the world.
> Lord, thy broken consort raise,
> And the musick shall be praise.

> ["Dooms-day"]

Measuring his lesser attempts at praise against this standard, the poet must steel himself against nature even while making use of its metaphors, and be prepared to discard metaphor in a direct naming of God ("Thy word is all, if we could spell")— presumably as he will discard the "gliding" nature of flowers in his own final garden.

At the same time, Herbert has lingering regrets over the world's destruction. In "Vertue," for instance, he mingles elegy and hymn as the soul is seasoned by its entanglement in nature and yet also proves itself more durable than nature:

> Sweet day, so cool, so calm, so bright,
> The bridall of the earth and skie:
> The dew shall weep thy fall to night;
>   For thou must die.

> Sweet rose, whose hue angrie and brave
> Bids the rash gazer wipe his eye:
> Thy root is ever in its grave,
>   And thou must die.

> Sweet spring, full of sweet dayes and roses,
> A box where sweets compacted lie;
> My musick shows ye have your closes,
>   And all must die.

> Onely a sweet and vertuous soul,
> Like season'd timber, never gives;
> But though the whole world turn to coal,
>   Then chiefly lives.

The speaker's attachment to the three elements of nature that he enumerates, days, roses, and springs, is based on a partial parallelism between them and humankind. The extent of the implication remains somewhat doubtful behind the cool precision of the songlike form. How are we to read our fate in their mirror? Clearly we do live partly in and for sweet days, the beauty of which the poet intensifies with the repetition of "so," the figure of the bridal, and the gentle exaggeration of the weeping dew—and perhaps even more immediately we find ourselves involved with roses, whose life cycle is like ours and whose grave is too near human for comfort. The speaker appears to be not fully committed to the elegy, however: it is the rash gazer who weeps—one who does not realize the implications of nature's dying—and even the cumulative good things of the third stanza do not force him to abandon his cool economy. Though we do not realize it at first, the progression from enumerated particulars to the generalized mortality of stanza three ("*all* must die") is a step toward a final extrication from nature's various items. We progress toward a categorical difference between souls and roses by this means, and thus toward an emergent triumph that eventually explains the limitations of the speaker's identification with nature.

The final stanza exploits the parallelism of the stanzaic structure to drive home that contrast: time rules the enumerated items—the day, the rose, the spring—while the soul rises beyond them. Although Herbert continues to draw upon metaphors from nature in the parallel between souls and seasoned timber, sympathy for timber is uncalled for. (Timber is also tougher than roses and does not bend in the building of structures.) Whereas the third stanza sets a universal dying to the "closes" (finished units and sacred precincts) of music, the last stanza alludes to a total conflagration, the mystery of the divine will, and the potentially terrifying conditions of the soul's doomsday judgment. The burning of a world still "whole"— not coming apart piece by piece as natural objects do but still "entire" and "healthy" when God destroys it—is a metamorphosis, a "turning," that surpasses any change in the daily and seasonal cycles that the soul has seen. It is a transformation as beyond "seasoning" as dried timber is beyond changes of leaf or weather. Yet the soul must indeed be seasoned, in the sense of "toughened," by virtue, if it is to withstand this absolute and "unnatural" destruction. As the dying of the universe surpasses any imaginable cause, so the life of a soul surpasses any imaginable natural life. If we have been lulled into thinking that being alive on a cool day in the company of roses, in spring's compact offering of gifts, is the zenith of paradisal joy, we have been mistaken; beyond the enumerated sweets of the seasons lies an indescribable condition in which the soul will chiefly live. The final refrain seals the contrast, and each of its three words is capable of bearing the stress of that contrast:

beyond the appointments of death that every natural thing keeps, the soul moves toward a point of liberation "then"; by contrast to the limited life it has experienced, it will then "chiefly" live, unencumbered by the checks of time; and, finally, it simply "lives," by contrast to the sympathetic dying it has had to do heretofore.

Despite this expansion of perspectives and despite hints of a paradisal life beyond nature, the final stanza does not take leave of the precision or the basic modesty of the poem, which are its most remarkable aspects. Though Herbert suggests a momentary expansion of the voice in the large vowels and mounting movement of the last stanza ("But though the whole world turn to coal"), he forces us to go slowly in the final line, which is effectively brief and quietly summary, as though the habit of precise observation established in the first three stanzas were transferable to observations of a quite different kind. My impression also is that "coal," in the poem's most expansive line, has a kind of domesticity about it that checks apocalyptic speculation; certainly "though" refuses to terrify us with sure prophecies. The ruin of the world is merely a possibility, the life of the soul a certainty.[4]

[4] "Vertue" has several echoes of the kind that the echo-poem "Heaven" makes more explicit. Gazers may be "rash" and roses have "angry and brave" hues (red and well-decked out), but in "The Rose" Herbert also watches the sacrifice reenacted in the rose. The red hue of the pagan rose is colored with "griefs" blushing "with woes,"; the redness of the Christian rose is stained with sacrificial blood, as D. C. Allen points out in *Image and Meaning* (Baltimore: Johns Hopkins Press, 1960), pp. 69 ff. The thornless rose of Eden becomes through Adam's fall a crown of briars, but redemptive blood suffused through it gives it the red of new life. The "bridal" (and bridle) of earth and sky in the first stanza of the poem joins heaven and earth and suggests the bridegroom trope. Christ is also the day-spring, the source of days and roses, even at times in the tradition the "box" in which they are summed up (as in Edward Taylor's "Oh! Wealthy Theam!"). These grace notes partly transform the bittersweet music of natural objects into dim predictions; there are strains of doomsday music in their "closes" (the ends of musical phrases, enclosures, and perhaps "cloistres").

The ambivalence of the soul engaged in but also disengaging itself from nature, looking forward to its own de-creation and resurrection, is perhaps characteristic of all measurements of temporal nature by eschatological visions. When that measurement is lacking, we have an entirely different sense of the botanical parallel, as, for instance, in Herrick's linking of the human observer to companionable flowers:

> Faire Daffadills, we weep to see
>   You haste away so soone:
> As yet the early-rising Sun
>   Has not attain'd his Noone.
>   Stay, stay
>   Until the hasting day
>   Has run
>   But to the Even-song;
> And, having pray'd together, we
>   Will goe with you along.
>
> We have short time to stay, as you,
>   We have as short a Spring;
> As quick a growth to meet Decay,
>   As you, or any thing.
>   We die,
>   As your hours doe, and drie
>   Away,
>   Like to the Summers raine;
> Or as the pearles of Morning dew
>   Ne'r to be found againe.

In a sense the song is the poet's only compensation, his only device for handling a nature that knows no transformation except decay and offers no hint of unfading beauty "fast in . . . Paradise, / Where no flower can wither." Recurrences of sound; the controlled pace (the lingering isolation of "stay, stay," "away," "we," and "drie"); the ceremonial second-person address; the reiterated comparisons of the second stanza: these contribute to a sense of formal play that suggests the conversion of time's flow into measured song. Threatened with evaporation as allotted time shrinks from a day to a few morning hours, the poet offers only the act of singing as a consolation:

we are not to reinterpret "flowers" as figures for something beyond them or make the poem into a double instrument, a purgative rehearsal of death followed by restoration.

The difference between a pastoral nature whose dying occasions a dirge and Herbert's redefinition of nature as an occasion for the soul's seasoning and at the same time a reminder of Christ's death and rebirth is still clearer in the word-shape poem "Easter-wings." Here the shrinking of the poet-sinner, the poem itself, and by implication the natural world is followed by a rejuvenation of all three. Each stanza is first plangent and evaporating and then full-voiced in petitioning Christ for the rebirth epitomized in the final event of Easter:

> Lord, who createdst man in wealth and store,
>   Though foolishly he lost the same,
>   Decaying more and more
>   Till he became
>   Most poore:
>   With thee
>   O let me rise
>   As larks, harmoniously,
>   And sing this day thy victories:
> Then shall the fall further the flight in me.
>
> My tender age in sorrow did beginne:
>   And still with sicknesses and shame
>   Thou didst so punish sinne,
>   That I became
>   Most thinne.
>   With thee
>   Let me combine
>   And feel this day thy victorie:
>   For, if I imp my wing on thine,
> Affliction shall advance the flight in me.

In the context of the opening sequence of poems, "Easter-wings" suggests also an imitation of Christ's recapitulation of history, as he is sacrificed in place of the old Adam and resurrected as the new, as he concludes the Old Testament and begins the New. If in "The Sacrifice," the events of the day of Passion establish the original patterns for the liturgical calendar of Easter, in the ascension Christ here adds to those patterns a blueprint for the poet's rites and for the physical shape of the poem. New life is engrafted at the center of the visual diagram, at the full stop between the doom inherited from Adam and the renewed appeal that brings more words for flight.

Given this possibility of "imping" on Christ's wing, the poet is justified in claiming a higher purpose for poetry than the poet of "The Thanksgiving" and "The Flower" manages to discover. As "The Quidditie" says, a poem is "not a crown,"

> No point of honour, or gay suit,
> No hawk, or banquet, or renown,
> Nor a good sword, nor yet a lute.

That is, it does not make one a king, establish a courtly caste, hunt down prey, cook one's meals, give one fame, strike down enemies, or even, finally, sing sweetly to ladies. Further,

> It cannot vault, or dance, or play;
> It never was in *France* or *Spain;*
> Nor can it entertain the day
> With my great stable or demain:
>
> It is no office, art, or news,
> Nor Exchange, or busie Hall.

But the poet gladly surrenders these social advantages. For him, poetry is "that which while I use / I am with thee, and *most take all.*" As an essence or quidditie, it enables the poet to seize the essences of all things and at the same time take the "All" that is with "thee." It is a visible "that which," an artifact definable mainly by what it procures, by its instrumental function: "I am with thee while I *use* it."

In thinking of poetry as a divine conveyance in these respects, Herbert is obviously giving it an important place in the various means of communion at one's disposal in the temple. At the same time, he is less forward in setting aside what tradition and dogma reserve for church sacraments than Milton, whose sense of divine visitation has behind it the iconoclasm of the Puritan revolution and the removal of all institutional means of communion. For Herbert, poetry is never the sole means of petitioning Christ nor is it ever wholly adequate to the ideal functions the poet would assign it. In a sense, the poet's suit must be granted even before he asks, for the asking itself will not change God's mind. In "Redemption," for instance, the petitioner's bold search for a new dispensation carries him fruitlessly over the universe and into heaven before he discovers Christ where he least expects to, purchasing that dispensation on the cross. Before he can muster words to present his case, Christ speaks ironically from among the ragged sounds and torments of the passion—using the suitor's own terms but correcting them: "your suit is granted" ("Your 'bond,' as you think of it, is honored; you've cashed it in, or rather I've done so before you could ask, paying dearly for coming to terms with you"). The difference between the suitor's agitated journey to make his bold petition and Christ's anticipatory "is granted" is almost absolute, like the difference between the poet's initial wish and its granting in "A true Hymne":

> if th' heart be moved,
> Although the verse be somewhat scant,
> God doth supplie the want.
> As when th' heart sayes (sighing to be approved)
> *O, could I love!* and stops: God writeth, *Loved*.

Wishing to command approval by loving, the speaker finally is served, loved, redeemed in a critical shift from the active to the passive voice. God's addition to the scant verse answers the petition ironically; it comes both as hoped for and as something beyond hope, as the terms of the poet's proposed bond are both accepted and transcended. The colon in the last line, like the full stop at the center of each diagram of "Easterwings," marks the pause between two quite different moods, one elegiac, mortifying, self-pitying, subjunctive, hopelessly active (poetry "runneth mutt'ring up and down" Herbert remarks earlier in "A true Hymne"), and the other unqualified, perfect, capable of drawing the listener into its perfection. Though the hand of Herbert writes *"Loved"* as surely as it writes *"O, could I love,"* in any true hymn it is merely transcribing what God offers for a conclusion.

Herbert's final assessment of Christ's capacity to define the poet's meaning for him is left to "Heaven," which is strategically placed before the priest's successful and summary approach to Love's communion in "Love III." In this case, the genre that requires rewriting is the conventional appeal to oracles in classical and neo-Latin pastorals. Rather than seeking an echo response from a valley or cliff, the poet directs his words to the vault of heaven. They travel to a point of vanishing and then return on the echo, not as they were, but as renewed vehicles, as heaven's rider. Herbert here discovers a compressed example of the double stance of poetry much like the twofold visual diagram of "Easter-wings," whose rejuvenated second halves are like the first halves, only in reverse. So here God makes use of the poet's very words and mistaken genre but corrects them.

The poet's initial ambitious appeal is necessary because without an urge to search out the truth, he would not make the gesture that becomes God's conveyance:

> O Who will show me those delights on high?
>   *Echo.*   I.
> Thou Echo, thou art mortall, all men know.
>   *Echo.*   No.
> Wert thou not born among the trees and leaves?
>   *Echo.*   Leaves.
> And are there any leaves, that still abide?
>   *Echo.*   Bide.
> What leaves are they? impart the matter wholly.
>   *Echo.*   Holy.
> Are holy leaves the Echo then of blisse?
>   *Echo.*   Yes.
> Then tell me, what is that supreme delight?
>   *Echo.*   Light.
> Light to the minde: what shall the will enjoy?
>   *Echo.*   Joy.
> But are there cares and businesse with the pleasure?
>   *Echo.*   Leisure.
> Light, joy, and leisure; but shall they persever?
>   *Echo.*   Ever.

The rhymes unite human and divine words, and though the connection is incongruous and the echo proves to be quite unlike the first of the rhymed pair in meaning, the verbal body is similar. The puns remind us that the ambiguity of Herbert's abstract nouns frequently allows for a similar union of disparate meanings: "Love," "Life," "Prayer," "Death," "Redemption." These broad titles that stand over the substance of the poems in which they are defined refer equally well to corporeal life or eternal life, the redemption that the petitioner seeks and the kind that Christ gives him, death as "termination" and death as "transformation," and so forth. In the poem "*Ana-* $\left\{ \begin{array}{c} \text{Mary} \\ \text{Army} \end{array} \right\}$ *gram*," Herbert is astounded that a simple word can "present" Christ, as though letters were magical runes capable of the same miracle of incarnation that Mary herself served as conveyance: "How well her name an *Army* doth present, / In whom the *Lord of Hosts* did pitch his tent!" Similarly, in "Heaven" each rhyme echo converts the meaning that the poet sends forth into a new substance.

Normal pastoral "leaves," for instance, give way to scriptural leaves. This example is especially rich in implications because it depends upon a group of ideas and images that *The Temple* connects into an extensive system of cross references. Headed initially toward nature, the word is redirected in midcourse and pointed toward an anagogic referent explicated by scripture. There perceptive readers discover that "heaven's" full "configuration of glorie" is invested not in one "leaf" but in the entire text:

> Oh that I knew how all thy lights combine,
>> And the configurations of their glorie!
>> Seeing not onely how each verse doth shine,
> But all the constellations of the storie.
> This verse marks that, and both do make a motion
>> Unto a third, that ten leaves off doth lie:
>> Then as dispersed herbs do watch a potion,
> These three make up some Christians destinie:
> Such are thy secrets, which my life makes good,
>> And comments on thee: for in ev'ry thing
>> Thy words do finde me out, & parallels bring,
> And in another make me understood.
>> Starres are poore books, & oftentimes do misse:
>> This book of starres lights to eternall blisse.

Like patterns of physical stars only surer, constellations of divine light confirm the meaning of any one part by linking it to the meaning of the whole book (as individual poems in *The Temple* are linked). "Truth" is the verified connection among things "ten leaves off." Thus as the special properties of herbs in a healing formula are drawn into their combination by the affinities they develop only in this particular company, so individual adages, images, and episodes of scripture join to cure what ails the reader and show him a destiny that the entire book defines. If the reader has wit enough to put together the parallels and explicate the text in all its configurations and systematic affinities, divine words will "find him out" and light his way to bliss.

And so the echo-poem, as its words return from heaven, presumably become less riddling and more scriptural. But again the firmest declaration that the poet can receive from the voice that joins his is merely a prediction: attuned to the double vision of the present and the future, the words sent out and the words received, the poem remains basically a set of ironic analogies and echoes; the state of the listener is uncertain despite heaven's inevitability, though the sureness of the echoes obviously qualifies his suspended state significantly.

The implications for poetry of that suspension between heaven and earth are more fully spelled out in "The Temper I," which I should like to consider as a final example both of Herbert's sense of the kind of paradisal "real presence" he may expect and the stylistic repercussions that it has. An initial exuberance over the prospect of soaring above all heavens is qualified in this case by a contrary-to-fact conditional:

> How should I praise thee, Lord! how should my rymes
>   Gladly engrave thy love in steel,
>   If what my soul doth feel sometimes,
>   My soul might ever feel!
>
> Although there were some fourtie heav'ns, or more,
>   Sometimes I peere above them all.

The suggestion that if permitted to feel this way more often he would write such poems as a deity would be proud to re-

ceive is implicitly a bribe. As it is, however, the poet sometimes "hardly reaches a score" of heavens and sometimes falls
"to hell." Unlike a plotted pilgrimage to paradise, his wild
poetic journeys lead nowhere; his time is unstructured and his
cycles irregular, and this seemingly radical purposelessness
leads to praise and lamentation without measure or "temper."
Caught in a temporal life of boundaries and limits, he cannot
use them to define his condition when his true home and subject of praise seemingly lies altogether beyond those limits.

In the third and fourth stanzas, Herbert suggests that it is
not worth God's while to rack so small a creature to "such a
vast extent":

> Wilt thou meet arms with man, that thou dost stretch
>   A crumme of dust from heav'n to hell?
> Will great God measure with a wretch?
>   Shall he thy stature spell?

The questions are obviously rhetorical since it is absurdly disproportionate to levy God's full might against a "wretch."
Though the poet's independence is guaranteed by that hostility,
no mutual adjustment can come of it. Hence, he proposes another course of action: to move into God's camp and roost
under his protection. Implicitly, he still "measures" with God
in bargaining with him, but on the surface, the proposal has
the virtue of making an exact exchange possible: God will be
free of a bothersome sinner and the poet of the hope and fear
that send him soaring and plummeting.

Such a bargain would have the disadvantage of reducing the
sinner to an unexciting dependency and of requiring major
changes in God's practice. Realization of this brings the reversal of the final two stanzas and the emergence of a music
less dependent upon inspirational flight:

> Yet take thy way; for sure thy way is best:
>   Stretch or contract me, thy poore debter:
> This is but tuning of my breast,
>   To make the musick better.
>
> Whether I flie with angels, fall with dust,

> Thy hands made both, and I am there:
> Thy power and love, my love and trust
> Make one place ev'ry where.

As a debtor the poet has no bargaining power; he owes everything and has nothing to give. Hence he does not offer even
this improved music for God's consideration; instead he finds
the tempering of extremes cause for consolation. He will not
have to alternate wildly between heaven and hell because all
ranks of the universe and all notes on the tempered scale are
touched by a divine omnipresence. God is both measured into
the capacity of the musician and yet beyond measure, extending everywhere. Even the wilderness thereby becomes, paradoxically, paradise. In his newly discovered tempered style, the
poet thus responds to his exile from God's closest proximity
with equilibrium and stands fast in governing abstractions,
"power," "trust," and "love," which fill all space and make all
successive moments basically the same. With "love" as the
pivotal center of a line joining divine power and human
trust, the human and the divine conditions overlap, like harmonic notes that include one another but remain different.
What "Easter-wings" and "Heaven" treat as a narrative movement from a despairing exile to paradise regained, "The Temper" thus fixes in a mixed co-presence, serving as a verbal
conveyance that renders the most extreme of all pastoral contrasts in Herbert—heaven and hell, complete divine presence
and complete absence—in a single encompassing state.

II

This tension between the wilderness in which the poet lives
and the paradise that he envisions and seeks to epitomize in
sacramental poems is basic to other Christian pastorals as well.
It is repeated in "Lycidas," "Comus," *Paradise Lost, Paradise
Regained,* and in much of Marvell, Vaughan, and Traherne,
though with different emphases in each case. In Marvell, in
place of the temple as the mediating instrument of the divine
presence, particular historical events, places, natural symbols,
and even people are assigned the task of "epitomizing" para-

dise. All become potentially sacramental, as the poet seizes them and transforms them into the illuminating icons of the poem:

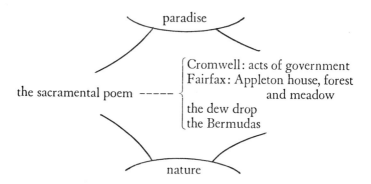

In "On a Drop of Dew," making the dewdrop an image both of paradise and of the soul requires that Marvell allow it very few natural properties beyond purity, circularity, and homesickness. He must tactfully suppress the fact that dew in nature does not return to the sun, stains what it touches, and unlike the soul does not move its flower-body. Despite its descriptive amplitude, the poem is therefore a spare and disciplined statement whose style accords well with the soul's own carefully maintained shape and rejection of material entanglements.[5] The poem itself is a necessary part of the process by which dew is transformed into an epitomizing symbol: it points the way, clears away irrelevancies, and purifies the objects it directs us to focus upon. The original of both souls and well-shaped artifacts, of course, is the archetypal circle of heaven that they seek to "express" in their lesser heaven:

> So the Soul, that Drop, that Ray
> Of the clear Fountain of Eternal Day,
> Could it within the humane flow'r be seen,
>   Remembring still its former height,
>   Shuns the sweat leaves and the blossoms green;
>   And, recollecting its own Light,

[5] I have recapitulated here from a different angle readings given to these poems in my *Marvell's Ironic Vision* (New Haven: Yale University Press, 1965).

Does, in its pure and circling thoughts, express
The greater Heaven in an Heaven less.

Having been ready to ascend but attached to their bodies, souls
and poems alike eventually dissolve their links with earth:

> In how coy a Figure wound,
> Every way it turns away:
> So the World excluding round,
> Yet receiving in the Day.
> Dark beneath, but bright above:
> Here disdaining, there in Love,
> How loose and easie hence to go:
> How girt and ready to ascend.
> Moving but on a point below,
> It all about does upward bend.
> Such did the Manna's sacred Dew destil;
> White and entire, though congeal'd and chill.
> Congeal'd on Earth: but does, dissolving, run
> Into the Glories of th' Almighty Sun.

"On a Drop of Dew" represents a Platonist extreme that
attempts to sever the idea of perfection from seasonal nature
and tangible aspects of metaphor and denies implicitly any un-
distorted incarnation of that idea until the poem and its act
of pointing and seeing have freed themselves from the body
of the metaphor. As in Shelley's "Adonais" and "Ode to a
Skylark" and in Emily Dickinson's "As Imperceptibly as
Grief," the poet can follow the logic of the concrete metaphor
only so far before it shatters—or an unembodied radiance
consumes it:

> without a Wing
> Or service of a Keel
> Our Summer made her light escape
> Into the Beautiful.

Thus for Dickinson, too, true "beauty" appears at the point
at which the seasonal conveyance, summer, disappears (an
imperceptible "light" escape, and an escape of light into imperceptible Light). Marvell's image of the dewdrop soul
handles the tension between invisible essence and concrete

body with similar skill: even as we watch, the soul, and with it the "pure" meaning of the poem, presses away the flower's contamination, until like heaven itself—which is not a real fountain but a fountain of "eternal Day"—both soul and poem are absorbed into an all-seeing Intelligence.

One quesitons whether in any Platonist poetic, however, the poet can actually remove the body of the metaphor once he has used it as a conveyance of ideas. "On a Drop of Dew" fixes our eyes on relatively concrete dewdrops and flowers initially, just as Dickinson's "escaped" summer requires first our experience of the real season in passage. (In generic terms we notice that most renaissance Christian and Platonist poetry begins with the concrete body of Arcadian imagery, using it not only dia-lectically—as something to be discarded in the course of dis-covering paradise—but also substantially, as the body of para-dise itself.) If Marvell's invisible "circle" of heaven were really to draw the poem all the way into itself as it draws the soul, the structured stages of the poem's unfolding would have to be treated as illusions. Yet the elaborate balance and symmetry and the analogies between parts of the poem all depend upon the firm establishing of the image and upon the linear narra-tive initiated by the pointer "see." Marvell thus gives us a very tangible and well-defined artifact finally, realized stage by visual stage, and the poem eventually falls back upon a final image, the sun, in order to give natural underpinnings to the idea of God.

We would be less inclined to stress the sensuous surface of Marvell's metaphoric conveyances of paradise were Marvell himself not so insistent upon it in so many poems. Unlike the more rigorous Platonism of Shelley, his Platonism ordinarily does not discredit the visual emblems it uses. In fact, Marvell is capable of urging us to forget altogether what lies beyond the moment and nature's sensuous vitality. The speaker of "To his Coy Mistress," for instance, dissolves the soul in pas-sion (*there* disdaining, *here* in love), making the sun not an emblem of infinity but a measurement of time; the poem turns outward as a rhetorical appeal for action within time rather than mirroring the timeless inaction of a celestial Sphere.

Two such widely divergent poems as "To his Coy Mistress" and "On a Drop of Dew" offer little chance for compromise—one arguing for the soul's self-enclosed existence, immune to time, and the other presenting negotiations between two people entirely governed by the natural seasons and love.

If we remember Herbert's perishing word-conveyances and the divine echo-rider, however, we can anticipate one of Marvell's alternatives to these two mutually exclusive positions. Like Herbert, Marvell sometimes finds it possible to engage the world's body and still be rescued from its temporal nature, and thus to conceive of a pastoral that uses nature to prefigure another kind of paradise while remaining basically itself. Clorinda and Damon find echoes of the Word in nature and address their final song to it rather than to each other. Though Damon resists Clorinda's enticements on her terms—basically the terms of the rhetorical appeal of "To his Coy Mistress"— he convinces her to join him on his terms, which draw all nature into a song to Christ:

> *D.* These once had been enticing things,
> *Clorinda,* Pastures, Caves, and Springs.
> *C.* And what late change? *D.* The other day
> *Pan* met me. *C.* What did great *Pan* say?
> *D.* Words that transcend poor shepherd skill,
> But he ere since my Songs does fill:
> And his Name swells my slender Oate.

They may encounter nature, then, but Damon does not specify precisely how or in what way Pan's words apply to it. They encounter it merely in the transcendent Name that all things sing as Pan's subjects:

> *Of* Pan *the Flowry Pastures sing,*
> *Caves eccho, and the Fountains ring.*
> *Sing then while he doth us inspire;*
> *For all the World is our* Pan's *Quire.*

From the Platonist's standpoint, the difficulty with Damon's position is that if the poet seeks divine vestiges in nature he must also look eventually into historical affairs: "All the

World" presumably includes other things besides fountains and pastures. Once the concept of a temporalized paradise is accepted, as it is in "Upon Appleton House," "Bermudas," "The Garden," and "The First Anniversary," the histories of particular times and places may begin to overpower the mirrored reflections they contain of "the greater Heaven" expressed in them.

In "Upon Appleton House," Marvell finds the several elements of the Fairfax estate involved both in history and in the emblematic modeling of perfect forms. The house itself reflects the circularity of the virtuous soul:

VI.

> *Humility* alone designs
> Those short but admirable lines,
> By which, ungirt and unconstrain'd,
> Things greater are in less contain'd.
> Let others vainly strive t'immure
> The *Circle* in the *Quadrature!*
> These *holy Mathematicks* can
> In ev'ry Figure equal man.

As the house shapes itself around its master, it is set "as a Mark of Grace" that others may emulate. At the same time, only by retreating from active power could Fairfax stay "circular": he has had to seek detachment from recent history, which is deprived of his imprint. Even close by the house, the garden and the meadow offer a pageantry of violence that belies its pastoral surface and the order and proportion for which Fairfax stands. At the same time, the garden and meadow retain their capacity to remind us of an initial paradise before the "luckless Apple," when the world was first created, which passes judgment on what they have become. In both sections Marvell experiments with perspectives from which historical violence can be controlled, moving close in for a moment and then backing away to a larger prospect that diminishes violence and renders vistas of paradise, glimpsed beyond the immediate landscape.

The poet so controls and directs his survey of the scenes as he moves images on and off stage that he can cause to be seen, through and beyond the landscape, the beginning of the paradisal world:

LVI.

This *Scene* again withdrawing brings
A new and empty Face of things;
A levell'd space, as smooth and plain,
As Clothes for Lilly stretcht to stain.
The World when first created sure
Was such a Table rase and pure.
Or rather such is the *Toril*
Ere the Bulls enter at *Madril*.

LVII.

For to this naked equal Flat,
Which *Levellers* take Pattern at,
The Villagers in common chase
Their Cattle, which it closer rase;
And what below the Sith increast
Is pincht yet nearer by the Beast.
Such, in the painted World, appear'd
Davenant with th' Universal Heard.

LVIII.

They seem within the polisht Grass
A Landskip drawn in Looking-Glass,
And shrunk in the huge Pasture show
As Spots, so shap'd, on Faces do.
Such Fleas, ere they approach the Eye,
In Multiplying Glasses Lye.
They feed so wide, so slowly move,
As *Constellations* do above.

Rather than enacting the creation as Davenant's universal herd does, however, these creatures of the meadow miscreate a world that began pure and "untabulated," and Marvell must manipulate the mirror image so as to diminish the miscellany that appears in it. The effect is like that of the painting in *Gondibert* itself, which is twice removed from the primary world, once as a painting and once again as a verbal description of a painting. All motion is calmed by the shrinking and then virtually frozen, like stars that seem stationary in their orbits. The function of these two techniques, the manipulation

of perspectives and the allusive glimpsing of the original creation in the landscape, is to absorb the meadow into the controlled world of symbolic playfulness. There it yields some of
its reality to the fictions of the imagination and the poet's
verbal inventiveness. Despite its quite unarcadian warfare and
disorder, it prepares to be "pastoralized" like the fiction of
conventional Arcadias.

As the meadow is flooded, however, the poet must relinquish
the ground he has controlled by these maneuvers and mannerist techniques. He is driven into retreat in a forest sanctuary
where the controls come primarily not from him or from the
mirror games of art but from another kind of power that
speaks more directly through nature itself. In a sense we pass
from a playful allegory invented by the poet to a kind of
augury in which divine messages are expressed—again teas-
ingly—in birds, trembling leaves, and other items of nature's
book—a mystic book, as Marvell insists. As such a book, nature
allows the poet to shed his thought, his contrived wit, and
even his reason, because "Chance's better wit" and the enigmatic language of topography can "with a Mask" his "studies
hit" more aptly (LXXXIV). Even in saying so, however,
Marvell continues to display oddities of wit and manipulated
distortions of visual imagery and perspective. Oak leaves are
embroideries of meaning, trees yield strange prophecies of "one
History" beyond the local conflicts of England, we know not
how, and birds speak in a language in which only attentive
ears divine special meanings:

LXXIII.

Out of these scatter'd *Sibyls* Leaves
Strange *Prophecies* my Phancy weaves:
And in one History consumes,
Like *Mexique Paintings,* all the *Plumes.*
What *Rome, Greece, Palestine,* ere said
I in this light *Mosaick* read.
Thrice happy he who, not mistook,
Hath read in *Natures mystick Book.*

Marvell's entanglement in this revelation of leaves—which sum
up classical wisdom and holy scripture—draws him into phe-

nomenal nature as an encyclopedic message, as an *enumeration* of paradise.

For fancy, there are these patterns of leaves; and for the body, the river banks, branches, and roots. Returning to the meadow after the stream has become a crystal mirror in which "all things gaze themselves, and doubt / If they be in it or without" (LXXX), the poet finds further revelations that require no study and allow him to sink into passive receptivity. He is doubly safe in doing so because of nature's reassurance and because of Maria Fairfax, who tightens and clarifies the somewhat haphazard materials of all elements of the poem's topography. She enables Marvell to recapitulate the poem in a single image, bringing the celestial perspective into the natural world with special force:

LXXXVI.

Maria such, and so doth hush
The World, and through the Ev'ning rush. . . .
But by her *Flames,* in Heaven try'd,
Nature is wholly *vitrifi'd.*

Thus beyond the ordinary sun, this flame. The word vitrify is strangely violent for the relaxed atmosphere, but we remember that Marvell in "Upon Appleton House" seeks an accord between the ampler strain of heroic panegyric and the humbler activities of meadow and forest. Its violence is a measure of the re-creation required of anyone who would "annihilate" all that's made to green thought and as central in its way to the poem as the stanza on the mind's activities in "The Garden," because it indicates how miscellaneous materials, in topographical enumeration, are to be made into a single reflective glass and heated into a mirrored image of heaven. What has remained somewhat enigmatic in the analogies and concealed meanings of the meadow, garden, and forest thus becomes in Maria "crystal" clear: she succeeds in impressing herself on nature—in a way that the dewdrop soul, in shunning contact with its flower, cannot do. The poem's variety of moods yields momentarily to eulogistic crescendo:

LXXXVII.

'Tis *She* that to these Gardens gave
That wondrous Beauty which they have;
She streightness on the Woods bestows;
To *Her* the meadow sweetness owes;
Nothing could make the River be
So Crystal-pure but only *She;*
She yet more Pure, Sweet, Streight, and Fair,
Then Gardens, Woods, Meads, Rivers are.

The catalog finds its unity in her perfection, which has logical priority as the clearer image of heaven. Hence, under her influence, the lesser world of the Fairfax estate becomes "Heaven's Center, Nature's Lap. / And Paradice's only Map." Marvell can abandon for the moment the playful distortions of perspective and odd metaphor that have heretofore dispersed suggestions of paradise disconnectedly through the landscape.

Having gone this far in seeking emblems of paradise in nature and in political affairs, Marvell pushes a step farther in the Cromwell poems that (in all probability) follow. There the scene becomes the greater domain of England and the map of paradise is sketched out by the interregnum government. Likewise, the circle has expanded from the self-enclosing soul refusing contamination and from the controlled, modest form of Fairfax's house and estate to the greater architecture that Cromwell practices on the English people. He himself "the force of scatter'd Time contracts" and "shines the Jewel of the yearly Ring"; he prevents not only himself but a nation from declining "in the weak Circles of increasing Years," drawing it into the pattern that providence designs for it.

Only when his social reform is finished and the governmental instrument is perfected, however, will providence be fully revealed and the work below resemble the pattern above. The promise of the millennium hovers uncertainly about Cromwell's first year. Marvell imagines the election of a divine agent to be in the offing, but the fulfillment of "the mysterious Work" remains problematic:

Hence oft I think, if in some happy Hour
High Grace should meet in one with highest Pow'r

And then a seasonable People still
Should bend to his, as he to Heavens will,
What we might hope, what wonderful Effect
From such a wish'd Conjuncture might reflect.
Sure, the mysterious Work, where none withstand,
Would forthwith finish under such a Hand:
Fore-shortened Time its useless Course would stay,
And soon precipitate the latest Day.
But a thick Cloud about the Morning lyes,
And intercepts the Beams of Mortal eyes,
That 'tis the most which we determine can,
If these the Times, then this must be the Man.

[131–143]

The "if" is large, and what the elected agent tries to enact, the
people still resist; good designs hang in the balance that if
executed would make of England an effigy, in time, of the
sphere above.

As Cromwell extends the song of creation, Amphionlike, to
a whole people, he attempts to restore the work of the days
and the eternal spring of the first creation:

Cromwell alone with greater Vigour runs
(Sun-like) the Stages of succeeding Suns:
And still the Day which he doth next restore,
Is the just Wonder of the Day before.
Cromwell alone doth with new Lustre spring,
And shines the Jewel of the yearly Ring.

As the hard, circular jewel of the cycle, he thus tries to convert
events into emblems, returning history to form by active
labor. In this respect, he makes the enclosed poem still possible—or would if the rest of its materials would take shape accordingly and an earthly version of paradise were truly con-
structed in the commonwealth:

Thus (Image-like) an useless time they tell,
And with vain Scepter, strike the hourly Bell;
Nor more contribute to the state of Things,
Then wooden Heads unto the Viols strings.
    While indefatigable *Cromwell* hyes,
And cuts his way still nearer to the Skyes,
Learning a Musique in the Region clear,

To tune this lower to that higher Sphere.

[41–48]

Since to be wholly effective Cromwell's incarnation of the "holy image" requires that England itself become an icon of ultimate harmony, "tuned to that higher Sphere," Marvell implicitly addresses an audience that must be swayed and persuaded to be worked upon. The poem becomes not only an imaging of paradise but a rhetorical instrument to bring about continued reform. Rather than offering static icons of the greater Heaven in the heaven less, it applies its icons to the shaping of the state. Where "On a Drop of Dew" asks for an intransitive understanding of a radiant glory outside time, "The First Anniversary" asks implicitly for participation in a cause and therefore stretches its shape to include satire and the strategies of argumentative discourse (as John Wallace argues persuasively in *Destiny His Choice,* pp. 106–145).

Judging after the fact, we can see that Marvell's most comprehensive idea of the poem's imitation of paradise required a compromise between static emblems that close out the world (while admitting the divine image) and reformative agents that seek to change a faulty reality. We see him seeking that compromise not in the Elizabethan way, in images of royalty or in the militant church of a Red Cross Knight but in those historical reforms of his time that press for spiritual renewal—in what we might call Puritan-Platonist "actional emblems." They offer a progressive revelation of the sphere above in yearly accomplishments and regard time as the stages of renewal. The pilgrims of "Bermudas," to take an instructive example, leave prelate-torn England and travel to an eternal spring where nature is "enamelled," where rocks bespeak gospel, and where the grassy scene itself is a divine "stage." Their work in rowing the boat across the "watry maze" keeps them from sinking in time's circles; it is accompanied by their own art, a kind of work song, which is an important part of their "doing": "What should we do but sing his Praise / That led us through the watry Maze." The reformed church-boat, returning to an earthly version of paradise, is thus, like Cromwell, an active instrument of historical transformation in which all pull together for change. Like their cousins the Arcadian shepherds, the pilgrims are free of masters, but unlike Arcadians they are no longer tied to purely natural seasons: their paradise transcends time even though it can be realized only in time.

The paradisal island and the Protestant craft are obviously a quite different locality and "conveyance" than Herbert's temple, from which the poet invokes God to descend into institutional and sacramental embodiments. But despite this difference, the poem itself in both Herbert and Marvell seeks to provide a sacramental image of paradise, to model the divine pattern and render the praise due it; and the tension between temporalized images and eschatological reality is basically unresolvable. For Marvell in the later satires, the pastoral element shrinks in proportion before a multitude of follies and England's general failure to attain the goals of the Reformation. The bond between the greater and lesser heavens is broken, and poems are no longer effigies of paradise. Whereas for Herbert the temple as purified heart, sacramental poem, and church is not vulnerable to so general a failure and the poet can find security in its epitomizing enclosure, for the later Marvell the poet is forced to conceive of poetry as a rhetorical weapon in the chastisement of follies and the implanting of moral standards.

Historical incarnations of divine harmony are the subject also of much of Milton's pastoralism, especially in the early poems. I will now turn to their identification of royalty with temporal emblems of divine order, before Milton had begun to remove social mediation between the poet and his paradisal vision. Where Marvell eventually abandons a poetry of "actional emblems," such as Cromwell and the rowing pilgrims, for satire and a career in Parliament, Milton, moving in the opposite direction, seeks for an increasingly comprehensive way of treating the return to paradise. In *Paradise Regained,* paradise is freed of all institutional attachments and founded in the manifestation of God in the desert: Christ renews paradise by that manifestation alone as he brings the Father's image to the wilderness and thereby transforms it into a reflection of "light of light . . . enshrin'd / In fleshly Tabernacle, and human form." Thus both in Marvell's gradual abandonment of visionary politics for practical politics and in Milton's view of paradise regained, we see an acute stage of the dissociation of those levels of pastoral that Marvell in "Upon Appleton House," Milton in "Arcades," and Herbert in *The Temple* labor to join. That dissociation, which includes the divorce of social and transcendental pastoral, will be reconsidered in Pope, Thompson, the romantics, and eventually Frost and Stevens. Each of these in his own way questions anew the possible reunion of the sacred and the natural in the *locus amoenus*— and what such a reunion might portend for the poem and visitants to its mirrored landscape.

SEVEN

Milton: Platonic Levels
and Christian Transformation

I

Because positions on each plane of Milton's hierarchy are assigned and unchangeable in *Paradise Lost,* tropospheric flights of the imagination are hazardous. Personal transcendence and certain ranges of knowledge are forbidden to Adam and Eve, for instance, though Eve expects to benefit from them when the apple works its marvelous and sudden change upon her. Nature's set of harmonious forms leads Adam to infer first principles almost as soon as he springs from the dust; but at the same time nature constitutes the inescapable conditions of his existence: his setting remains fixed and he in it, tracing the creator in the serpent and the unwieldy elephant. Everything implicitly argues the need for exactly its own place in the order. The postlapsarian wilderness is even more inescapable as Adam's bounded condition. His range of choices is narrowed, and he is sentenced to close entanglement in a landscape of hardship and trial. The seasons turn extreme to plague him, and the soil yields its bounty only with labor.

In contrast, the poet in Milton's early poems—like the Attendant Spirit who guides the hapless brothers and the Lady through Comus's tangled forest—is frequently aloft and thinks in terms not of "georgic" labor and hierarchical placement but of Platonist cycles of descent and return. As we have noticed with respect to other pastoralists who stress Ovidian transformation and vertical differences among pastoral landscapes, he maps out courses of personal ascent which will bring paradise almost within reach. He also develops stylistic levels appropriate to that ascent, beginning with lowly pastoral and rising to exalted forms of hymn and divine celebration.

The difference between these two views of the good place

can partly be explained by the natural growth of the poet from youthful confidence and untested innocence to well-tested experience. But it is also typical of the period between the 1630s and the 1660s, in which social pastoral of the courtly kind and the conventions that "Arcades" accepts are transformed and fused with Hebraic and Christian thought concerning the wilderness, the conflict of good and evil, and paradise. In retrospect, it seems only a matter of time before the early Milton would have had to reconceive the concept both of the *locus amoenus* and the function of poetry, even if he had not been inclined to by nature. As they appear in "Arcades," the Nativity Ode, "L'Allegro," "Il Penseroso," and "Comus," these concepts are inadequate to the 1640s and 1650s. "Lycidas" is the pivotal poem in which Milton first turns about, enacting the struggle between classical pastoral and the Christian vision as a conflict of voices—the swain's, Apollo's, Camus's, and St. Peter's—and resolving that conflict in a redefinition of the good place that will be sustained in the idyllic vision of all the later poems. Under the influence of both his own growth and the times, then, the genres he took up and explored in turn—the ode, the pastoral masque and elegy, the epic, and the tragedy—revealed different and expanding dimensions of his pervasive view of things; the later genres continually absorbed and transformed the earlier.

One of the poet's functions in the early poems is to reconcile the levels of a still basically Platonist universe; another is to apply divine harmony as therapy to his listeners and suggest its embodiment in contemporary institutions—especially in a decorative and symbolic royalty. The music of the shepherd-poet is psychologically cleansing and has social benefits of a special kind. This alliance of music and local-divine social order is first evident in the visual pageantry of the court masque "Arcades," in which the Countess Dowager of Derby transforms England into a new Arcadia as the Genius of the Wood (the poet) recites correspondences between her royalty and celestial harmony.[1] Milton ends by enjoining common shepherds to kiss the "sacred vesture's hem":

[1] As George Sandys illustrates in his commentary on *Ovid's Metamorphoses,* Platonist magic continued to be used into the

> in deep of night, when drowsiness
> Hath lockt up mortal sense, then listen I
> To the celestial *Sirens'* harmony,
> That sit upon the nine infolded Spheres
> And sing to those that hold the vital shears
> And turn the Adamantine spindle round,
> On which the fate of gods and men is wound.
> Such sweet compulsion doth in music lie,
> To lull the daughters of *Necessity,*
> And keep unsteady Nature to her law,
> And the low world in measur'd motion draw
> After the heavenly tune, which none can hear
> Of human mold with gross unpurged ear;
> And yet such music worthiest were to blaze
> The peerless height of her immortal praise,
> Whose luster leads us, and for her most fit,
> If my inferior hand or voice could hit
> Inimitable sounds; such as we go,
> Whate'er the skill of lesser gods can show,
> I will assay, her worth to celebrate,
> And so attend ye toward her glittering state;
> Where ye may all that are of noble stem
> Approach, and kiss her sacred vesture's hem.
>
> [61-83]

A critical turn from mythopoeic to eulogistic aims comes at "And yet such music. . . ." Milton manages the exalted style so well that technical excellence does much to conceal the difficulty of that transition. The juxtaposition of different levels of diction in "hit" (both "strike as planned" and "accidentally connect with") and "inimitable sound" suggests that the union of the rustic poet and his high subject is purposely incongruous; and yet, since celestial harmony and the countess are equally far above him, he might well link them. "Attend"

---

later Renaissance for political eulogy. Sandys equates chaste love with Charles I as the controller of chaos and restorer of the Golden Age. The royal prerogative issues from the leaden mass of the body politic like gold under the coaxing of reason. The chief task of the muses is therefore to restore "wretches doomed to die to light" by imitation of the king's own penetrative light, symbolized by Mercury and Apollo, the guardian spirits of Sandys' translation. See Ovid's *Metamorphosis, Englished, Mythologiz'd, and Represented in Figures* (Oxford, 1632). "A Panegyricke to the King" is attached.

is effectively ambiguous, uniting "see" with "pay deference to,"
as though the countess has only to be seen to be truly understood and obeyed. Then the voice drops into a concluding
hush as they approach the sacred presence, and the tone is
controlled by a sense of conclusive logic in "And so attend,"
the privileged position of "Approach," and the final association
of divine harmony with the countess.

But the use of a countess as a means of divine manifestation
would obviously not please the later Milton, for whom glitter
and pageantry tend to be idolatrous; and even here the sonori-
ties of the high mode do not quite fuse with the shepherd-
poet's humility. Though tradition helps confirm the analogy
between celestial order and royalty, the speaker's modesty
strikes us as little more than convention and artifice. The
situating of "Approach" (which is half command) and the
subtle mixing of exalted and plain levels of diction promise
a finer poetry than the subject permits. Milton cannot exploit
the irony of noble masquers wearing rustic costumes; any
reciprocity between reverence and irony that a Quince or
Snout might produce is out of the question.

"Arcades" makes the most explicit link between poetry and
political emblems in the early poems, but "L'Allegro" and "Il
Penseroso" are probably more central to the characteristic
pattern of pre-Lycidas poems, in which the poet or individual
hero himself progresses to regions that entertain "the immortal mind." Taken together the two poems also combine
Platonic and Christian means of liberating the poet, whose
higher art is governed both by "the spirit of Plato" and by a
Christian "prophetic strain." The goddesses Mirth and Melancholy cut across this programmatic development as states of
mind assumed to be efficient and contrasting causes of the
poet's progress but actually little more than mood-accompani-
ment. As Cleanth Brooks and D. C. Allen have argued, the
structure of the two poems is based less on the contrasts cen-
tered in them than on the sequential passage from one level of
experience to another.[2] Though the rural muses of "L'Allegro"

[2] Cleanth Brooks in *The Well Wrought Urn* (New York: Harcourt, Brace, 1947) and D. C. Allen in *Harmonious Vision* (Balti-

are obviously quite different from the muses of "Il Penseroso" arranged around Jove's altar, they do not really function as opposites. The urban art that the poet discovers at the end of "L'Allegro" is already several steps in sophistication beyond rural dances, and both kinds of art are good in their way. Mention of Eurydice, half-regained but lost, bridges joy and melancholy without a break in the narrative progress or the poet's programmatic development.

The goddesses also obscure the part played by the poet's passivity in the transformation, the true cause of which seems to be the hierarchical structure of experience itself, which draws the poet continually onward:

> And as I wake, sweet music breathes
> Above, about, or underneath,
> Sent by some spirit to mortals good,
> Or th' unseen Genius of the Wood.
> But let my due feet never fail
> To walk the studious Cloister's pale,
> And love the high embowed Roof,
> With antic Pillars massy proof,
> And storied Windows richly dight,
> Casting a dim religious light.
> There let the pealing Organ blow
> To the full voic'd Choir below,
> In Service high and Anthems clear,
> As may with sweetness, through mine ear,
> Dissolve me into ecstasies,
> And bring all Heav'n before mine eyes.
> And may at last my weary age
> Find out the peaceful hermitage,
> The Hairy Gown and Mossy Cell . . .
> Till old experience do attain
> To something like Prophetic strain.
> ["Il Penseroso," 150 ff.]

At this stage it cannot be Melancholy alone that brings the poet's response to the scene. "Spirit" is a vague source of music, and the "Genius of the Wood," though a figure for the poet in "Arcades," is indefinite here. The feet are invested

---

more: Johns Hopkins Press, 1954) read the two poems as a single process.

with a religious duty that seems to consist of walking where
the architecture is impressive, where one is put in the way of
religious feeling. (They are also oddly invested with power to
love roofs.) In "Arcades," the attaching of duty and veneration
to a sacred vesture is appropriate to the ornateness and costuming of the masque—and to the embodiment of cosmic
necessity in visual symbols that command authority; here the
poet's devotion to atmosphere merely renders him passive
before it. His love of massy pillars and storied windows serves
as an initial stage in aesthetic perception, followed one knows
not how by a dissolving of the senses and an ecstasy that leaves
behind the surface of art and music. "Weary age" rather than
a willed course of action will bring the poet to a peaceful
hermitage; and "experience" rather than a prophet devoted to
a calling will attain the "prophetic strain."

Milton handles stylistic shifts with confidence, however.
After establishing a pattern of light joy in the quick rhythms
of "L'Allegro," he extends the verse units into larger, mellower
paragraphs. The structural principle of both poems is a transposing of keys and modes that correspond to the soul's gradual
liberation. Thus "joy" is both continuous and well shaded, and
the mood of the goddesses is keyed to ever new and higher
epiphanies:

> And ever against eating Cares,
> Lap me in soft *Lydian* Airs,
> Married to immortal verse,
> Such as the meeting soul may pierce
> In notes, with many a winding bout
> Of linked sweetness long drawn out,
> With wanton heed, and giddy cunning,
> The melting voice through mazes running;
> Untwisting all the chains that tie
> The hidden soul of harmony.

[134–44]

The style is typically Miltonic in its accumulation of clauses by
loose association rather than by strict logical subordination and
development. As in the concluding passage of "Il Penseroso,"
the soul's marriage to harmony depends upon the melting
away of corporeal sound and the discovery of the hidden soul

of harmony behind it. The *"Lydian* Airs" that replace "eating Cares" are both pleasantly physical and capable of carrying the soul beyond their own linked sweetness. At the critical point in the soul's penetration of music, its notes "untwist" from the soul of harmony, and the marriage of soul and art is complete. The sentence, itself a "winding bout of linked sweetness" building into a long-breathed period, proffers that music, as though art simply happened and one got entwined in it. The approaching fullness of religious prophecy is already swelling, independent of the goddesses.

Both the programmatic growth of the poet in "L'Allegro" and "Il Penseroso" and the approach of humble shepherds to the countess in "Arcades" depend upon the ready fulfillment of the idyllic vision and the availability of exalted spiritual experience, which is somehow inherent in the landscape. All resistance to that spiritual fulfillment is overcome as easily as light vanquishes dark in the Nativity Ode. Though all of Milton's poetry, early and late, is controlled by his idyllic imagination, we have only to recall the hard choices and complexities of spiritual trial in *Paradise Regained* and *Samson Agonistes* to see how staged the pastoral contrasts are in these early performances.

In "Comus," however, Milton makes the first of his several temptation dramas the central matter and binds the poet's transformational power to the outcome of its lonely moral trial. It is true that once again Milton finds it difficult to bring together all the contributing elements of poetic harmony in a single coherent "schedule" by which the soul is taught to transcend nature: though Sabrina, divine philosophy, the Attendant Spirit, and the Lady are a formidable array for Comus to manage, he escapes—presumably to ambush other wanderers in the forest. But despite that escape, two additions to the soul's volitional powers suggest a growing confidence in its capacity to contain nature and perhaps turn it to advantage: the poet's knowledgeable imitation of a higher harmony and the notion emphasized in the Florentine Platonists that the soul's protean changes are entirely dependent upon the rational mind.

As Milton later wrote in *The Reason of Church Govern*

ment, poetry provides an effective complement to the pulpit
in making celestial harmony useful as therapy: it hymns divine
glory, sings of victorious agonies of saints (martyr tragedy),
deplores moral relapses (satire), and describes "the wily sub-
tleties and refluxes of man's thoughts from within" (lyric
monodrama). Primarily it undertakes to "allay the perturba-
tions of the mind and set the affections in right tune." Its
means of doing so Milton habitually describes in terms that
suggest the Pythagoreans and the *Timaeus,* which link thought
with the controlled movements of the spheres on the basis of
their harmony: "the motions akin to the divine part in us are
the thoughts and revolutions of the universe; these, therefore,
every man should follow, and correcting those circuits in the
head that were deranged at birth . . . he should bring the
intelligent part . . . into the likeness of that which intelligence
discerns." [3] To make these corrections one must hear as well
as reason correctly:

For not only was speech appointed to this same intent . . .
but also all that part of Music that is serviceable with respect
to the hearing of sound is given for the sake of harmony; and
harmony, whose motions are akin to the revolutions of the soul
within us, has been given by the Muses to him whose commerce with them is guided by intelligence, not for the sake of
irrational pleasure . . . but as an ally against the inward discord that has come into the revolution of the soul, to bring it
into order and consonance with itself. [*Timaeus* 47D]

For Milton, such therapeutic effectiveness has the advantage
over the pulpit of requiring no other intermediaries. The poet
is his own priest of harmony. Since he employs mysteries and
charms to set the affections straight, Milton tells his father,

you should not despise the poet's task, divine song, which pre-
serves some spark of Promethean fire and is the unrivalled
glory of the heaven-born human mind and an evidence of our
ethereal origin and celestial descent. The gods on high love

[3] *Plato's Cosmology: The Timaeus of Plato,* trans. Francis
Macdonald Cornford (New York: Liberal Arts Press, 1957), p.
354 (*Timaeus* 90D).

song and song has power to move the frightful depths of Tartarus and to bind the gods below and control the implacable shades with triple adamant. By song Apollo's priestesses and the trembling Sibyl, with blanched features, lay bare the mysteries of the faraway future. . . . Even now the fiery spirit who flies through the swift spheres is singing his immortal melody and unutterable song in harmony with the starry choruses.[4]

The plot and embodied musical effects of the masque in "Comus" suggest that not so much the liberating power of virtue or divine grace (the Lady already knows all about them and Comus is the only nonbeliever) as the curative and restorative powers of song are responsible for the Lady's success in breaking Comus's spell. What she requires is a magic to counter black magic, *to make harmony operational,* and only song of a certain kind has that power, quite literally a power to set "the affections in right *tune."* Accordingly, it is nature spiritualized by art that constitutes the restored order of the forest. Ultimately, the transformational power of music is focused in Sabrina.

Both the function of poetry in the masque and Sabrina's rescue of the Lady, however, lead us beyond the Platonist concept of music because they both require allies. Harmony without moral purpose and philosophical guidance is helpless. Like Italian pastoralists, Milton draws upon the Florentine belief that the soul, by exercising or failing to exercise its moral power to say no, can become either angelic or brutish. Pico remarks that the first words of God to Adam concerned his potential for good or bad changes of shape:

Neither a fixed abode nor a form that is thine alone nor any function peculiar to thyself have we given thee, Adam, to the end that according to thy longing and according to thy judgment thou mayest have and possess what abode, what form, and what functions thou thyself shalt desire. . . . Thou shalt have the power to degenerate into the lower forms of life, which are brutish. Thou shalt have the power, out of thy soul's

---

[4] "Ad Patrem" quoted from *John Milton, Complete Poems and Major Prose,* ed. Merritt Y. Hughes (New York: Odyssey Press, 1957).

judgment, to be reborn into the higher forms, which are divine.[5]

From this moment on, Pico suggests, man has the power to alter himself: "It is man who Asclepius of Athens . . . says was symbolized by Proteus in the mysteries. Hence those metamorphoses renowned among the Hebrews and Pythagoreans" (pp. 225–226). The very word *mageia* means "worshiper of the divine," so that magic is linked to perfect cognition, discovery of the "affinity of nature" or esoteric correspondences between things. Magic and art are the means of epiphany. Drawing wisdom from nature is the function of philosophy and making that wisdom operative for the soul's advance is the function of enchantment or the magician's *iugges,* which "brings forth into the open the miracles concealed in the recesses of the world, in the depths of nature, and in the storehouses and mysteries of God": as the farmer weds his elms to vines, the *magus* weds earth to heaven, countering the evil of demonic magic, which discovers secret identities between man and the brutes (p. 249).

The Florentine concept of transformation accounts for Comus more easily than for Sabrina. For Comus obviously derives from the class of shape-changers which the Greeks called *goeteia,* who love the earth but not its creator. When Phoebus (reason) is quenched, the victim promptly sinks in the scale of being, losing his capacity to wed himself to the mysteries and secret affinities that enable the soul to be "reborn into the higher forms." Comus

> Excels his Mother at her mighty Art,
> Off'ring to every weary Traveller
> His orient liquor in a Crystal Glass,
> To quench the drought of *Phoebus,* which as they taste,
> (For most do taste through fond intemperate thirst)
> Soon as the Potion works, their human count'nance,
> Th' express resemblance of the gods, is chang'd
> Into some brutish form of Wolf, or Bear,
> Or Ounce, or Tiger, Hog, or bearded Goat.

[63–71]

[5] *Renaissance Philosophy of Man,* ed. Ernst Cassirer et al. (Chicago: University of Chicago Press, 1948), p. 224.

To prevent demonic transformation in the Lady's case, the Attendant Spirit descends from the realm of the Untransformable—"where those immortal shapes / Of bright aerial Spirits live inspher'd"—and metamorphoses himself into a guide. (Henry Lawes as servant of the Bridgewater estate composed the music for the masque and acted the part of the Spirit.) Initially, then, the conflict is between an immortal shape immanent in song—"Who with his soft Pipe and smooth-dittied Song/Well knows to still the wild winds when they Roar" (87–88)—and the degrading magic of Comus, and it is primarily by comparison with the Spirit's honied art, that we know Comus's antimasque music to be a barbarous din:

> I sat me down to watch upon a bank
> With Ivy canopied, and interwove
> With flaunting Honeysuckle, and began,
> Wrapt in a pleasing fit of melancholy,
> To meditate my rural minstrelsy,
> Till fancy had her fill; but ere a close
> The wonted roar was up amidst the Woods,
> And fill'd the Air with barbarous dissonance,
> At which I ceas't.
>
> [543–551]

The first and encompassing antinomy is that of the "Palace of Eternity" and "this pinfold here."

But Spirit's opening assertion is deceiving because earth is more than a place of "smoke and Stir," a "dim spot" where men are "with low-thoughted care / Confin'd and pester'd"; it is also the realm of Neptune, who

> Took in by lot 'twixt high and nether *Jove,*
> Imperial rule of all the Sea-girt Isles
> That like to rich and various gems inlay
> The unadorned bosom of the Deep;
> Which he to grace his tributary gods
> By course commits to several government
>
> [20–25]

After complaining of "the rank vapors of this Sin-worn world," the Spirit finds it a delightful place of "Sapphire crowns" and "blue-hair'd deities." Nature is obviously radically transformable, depending on which enchantment one applies to it. The contest between the Spirit and Comus is thus soon transmuted into a series of local contests between Comus and other representatives of nature. The spirit world that most concerns the Lady herself is that of the "natural" fairies, Comus and Sabrina, who employ music and charms to free or entrap people. The Lady's own immediate goal is not to escape the realm of Neptune (the Attendant Spirit takes no one with him when he leaves and offers only vague instructions to those who would follow) but to escape one element of it and to arrive safely where the most noble revels are held. The songs of the immortal Spirit, the Lady, and Comus are staged in a succession that leads "deductively" from the cosmic to the local scene, presided over by the Earl of Bridgewater like royalty in a Jonsonian masque. Comus's song seems at first to have the greatest vigor and excitement, but then it is native to that scene:

> Meanwhile welcome Joy and Feast
> Midnight shout and revelry,
> Tipsy dance and Jollity.
> Braid your Locks with rosy Twine
> Dropping odors, dropping Wine.
> Rigor now is gone to bed,
> And Advice with scrupulous head,
> Strict Age, and sour Severity,
> With their grave Saws in slumber lie.
> We that are of purer fire
> Imitate the Starry Choir,
> Who is their nightly watchful Spheres,
> Lead in swift round the Months and Years.
>
> [102–114]

His philosophy is secondary to the cleverness of his art—his "charming Rod," his glass, and the "dazzling Spells" that he hurls "into the spongy air" to "cheat the eye with blear illusion" (154). The rites are dedicated to "love," the omnipresent agency of metamorphosis among the Platonists—presided over by Venus Pandemos, the sensual goddess:

> *Venus* now wakes, and wak'ns Love.
> Come let us our rites begin,

> 'Tis only daylight that makes Sin,
> Which these dun shades will ne'er report.
> Hail Goddess of Nocturnal sport.
>
> [124–128]

But the exhilaration of Comus's rites is false, as will be clear
later when Sabrina's song replaces them; and even in the earlier encounters the Lady's own power have profound effects
on Comus. The "different pace / Of some chaste footing"
causes him to break off his own celebration to listen to her
song in praise of song, and he is startled into changing his
plans. Having set out to metamorphose the Lady into a beast,
he decides to make her queen:

> Can any mortal mixture of Earth's mold
> Breathe such Divine enchanting ravishment?
> Sure something holy lodges in that breast,
> And with these raptures moves the vocal air
> To testify his hidd'n residence.
>
> [244–248]

At this stage in the masque, however, the power of song can
be no more than a gesture. The Lady is lost in darkness, deprived of allies:

> A thousand fantasies
> Begin to throng into my memory,
> Of calling shapes and beck'ning shadows dire,
> And airy tongues that syllable men's names
> On Sands and Shores and desert Wildernesses.
>
> [205–209]

With the confrontation of the respective proponents of song,
Milton sets the contest of styles, but in keeping with the technique of the allegorical masque, he delays the completion of
the pattern until the requisite doctrinal elements can be gath-
ered into the symbols. We know that the best of art contains
a magic compared with which Circe's and Comus's "dazzling
Spells" are mere sleights of hand accompanied by pulsing
drum beats; but we do not know how to distinguish between
the two, what their differences in content are, or what use each
makes of nature. Since Milton expects art to be about some-

thing besides art, the middle section is devoted primarily to philosophical questions. The upward path leads through abstraction, discursive reason, and intellectual enlightenment—the path downward to "pleasing slumber" through the appearance of reason and sweetly coated sensuality.

If music is inadequate without the guidance of reason, however, philosophy also has its limits. The elder brother stretches its capabilities in holding that it has a transformative power of its own (ll.453 ff.), requiring no particular effort to work. He looks forward to a decisive end of trials, when evil will recoil on itself and mix "no more with goodness":

> Gather'd like scum, and settl'd to itself,
> It shall be in eternal restless change
> Self-fed and self-consum'd; if this fail,
> The pillar'd firmament is rott'nness,
> And earth's base built on stubble.
>
> [593-597]

For those caught in the throes of chaos, this will be the beginning of a never-ending change like the turbulence of formless matter before reason imposed order upon it. To the elder brother, the wilderness of Comus's rites is thus the first step toward primal disorder, but for those who escape, the cycle will be completed by a return to perpetual feasts of "nectar'd sweets" that never "surfeit."

Too easily convinced by this vision, the second brother concedes that chastity has some such inherent power and that divine philosophy is indeed "charming" in its own right,

> Not harsh and crabbed as dull fools suppose,
> But musical as is *Apollo's* lute,
> And a perpetual feast of nectar'd sweets,
> Where no crude surfeit reigns.
>
> [477-481]

By establishing this basic analogy between music and philosophy, he incorporates the discursive matter of the masque into its central concern for pageantry, dance, and music. Though the doctrines of virginity and chastity prevent the Lady's

change into a beast, they are not capable of bringing her release. The Attendant Spirit applauds the brothers' philosophy
but cautions against overconfidence: "far other arms and other
weapons must / Be those that quell the might of hellish
charms." Comus "with his bare wand" can unthread their
joints and crumble their sinews.

New weapons are obviously called for, and the Spirit produces one from the "Shepherd Lad" whose words reinforce
the Spirit's own music (617–628). Whereas the brothers' rap-
turous philosophy lacks recognition of the usefulness of nature,
the poet's words come from a "leathern script" filled with nature's images and names. That his contribution is an "unsightly
root," "dark and prickly," suggests the elder brother's *con-
temptus mundi* but acknowledges, too, that the poet is situated
in the realm of Neptune.

With the uniting of the Attendant Spirit as the divine musician, the brothers with their quantity of doctrine, and the
namer of plants as poet-magician, the rescue of the Lady appears imminent, her own chastity and unshakable will to
endure having forestalled the effectiveness of Comus's "wit
and gay Rhetoric." Some ingredient, however, is still missing.
Comus's charming rod has a power of wizardry that neither
philosophy nor the shepherd lad's herbs possess, sovereign as
they may be " 'Gainst all enchantments, mildew blast, or
damp / Or ghastly furies' apparition." One can reverse it, but
to do that would suggest that black and white magic are two
sides of the same power. Milton's strategy is typically masque-
like; he unites all of these forces in a single visual symbol of
ideal art, the song of Sabrina, and thus replaces the magic rod
with a consummately natural ritual. It is toward this model of
beauty and song that the entire masque points. The drink
that Comus proposes, the sip from the enchanted glass that
"will cure all straight / . . . will bathe the drooping spirits in delight," Sabrina symbolically surpasses in her association with
the transformational powers of the sea. (It is the sea, not a
baptismal fount of grace, that has laved and purified each of
her senses: through "nectar'd lavers strew'd with Asphodel, /
And through the porch and inlet of each sense" Nereus "Dropt

in Ambrosial Oils till she reviv'd / And underwent a quick
immortal change" [838].) As in the sea-change of Ariel's song,
all that dies is immortalized in her and she in turn immortal-
izes others with "precious vial'd liquors," the stuff of her art:

> For which the Shepherds at their festivals
> Carol her goodness loud in rustic lays,
> And throw sweet garland wreaths into her stream
> Of pansies, pinks, and gaudy Daffodils.
> And, as the old Swain said, she can unlock
> The clasping charm and thaw the numbing spell,
> If she be right invok't in warbled Song.
>
> [848–854]

The "old Swain" (Meliboeus) recalls Spenser and perhaps
through him Neoplatonist pastorals in which faithful shep-
herdesses are saved by miraculous conjuring. But the chief
significance of the stream and of Sabrina's laving as medicinal
ritual is suggested by the Attendant Spirit's invocation in the
name of Oceanus, Tethys, Nereus, the "Carpathian wizard,"
Triton, Glacus, Leucothea, Thetis, "The Songs of Sirens
sweet," Parthenope, and "all the *Nymphs* that nightly dance /
Upon thy streams with wily glance" (868): all shape-changers,
artists, or wizards, who compose a strange group if Sabrina
is meant to represent divine grace, but who are entirely appropriate as associates of an ideal magical poetry.[6]

Having arrived at a crystalline style suitable to the kind of
engagement the chaste soul can make of nature, Milton is
ready for the formal celebration. The Attendant Spirit presents
the two brothers and the Lady to the audience, and they replace the clumsier art of the rural dances with a sophisticated
(royal) art permeated with the spirit of Sabrina:

> *Spirit.* Back Shepherds, back, enough your play,
> Till next Sun-shine holiday;

[6] Nereus, the son of Oceanus, fathered the fifty dancing Nereides
and had a gift of prophecy and shape-changing. Proteus, the Carpathian wizard, was for Milton, as for Wordsworth, apparently a
symbol of mythic beauty and the metamorphosing powers of the
sea. Glacus was a spell-weaver of first rank, while Leucothea presided over the discovery of speech. The rest are an assortment of
singers and dancers suitable to replace Comus's tipsy antimasque.

Here be without duck or nod
Other trippings to be trod
Of lighter toes.

                                        [959–963]

As the contract between art and philosophy is summed up and
the children are presented to their parents with their "crown
of deathless Praise" (the masque itself), the Attendant Spirit
rises to an ascending series of Good Places, the source of all
celestial harmony, leaving the realm of Neptune the better by
one musical performance, harbored in a graceful court that
once again demonstrates the analogy between social and divine harmony.

To recapitulate: the structure of the work follows that of a
proper musical, poetic, philosophic education as translated into
the fluid pageantry and shape-changing of the masque. The
beginning and ending offer an encompassing perspective on
the Platonist cosmos, but, in the interior drama of the forest,
Milton mixes masque pageantry and music with moral dialectic, as nature forces the soul to defend itself on nature's own
ground. The right kind of musicians, however, "bring down"
the aid of immortal music, which attends the soul and helps
liberate it from the deranging rhythms of Comus's antimasque.
Eventually poetry is purged of its demonic elements as Sabrina
and the dancing royal masquers come forward. Finally, the
Attendant Spirit reaffirms the connection between heaven and
earth and then leaves, his task accomplished. Though Milton
has exposed the soul to drama, he has not had to sacrifice the
idea that music prevails for those attuned to it. Thus although
"Comus" predicts the temptations and contests to which later
Miltonic protagonists are subjected, it obviously does not have
the same Christ-centered means of epiphany nor is its trial, a
temporary exposure to the wilderness, as severe as Adam's
exile from paradise.

                                   II

In "Lycidas," despite a similar equilibrium in the relationship
between heaven and earth, the purifying rites of art and
Platonist harmony have lost their power and prove ineffectual

in handling the disruptive forces that destroy the harboring landscape of Lycidas. Though Milton had written elegies on the Bishop of Wincester, the Bishop of Ely, and other acquaintances, he had not yet considered the full impact of death on the idyllic imagination and especially on the therapeutic powers of poetry. One result of his doing so in "Lycidas" is the emergence of an authentically dialectical style, which stems not merely from the broadening of nature's disruptive power but also from the interior focus of the poem, whose speaker, unlike the speaker of "L'Allegro" and "Il Penseroso," is himself threatened by a disintegrating world. Actually, the poem has not one but several styles that overlay one another in the manner of a dramatic meditation that begins in one key, transposes to another, and doubles back. The transitions are seldom marked by explicit shifts in thought or syntax or by grammatical or logical signals; when these become noticeable, new movements are already well underway. The result is a complex interweaving of an initial innocent pastoralism, a countering realism, and a revised version of Christian pastoral that collects several elements of what precedes.

The structural result of this mixture will perhaps be clearer if we think of the syntactical countermoves and dramatic progression of certain passages in *Paradise Lost* in which motives rise to visibility only after they have been working for some time. Consider, for instance, Satan's manipulation of Beelzebub in the first approach to him in Hell:

> If thou beest hee; But O how fall'n!
> From him, who in the happy Realms of Light
> Cloth'd with transcendent brightness didst outshine
> Myriads though bright: if he whom mutual league,
> United thoughts and counsels, equal hope,
> And hazard in the Glorious Enterprise,
> Join'd with me once, now misery hath join'd
> In equal ruin; into what Pit thou seest
> From what highth fall'n, so much the stronger prov'd
> He with his Thunder.
>
> [i.84–92]

(On from there to "fixed mind," high disdain, and proposals for eternal war). We cannot impose logical direction on such passages, assuming, for instance, as Bentley, Pearce, and Empson do, that Satan's main objective is to comfort Beelzebub. Such an assumption forces a definite set of motives and a rhetorical order on the passage at the expense of its devious movement. The density of texture is the result of Satan's interweaving of multiple threads, which he causes to appear and disappear as the fabric of his design requires. As usual when Satan talks, the speech is filled with implicit ironic likenesses to God's pronouncements to his creatures, but unlike divine epiphanies, Satan's truths fade into illusions and prove to be timely elements of his political and psychological manipulations. Because it will be obvious to Beelzebub that something has gone wrong, Satan does not try to conceal their ruin; he uses it to promote their alliance. If the two of them came there equally, under their own free wills ("You chose to come along, remember?"), they are both to blame and the disaster confirms their league. This use of their mutual guilt and misery, however, may well be an afterthought: Satan begins with the plain truth and a trailing clause that remembers nostalgically their former glory. He says no more than he can prove and avoids nothing, as a merely shrewd leader might have: sharing responsibility is much more effective than denying it because it helps burn away regret and short-circuit resentment, converting them into energy against the unjust thunderer.

The structural point is that the shift from truth to politics is subtle and buried in a skillfully manipulated range of styles. The movement of the passage is uniquely Miltonic and yet also reflects the particular situation of Satan as he remembers a grander style from the place he lost and adapts it to his dilemma. We can locate no opening for Beelzebub's escape; given the circumstances, he would find it difficult to set aside Satan's plan for regaining lost glory on behalf of a plan designed for truly repentant sinners; to resist the league Satan seeks would require that he deny both his leader's compassion and the truth it makes use of. Abdiel's "no" at the original gathering of the rebellious host might suggest a path for him, but he has already substituted glorious "enterprise" for glorious worship and is therefore forced now to let the rhetoric and values of satanic enterprise define the rules by which they play.

The monodrama of "Lycidas" is Milton's first experiment in such a mode, which conceals its working motives until they erupt, and entangles one set of values and one perspective in another. While the poem moves successively from the idyllic life of Cambridge to a restored and raised paradise, it constantly anticipates what is to come, not explicitly but in its issuing images and sound (which suggest a musical technique that Gretchen Finney likens to the operatic versions of the Orpheus legend that Milton may have used).[7] At the same time, the drama is also marked by the main movements of the poem: the ceremonial decorum and Sabrina-like music appropriate to pastoral recollections of Cambridge are followed by a more explicit awareness of death, bringing with it tonal complexities and a harsher dissonance; and finally, after two returns to the manner of the "oaten flute" and two further disruptions, the vision of Lycidas in paradise evokes a full-voiced hymn. This hymn emerges with commanding organizational force just as the swain appears about to surrender to the unavoidable thought of Lycidas submerged in the sea. It emerges as a structural reversal, but it also resumes and reorders previous images and themes.

Technically, Milton mixes voices by quoting the uncouth swain, St. Peter, Jove, and others. But these voices succeed one another in decisively marked passages, and the most effective interplay of moods consists of a simultaneous interweaving of harmonious and dissonant elements in the primary voice of the poet. The mixture of tones in the flower passage is typical.

It is sometimes assumed that the flowers symbolize rebirth and are so appealing in their profusion and fragrance, as J. H. Hanford sums up, that we find them ample recompense for the harshness of the dread voice that precedes: they allow us to "sink back again into the tranquil enjoyment which comes from the contemplation of pure beauty, unmarred by any

[7] Gretchen Finney, "A Musical Background for 'Lycidas,'" *HLQ,* 15 (1952), 325–350.

newness of idea, unclouded by overmastering emotion." [8] The flowers are anything but carefree themselves, however:

> Ye valleys low were the mild whispers use
> Of shades and wanton winds and gushing brooks,
> On whose fresh lap the swart Star sparely looks,
> Throw hither all your quaint enamell'd eyes
> That on the green turf suck the honied showers,
> And purple all the ground with vernal flowers.
> Bring the rathe Primrose that forsaken dies,
> The tufted Crow-toe, and pale Jessamine,
> The white Pink, and the Pansy freakt with jet,
> The glowing Violet,
> The Musk-rose, and the well-attir'd Woodbine,
> With Cowslips wan that hang the pensive head,
> And every flower that sad embroidery wears:
> Bid *Amaranthus* all his beauty shed,
> And Daffadillies fill their cups with tears.

The technique in "L'Allegro" of casting a sober light over vernal pleasures is here turned to better advantage. Despite an apparent riot of color, the flowers are not of a thousand hues but predominately pale and overly sweet. There is a suggestion of blight in the "swart Star" (Sirius) that scorches fields in August, in the forsaken primrose, the wan cowslip, and in an Amaranthus that sheds all its beauty though supposedly immortal. The tension between idyllic celebration and blight suggests that both the beauty of flowers and the elegiac consolation that they bring are fragile: the death of Lycidas requires greater recompense than that which pagan shepherds receive or pastoral conventions offer.

The description of Lycidas which follows breaks through whatever tranquillity the flowers have: the resistless, unsympathetic force of the Irish sea, as Shumaker writes, "deals with the body of the poet-priest-shepherd exactly as the Hebrus has the severed head of Orpheus, tossing it about with the indifference with which it would toss a plank broken from the

[8] James H. Hanford, "The Pastoral Elegy and Milton's *Lycidas*," *PMLA*, 25 (1910), 446–447.

hull of the wrecked ship." [9] All brooks are submerged in the
sea, and the poet is forced to confront nature's inability to re-
claim itself, whatever myths of renewal may be imposed on it.
To find the flower passage "too pretty-pretty, too convention-
ally poetic" to carry emotional weight and therefore "deliber-
ately delusive" (as Shumaker does), however, is to drive nature and grace farther apart than the poem warrants. Nature
as beauty and nature as blight are simply left suspended without an explicit connective; as the swain has earlier argued, in
effect, "Those who deserve will be smitten at the door of paradise with the two-handed engine; let us (nonetheless? therefore? anyway?) proceed to scatter flowers." While the voice
changes to accommodate these shifts, the ambivalence remains
unresolved—until it is clear that nothing in either the pastoral
tradition or in the therapy of ceremonial song will invoke
grace.

Similar contrasts of beauty and blight, ceremony and disruption, are evident in other abrupt transitions and movements
of partial insight into the futility of pastoral rites. The disruptive effect that St. Peters' voice and the conclusion of the
flower passage have is implicit initially in the violence of the
invocation and the speaker's address to nature. The difference
is that in the earlier passages the dissonance surfaces more
distantly. The attempt to produce "melodious tears" and to
offer mead to one who "must not flote upon his watry bier /
Unwept, and welter to the parching wind" proves futile, but it
is not clear at first why it should be or even that it must. It
is ironically to be Lycidas, not the swain, who protects "all
that wander in that perilous flood" and Lycidas who discovers
a more suitable music in the celestial choirs; but meanwhile,
the effort to produce an appropriate song merely forces the
swain to "somewhat loudly sweep the string," to put aside his
reluctance and proceed as the tradition suggests.

In the "But O the heavy change" section and the Orpheus
passage, Milton brings the collision of pastoral ceremony and
the disruptions of a more strident and realistic voice to a pitch,

[9] "Flowerets and Sounding Seas: A Study in the Affective Structure of Lycidas," *PMLA,* 66 (1951), 485–494.

and we discover that the poem's concern is not merely death but the poet's inability to control nature, whatever enchantment he may command. These seem to me the really critical passages in Milton's early development. Implicitly, the magical rites of "Comus" as well as the conventional consolations of the pastoral elegy are called into question in them. The river Deva, as Camden says, was believed to foreshadow a "sure token of victorie to the inhabitants upon it" who "attributed Divinitie" to it. But whereas Spenser makes it the haunt of magicians[10] and tutelary deities may be supposed to offer protection there, Milton's adjective "wizard" suggests that any Sabrina-like enchantment will be ineffectual before nature's ruthless power. If the son of a celestial being was helpless before the furies, a mere uncouth swain is doubly so:

> What could the Muse herself that *Orpheus* bore,
> The Muse herself, for her enchanting son
> Whom Universal nature did lament,
> When by the rout that made the hideous roar,
> His goary visage down the stream was sent,
> Down the swift *Hebrus* to the *Lesbian* shore?[11]

[10] See Hughes's note to line 55 in *John Milton, Complete Poems and Major Prose.*

[11] The Orpheus figure appears frequently in classical and renaissance pastoral. See Moschus; Alamanni (first eclogue); Sannazaro (second eclogue); Spenser (October eclogue); Boccaccio's comments on Orpheus' power of song in *Geneologie deorum gentilium;* Henry Reynolds, "Mythomystes." Milton characteristically thinks of Orpheus as an example of poetic capacity, but references grow increasingly less flattering after "Lycidas," especially in *Paradise Lost,* 3.17.

That Milton intended to stress the helplessness of Orpheus as a nature poet is clear from the revisions of the Trinity manuscript:

. . . .
what could the golden hayrd Calliope
for her inchaunting son ——————
when shee beheld (the gods farre sighted bee)
his goarie scalpe rowle down the Thracian lee
. . . .
↳whome universal nature might lament

"Universal nature" laments Orpheus, its representative and musical voice, but its lament is drowned by the roar of his slayers.

In the apotheosis of Lycidas, the swain discovers an answer to that "hideous roar" in a combination of apocalyptic and pastoral conventions capable of "retuning" nature and transmuting its streams and flowers to another kind of pastoral celebration, another kind of musical therapy. All the things that have been threatening and dangerous to Lycidas and Orpheus Milton has contribute now to the realization of the idyllic vision. This vision prevents a total severing of nature and grace and reclaims some aspects of the convention while subordinating them to a new purpose. Chief among nature's contributions to this Christian calculus is water. Lycidas has been submerged in it at the bottom of the "monstrous world"; Orpheus has gone to it with lamentation and discordant rout; the sea has overwhlemed the brooks of the Sicilian muse and

> *and heaven and hel deplore*
> *when his divine head downe*
> the streame was sent
> down the swift Hebrus to the
> Lesbian shore

(Italics indicate crossing out.) Milton inserted "Universal nature" and allowed it to stand, but rejected "heaven and hel," "divine," and the original notion that the gods are farsighted enough to see mortal events. Then turning to a separate piece of paper (apparently because the revisions were becoming too involved for the manuscript page), he further heightened the discrepancy between the ineffectual powers of art and the rout it must try to control:

> what could the muse her selfe that Orpheus bore
> the muse her selfe for her inchanting son
> *for her inchanting son*
>   did
> whome universal nature *might* ∧ lament
> when by the rout that made the hideous roare
>   goarie
> Goarie   his *divine* ∧ visage downe the streame was sent
>   downe the swift Hebrus to ye Lesbian shoare.

Milton changed "Calliope" to "the Muse her selfe," again emphasizing the helplessness of poetry, and added "rout" and "hide-the fountains and rills of Cambridge, and it has floated and sunk that "perfidious Bark / Built in th' eclipse" but refused to be the "bier" that floats Lycidas; and even the Pilot who comes from the Galilean lake was once himself in need of rescue. But water is also the element that Christ walks upon in a miracle that both uses and transcends nature. Normal pastoral streams are replaced by those "other streams" that "solemn troops, and sweet societies" walk beside in a paradise where the host replaces the initial society of Cambridge and the chaotic rout that surrounded Orpheus. Other images are also transformed in Milton's reconceiving of the convention. Images of the "eye-lids of the morn" and the sinking evening star (lines 26, 30) are replaced by the rising "day-star" that flames in the forehead of the morning, a symbol of the resurrection, and what in the original pastoral decorum were rough satyrs' dances and the melody of the poet's ceremonial "tear" are metamorphosed into the dance of societies that "sing, and singing in their glory move" and into the "unexpressive" nuptial song that greets Lycidas. The harsh justice of the ecclesiastical section that comes forth to shatter the pastoral surface is also softened in the "might" of the atonement and in the "joy and love" of the "blest Kingdom." The threat of St. Peter's judgment may thus be safely put behind (though it has by no means been irrelevant to the choosing of the blest society).

This series of translations from the realm of nature to the realm of grace does not find a place for poetic enchantment and magic as the defeat of Comus does, nor does nature itself prove immediately changeable for those who still wander in "the perilous flood." But Lycidas's new state is a pledge for the future and sets a pattern for similar transformations; and it reassures the poet-swain of his own course by suggesting a function for poetry—the elaboration of the means by which paradise is lost and then restored in the wilderness. In *Para-*

---

ous roare," crowding out the last vestige of the idyllic life and the last suggestion that farsighted gods watch over nature. "Divine" returns to "goarie" which strengthens the link between Orpheus's death and that of Lycidas as described after the flower passage.

dise Lost and *Paradise Regained* such an extension of the pattern of Lycidas is inherent in the concept of the fortunate fall that expels Adam from paradise. The death that Adam brings to Eden will require a more ambitious fusion of Christian, heroic, and pastoral modes than the early Milton predicts, especially in "L'Allegro" and "Il Penseroso"; but in "Lycidas" the basic elements of that combination have come together decisively enough to justify the poet's sense of purpose: "To-morrow to fresh Woods, and Pastures new."

EIGHT

The Augustan Balance
of Nature and Art

BELINDA AND THE GARDEN

Sol thro' white Curtains shot a tim'rous Ray,
And op'd those Eyes that must eclipse the Day.

. . . .

This the *Beau-monde* shall from the *Mall* survey,
And hail with Musick its propitious Ray.

The disruption in Pope's "The Rape of the Lock" of Belinda's
delicate existence by the violent assault of the normally well-
bred baron demonstrates the fragility of beauty in a world
in which disinterested contemplation is helpless before the
desire to possess. That disruption is typical of the plight of
potential aesthetic objects generally: appealing and seemingly
available for the "snipping," they invite the beholder to take
liberties with them, to pull them away from the self-contained
and enclosed world of the artifact into another kind of world,
where objects are consumed with use and worn by time. Indeed, the parallels between the lock's detachment and eventual
escape from "the *Beau-monde*" and the condition of poems
are strong enough to suggest that Pope found many of the
same aesthetic principles applicable to each, especially those
that apply to the transformation of nature into art. The lock's
ornamentation, its defense by the organized hand of sylphdom,
and its eventual enshrinement are what one might expect of
poetry, or at least want for it. Before Pope has Ariel's lucid
squadrons escape with it and make it a distant star, however,
he acknowledges the difficulties of its transformation. While

it hangs temptingly among Belinda's other locks, it is a delightful piece of nature, human and vulnerable.

Perhaps the most surprising part of Belinda's ambiguous role in the making and display of that work of cosmetic art is her nymphlike purity and simplicity in spite of everything. Her love of artifice never quite smothers all naturalness in her, and in fact, with Ariel's help, she improves nature significantly. (Allen Tate, Cleanth Brooks, and Murray Krieger have noticed the pastoral quality of her innocence and of the social idyll generally.) [1] Ariel himself remarks that his revelations are only for "the Fair and Innocent," for "Maids alone and Children" (i.38). Belinda's entrance into the social world puts on display the best of nature reshaped by art:

> While melting Musick steals upon the Sky,
> And soften'd Sounds along the Waters die.
> Smooth flow the Waves, the Zephyrs gently play,
> Belinda smil'd, and all the World was gay.
>
> [ii.49–52]

The references to breezes, vernal flowers, sun, moon, and stars are numerous, many of them associated with Belinda; Ariel's language especially overflows with the particulars of the outdoor world. As Emerson suggests in another connection: "The smoothest curled courtier in boudoirs of a palace has an animal nature, rude and aboriginal as a white bear, omnipotent to its own ends, and is directly related, there amid essences and billets-doux, to Himmaleh Mountain-chains, and the axis of the globe." And just so, Belinda's boudoir-workshop savors

---

[1] Cleanth Brooks, "The Case of Miss Arabella Fermor," *The Well Wrought Urn* (New York: Harcourt, Brace, 1947), pp. 80–104; Murray Krieger, "The 'Frail China Jar' and the Rude Hand of Chaos," *Centennial Review*, 5 (1961), 176–194. As Brooks writes, "Belinda is, after all, an artist, and who should be more sympathetic with the problems of the conscious artist than Pope himself?" Krieger carries that analogy further and finds the lock "metonymic" for the beau monde. The frail lock and the artifice that it models are "powerless against chaos" but are eventually inscribed among the stars, winning "immortality with the very evanescent quality" that dooms them on earth.

of jungle and desert, turtle and elephant, marvelously liberated
from solidity and locked into the controlled glitter of her social
display, almost no longer themselves:

> This casket *India's* glowing Gems unlocks,
> And all *Arabia* breathes from yonder Box.
> The Tortoise here and Elephant unite,
> Transform'd to *combs*, the speckled and the white.
>
> [i.133–136]

As the light militia transforms each of these things, it distills
essences from them, extracting some glow formerly concealed
by their earthy styles. Nothing is allowed to take its own crude
way uncorrected but is prepared for paradise by this purification, "pastoralized" into perfection, freed from the world of
birth and organic growth, fixed in the permanence of the artifact—as is fitting for its presence beside the angelic coquette.
Ariel promises Belinda a similar translation into pure celestial
Form, a preview of which greets her awakening:

> If 'er one Vision touch'd thy infant Thought,
> Of all the Nurse and all the Priest have taught,
> Of airy Elves by Moonlight Shadows seen,
> The silver Token, and the circled Green,
> Or Virgins visited by Angel-Pow'rs,
> With Golden Crowns and Wreaths of heaven'ly Flow'rs,
> Hear and believe! thy own Importance know.
>
> [i.29–35]

As in epics that encompass Earth with Heaven and Hell,
two worlds converge in Belinda's, the cosmos of sunlit, airy
imagination presided over by Ariel's squadrons and the subterranean world of distorted forms presided over by the Goddess of Spleen. The first of these Ariel here describes to her as
nature perfected and heightened, and the second comes to her
later as a warped nature brought on by her own anger. Ariel's
marriage of nature and art is clearly a kind of idyll that he
gives to sleeping maidens in dreamy visions. The counter-
parts of silver tokens and golden crowns—crafted artifacts—are
nature's circles in the green and in wreathes of flowers, shaped
like artifacts but of organic materials. The elves that dance

by moonlight are earthly versions of angels, who offer the highest models for maidens who would make *themselves* artful-natural objects.

In contrast, in the realm of gnomes, the dusky spirit Umbriel finds a confusion of forms—where "Unnumber'd Throngs on ev'ry side are seen / Of Bodies chang'd to various Forms by *Spleen*" (iv.47–48). Here too is a marriage of art and nature of sorts, but of misshapen art under the influence of Affectation and "Ill-Nature," personified as an ancient maid,

> Her wrinkled Form in *Black* and *White* array'd;
> With store of Pray'rs, for Mornings, Nights, and Noons,
> Her hand is fill'd; her Bosom with Lampoons.
>
> [iv.27–30]

The arts that Affectation practices are akin to Belinda's rites of vanity, but they sacrifice charm and beauty for self-advancement. The scene surrounding Ill-Nature and Affectation is a counterpastoral world of bizarre miscreations:

> A constant *Vapour* o'er the Palace flies;
> Strange Phantoms rising as the Mists arise;
> Dreadful, as Hermit's Dreams in haunted Shades,
> Or bright as Visions of expiring Maids.
> Now glaring Fiends, and Snakes on rolling Spires,
> Pale Spectres, gaping Tombs, and Purple Fires:
> Now Lakes of liquid Gold, *Elysian* Scenes,
> And Crystal Domes, and Angels in Machines.
>
> [iv.39–46]

The perfecting of nature in the formality of Ariel's deft art is lost to extremes of wild disorder and rigid imprisonment in this sullen realm. Affectation's rosy cheeks and the gold of the lake are perversions rather than fulfillments of nature. Obviously, if popular plays, lamentations and lampoons, swan songs, victory speeches—not to mention epic sneezes and other weapons in love's wars that enable beaux and witlings to perish in metaphor and song—are products of the imagination, not all poetic inspirations can be trusted. Everything that comes from the "Parent of Vapours and of Female Wit, / Who give th' Hysteric or Poetic Fit" (iv.59–60) is warped.

Until death purifies coquettes beyond Spleen's influence and installs them in the ethereal realm, they remain ambiguous creatures subject to that hysteric fit. To be totally free of such vile distortions of nature, Belinda must reject "mankind," as Ariel warns; but for the moment she and her lock are still the bodily vehicles of beauty, not yet evaporated into crystal sylphdom where they would be safe. Within the limitations of Belinda's social and corporeal state, Ariel can only try to transform and displace nature, as Belinda's white curtains diffuse and soften the sun. Yet screened and primped as it is in her boudoir, nature is also threatened from another direction, by suffocation in art. As a product of sylphdom, Belinda illustrates the difficulty of finding a proper balance between Ariel's aesthetic distillation of nature and the human usefulness of his craft, which requires that its products be risked in the full view of rapacious barons. As Clarissa indicates, the rites of art dare not be completely "pure": even coquettes must work for a purpose. Like epic heroes, nymphs assume a style according to the manners expected of them, and, in so doing, they inevitably allow mankind to enter their calculating hearts and affect the strategies by which they prepare and then "publish" their beauty. It is true that for coquettes who try not to be owned, a variety of roles may prevent any one beau from laying claim to them. Like true works of art, they are uncapturable: they belong to everyone and so to no one. (In Ariel's metaphor, "With varying Vanities, from ev'ry part, / They shift the moving Toyshop of their Heart" [i.99].)

But Ariel has seen something else in the mirror of her ruling star: enshrined in her heart is the image of mankind, which obviously she seeks to please. As art for art's sake critics might have warned her, one who would make locks into "pure" artifacts should transcend the temptation to make public use of art. Exposed to the outside world, art is vulnerable to its voracious lovers, who sell, barter, or "rape" it. And so, having put herself in the way of assault, Belinda regrets too late her own exposure to rivals, who call her a degraded "toast." Her "eyes dejected, and her hair unbound," she would then rather have remained a mute inglorious poet "in some lone isle, or distant

northern land," where she could have kept her "charms conceal'd from mortal eye, / Like roses, that in deserts bloom and
die." This wish, as readers of pastorals immediately recognize,
is a common pose among poet-swains. Its function is to divert
punishment for poetic hubris and allow a call for attention to
rest at ease alongside modest disclaimers of talent. Though
Pope himself adopts it at the end of "Windsor Forest" and
again in the Spring eclogue, it seems questionable that we are
meant to take it seriously here. Unlike the obscure swain of
the pastorals, Belinda is the apex of an aristocratic order capable of appreciating a well-made article: she should come forth
as she does; the world awaits her entry. She is drawn into the
card game by a thirst for fame (iii.25), and conquest is in her
blood. Though her excess of ambition is not defensible, where
the choice is either art for art's sake or a public mauling, art
must be made to engage mankind and suffer the consequences.

Despite its prominence in the poem, Clarissa's advice offers
no real solution to the dilemma of the product, too ravishing
to be resisted and too much a part of nature to be irrelevant. In
treating Belinda's art as a commodity like any other, Clarissa
merely gives the raping of the lock a middle-class sanction.
Arguing necessity, she denies that beauty has any but pragmatic reasons to exist:

> But since, alas! frail Beauty must decay,
> Curl'd or uncurl'd, since Locks will turn to grey,
> Since painted, or not painted, all shall fade,
> And she who scorns a Man, must die a Maid;
> What then remains, but well our Pow'r to use,
> And keep good Humour still whate'er we lose?
>   [v.25–30]

If it were otherwise, "who would learn one earthly Thing of
Use?"—so need teaches the hand that curls the lock. We
would expect to find Clarissa busy among those who search
for the severed lock on earth or who look for it to land in
some lunar sphere where heroes' wits are stored,

> in pondrous Vases,
> And Beaus' in *Snuff-boxes* and *Tweezer-Cases*.

> There broken Vows, and Death-bed Alms are found,
> And Lovers' Hearts with Ends of Riband bound;
> The Courtier's Promises, and Sick Man's Pray'ers,
> The Smiles of Harlots, and the Tears of Heirs.
>
> [v.115–120]

—all obviously forms of address designed for courtship or uses of rhetoric, remnants of a subheroic order defined by their specific functions. In effect, Clarissa would replace the ailing system of courtly advancement with vulgar directness.

Speaking in his own voice both in the prefatory note to Mrs. Arabella Fermor and in a later rhetorical address to the poem's audience, Pope offers another kind of apology for the use of locks and another place of residence. These in a sense solve the dilemma of locks that both are and are not aesthetically transcendent. (It also lets critics off the hook by allowing them to see and talk about the aesthetic object without having it in hand, offering a compromise as it does between nature and art or between imitative and rhetorical dimensions, on one hand, and aesthetic distance, on the other.) Locks of real hair such as Mrs. Fermor's must not only be curled, adorned before the mirror, clipped, and displayed: they must also be enshrined, beyond the reach of the baron and Clarissa. Before it can be carried off and fixed in its firmament by sylphdom, the lock must be cut "from the fair head, for ever, and for ever!" But that means being lost not so much *to* as *from* the world: it still exists in its special way, both detached and influential. In a similar manner, the poet (true sylph) has snatched a real lock from Mrs. Fermor's hectic life and installed it in the firmament of the poem, in effect giving us a symbolic mirroring of real-life incidents, yet transforming them into something permanently radiant. As a star, the lock rains a timeless divine influence down upon those who "survey" it correctly: we both have it and do not have it, snip and possess it—and then lose it to a better possession. It beckons to us from inside the poem as the star beckons to the beau monde—misreadings no doubt abounding in both cases:

> This, the blest Lover shall for *Venus* take,
> And send up Vows from *Rosamonda's* Lake.

> This *Partridge* soon shall view in cloudless Skies,
> When next he looks thro' Galilæo's Eyes.
>
> [v.135–138]

From the vantage point of this safety, the poem mocks the single-minded practicality of Clarissa's desperate advice:

> Then cease, bright Nymph! to mourn thy ravish'd Hair
> Which adds new Glory to the shining Sphere!
> Not all the Tresses that fair Head can boast
> Shall draw such Envy as the Lock you lost.
>
> [v.141–144]

Liberated into art, the lock is beyond both the narrow utility and the warmth of real life, made glittery and cold.

Insofar as Mrs. Fermor can take pride in having provided the occasion for the poem, Pope provides an indirect apology for the rites of the mirror that produce the well-groomed lock that becomes a star. Though its satire of social trivia is unstinting and the distance between modern and ancient heroes is vast, the poem allows its society a special glory. The transformed lock speaks for itself.

But the contribution that Augustan society and Augustan taste make in the production of the glittering artifact is perhaps more problematic than this. One might equally argue that it takes a great labor and much wit indeed to extract a poem from Mrs. Fermor's lock, and that no poem which was not ironic could be honest on such a subject. To explore the problem fully we would have to look into Pope's verse epistles and essays. Without recourse to such an extended detour, however, one can cite evidence that Pope had for some time been seeking a workable compromise between nature and Augustan "cosmetic" improvements on it. In both his eclogues and in the early poem "The Garden" (an imitation of Cowley in a mock-humble manner), he finds a just balance between art and nature in the works of those whom he admires, which are like "The Rape of the Lock" in fusing the aristocratic boudoir with the natural garden. "The Garden" is especially useful here because it, too, implicitly mirrors its own method as it describes the arts of the gardener:

> Fain would my Muse the flow'ry Treasures sing,
> And humble glories of the youthful Spring;
> Where opening *Roses* breathing sweets diffuse,
> And soft *Carnations* show'r their balmy dews;
> Where *Lillies* smile in virgin robes of white,
> The thin Undress of superficial Light,
> And vary'd *Tulips* show so dazzling gay,
> Blushing in bright diversities of day.
> Each painted flouret in the lake below
> Surveys its beauties, when its beauties grow;
> And pale *Narcissus* on the bank, in vain
> Transformed, gazes on himself again.

The poet's approach in "Fain would my Muse . . . sing" combines an echo of large epic beginnings with the deferential stance of the swain content with gardens and bowers. The high tone of "treasures" is echoed in "humble glories," both pointing toward a fusion of high society and nature in a slightly ironic manner. The urbanity is agreeable both to the Augustan sensibility generally and to Pope, who has very little shaping to perform on the material set so well formed before him, by a society that habitually dresses nature to advantage. Like the gardener who has arranged the reflecting water to double the beauty of the flowers, he mirrors these bright diversities in the verbal means of the poem. Though a hint of melancholy narcissism creeps in, as again in Belinda's self-involved rites of vanity, the predominant note is innocence: coming forth like nymphs at their first outing, the flowers are caught in moments of blushing delicacy halfway between reluctance and desire for admiration. Though "undress" points toward an unadorned nature, the mode is half witty from the beginning and can easily accommodate a teasing contrast of this kind. In fact the contrast is heightened by "superficial," which suggests both an artificial light of the surface and an essential inner nature not quite revealed. The poem is a poem of surfaces that transforms organic, growing things into artifacts; its profusion is pleasing to the "superficial" eye, which seizes upon profusion and makes it submit to art and arrangement. The flowers thus come forth in couplet enumeration, at a processional pace that allows each participant to register clearly and display itself like an innocent floral model.

Subsequently Pope keeps nature and the civil graces of these flower-maidens distinct by exaggerating the "social" metaphor. But they continue to reinforce one another, nature providing the substance for art and art turning aside its blunt thrust. The progression of the poem is a tightening of their tension until they are thoroughly defined and locked into place. A final Ovidian metamorphosis suggests that the laurels were really once a nymph and that nature is capable of being tamed even when passions seem to have gotten out of hand. Pope thus gives us a glimpse of a stronger reality behind the plants, only to demonstrate thereby the greater strength of the gardener's art:

> There in bright drops the crystal Fountains play,
> By *Laurels* shielded from the piercing Day:
> Where *Daphne,* now a tree was once a maid,
> Still from *Apollo* vindicates her shade,
> Still turns her beauties from th' invading beam,
> Nor seeks in vain for succour to the Stream.
> The stream at once preserves her virgin leaves,
> At once a shelter from her boughs receives,
> Where *Summer's* beauty midst of *Winter* stays,
> And *Winter's* Coolness spite of *Summer's* rays.

As in "The Rape of the Lock," nature's masculine violence requires this civilized arranging of natural resources so that they collaborate in bringing forth the best from one another. Daphne must "vindicate" ("protect") herself from the "rape" of the sun, as sunlight must be diffused by Belinda's curtains to be admissible to the boudoir. The act of turning from the sun, caught by the gardener-poet in such a telling moment, lies at the heart both of Pope's pastoralism and of Augustan poetic, which depends upon the balance between reckless nature and careful art. In setting summer and winter against each other, the gardener has removed the sting from their hostility and converted their warfare into an architectural symmetry: winter and summer, beauty and coolness, masculine invasion and feminine retreat assume their places—exactly corresponding places in the last couplet with its reversal of positions. All told, the final lines offer a gentle image of cooperation among elements in the control of an artist capable of diverting fierce onslaughts into an energy-charged form.

If we return to "The Rape of the Lock," with this reconciliation of art and nature and the transformation of brute power into structured grace in mind, it becomes clear that Belinda and the baron err in pursuing artifice and primitive aggressiveness separately. What nature and art require is a balanced reciprocity. The incipient order of nature makes the aesthetic transcendence of nature possible, as Belinda's beauty makes a beautiful poem possible. But it is not enough in itself, and again a defense of eighteenth-century gentility is implicit in the further advance that such gentility makes toward art in its mannered imitations of art. The relapse of the two principal actors is surprising because so uncharacteristic. Good breeding and gentility distinguishes them from the countryfild types that Pope satirizes in realistic pastoralists like Ambrose Philips —whose subjects stand much too far off from poetry to be enshrined in it, especially in the artifices of pastoral convention. An assault by one of Gay's mock-realistic rustics, for instance, would not be surprising or even necessary, because such nymphs as Blouzelinda do not "vindicate" themselves from nature's assault: they embrace it willingly. Belinda's lord, however, is compelled by "strange" motives, and Belinda herself takes leave of her manners when, rather than remaining passive and admirable as she should, she rises from the cosmetic table burning to encounter knights and defeat them.

It is interesting that she makes a card game the instrument of her attack because, in their reflections of the aristocratic order, the cards themselves mirror a latent potential for envious strive in a competitive society—even while they normally render that potential harmless. Releasing that potential and destroying the safeguards of the game, Belinda allows the vanity of the private rites of the boudoir to erupt in a full-fledged public sniping at rivals and superiors. Intrigue, cheating, and open rebellion are in a sense "in the cards" waiting to be released. Naturalistic impluses (including the repressed sexual energy of Belinda herself) shake loose the restraints ordinarily

imposed by the public masquerade. The "rebel-Knave" en-
gages his prince, and "The Knave of Diamonds tries his wily
arts / And wins (oh shameful Chance!) the Queen of Hearts":

> *Clubs, Diamonds, Hearts,* in wild Disorder seen,
> With Throngs promiscuous strow the level Green.
> Thus when dispers'd a routed Army runs
> Of *Asia's* Troops, and *Africk's* Sable Sons,
> With like Confusion different Nations fly,
> Of various Habit and of various Dye,
> The pierc'd Battalions dis-united fall,
> In Heaps on Heaps; one Fate o'er whelms them all.
>
> [iii.75–86]

The poet sees that an upset hierarchy is chaos on all levels,
from disrupted government to miscegenation. Rather than
holding opposites apart and in structure by social arrangement,
this promiscuity creates confused variation, disunited lumps of
reality. Black, yellow, and white men run to a single fate, un-
making both nature and artifice.

But it is fortunate, too, that a relatively polite society (which
in spite of everything this still is) wars only at cards rather
than taking up the sword in earnest. There is consolation in
one's not requiring epic heroes and in not encountering "various habit" and "various dye" in vulgar person. In a sense, then,
Pope renders the assault on propriety as harmless as he can
by treating it in mock-heroic spirit. Game is enfolded within
game until the light wand of poetry is felt to have cleansed
the entire social fabric with wit and aesthetic distillation—
without having been untrue to the bitter realities underneath.
If Belinda invites the assault (much as Tasso's Silvia, according to the worldly-wise Thyrsis, wants Aminta to be forceful
and that is why she flees), the assault when it comes is after all
still no more than the snipping of a lock. Nothing is at stake
beyond a momentary shattering of decorum.

And that mild disturbance certainly is too little to justify
Clarissa's moralistic stance, which is nearly as disrupting as the
dreadful act itself—not because she is wrong but because she
has the bad taste to wreck a masquerade. It does not matter to
her whether locks are curled or uncurled, whether faces are

painted or unpainted, so long as the soul has merit. By destroying Ariel's "charms" in a drab and imageless virtue, Clarissa would remove all that stands between a well-adorned coquette and a mere Blouzelinda, who knows only too well that one who is perishable must barter quickly. Pope allows this intrusion of common sense to stand as good counsel for those who prefer plain nature; but meanwhile the muse has seen the ascension of the lock with "quick poetic eyes"—and with it the possibility of making something that will last forever:

> When those fair Suns shall sett, as sett they must,
> And all those Tresses shall be laid in Dust;
> *This Lock,* the Muse shall consecrate to Fame,
> And mid'st the Stars inscribe *Belinda's* Name!
> [v.147–150]

Only such an inscribing is consecrated enough that in desiring it even adventurous barons may transcend the possessive self. When they reach for actual possession, they merely tear at the thin fabric of social artifice; but in beholding the unreachable star they are tempted out of themselves, teased into thoughts of eternity. If in gardening, the shade of well-placed trees prevents the assault of "piercing Day," in poetry the muse carries its subject beyond assault altogether and turns back to rain gentle light upon us. Thus the muse holds the crystal equipage of the poem mocking and unreachable and at the same time leaves the poem in communication with the world it has transformed. The poem is "propitious" and displays a consoling permanence to those who realize that nature lays all things in dust, and in this final aspect of art's holy rites, cosmic and cosmetic dimensions meet: the lock at least, if not the coquette herself, belongs to Ariel, who holds it rapt (carried off from reality) where nothing will violate it again.

RUSTIC PARODY

Pope's mock-epic version of the ascendant lock is a brilliant adjustment between high art and the beau monde, central to which is the civilizing function of the poem that patches up a quarrel and at the same time purifies its materials and enshrines them in the firmament. But this transformation of the lock is also ambivalent inasmuch as both makers and readers of poems remain earthly creatures gazing at the finished product from a distance; if art is an enclosed and remote order untouchable by shock and change, it may strike us as Keats's urn strikes the poet, as "cold pastoral," beyond use as well as beyond time. The romantics will wish to take poetry more earnestly, and the effects on the audience, too, will be stronger when Keats and Shelley turn back to the audience and suggest that what the ideality of art reveals and is we may ourselves become. Keats's heaven's bourne and Shelley's golden age partake of the permanent radiance of poetry but are intended as achievable conditions. The distinction between Augustan and Romantic views of both the poem and the ideal reciprocity of art and nature is not as firm as the terms Augustan and Romantic suggest, however. Nor does Pope indicate the variety of eighteenth-century pastoral, which from one point of view is a series of skirmishes between variously allied and opposed camps. Thomas Tickell, Ambrose Philips, John Gay, Jonathan Swift, and James Thomson represent quite different views of pastoral, while George Crabbe passes judgment on all aspects of the tradition from his own perspective. These elements of eighteenth-century pastoral are too numerous and too complex for us to examine closely (in what is intended as a bridging chapter between renaissance and romantic pastorals), but to understand the romantic reaction to them we should be aware of them.

In the general disagreement between what James E. Congleton describes as "rationalist" (realist) and "neo-classical" (formalist and ornamental) theories of pastoral, Pope sides with the latter and offers mock praise of Ambrose Philips's brand of rusticity. He cites such lines as "Rager go vetch tha Kee, or else tha Zun / Will quite be go, be vore c'have half a don" as models of eloquence. (A few years later he might have done well with Ramsay's "Me dorty Jenny looks upon asquint / . . . an' unco blate.") But the main scrimmages in the mock-rustic

vein fall to Swift and Gay, who expand the scope of the eclogue to encompass all manner of crudeness in both country
and town scenes. Swift's "A Description of the Morning" and
"A Description of a City Shower," for instance, upend the
sense of reverence and comfort that usually accompanies pastoral description with images of water washing from a con-
duit and sweeping out "Drown'd puppies, stinking sprats,
all drench'd in mud, / Dead cats, and turnip tops . . .
tumbling down the flood." "A Town Eclogue" presents a
loose-living nymph and her "shepherd" in a compromising
light. In "Strephon and Chloe," a nymph who has never felt
the call of nature until her wedding night scatters the amazed
Cupids who hover around her, "For fine ideas vanish fast, /
While all the gross and filthy last." Such is the "universal
light" of nature. The satiric effect of these shifts of scene and
descriptive detail is to mock both pastoral conventions in general and the comparative realism of the rationalist theory, as
though to say, "if you are going to be truthful about common
people, this is what you come to."

When all pretense is stripped aside, however, "civilization"
too, as Gulliver discovers, becomes a nightmarish rather than
a rational alternative to primitivism. Not content merely with
burlesques of rusticity, Swift tends to cross party lines and
expose human failings in general. Barbarism and civilized
crudeness, whether the barbarism of the Yahoo or of "the
politest court of Europe," are both ever-present and inevitable.
Hence, whatever Swift's position with respect to the difference
in taste between the neoclassical and rationalist pastoral theo-
rists, he offers little consolation either to those who find hope
in the "natural" man or to those who look to the tinsel politeness of Belinda-like society to extract something divinely
bright from nature.

Much closer to Pope's own satiric spirit is the burlesque of
Gay's pastorals. The difference between Swift and Gay in this
respect can be seen in part in the proper names they give to
the places and types they attack. Lilliput, Blefuscu, Laputa,
Glubbdubdrib, Luggnagg, and Struldbrug multiply vulgarity
with polysyllabic, spitting, gutteral, and quasi-scientific labels,

like forms of verbal nosethumbing appropriate to universal corruption and violence. More in the manner of Fielding's "Huncamunca," Gay's names suggest pretentious elegance: whereas "Hunc" or "munca" alone might suggest a merely sensual and rather forward nymph, "Huncamunca" gives her insufferable airs as a social pretender. Thus with Cloddipole, Buxoma, Blouzelinda, Sparabella, Hobnelia, Clumsilis, Bumkinet, Grubbinol, and Bowzybeus, which graft Virgil onto Spenser as if milkwomen, cobblers, local plowboys, and raisers of pigs were claiming a Latinate cultural elegance. It is partly intended as medicine for those inclined to make poet-laureates out of the likes of Stephen Duck.

Despite this discrimination in Gay's satiric aim, the social attitudes that he embraces are by no means simple. It is difficult to describe the point of such exercises in ambiguity as *The What D'Ye Call It: A Tragicomi-pastoral Farce,* a bad play with a good preface, which parodies a plenitude of literary attitudes and forms. Gay remarks that because its youths are amorous before wedlock and the damsels prodigiously fruitful, it is a pastoral (in keeping with the wholesome lustiness of the clods in *The Shepherd's Week*); its sentiments are those of the meanest clowns, which aligns it with farce, and being pompous as well, it is forced beyond a creditable imitation of nature, which adds the inflated manner of the "heroic" modes as a prime target. All these taken together suggest that Gay was taking aim at staginess in all forms. Pastoral is only a prominent example.

It may also be that Gay's ironic playing with various genres is meant merely to throw readers off the scent of some much simpler proposition—as that, in whatever form, rustics are still rustic and hence inappropriate subjects for serious art. But if the attitude of *The What D'Ye Call It* is that simple, Gay makes an elaborate joke of it; and one could counter with his more or less straightforward pastorals, such as *Dione* and *Acis and Galatea,* which portray unironically refined nymphs and golden age shepherds without giving them Pinocchio's privilege of changing from puppets to live creatures.[2] Likewise, the

[2] Bertrand H. Bronson appropriately suggests concerning *Acis and Galatea* that "full realization of character is not . . . the

genuinely rustic plowmen and damsels of "Rural Sports" are presented straightforwardly, in this case as models of the simple life. There seem to be adequate grounds for saying, then, that rather than merely demonstrating disdain for rustics, Gay's mock-humble forms exploit discrepancies among classes and require the incongruity of sophistication and country simplicity—or of thieves who are noble and nobles who are rogues —to furnish the front and back sides of wit. The central target is as often the hypocrite as the farmyard lout or the damsel of loose virtue. As *The Beggars Opera* illustrates, Gay managed to play one social attitude off against another with great dexterity and involution; but it is not surprising that he managed that complexity with complete success only once, or that other eighteenth-century pastoralists never quite managed it at all.

His ambivalence toward rusticity and artifice produces interesting if less impressive results in *The Shepherd's Week*. Published a year after "Rural Sports" and two years before "Trivia" (which concerns city diversions), it derives too much pleasure from the burlesque and from the lusty crudeness of rustics to be taken seriously as a satire of rusticity only. The preface is a mock pretense of distaste for polite pastoral, but as so often in Gay's complex tactics, the parody cuts both ways: mock objections to elegance are allowed to become effective before the mock praise of "downright" peasants has had a chance to register. All satiric points are reduced to playfulness:

Verily, as little pleasance receiveth a true homebred taste, from all the fine finical new-fangled fooleries of this gay Gothic garniture, wherewith they so nicely bedeck their court clowns, or clown courtiers . . . as would a prudent citizen journeying to his country farms, should he find them occupied by people of this motely make, instead of plain downright hearty cleanly folk.

---

object of this kind of writing, and indeed could only defeat it" and that Gay's strategy "to represent a single state of mind in each aria, so that by the sum of these successive personifications of emotion the whole character becomes known." "The True Proportions of Gay's 'Acis and Galatea,' " *PMLA*, 80 (1965), 327–328. The pleasure of the opera lies chiefly in its theatricality and musical form.

Likewise, much of the parody in the eclogues themselves is directed toward the conventions of pastoral verse in general, so that the correction of taste can work two ways: it can suggest either that poets find more suitable modes for the imitation of gentility than pastoral offers, or that, if they insist on writing about such rustics as Lobbin Clout, they do so in an appropriate realistic style.

In point of emphasis, of course, Gay gains more diversion in *The Shepherd's Week* from parodying rural realism than from other satiric exercises, and he does so primarily by moving the focus of pastoral description to closeups—to sniff the breath of cows, savor Buxoma's thick food, and listen to the wail of Sparabella's songs. He makes the concept of "humble glory" appear a contradiction in terms:

> But now, alas! these ears shall hear no more
> The whining swine surround the dairy door,
> No more her care shall fill the hollow tray,
> To fat the guzzling hogs with floods of whey.
> Lament, ye swine, in grunting spend your grief,
> For you, like me, have lost your sole relief.
>
> ["Friday"]

Typically, the main sport is to exploit the contrast between the formal movement (of the pastoral dirge in this case) and the guzzling and grunting of rural life. The damage done to pastoral conventions is secondary to that done to the glorification of rustics; but Gay also gives a slight twist to many of the elegancies of Pope's couplet so that nothing fits quite snugly. Merely by changing swine to sheep and whining and grunting to tender bleating, we would have an elegant if somewhat mechanical period pastoral, cast in creditable heroic couplets. The excess of *r*'s and *d*'s in the second line might pass unnoticed, but the dissonance of "whining swine," is calculated to set the nerves on edge. The animality that underlies the final description of appetite spins elegiac grief into laughter. Thus Gay serves it all up with such polish (almost with beauty), that we are led to ponder the form itself, which is too obviously exploitable for the adornment of such things.

THOMSON AND CRABBE

For poetry was all written before time was, and whenever we
are so finely organized that we can penetrate into that region
where the air is music, we hear those primal warblings, and
attempt to write them down, but we lose ever and anon a
word, or a verse, and substitute something of our own, and
thus miswrite the poem. . . . For nature is as truly beautiful
as it is good. [Emerson, "The Poet"]

At the opposite extreme from Gay's detached, ironic play
with pastoral's attempt to combine artifice with rustic nature is
the unplayful seriousness of Thomson and Crabbe, one predominantly a poet of natural sublimity, the other of rural and
village realism. In a sense Thomson and Crabbe represent
extremes in the spectrum of possibilities that one could imagine for pastoral in their times. Whereas Pope's attendant spirits
are minor genii who carry a modest but beautiful lock into the
galaxy, every object that Thomson's attendant graces collect
is aggrandized by its inclusion in the poetic firmament, yet
Thomson is totally without Pope's sophisticated sense of the
transformations that art imposes on nature in arranging it,
decorating it, and saving it from the world of time and decay.
And whereas Swift and Gay are astutely aware of the problem
with rustics and treat them with a disdain that places all the
blame on any man who chooses to be animalistic, Crabbe has
an unironic sympathy with his workers and villagers. Both
Thomson and Crabbe at times thus drop (or rise, depending
on one's point of view) out of the range of pastoral contrasts;
they exclude each other and they exclude the mixed pastoral
attitudes that enable Swift, Pope, and Gay to juxtapose the
standards and decorum of graceful elegance with the actualities
of rustic life—and sometimes the grander potentials of sublimity. At the same time they might be said to prepare separately for Wordsworth's fusion of rustic realism and natural
sublimity. From this angle, both of them appear one dimen-
sional and sometimes inadequate as pastoralists and yet necessary to the freeing of pastoral from its conventions and to the

evolution of a new pastoral in Wordsworth and the romantics. Certainly they play a more vital role in future pastoral contrasts than the Augustans, who in retrospect represent the last gasp of aristocratic attitudes originating in Italian and French court pastorals.

That Thomson illustrates typical pastoral attitudes without the old conventions or much stress on pastoral contrasts is evident enough to need no demonstration. What is more interesting is the manner in which he elevates and transforms landscapes without recourse usually to myths of Eden, the golden age, or other pastoral fictions. The mood of *The Seasons* is idyllic in the sense that the poem absorbs nature into a preconceived style that dissolves its contrasts and antitheses, its temporal movement, and its moments of harshness into a single sublime continuum. Though Thomson was taken in the eighteenth and nineteenth centuries as a realist whose subject was "nature as it is" (J. Logie Robertson, for instance, writes of his "fidelity to nature" and concludes that "a love for nature is synonymous with a love for Thomson"),[3] his descriptive technique does not set precisely defined objects off from one another. The poem creates its impressions of the good place partly by doing away with boundaries and partly by attaching an emotion proper to large prospects to each part in them, "aggrandizing" the part into the whole. Although the admission of one item at a time to a typical landscape appears to make certain passages catalogs of dividual items, the bounded particles flow toward a point of fusion in the sublimity of the total prospect, which is Thomson's real interest. This sublimity implicitly rejects the Augustan balance of art and nature and its companion assumption that nature's crudeness requires the controls and improvements of art. Whereas transcendentalists such as Thoreau and Emerson often oppose the unity of a landscape to the petty holdings of farmer Jones and Smith (who have fenced parts of it), the owners of Thomson's nature are seldom visible: topography remains independent of any household, landed gentry, or the skills of the gardener.

[3] J. Logie Robertson, ed., *The Complete Poetical Works of James Thomson* (London: Oxford University Press, 1908), p. xi.

Distinctions between science and poetry also dissolve as both are drawn into the divine continuum beyond partitioned time and space, distinct properties, or structured relationships. Partition, enumeration, parallels and contrasts, causal sequences, and other devices of analytical thought and expression that deal with the many give way to a language appropriate to a celebration of the one.

Where Thomson's interest in science is involved, however, they do not always do so gracefully because science depends upon enumeration and boundary and these consort strangely with poetic enthusiasm. The poet's invocations, which are ode-like anticipations of sublimity, frequently lead merely to encyclopedic lists, and the seer and the enumerator remain somewhat at odds:

> Say, then where lurk the vast eternal springs
> That, like creating Nature, lie concealed
> From mortal eye, yet with their lavish stores
> Refresh the globe and all its joyous tribes?
> O thou pervading genius, given to man
> To trace the secrets of the dark abyss!
> Oh! lay the mountains bare, and wide display
> Their hidden structure to the astonished view.
>
> ["Autumn," 773-780]

Following this preparation, though the emotion remains appropriate to a Prospect-of-the-World, Thomson offers an anticlimactic description of fluids seeping into rock strata, of chalk, retentive earth, and condensed vapors.

Ordinarily, the speaker, fully prepared to be transported, knows that wherever he begins—among groves or hay fields—the prospect will draw him toward the universal Poem. The lists are designed to make a gesture toward that totality, whether the scene is attractive or desolate:

> Fled is the blasted verdure of the fields;
> And, shrunk into their beds, the flowery race
> Their sunny robes resign. Even what remained
> Of bolder fruits falls from the naked tree;
> And—woods, fields, gardens, orchards, all round—
> The desolated prospect thrills the soul.

> He comes! he comes! in every breeze the Power
> Of Philosophic Melancholy comes!
>
> ["Autumn," 998–1005]

Overlaying Thomson's response to the particulars of desolation is again the sense of a universal energy or "power" that melts each scene and each season, until discrete details abandon their properties and join the harmonious aggregate; the seasons flow into an endless Golden Age perpetually forming itself, even out of "blasted verdure" and melancholy.

Echoes of Milton further demonstrate this transformational fluidity, ironically by contrast to Milton's usually distinct properties, which Adam, for instance, names one by one. Thomson's sun is less a member of an articulated cosmos whose hierarchy requires the exact stationing of every created object than a spiritual overforce drawing what is below up to it in its oneness:

> Lo! now, apparent all,
> Aslant the dew-bright earth and coloured air,
> He looks in boundless majesty abroad,
> And sheds the shining day, that burnished plays
> On rocks, and hills, and towers, and wandering streams
> High-gleaming from afar. Prime chearer, Light!
> Of all material beings first and best!
> Efflux divine! Nature's resplendent robe,
> Without whose vesting beauty all were wrapt
> In unessential gloom, and thou, O Sun!
> Soul of surrounding worlds! in whom best seen
> Shines out thy Maker! may I sing of thee?
> 'Tis by thy secret, strong, attractive force,
> As with a chain indissoluble bound,
> Thy system rolls entire.
>
> ["Summer," 85–99]

Whereas nature's emblems operate on two levels in Milton, reflecting God but also maintaining their distance, in Thomson the sun itself becomes godlike, a "strong, attractive" quickener of "brute unlovely mass, inert and dead." Light is the inward "Soul" and "informer" as well as the outer clothing of the scene, instilling life in the mass not by ordinary chemistry but by a "quickening glance." [4] Thomson does not alter the separated, geographical aspect of these items; he moves the focus ever upward.

It is true that despite the continual collapse of "part" into "all," the poem is often dualistic. On one hand, Thomson thinks of "evil" in terms of chronological succession, from the Golden Age to "these iron times" ("Spring," 274) and in terms of the traditional dualism of passion and reason. On the other hand, these suggestions of nonidyllic elements are seldom allowed to intrude upon the celebration of nature's inherent Poem; they are a "forbidden" subject:

> High Heaven forbids the bold presumptuous strain,
> Whose wisest will has fixed us in a state
> That must not yet in pure perfection rise.
> ["Spring," 374–376]

Within the framework of the sublime idyll, the poem can paint winter horrors and express sympathy with the "good distressed" without calling into question the fundamental bounty of the universal garden. Thus the hardships of shepherds in the cold are submerged in the general celebration of winter's animating power:

> What art thou, frost? . . .
> Is not the potent energy, unseen,
> Myriads of little salts, or hooked, or shaped
> Like double wedges, and diffused immense
> Through water, earth, and ether . . .
>   The loosened ice,

[4] Thomson makes use of Miltonic rhythm, syntax, and shifts in perspective to lend such passages a sense of epic dignity. The appearance of "The powerful king of day" is set off by "Lo!" and prepared for by two adjective phrases, "apparent all" and "aslant the dew-bright earth and coloured air." Thus announced with a flourish, it "looks in boundless majesty abroad." At the same time, short exclamations counteract the long sentence and the intellectual sobriety of Latinate phrasing so that pensive joy and joyful melancholy fuse; they become in a sense emotional solvents answerable to a grandeur to which one reacts with awe rather than a light heart.

Let down the flood and half dissolved by day,
Rustles no more; but to the sedgy bank
Fast grows, or gathers round the pointed stone,
A crystal pavement, by the breath of heaven
Cemented firm; till, seized from shore to shore,
The whole imprisoned river growls below . . .
      Then appears
The various labour of the silent night—
Prone from the dripping eave, and dumb cascade,
Whose idle torrents only seem to roar,
The pendent icicle; the frost-work fair,
Where transient hues and fancied figures rise;
Wide-spouted o'er the hill the frozen brook,
A livid tract, cold-gleaming on the morn;
The forest bent beneath the plumy wave;
And by the frost refined the whiter snow
Incrusted hard, and sounding to the tread
Of early shepherd, as he pensive seeks
His pining flock, or from the mountain top,
Pleased with the slippery surface, swift descends.

                                ["Winter," 714-759]

Frost energy is another manifestation of the Poem's life-force,
disclosing "infinite worlds" intensely "keen." Though the question "What art thou, frost?" is answered semiscientifically, in
terms of energy and molecules, the gale is a kind of quickening spirit. Frost creates new shapes, make the brook a "livid
tract," and covers the forest with "plumy" wave. The shepherd's labor, amid the bright solidity of the frost-poem, is a
joy to him. The erasing of distinctions in sublimity thus works
on behalf of contentment; each alike has the sun in the morning and the moon at night:

    Ye good distressed!
Ye noble few! who here unbending stand
Beneath life's pressure, yet bear up a while,
And what your *bounded* view, which only saw
A little part, deemed evil is no more:
The storms of wintry time will quickly pass,
And one *unbounded* Spring encircle all.

                                 ["Winter," 1063-1069]

Though *The Seasons* looks forward to the romantic concept
of the dignity of the "natural" man in this way and anchors

that dignity in nature's sublimity, in other respects it is as conservative as "The Castle of Indolence," in which Thomson
awkwardly transfers the energy of the "universe" to the
Knight of Arts and Industry. In the latter poem, the poet pic-
tures himself as a humble worker as well as a nature enthusiast:

> I care not, fortune, what you me deny:
> You cannot rob me of free nature's grace;
> You cannot shut the windows of the sky,
> Through which Aurora shows her brightening face.
> [2.3-7]

(Thomson retracts part of it later: "But now, alas! we live too
late in time: / Our patrons now even grudge that little claim,
/ Except to such as sleek the soothing rhyme" [2.22].) Assuming that the enterprise of the knight of industry taps the same
powers as the poet who transforms individual phenomena into
universal beauty, Thomson can celebrate them both together.[5]

The difficulty in praising both nature and industry, as the
American transcendentalists discover later, is that industry ap-
propriates the poet's nature for use, removing it from the continuity of forms that points the poet toward the "efflux divine."
As soon as one begins to think of a productive economy, the
fictions of pastoral, especially the character of the humble or
rustic figure, undergo a profound change. Actually, in both

[5] Alan Dugald McKillop points out that "The Castle of Indolence" concerns two kinds of indolence, luxuriousness and philosophic quiet. Hence, "on one level *The Castle of Indolence* repudi-
ates ambition and indulges in reverie, on another level it disowns
the reverie and reasserts ambition." *The Castle of Indolence and
Other Poems* (Lawrence: University of Kansas Press, 1961), p. 6.
The ideal combination of (social) art and nature Thomson describes in a letter to Elizabeth Young (August 29, 1743) concerning Lyttelton's Hagley Park: "Nor is the Society here inferior to
the Scene. It is gentle, animated, pleasing. Nothing passes but
what either tends to amuse the Imagination, improve the Head,
or better the Heart. This is the truly happy Life, this Union of
Retirement and choice Society: it gives an Idea of that which the
Patriarchal or Golden Age is supposed to have been" (p. 39).
Cf. Raymond D. Havens, "Primitivism and the Idea of Progress in
Thomson," *SP*, 29 (1932), 41-52.

georgic and pastoral, the tension between the industrial use of nature and nature as an avatar comes to focus in the rustic, who may be either a victim of an economic condition or the first recipient of nature's spiritual blessings, depending upon whether one thinks "poetically" or "realistically."

When Thomson pauses to sympathize with simple life, *The Seasons* anticipates not only Wordsworth's romantic enthusiasm for nature as a spiritual revelation but also the concern with the daily life of the humble, which characterizes George Crabbe. The moments when he does so are comparatively rare, however, and it is left to Crabbe to make a pronounced break with conventional expectations of rusticity and to concentrate on the economic man exclusive of pastoral fictions and the landscapes of indolent pleasure and sublimity. Whereas in Thomson the admixture of realism is not allowed to undermine the natural Poem that the aggregate of objects and the seasonal flow compose, to Crabbe the particulars of nature accumulate into a detailed correction of "mechanic echoes of the Mantuan song." They bring with them no sense of the "efflux divine" that Thomson finds finally the supreme consolation for poverty (as Frost and Stevens later will seek for consolations for modern economic men in the blessings of imaginative fictions). If "The muses sing of happy swains," Crabbe suggests, it is only "because the muses never knew their pains." As to industry and the economic order generally, he stresses their debilitating realities and grim future. Whatever bounty nature yields—and it is never sufficient—it seldom finds its way into the hands of the village poor. Crabbe's pastoral is thus largely without ceremony, and his georgic elements are without those answerable responses between men and nature that make the georgic life so rewarding in Virgil. Nor is "art" likely to dress nature to advantage for the average villager. Neither the Augustan garden nor the wide prospect of eighteenth-century sublimity is of any use to those whose lives are a sequence of drunkenness, sickness, and hunger.

That the "luxurious lord" is as wretched in his way as his servants exposes any pretense one might make to "natural" elegance or the superiority of a cultivated life:

> Yet why, you ask, these humble crimes relate,
> Why make the poor as guilty as the great?
> To show the great, those mightier sons of pride,
> How near in vice the lowest are allied;
> Such are their natures and their passions such,
> But these disguise too little, those too much:
> So shall the man of power and pleasure see
> In his own slave as vile a wretch as he;
> In his luxurious lord the servant find
> His own low pleasures and degenerate mind:
> And each in all the kindred vices trace,
> Of a poor, blind, bewilder'd erring race,
> Who, a short time in varied fortune past,
> Die, and are equal in the dust at last.

Though the last couplet treats the discrepancy between low and high as a merely temporary affair, the satire is nonetheless pointed and the elegiac note enriches it rather than diverting it into helpless resignation. The case for the humble villager is weakened, however, by stylistic concessions to those whom Crabbe expects to judge him as a poet. Descriptive passages, as opposed to didactic passages like the one quoted, are frequently a mixture of elegance and bluntness:

> Here, wand'ring long, amid those frowning fields
> I sought the simple life that Nature yields;
> Rapine and wrong and fear usurp'd her place,
> And a bold, artful, surly, savage race;
> Who, only skill'd to take the finny tribe,
> The yearly dinner, or septennial bribe,
> Wait on the shore, and, as the waves run high,
> On the tost vessel bend their eager eye,
> Which to their coast directs its vent'rous way;
> Theirs, or the ocean's miserable prey.

"Finny tribe" is somewhat too comfortable for the scene, and "bend their eager eye" is what sportsmen might do rather than rapacious and hungry fishermen hoping for a shipwreck. Other details suggest a certain shrewdness in Crabbe's tactics, however. Certainly "tribe" rings queerly against "bribe": the fishermen have skill in "taking" either kind of game. The sequence "bold, artful, surly, savage," while it does not expose hypocrisy or parody pretensions to elegance, clearly crosses over from one's initial expectation of polite rusticity to an unpoetic frankness. As sharp bargainers, the fishermen must be artful in order to make savagery work for them—which suggests that those who give the yearly dinners and own the tossed vessels may be more closely observed than they realize. Though Crabbe is clearly repelled by the rapacity and callousness of the fishermen, he also sees them as socially problematic and beyond patronizing satire.

We should probably not make too much of Crabbe's self-consciousness in such matters, which seems likely to have been less than Gay's; but that sly ironies are not out of keeping with his manner of approaching what he assumed would be cultivated readers (and possible patrons) is revealed by "The Birth of Flattery," in which a sturdy swain named Poverty, from the humble cottage of Care, marries Cunning, who gives birth to Flattery. Whether such passages as the one quoted are designed to "lift the veil between classes" gently, as a critic in the *Quarterly Review* suggested, or to demonstrate that realism and elegance of style are not incompatible, Crabbe's avowed counterpastoral is cast in a conventional Augustan style. It contains much of the standard diction of eighteenth-century nature poetry, and its artifice suggests the combination of politeness and bluntness in Crabbe's letters to potential patrons, to whom he had to write as a man who has experienced destitution and yet could be counted upon to discuss it in an acceptable manner:

Forgive, my Lord, a free, and perhaps, unusual address; misfortune has in it, I hope, some excuse for presumption. Your Lordship will not, cannot, be greatly displeased with an unfortunate man, whose wants are the most urgent; who wants a friend to assist him, and bread.

I will not tire your Lordship with a recital of the various circumstances which have led to this situation. . . . Starving as an apothecary, in a little venal borough in Suffolk . . .

And so in poetry he adjusted what the cultivated ear expected to hear to what his subject demanded that he say:

> Lo! where the heath, with withering brake grown o'er
> Lends the light turf that warms the neighbouring poor;
> From thence a length of burning sand appears,
> Where the thin harvest waves its wither'd ears;
> Rank weeds, that every art and care defy,
> Reign o'er the land, and rob the blighted rye:
> There thistles stretch their prickly arms afar,
> And to the ragged infant threaten war.

It is a prickly, hostile nature that yields very sparse returns for labor, yet Crabbe precedes his description with a conventional "lo!" and finds an odd friendliness in withered ears that "wave" to us. These details come from a decorum linked to another kind of nature and intended for a "gentle" reader. That the combination was successful in at least part of its intent is indicated by Jeffrey's comment that "Mr. Crabbe exhibits the common people of England pretty much as they are . . . at the same time that he renders his sketches in a very high degree interesting and beautiful." A *Quarterly Review* critic speaks of "that exquisitely finished, but heart-sickening description" of the poor-house in "The Village." [6]

Whether or not the combination of Augustan taste and sympathy for common people works effectively, when we consider Crabbe and Thomson together and review the drift of eighteenth-century pastoral, it becomes clear that any attempt to bring together particularized accounts of nature and the universal spirit of nature with the artifices of conventional pastoral would involve significant stylistic and conceptual difficulties. When later poets seek to combine romantic enthusiasm and realism, they discover that these have all along implied quite different views of historical progress and nature. From Wordsworth's standpoint, much in Thomson's pantheism proved useful and some elements in Crabbe were clearly compatible with his own sympathy for humble figures; but both the meaner realism of Crabbe and the conventional rusticity of Augustan pastoral fail to reflect the spiritual elevation of

[6] George Crabbe, *The Life and Poetical Works* (London, 1901), pp. 116–117.

his subjects. And despite his significant Wordsworthian elements, Thomson does not consider the problems of memory, mortality, and age that are so central to Wordsworthian experience, both in rustic figures and in the poet himself.

The dilemma for each of the romantics in his own way is to reconcile an urge toward transcendence with social entanglements and economic problems, and to evolve a view of historical progress and growth capable of linking personal, spiritual experiences to possible cures of social problems. In neither Thomson nor the eighteenth-century generally is the rustic's inherent, or potential, goodness linked to historical and social progress and given institutional expression. The seasons for Thomson do not unfold a possible new state or spin out cycles of historical recurrence that may return a golden age. They display instead the orderly working of a cosmic creator who constantly attends his works and infuses them with his own energy without close attention to particular instances or the social order. Since any possible personal fulfillment depends upon that dynamic power invested in nature's bounty, the cure for those who are victims of social ills is simply to rediscover divine purpose day by day in its continuous unfolding. Crabbe also ignores both cyclical renewal and progressive or linear movement toward a better time: corrective powers diminish to social institutions, which need first of all to realize what humble life is like. The romantics seek a more encompassing pastoral, free of conventions, capable of drawing together those elements of nature and rustic figures that the eighteenth century left divided.

From another direction, too, eighteenth-century pastoral is a miscellany of dying traditions and of generating but uncrystallized new movements. Whereas the pastorals of the seventeenth century as written by Herbert, Marvell, Milton, Vaughan, and Traherne represent the *locus amoenus* in terms of the cycle from Eden to paradise restored, in contrast, the pastorals of the Restoration and of Swift, Gay, Pope, Thomson, and Crabbe obviously conceive of it as a variety of pleasant places, in a variety of ways, no longer dominated by the Christian-Platonist view—though of course not unmindful of it. Neither Thomson nor Crabbe agrees with the Augustan position that fragments of Eden are restorable by the "gardener" and the poet, who both disclose nature's universal laws and dress them to advantage. (Eden lives again in song, as Pope remarks in "Windsor Forest," and in those special elements of topography properly owned and controlled by one's patrons.) Nor do Swift and Gay suggest any common ground among pastoral's various possibilities in their satiric exploitation of its discrepant ideals and realities and of the perspectives that "rustics" and men of cultivated taste take upon one another. The romantics are therefore forced to forge their own new combinations of humble life, art, and transcendental views of nature. They seek to reconcile the notion of historial progress toward an ideal time with a social consciousness as insistent as Crabbe's. Inevitably, that progress is described in ways more personal and less commonly accepted than Christian and classical views of a golden age that has been or will be. Romantic progress is first of all an individual and personal spiritual growth, as in Keats's "pleasure thermometer" and programmatic realization of heaven's bourne, Wordsworth's growth of a poetic mind in *The Prelude,* and the mind's pursuit of Platonist ideality through and beyond nature's forms in Shelley. The problem is to make these individual psychological and spiritual evolutions also paradigms for a more general progress—and thus to find in them cures for the kind of social ills which Crabbe demands that poetry confront.

These are matters that the next chapter will examine more broadly, but in looking ahead from eighteenth-century versions of pastoral from this modest vantage point, we notice that the tangled legacy they left carries into the nineteenth century. Insofar as the postromantics tend to ignore Platonist idealism and pantheism in the interest of more humanized and limited concepts of the good place, Crabbe has a somewhat larger stake in the future than Thomson: Hardy, at least, entertains little hope of dignifying rustics by association with the "efflux divine" of the seasons. At the same time, later nineteenth-century poets, like the romantics, continue to reject conventional pastoral and to focus upon present nature rather

than fictions of a past or future golden age. Pastoral henceforth finds part of its usefulness in its availability for such
rejection. Its artifice and fictions serve as a convenient foil for
whatever view of harsher realities or whatever rival social idyll
(such as a classless society) that one proposes—though many
rival idylls, Marx's included, look with longing at a noncompetitive, tribal peacefulness—in a sense to a renamed pre-
industrial "Arcadia"—for an ideal model. With the departure
of the idea of an evolved heaven or some other final state at
the end of historical progress, it also becomes possible for the
poet to see the relationship between pastoral fictions and reality
in a new light—to consider, as Stevens suggests, the contribution that such fictions make to limited natural blessings.

Thus by the end of the century, the conflict between pressing social realities, such as Crabbe's rural poverty, and the
kinds of elevated experience that Thomson and the romantics
seek in nature can be explored from a new viewpoint. Whereas
the function of the poet in Thomson is to celebrate an exterior
Poem that he believes discoverable in nature, and in Crabbe
to point out widespread distress (but to do so in an elegant
style somewhat out of keeping with the subject), in Frost and
Stevens the function of the poet becomes in part the use of
fictions to achieve insights into "reality," to try to discover
what it is and how we may conceive of it. The poet in creating fictions can regard imagination and verbal adornment
as vital to those insights. Pastoral more and more links social
affairs not to divine influence and far-off ideal models but to
epistemological problems and levels of the mind; it looks for
the source of the pleasant place in the reconstruing and perfecting vision of the imagination and thus reviews reality from
the perspective of its own inventions. The poet's task in Wallace Stevens's words is to suggest "the possibility of a supreme
fiction, recognized as fiction, in which men [can] propose to
themselves a fulfillment." [7] As one of our more habitual fictions, pastoral is a vital instrument in taking the measure of
reality and proposing new ways of seeing it. Rejected as in

[7] Wallace Stevens, *Letters,* ed. Holly Stevens (New York: Alfred A. Knopf, 1966), p. 820.

any way a mode concerned with literal truths, it may become one of several strategies for placing constructions on reality.

Actually pastoral has always been something like that if my view of it is not entirely wrong, but that fact (if it is a fact) is concealed initially by its traditions and shepherd conventions, concealed again in the literalness with which the Eden myth is taken in the Renaissance—and then concealed still again by the fragmentation of its possibilities in the eighteenth century. Basically, even in these periods, pastoral is a mode for the proposing of a fulfillment, in the context of reality's many inventive ways of forcing its way into the best of dreams. It implicitly sets the artfulness of imaginative visions and poetic enclosures against the threats of an actual nature: it sets the dream of perfect landscapes (such as poets invent) against a resistant land of tillage, warfare, class division, and industry.

Looking backward from the perspectives on pastoral fictions that Frost and Stevens provide, we find both the singular unity of the seventeenth-century's idyllic vision and the diversity of eighteenth-century pastoral to be rich in resources but awaiting an exploration of the special nature of poetic myths and their usefulness in testing reality. The versions of the *locus amoenus* that Pope, Gay, Crabbe, and Thomson give us are individually partial and incomplete, and collectively irreconcilable; we could not really expect them to be sorted out until pastoral fictions were allowed to take their place beside other poems "of the mind in the act of finding / What will suffice." My historical point is that in a sense, we, too, cannot understand them unless we step outside them and see their total movement—see that their nature is revealed not just in themselves but in what happens next and in what continues to happen to pastoral fictions. If, even after a century and a half since the romantics and after a prolonged period of serious questioning about the nature of poetry and linguistic structures, we have only begun to understand the use of fictions, it should not surprise us that no pastoral theorist or poet in so divided a period as the eighteenth century ever quite reached all the way around the genre, or that the debate over pastoral took enumerable paths away from the center.

NINE

Industrial and Romantic
Versions of Nature

JOURNEYS TO ARCADIA AND BACK

In this chapter I plan to survey the historical ground of the following chapters in a broad enough fashion to suggest that for various reasons social and transcendental themes and motives have a natural inclination to separate after the eighteenth century, and that they do so more than formerly despite attempts by the romantics to reconcile them. Their separation can be seen in the conflict between romantic and industrial views of nature and in the collision in certain novels between owning nature and experiencing nature as a symbolic landscape. Postromantic pastoral, too, consists to some extent in an attempt to find a means to unite them—or at least minimize the impact of their separation.

Unlike romance heroes and royal shepherds who journey to or dwell in a dreamlike atmosphere immune from many of the problems of complex societies, the heroes of Daniel Defoe, Samuel Richardson, and Jane Austen pursue largely contractual ends—an advantageous marriage, a middle-class standing, a productive plantation in Virginia, a string of island enterprises in the New World. Equally distant from older heroes of romance but in the opposite direction is the hero of the romantics who seeks a spiritual completion, usually beyond social or institutional endowments, perhaps beyond even time and change. The heroes of Shelley and Keats often aim at a match with a symbol of transcendence such as Endymion's moon goddess or Alastor's "kindred spirit." Their programs of spiritualization rely largely on the tutelary powers of the imagination and Platonist idealism.

210

Such a distinction among heroic types and among modes is too broad and commonplace in itself to be of much value, but it is instructive in gauging the difficulty that romantic figures have in returning to the habitual self after their transcendental adventures. A generic association as firmly settled as that between romantic idealism and social realism provides both novelists and poets with opportunities to work against the grain, as when Keats's mortal fever and time obstruct the poet's realization of "heaven's bourne," or as in Wordsworth's impairments of the imagination and Blake's London, industry, authority, and sexual strife.

As we have seen, the predecessors of romanticism were not entirely successful in finding a suitable agreement between social organizations and idyllic dreams. When allowed to follow his own inclinations, Spenser's Colin Clout stands apart from society conjuring visions of dancing graces in the land of Pastorella, and Calidore, too, takes leave of the duties of a defender of courtesy in order to approach those visions; in returning to court he cannot take the simple life of Pastorella with him. Likewise, Sidney's Musidorus and Pyrocles must leave Arcadia in order to resume their chivalric functions. In Shakespeare's pastoral comedies, the exiled society gains a good deal from nature and the forces of imagination and magic to which it has been exposed. But a miraculous reversal of society's disrupters is required before its problems will disappear, and its courtly elements obviously consider the green world only a temporary retreat despite the advantages one may gain from it.

The difficulty in finding an effective balance between idyllic dreams and the everyday functions of complex societies is increased when paradise becomes a distant Eden or future paradise, which are all the more unreachable and hostile to business as usual. We have seen Marvell's difficulty in uniting pastoral myth and politics, and glanced at Milton's abandonment of politics in *Paradise Regained*. The Augustan pastoralists set an easier task for themselves by seeking models of an ideal nature closer to home, in their own gardens, perhaps, or close by in someone's estate, which they find analogous to

Eden but much more available. Most topographical poetry of
the eighteenth century, in fact, retains some possibility of mirroring the social order in nature and in doing so methodizes
nature according to its taste. The river Thames in Sir John
Denham's *Coopers Hill,* for instance, mirrors divinity, monarchy, and an ideal poetry all at once:

> But God-like his unwearied Bounty flows;
> First loves to do, then loves the Good he does.
> Nor are his Blessings to his banks confin'd,
> But free, and common, as the Sea or Wind. . . .
> O could I flow like thee, and make thy stream
> My great example, as it is my theme!
> Though deep, yet clear, though gentle, yet not dull,
> Strong without rage, without ore-flowing full.

The river is comparable to God because bountiful, to kings
and to poetic styles because majestic and contained within rational bounds. Again in "Windsor Forest," the scene is "so-
cialized" and provides the poet with an easy return to society
—which he has never really left. Nature itself models the best
of art and politics and invites a particular kind of song:

> Thy forest, Windsor! and thy green retreats,
> At once the Monarch's and the Muse's seats,
> Invite my lays. . . .
>   Thy groves of Eden, vanished now so long,
> Live in description, and look green in song:
> These, were my breast inspired with equal flame,
> Like them in Beauty, should be like in Fame.

Insofar as the poet is successful in discovering the original
Forms of nature in Windsor that were once manifest in Eden,
he undoes the fall and establishes, not an adamic frame of
mind perhaps but a proprietor's fame and a symbolic model
of order-in-variety applicable to other areas of social activity.

The romantic shift to private experiences of nature does not
change the basic difficulty of adjusting natural, transcendent,
and social standards to one another. It makes the journey out
and back more dramatic and minimizes direct transactions

between the social contract and poetry's high aspirations. The poet's symbolic pursuit of the skylark, nightingale, or west wind is essentially a movement of mind and imagination, as he speaks lyrically to himself or in odic address to the object.

That movement and address are typical of others besides the romantics, of course. Yeats's journey to ancient Byzantium, for instance, also leaves behind the ordinary condition of nature and in its final stage requires timely help from sages standing in "God's holy fire," beyond temporal process and mortal sickness. The aging speaker calls down these divine agents as the muses of his art and the means of his transformation. His own "studied" words are thus an incantation or invocation to induce them to descend, and Byzantium is a stage for singing, the scene of his transfiguration, where he will sing of things in time—past, or passing, or to come. But there is no guarantee that the sages will perform or that the aging natural man can become golden handiwork. "The Circus Animals' Desertion" later confesses that such masterful figures as the sages are the inventions of the poet's own "pure mind" or improving imagination. In his more realistic moments, the poet knows that his condition calls for another kind of poetry, which begins in

> A mound of refuse or sweepings of a street,
> Old kettles, old bottles, and a broken can,
> Old iron, old bones, old rags. . . .

The pattern of Yeats's later poetry is typical of romanticism in that the farther the trip the poet takes to the ideal place of art and harmony, the greater the recoil when creaturely facts are recalled. Once the poet begins to realize that paradise is located in the private workshop of the imagination rather than those deities and sympathetic streams of Arcadia that the conventional shepherd addresses, he begins to question its validity. He also has a formal difficulty in that, having committed himself to an address to God's holy sages or the skylark, he must then maneuver the audience back into view and convince it of the validity of his private ideal. Yet, in turning aside to an audience, he threatens to break the form of the address and risks prophetic utterance that has no authority beyond his (or the Grecian urn's or west wind's) power of assertion. Whereas the old eclogue expresses a continuous, usually low-key dramatic negotiation between the ideal and the real, the romantic ode and mythological narrative are high modes of supplication, followed frequently by ironic recognitions of the poet's mortal capabilities. The high tone is dramatically appropriate and grows out of the ascending impulse of the poem, but it is also based on vulnerable private experience. Shelley's golden age, Wordsworth's evenings of extraordinary splendor, and Keats's heaven's bourne remain their special, private visions. If in fact Yeats's speaker becomes the immortalized singer of songs, what relationship does he have with drowsy emperors who receive his prophetic messages with scarcely open eyelids? Where is Shelley at the end of "Adonais," or the poet-shepherd at the end of "Endymion"? If the poet attempts to translate his vision into more definite public programs, becoming an "unacknowledged legislator of mankind," he claims a social therapy for poetry that places a very heavy burden upon private dreams. And the poet who does invite the public into the world of his ideals for its edification or entertainment, as Lycius does in "Lamia," may find his dream-labor shattered by the intrusion.

TRANSCENDENTALISM AND MAGIC

The transcendentalists illustrate perhaps the most conspicuous translation from one level of experience to another. Ralph Waldo Emerson remarks, "I leave village politics and personalities, yes and the world of villages and personalities behind, and pass into a delicate realm of sunset and moonlight, too bright almost for spotted man to enter without noviciate and probation. We penetrate bodily this incredible beauty." [1] Nature not only beckons him to it but changes its particular masks in a continual marvelous transformation of individual

[1] Ralph Waldo Emerson, "Nature," from *Essays* (New York, 1926), p. 383.

shapes. Standing before the various tablets of history, we are to say, Emerson advises, " 'Here is one of my coverings; under this fantastic, or odious, or graceful mask did my Proteus Nature hide itself' " (essay on "History"). Within this system of universal correspondences and shape-changings, the poet, the philosopher, and the historian are capable of metamorphosing themselves into myriad shapes—not precisely in a "negative capability" or self-annihilation before the fact like Keats's but in a discovery of the universal extensions of the self in other shapes. In the essay on the poet who "stands one step nearer to things" than ordinary men and "sees the flowing or metamorphosis; perceives that thought is multiform," Emerson thus finds both village economy and biological life legitimate subjects for poetic treatment: "all the facts of the animal economy, sex, nutriment, gestation, birth, growth, are symbols of the passage of the world into the soul of men, to suffer there a change and reappear a new and higher fact. . . . The poet alone knows astronomy, chemistry, vegetation, and animation, for he does not stop at these facts but employs them as signs." Mechanistic philosophy cannot touch this range of significance behind the material fact, and even the merchant becomes a poet of sorts, his true interchange being of souls *through* peppers and silks. Money and the objects of trade are thus components of the All, in its continually dramatic "flowing or metamorphosis."

In this manner, in what we might call the magic of tribal economy, "the facts of the animal economy" are "symbols of the passage of the world into the soul of man." In the enterprise of Walden Pond, Thoreau writes, "trying to hear what was in the wind" (punning on "gossip" between dealers, and on prophetic oracles), he has attempted to carry on his proper business; but "I well-nigh sunk all my capital in it, and lost my own breath into the bargain." An "acquisition" of nature (spiritually) is "minding my business," making "ventures," trading in "the celestial Empire." Thus Thoreau like Emerson emphasizes the wry irony inherent in describing transcendental relationships in terms of business. These two contraries set together send off a stream of sparks like an ax against grindstone. With respect to landscapes, he finds (in "Where I Lived, and What I Lived For") that he is monarch of what he "surveys" (which is unsurveyable):

I have frequently seen a poet withdraw, having enjoyed the most valuable part of a farm, while the crusty farmer supposed that he had got a few wild apples only. Why, the owner does not know it for many years when a poet has put his farm in rhyme, the most admirable kind of invisible fence, has fairly impounded it, milked it, skimmed it, and got all the cream, and left the farmer only the skimmed milk.

Concerning "economy":

Finding that my fellow-citizens were not likely to offer me any room in the court house, or any curacy or living anywhere else, but I must shift for myself, I turned my face more exclusively than ever to the woods, where I was better known. I determined to go into business at once, and not wait to acquire the usual capital, using such slender means as I had already got. My purpose in going to Walden Pond was not to live cheaply nor to live dearly there, but to transact some private business with the fewest obstacles; to be hindered from accomplishing which for want of a little common sense, a little enterprise and business talent, appeared not so sad as foolish. ["Economy," *Walden*]

To the transcendentalist, then, magic and science, science and poetry, beauty and truth, are identical: "Magic and all that is ascribed to it is manifestly a deep presentiment of the powers of science," Emerson asserts in summing up ("History"). We might, however, argue that rather than combining them as equals, Emerson and Thoreau really collapse the second term into the first. Magic and poetry claim prior knowledge of the secret correspondences between the mind and nature upon which romantic metaphor and symbol depend. In any case, among the romantics disbelief in the possibility of translating oneself from one realm to the other without loss is recurrent. In Keats, for instance, though the poet aims to discover permanent "essence" in particular objects, the entelechial impulse inevitably simplifies and reduces as it perfects. The processes of courtship depicted on the Grecian urn are reduced to the moment just before the lovers kiss; Keats essentializes temporal pursuit in a particular moment best suited to frozen, statuesque art. It is true that the oaten pipe, the nymphs and shepherds, and the realm of Pan (in leaf-fringed decoration) are all apparently captured in imitative art. But the closer they approach permanence in form, the farther they depart from the world of fever and loss, fleeting sounds of music, and nature's cyclical birth and death. The poem finally "fixes" them by abstracting them entirely—into the formula spoken by the artifact in disregard of the woes it sits among, a formula that in effect turns language back upon itself until it refers to nothing, totally sealed off from time and place. The desire to make truth beauty, then, leads to a "cold pastoral" that belongs to a world of art habitable only by the creatures of the imagination.[2] The birdlike qualities of Shelley's skylark disappear as the skylark becomes a symbol of Platonic ideality and pure song (only to reappear in Hardy's "Shelley's Skylark").

One of the central difficulties of romantic pastoral is evident in this escape from the tangible properties of the creatures that populate its landscapes: it brings about the elegiac mood that usually accompanies the urge to dwell beyond time and change. As Hegel indicates, a "sorrow of finitude" is the reverse side of any strong yearning for transcendence. (Edgar Allan Poe suggests the aesthetic side of the same yearning when he remarks, "the death of a beautiful woman is, unquestionably, the most poetical topic in the world": it combines ultimate perfection with ultimate deprivation and sorrow.) The mortal poet who remains in the midst of woe may be consoled by a grecian urn's identification of truth and beauty, but he is excluded from living under its mandate.

[2] Hegel remarks that the closer we approach "Being," the more we dispense with the tangible world; because we can point to nothing in that world as "Being," "nothing" is a necessary part of a definition of pure being. This law of "symbolicity" and the elegiac feeling often associated with it is discussed in Kenneth Burke, *The Rhetoric of Religion* (Boston: Beacon Press, 1961), p. 25, and in *Language as Symbolic Action* (Berkeley and Los Angeles: University of California Press, 1966), pp. 26 ff.

Having discovered some state where beauty and truth are the same, he must return to his "habitual self," as the knight of "La Belle Dame sans Merci" and the poet of the nightingale ode eventually do. Or if he escapes, he leaves those who observe him somewhat mystified, as in Shelley's pursuit of the transfigured Keats in the concluding stanzas of "Adonais." The critical moments of romantic pastoral are often those in which the poet discovers the cost and difficulty that his concept of paradise exacts and the loss of specific, temporal content in the vision itself.

DREAM AND NIGHTMARE

But how is paradise to be approached if not by abstraction from the flux of mortal life and the storm of particulars? Keats suggests that a dream-release from normality is one means. For like magic, dreams may establish a secret kinship between the mind and tangible things and suggest hidden analogies between imagination and reality. And for Blake's chimney sweeps locked in coffins, too, translation from one state to another is granted by the angel of sleep, whose dreamwork transforms one set of particulars into another. Though a transcendental change, their transfiguration remains tangible:

> As Tom was a-sleeping he had such a sight!
> That thousands of sweepers, Dick, Joe, Ned, & Jack,
> Were all of them lock'd up in coffins of black.
>
> And by came an Angel who had a bright key,
> And he open'd the coffins & set them all free;
> Then down a green plain leaping, laughing, they run,
> And wash in a river, and shine in the Sun.
>
> Then naked & white, all their bags left behind,
> They rise upon clouds and sport in the wind;
> And the Angel told Tom, if he'd be a good boy,
> He'd have God for his father, & never want joy.

The change is a point by point reversal: though in everyday life the chimney sweeps are sealed in coffins, in dreams they sport on the green; imprisonment becomes freedom; darkness becomes light; dirt, cleanliness; the oppressive "father," God the father; and weeping, laughter. The vision is apocalyptic in a literal way.

But it is also ironically undercut by the reality to which Tom must awaken. No matter how real they seem, dreams are merely dreams, and remaining inside them is as difficult as getting "inside" the grecian urn. "The Crystal Cabinet" suggests, in fact, that the mind's very act of reaching out for the dream brings about a reverse transformation:

> The Maiden caught me in the Wild,
> Where I was dancing merrily;
> She put me into her Cabinet
> And lock'd me up with a golden Key.
>
> This Cabinet is form'd of Gold
> And Pearl & Crystal shining bright,
> And within it opens into a World
> And a little lovely Moony Night.
>
> Another England there I saw,
> Another London with its Tower,
> Another Thames & other Hills,
> And another pleasant Surrey Bower,
>
> Another Maiden like herself,
> Translucent, lovely, shining clear,
> Threefold each in the other clos'd—
> O, what a pleasant trembling fear!
>
> O, what a smile! a threefold Smile
> Fill'd me, that like a flame I burn'd;
> I bent to Kiss the lovely Maid,
> And found a Threefold Kiss return'd.
>
> I strove to seize the inmost Form
> With ardor fierce & hands of flame,
> But burst the Crystal Cabinet,
> And like a Weeping Babe became—
>
> A weeping Babe upon the Wild,
> And Weeping Woman pale reclin'd,
> And in the outward air again
> I fill'd with woes the passing Wind.

The cabinet is a magic box (associated with dance and music and then with a poetic way of seeing) that translates all experience into wonder. As poems are disciplined forms, so the cabinet is a golden housing that transforms reality and leads to an intellectual seizing of "inmost Form." The merry dancer is imprisoned in it against his will, caught while in a wild state of innocence. His reaching out converts the dream into a nightmare and idyllic love into sexual strife; the innocent child becomes a "weeping Babe" and the lady a fallen creature.

For Keats's heroes, the dreamer in awakening usually finds that the vision has not foreshadowed truth but aroused false hope in the dreamer. In "Endymion" where a transformation is actually "materialized," the transition is arbitrary and abrupt, and Diana's explanation of how it comes about is less than inspired but more than reasonable:

> drear, drear
> Has our delaying been; but foolish fear
> Withheld me first; and then decrees of fate;
> And then 'twas fit that from this mortal state
> Thou shouldst, my love, by some unlook'd for change
> Be spiritualiz'd.

Like Adam, Endymion swoons, recovers, and vanishes "far away" to live out his materialized dream. But Poena remains behind, and though she is promised that she can visit the lovers after their honeymoon, she goes "Home through the gloomy wood" in wonderment, her condition representing the mortal bewilderment of the unliberated self.

Wordsworth's visionary "translations" of the ordinary world are similar to those of both Keats and Blake. In "To the Cuckoo" a contrast between the mortal and the visionary is resolved as the bird brings to the listener "a tale / Of visionary hours":

> Even yet thou art to me
> No bird, but an invisible thing,
> A voice, a mystery.

As the passive mind is enticed into believing in the symbol, the bird "begets" again the Golden Age of the Child:

> And I can listen to thee yet;
> Can lie upon the plain
> And listen, till I do beget
> That golden time again.

> O blessed Bird! the earth we pace
> Again appears to be
> An unsubstantial, faery-place;
> That is fit home for Thee!

Whereas in Blake such attitudes are stated in the voicing of someone of limited perspective and then countered with an opposing song, in this case the perspective of the visionary displaces all others. Transportation to childhood is equivalent to the dream-begetting of a fairy place and golden time now resident somewhere in the mind. Though we are aware that in a waking state the earth might well appear different, for the time being it seems a "fit home." Often in Wordsworth, however, the mind is divided, half following the blessed bird or butterfly to childhood and half holding back. As the recollecting mind approaches its former timelessness, the speaker realizes with new pain the fleeting losses of adult life. Also, the cause of dream conversions is often unstated, as shapes fade into one another without perceptible reason. The butterfly that comes to Wordsworth's orchard perches only momentarily within the boundaries of his property line; passing mysteriously forth among the trees, it suggests the spirit's flight in childhood, before reason and experience anchor the child to thoughts of mortality.

THE TRANSFORMING POWER

We have seen that romantic poetry is often an odic supplication to bring about the transportation of the speaker; but the transformation also requires the cooperation of dreams or of some external agent such as symbolic landscapes or creatures like the skylark, the butterfly, or the nightingale. Since that agent is often indefinable, the mind is likely to be passive before it. Keats's lines, "till we shine / Full alchemiz'd and free of space" (which Christine Brooke-Rose classifies as a "passive metaphor") [3] are a good example. The agent that liberates the human spirit could be any of a number of things. It is true that Pan, the "unimaginable lodge / For solitary thinkings," a "leaven" that "spreading in this dull clodded earth / Gives it a touch ethereal—a new birth" ("Endymion" [1.293 ff.]), is a primary stimulus. But Pan, like other gods and goddesses of romantic mythology, is a disguised, dreamlike figure, and the name by itself helps very little in defining the power that he wields. In the passage preceding the alchemization, a demonstrative pronoun apparently specifies a more particular catalyst: *"that which* becks / Our ready mind to fellowship divine / A fellowship with essence." Rather than beginning with a vision of Pan's "Allness," the poet holds up a particular rose leaf, sets his mind "in preparation," folds the petal around his finger, and the "airy stress / Of music's kiss" then "impregnates the free winds." With that alchemical penetration of spirit into matter, "with a sympathetic touch," the music unbinds "Eolian magic from . . . lucid wombs" (1.782), and the poet's music becomes a melodious prophecy. But this is an extraordinary rose leaf, and the real source of the transformative power, as opposed to its efficient agency, is in doubt, as it is again in the magical rites of St. Agnes Eve. Whereas in Christian pastoral the divine source for one's return to paradise is clear, in romantic pastoral it is infused in objects and cannot be addressed, named, or delegated to analogical institutions and mirrors of the creator. The poet's own contribution therefore becomes at best reflexive: rather than calling down a gift of grace from a definite power, he enchants himself with an incantation. Minds and objects properly prepared by incantation release the self until it shines "free of space," and the poet-shepherd escapes his imprisonment. But he escapes it in the poem itself and nowhere else; he is the sole maker of the journey away from habitual self.

In Wordsworth, passivity is often combined with volition, as in the assumption that forms of nature have "a passion in themselves / That intermingles with those works of man / To which she summons him" (*The Prelude,* 13.290 ff.). Occasion-

[3] Christine Brooke-Rose, *A Grammar of Metaphor* (London: Secker Warburg, 1965), p. 228.

ally the passive voice is mixed ambiguously with reflexive and
active verbs, as the mind works both on itself and on nature.
For glorious minds are "ever on the watch, / Willing *to work*
and *to be wrought* upon":

> in a world of life they live,
> By sensible impressions not enthralled,
> But by their quickening impulse made more prompt
> To hold fit converse with the spiritual world,
> And with the generations of mankind. . . .
> Such minds are truly from the Deity,
> For they are Powers; and hence the highest bliss
> That flesh can know is theirs—the consciousness
> Of Whom they are, habitually infused
> Through every image and through every thought
> And all affections by communion raised
> From earth to heaven, from human to divine.
> [*The Prelude*, 14.105–118]

They deal with the "whole compass of the universe" and send
abroad "kindred meditations," creating for themselves "a like
existence" outside them (i.e., discovering metaphors). Whether
"resemblance" is created for them or they create it, whether
they *"catch* it, or *are caught* / By its inevitable mastery," they
are exalted by it (*The Prelude,* 14.90 ff.).

Coleridge stands much more emphatically behind the power
of the mind itself. A definition of the primary imagination as
a *"living power* and prime *agent* of all human perception"
concedes a vitality to finite minds as self-sustaining as that of
the infinite I Am; and in agency and alchemical power, the
secondary imagination is identical to the primary: "it dissolves,
diffuses, dissipates in order to recreate." Where these functions
prove impossible, it still "struggles to idealize and unify." Insofar as it succeeds in "unifying," it establishes its own resemblances among things and hence metaphors by which subject
and object coalesce. But again idealizing extracts the concreteness from imagery and may do so in ways beyond rational
comprehension and volition; thus in a sense Coleridge, too,
finds metaphors and symbols operating like dream associations
on a passive mind. Their dissolving, diffusing, and dissipating
are annihilations of the normal outline and texture of things

in preparation for their re-creations in another context; and they are verbal rather than actual re-creations, of course.

Such passive, reflexive, and supplicational modes are ways of engaging directly, or being engaged by, the romantic landscape as an avatar. They reinforce both the sublime attraction of an ideal and the helplessness of elegiac resignation. A shadow passes over the features of that landscape, melting its usual identities and investing it with preternatural powers. The important matter from the standpoint of form and style, however, is not whether the fellowship between the poet and the object is of the mind's doing or nature's but what happens to the remainder of the consciousness and the historical world when the self is "by communion raised / From earth to heaven, from human to divine"—when a cuckoo becomes "a voice, a mystery." In symbols and figures of the kind that Pan, the skylark, and the butterfly illustrate, animal normality either drops silently out of sight or calls the power of imaginative transformation in doubt by insisting on its own reality.

As we have seen, these symbols stand outside the web of social relations, parliaments, and historical chronicles, perhaps outside embodiment, and having placed himself before them, a given speaker is left with a difficult return to normality. But the most effective romantic pastorals take due notice of this difficulty. Typically they do so in such patterns as these:

Visionary Future

"We will create paradise once we rid ourselves of our mortal curse. If we listen to poetry, we can do so now." ["Prometheus Unbound," "To a Skylark," "Ode to the West Wind"]

Nostalgic Reflection

"The glory was indeed splendid once. If it were to be so again, I should not lack ceremonies of joy":

> Oh, let thy grace remind me of the light
> Full early lost, and fruitlessly deplored;
> Which, at this moment, on my waking sight
> Appears to shine, by miracle restored.
> [Wordsworth, "Composed Upon an Evening of
> Extraordinary Splendour and Beauty"]

Instructional Dreams and Symbols

"This extraordinary beauty came in order 'that frail Mortality may see— / What is?—ah no, what *can* be!'" which suggests not a specific plan of action that the poet urges us to follow (to bring it back) but a way of measuring the distance between everyday reality and the dream. The grecian urn's credo gives similar instructions concerning a beauty beyond mortals. A sense of longing accompanies the symbol's message when the speaker is unable to recapture the vision it brings him, or again: the balmy sky, the stars, the moon, "I see, not feel, how beautiful they are!" "My genial spirits fail; / And what can these avail / To lift the smothering weight from off my breast?" (Coleridge, "Dejection: An Ode"). "Could I revive within me / Her symphony and song" I would "build that dome in air" by following the implicit instructions of the dream in making a poem ("Kubla Khan").

Narrative Alternation from
One Realm to Another

"The journey 'out' is exhilarating, but 'how crude and sore / The Journey homeward to habitual self!'" (Keats), as again in "La Belle Dame sans Merci" and "Lamia"; or in a mixed active and reflexive combination:

> Thou wast the charm of women, lovely Moon!
> O what a wild and harmonized tune
> My spirit struck from all the beautiful!
> On some bright essence *could I lean,* and *lull*
> *Myself* to immortality.
>
> ["Endymion"]

If these combinations of the idyllic imagination and fact are reasonably representative, ceremonies of resignation (elegies primarily) and hymnal means of ignoring the profane while celebrating the sacred are the strong points of romantic pastoral. Styles of colloquial conversation do not matter as they frequently do to renaissance pastoral, nor do the shepherd conventions that most earlier pastoralists observe when treating similar themes. The key to transformation is found not in a courtship of nature by art or of "Pastorella" by "Calidore," but in mysterious alchemical powers, which the romantics do not address familiarly. These ranges of moral and social concern, colloquial bargaining, domestic negotiation, and kindred ranges of ironic wit are the most obvious omissions of romantic pastoral; they will be the main contributions of modern revisions of romantic pastoral, especially in Robert Frost and Wallace Stevens.

OWNERSHIP AND INDUSTRIAL
TRANSFORMATIONS OF NATURE

These variations of romantic pastoral assume that the creations of the imagination take precedence over whatever physical changes one might make in an environment; they find the locality of "Arcadia" in poems, in transcendent objects, and in dreams, or if, as in Wordsworth, their locality has a proper name and can be located on a map, it is divided into a tangible surface and an intangible spiritual presence. The poet's passivity before nature and his movement, once he has been beckoned forward, toward a spiritual and intellectual transcendence of definite localities is more meaningful if we see it as a reaction to a quite different approach to nature, dynamically active, unspiritualized, and expressible as the power of industrial change and ownership. Speculation as to the causes of the romantic turn inward lies beyond our province, but we can assume that the rise of machine manufacture, the substitution of "crass cash nexus" for "idyllic feudal" relations (as Marx describes them), and myth-free science had something to do with it. As Yeats redefines Genesis, the eighteenth century had already converted Eden into a kind of factory or place of home manufacture where a spinning Jenny replaces Eve as the final creation of God and man:

> Locke sank into a swoon;
> The Garden died;
> God took the spinning-jenny
> Out of his side.

Adam-Locke is henceforth split by so radical a separation of the place of work and the place of beauty that nothing can put him together again.[4] While the courtier-shepherd could at least visit shepherdom and carry on transactions with it for a time, factories and romantic versions of the idyllic landscape are mutually exclusive.

The characteristic literature of an industrial approach to nature is opposite in most respects to the characteristic romantic ways of regarding the idyllic place and the transcendent symbols that it contains. It is something like encyclopedic classification. If in romantic odes the tangible properties of objects are subdued one by one by some spiritualized power, encyclopedias collect those properties as useful information that enables us to manage the thing in itself, or the thing as product. The nature of the industrial manual or the encyclopedia is to examine the way things work in an animal economy, and their categories are those appropriate to creatures as detached objects of study or as raw materials. (The encyclopedia in this respect resembles georgic.)

Encyclopedias are not our concern, of course, but the encyclopedic method is not entirely beyond literary use, as the documentary novel illustrates. More important is pastoral's reaction to the exploitation of natural resources, the modern tension between conservation and use, and pastoral modes shaped by tensions between work and poetry, as in Frost. It is mainly in novels with pastoral elements that we find combinations of the two, especially in the novels of Cooper, Hardy, and Faulkner. *The Pathfinder*'s pragmatic view of "Arcadia," to take one of the earliest examples in prose fiction, is both an encyclopedic index to the edible parts of the wilderness and a romantic appreciation of nature. It prepares implicitly for the settler's claiming of the land and what thrives on it:

Notwithstanding the remote frontier position of the post, they who lived at it enjoyed a table that, in many respects, kings

---

[4] In modern times the "natural" man is preserved or restored by vacations from industry—in Europe by the *villegiatura,* elsewhere by the equivalent of a trip to Yellowstone Park.

and princes might have envied. . . . The whole of that vast
region which has been called the West . . . lay, a comparatively unpeopled desert, teeming with all the living *produc-*
tions of nature that properly belonged to the climate, man and
the domestic animals excepted. . . . Oswego was particularly
well placed *to keep the larder of an epicure amply supplied.*
Fish of various sorts abounded in its river, and the sportsman
had only to cast his line to haul in a bass or some other member of the finny tribe, which then peopled the waters as the air
above the swamps of this fruitful latitude is known to be filled
with insects. . . . Of the different migratory birds that frequent forests and waters, there was the same affluence, hun-
dreds of acres of geese and ducks being often seen at a time
in the great bays that indent the shores of the lake. Deer,
bears, rabbits, and squirrels, with divers other quadrupeds,
among which was sometimes included the elk or moose,
helped to complete the sum of *the natural supplies* on which
all the post depended. [Chap. 9]

The members of this bestiary and aviary though not so fine
as delicacies as the buffalo meat that Leatherstocking consumes in *The Prairie,* are half zoo specimens and half candi-
dates for frontier cookery. In *The Pioneers*—which finds the
aged Leatherstocking surrounded by civilization—lawyers,
judges, legislators, clerks, shopkeepers, servants, and slaves
have all but conquered the wilderness, which is surveyed,
fenced, housed, and willed to the next generation. (The predominately legalistic concerns of the novel begin appropriately
with a dispute between a judge and a second generation
woodsman over the ownership of a recently slain deer.) Leatherstocking himself, together with his Christian-convert friend
Chingachgook, is not less obsolete in claiming "your titles
and your farms are all new . . . but laws should be equal,
and not more for one than another" than in reciting melancholy tales of freer days gone by. But despite his protest, the
movement of his own life is logical, given the naturalist's and
the hunter's cooperation with the landowner: it is the deer-
slayer who feeds the civilization that makes the wilderness
safe for its exploiters.

Much of the romantic view of nature remains in Cooper's

novels as well, as again in the novels of Hardy and Faulkner. Closely observed, the wilderness inculcates a natural virtue; it bespeaks a benevolent influence that makes its ruin a desecration. The energetic exploiters, the buffalo slayers, the conquerors of Indians, and the practitioners of European manners and customs are sometimes admirable in their own right, and the westward spirit makes a forthright conquest of the wilderness inevitable. But the losses are felt the more keenly because the romantics and transcendentalists have taught Cooper, Hardy, and Faulkner to see much that is beyond appropriation in nature. In Hardy's scenic novels, which are set in a nature that recalls romanticism, the protagonists are engaged in a similar unfruitful struggle against rigid social conventions, foremost among them the ownership of nature. The problem in a sense is to romanticize the conventions—or to put into them some of the spontaneous naturalness and democratic feeling that bucolic figures have—and at the same time to civilize the heath or woodland, which is far from tame or gentle.

Among modern novelists, Faulkner provides equally striking examples of the interaction between transcendent nature and industrial exploitation. *The Hamlet, The Town, The Mansion, Sartoris,* and *Go Down, Moses* each in its way explores the incompatibility of the wilderness and the area claimed for agricultural and industrial use. Each brings together local politics and an ancient wilderness beyond recorded history. As in Hardy, those who are caught between the two worlds have difficulty reconciling them. In "The Bear" Ike McCaslin's wilderness experience is a single and lonely confrontation between him and the forest, shared only by those spiritually akin and even by them only from a distance. It is an initiation into the transcendental spirit of the wilderness, which resists men with axes and encourages a "communal anonymity of brotherhood." The history that Ike reads in the commissary accounts—human events marked down in terms of money-changing—is the other half of his inheritance. In Ike's case these two ways of life, one expansive and heroic, the other constrictive and filled with violence and human greed, admit of no compromise. Under the encroaching expansion of the empire of contract, the hunt itself is corrupted and becomes a symbol of exploitation (in "Delta Autumn"). Roth Edmonds cheats on the hunting code and "hunts" people. The horn that he has inherited from a former generation of hunters Ike uses as a bribe in attempting to rid himself of reminders of his unintentional share in the McCaslin sins. Like the aging Leatherstocking, he can only renounce.

Even in the original hunt, the actual killing of the bear is meaningless except as an arbitrary test of courage; Ike must choose between seeing and slaying, expanding in vision and owning. As long as he carries a gun, he is tainted; and he must relinquish the watch and the compass, symbols of bounded time and direction-finding. In doing so, he submerges the possessive self in the universal "forest," alien and lost in the green and soaring gloom of the markless wilderness":

It rushed, soundless, and solidified—the trees, the bush, the compass and the watch glinting where a ray of sunlight touched them. Then he saw the bear. It did not emerge, appear: it was just there, immobile, fixed in the green and windless noon's hot dappling, not as big as he had dreamed it but as big as he had expected, bigger, dimensionless against the dappled obscurity.[5]

The rush into significance, the coalescing, the "dimensionlessness" of something described in dimension, the foreshadowing dream, the gliding disappearance, all these are dreamlike elements that, though beyond reason, can be glimpsed in symbols like the bear. Again, the basic difficulty is that these symbols "slay" the concrete things that they use as vehicles and therefore make possession incompatible with seeing. For the forest can be either possessed as timber or used as an instrument of romantic transcendence but not both at the same time.

Without resolving the conflict between the boundless wilderness and the contractual order, however, "The Bear" offers

[5] William Faulkner, "The Bear," from *Go Down, Moses* (London: Chatto and Windus, 1942), p. 159.

a perspective by which the problem can be defined. Ike's goal
is to understand and then merely to endure the processes of
history that are working themselves out as though under the
guidance of providence—mysteries inherent in the human condition from the beginning of time though localized in regional
myth, and fully explicable only when historical process itself
comes to an end. Faulkner's strategy is to superimpose the
providential view of things (which "pastoralizes" all history)
upon the politics of the Southern economy. The stylistic effect
of that combination can be seen in Gavin Stevens's hillside
view of Jefferson:

> Then, as though at signal, the fireflies—lightning bugs of
> the Mississippi child's vernacular—myriad and frenetic, ran-
> dom and frantic, pulsing; not questing, not quiring, but choir-
> ing as if they were tiny incessant appeaseless voices, cries,
> words. And you stand suzerain and solitary above the whole
> sum of your life beneath that incessant ephemeral spangling.
> First is Jefferson, the centre, radiating weakly its puny glow
> into space; beyond it, enclosing it, spreads the Country, tied
> by the diverging roads to that centre as is the rim to the hub
> by its spokes, yourself detached as God Himself for this mo-
> ment above the cradle of your nativity and of the men and
> women who made you, the record and chronicle of your native
> land proffered for your perusal in ring by concentric ring like
> the ripples on living water above the dreamless slumber of
> your past; you to preside unanguished and immune above this
> miniature of man's passions and hopes and disasters—ambition
> and fear and lust and courage and abnegation and pity and
> honour and sin and pride—all bound precarious and ram-
> shackle, held together by the web, the iron-thin warp and
> woof of his rapacity but withal yet dedicated to his dreams.
> They are all here, supine beneath you, stratified and super-
> imposed, osseous and durable with the frail dust and the phan-
> toms—the rich alluvial river-bottom land of old Issetibbeha, the
> wild Chickasaw king, with his Negro slaves and his sister's son
> called Doom who murdered his way to the throne.[6]

In a sense, Stevens discovers the wilderness still visible in
bourgeois life. The disjunctive "fireflies" of his life are seem-

[6] Faulkner, *The Town* (London: Chatto and Windus, 1958),
p. 272.

ingly random but withal "choir" together. The prospect of Jefferson unites distant dream and immediate rapacity. The spreading rings of his vision encompass and organize the past under something like divine providence. Though Stevens cannot escape the comedy of provincial life (even a shrewd man like Ratliff finds himself scratching for gold), the panorama extends the chronicle in time and space and tells of a perspective far enough beyond farce to justify rhetorical elevation.

Faulkner's tragicomic, humble-sublime style is based on just such simultaneous presences of the exalted and the comic in provincial life. It is a raising of the perspective in this manner that gives insignificant men like Mink Snopes a share in the destiny of all men and thus "pastoralizes" them beyond reach of the economic classes assigned them in the South's tarnished Arcadia:

it seemed to him he could feel the Mink Snopes that had had to spend so much of his life just having unnecessary bother and trouble, beginning to creep, seep, flow easy as sleeping; he could almost watch it, following all the little grass blades and tiny roots, the little holes the worms made, down and down into the ground already full of the folks that had the trouble but were free now . . . the folks themselves easy now, all mixed and jumbled up comfortable and easy so wouldn't nobody even know or even care who was which any more, himself among them, equal to any, good as any, brave as any, being inextricable from, anonymous with all of them: the beautiful, the splendid, the proud and the brave, right on up to the very top itself among the shining phantoms and dreams which are the milestones of the long human recording—Helen and the bishops, the kings and the unhomed angels, the scornful and graceless seraphim.[7]

Democratic death and fellowship with grass lead the thoughts of Mink, and the rhetoric of the novel, into a sublimity that sweeps past kings and on to angels in a single expanding sentence.

Except for its emphasis on the difficulties of maintaining

[7] Faulkner, *The Mansion* (London: Chatto and Windus, 1961), p. 399.

equilibrium between boundlessness and the provincial southern community, Faulkner's exploration of the social contract
is typical of the American wilderness novel, the clash between
the open wilderness and encroaching civilization having begun
sometime before sunset the first day a European flag was set
in Indian soil—or earlier still, if we honor Isaac McCaslin's
line of Dispossession:

He told in the Book how He created the earth, made it and
looked at it and said it was all right and then He made man.
He made the earth first and peopled it with dumb creatures,
and then He created man to be His overseer on the earth and
to hold suzerainty over the earth and the animals on it in His
name, not to hold for himself and his descendants inviolable
title forever, generation after generation, to the oblongs and
squares of the earth, but to hold the earth mutual and intact
in the communal anonymity of brotherhood. ["The Bear," pp.
55–56]

But more immediately relevant to Ike's vision than Adam's
experience is Emerson's view of the wilderness, which insists
that "Line in nature is not found; / Unit and universe are
round." "Time dissipates to shining ether the solid angularity
of facts." To Emerson, "no anchor, no cable, no fences avail
to keep a fact a fact," which dispenses with contracts and
deeds.[8] Again, as we saw with respect to the transcendentalist
transformation, "Everything is made of one hidden stuff; as
the naturalist sees one type under every metamorphosis," and
therefore "every occupation, trade, art, transaction, is a com-
pend of the world and a correlative of every other," which
makes each "an entire emblem of human life."[9] Property lines

[8] Emerson, "History," from *Essays,* p. 6.
[9] *Ibid.,* "Compensation," p. 73. Cf. Leo Marx, *The Machine in
the Garden: Technology and the Pastoral Idea in America* (New
York: Oxford University Press, 1964), pp. 229–265. Marx points
out that Emerson was more optimistic than Thoreau in believing
that technology could be assimilated into the romantic view of
nature. Emerson translated industry into idyllic terms in the
"rhetoric of the technological sublime" (p. 230). The key to their
harmonious combination was the spirit with which nature was
put to use, for one may work as well as perceive transcendentally—

mean nothing unless man first binds himself: "there is a property in the horizon which no man has but he whose eye can
integrate all the parts, that is, the poet," who has an "ownership" without "warranty-deeds."

But Emerson had little experience with the typical social
realities to which a modern wilderness journeyman such as
Ike returns when he confronts the commissary records. When
Archibald MacLeish thinks of these contrasts in "The Empire
Builders" and compares the pretentious rhetoric of business
enterprisers with the quiet romantic "poetry" of Meriweather
Lewis, he turns with something less than reverence to the
possessors of the wilderness:

You have just beheld the Makers making America
They screwed her scrawny and gaunt with their seven-year
    panics:
They bought her back on their mortgages old-whore-cheap:
They fattened their bonds at her breasts till the thin blood
    ran from them:
Men have forgotten how full clear and deep
The Yellowstone moved on the gravel and grass grew
When the land lay waiting for her westward people!

The first four lines could be printed as prose, the apposite
medium for their blunt realism. But the last three in remembering the reverence of the romantics for nature (as Lewis
himself did) are a strongly rhythmic, elegiac benediction. Together they reflect the prose-poetry of Whitman and other
"rough-transcendentalists" modes that yoke together industry
and the romance of unbounded nature.

Accompanying this dislike in romantic-realist modes for
fences and those who have built them is a general distrust of
domesticity and book learning, which the typical wilderness
hero shares with Wordsworth. Though a gentleman toward

---

or so it seemed to Emerson in the early period of technological
progress, though he valued consistency in this little more than in
other matters. In contrast, Thoreau's native blend of myth and
economic reality (in Marx's words) stresses the paradoxical relation of practical labor and romantic perception; inevitably, the
economic man and the poet often go separate ways.

the fair sex and even an occasional employee of the army, Leatherstocking would clearly be diminished by either parade drill or a passionate interest in John Donne. He confesses that his love for Mabel (in *The Pathfinder*) might convert him into an anxious money winner trying to give her Advantages, but we have difficulty imagining him as a member of the town council or a devotee of the theater. His moral fiber derives from a close observation of nature rather than the daily worries of a corporate people or their written histories and laws. If he kills, he does so swiftly and only in self-defense, as nature teaches, never for political power or as an extension of something so abstract as policy.

"Going west" or "westering" in John Steinbeck's phrase, permitted an unusually long survival of romantic myths of boundless space. But jurisprudence and social compromises of various kinds inevitably replaced in due time the nonlegislative codes, instinctive wisdom, and easy communion with the wilderness figure's version of the Great Spirit. Besides, as Frost realizes, there is a contradiction in those who seek total release from civilized boundaries: they court disorder and self-annihilation. To those less committed to solitude, the victory of civilization is not always a defeat; even Pathfinder broods over the prospect of a lifetime of solitude away from human discourse:

Pathfinder was accustomed to solitude, but, when the *Scud* had actually disappeared, he was almost overcome with a sense of his loneliness. Never before had he been conscious of his isolated condition in the world, for his feelings had gradually been accustoming themselves to the blandishments and wants of social life, particularly as the last were connected with the domestic affections. Now, all had vanished, as it might be, in one moment, and he was left equally without companions and without hope. [*Pathfinder,* chap. 30]

It is difficult to stay out too long. Sooner or later the frontier romantic, like his English predecessors, returns to the constrictions of lawyers, takes responsibility for his children, and seeks the services of trained specialists.

So profound a rift in pastoral—indeed in modern culture's

contradictory desire both to appropriate and to preserve natural resources, to maintain innocence and spiritual communion with nature while progressing deeper and deeper into industrialism—is not likely to be cured. (If it were, pastoral would survive on any of several related rifts.) If eighteenth-century pastoral is characterized by its fragmentation of issues and its failure to produce a comprehensive view of the collision of idyllic dreams and realities, modern pastoral fares little better except in its firmer sense of the central importance of fictions themselves. It has not discovered a way to reconcile pastoral landscapes, golden innocence, and other imaginative fictions with the experience of social complexities, with the factory, the slum, the despoiling of nature, nor can we expect that any period ever will. We have begun to understand the mind's own contribution to the fictions it tries to make real, then, but we have no more idea how to make them real than men ever have.

For this reason, among others, we cannot expect to find a definitive view of postromantic pastoral; we are still too involved in its repercussions and the problems that gave rise to it. The several themes and their historical unfolding that we have surveyed obviously do not lend themselves to an easy summing up, and we need not apologize for beating a retreat to more modest and detailed examinations of pastoral's romantic and postromantic variants. I plan to concentrate first on Wordsworth and Keats before going on to Hardy and Bellow for a look at two versions of pastoral in the novel, and then gather what threads Stevens and Frost allow. The latter two poets enable us to understand the romantics and the potentials for modern pastoral in ways that we could not have found without them. They will not of course provide us with final controls over the variety of pastoral visions that the tradition generates, but they are nonetheless very encompassing. They bring into the open and revitalize much that has lain dormant in pastoral, even as they lean heavily on the romantic redefinition of pastoral in Wordsworth and Keats, without which their versions of pastoral would be unimaginable.

TEN

Wordsworth's Two Natures

The speakers of Wordsworth's poems often confront two quite different versions of nature, a nature of concrete materiality (hereafter "A") and a nature composed of types and symbols of eternity, or "Characters of the great Apocalypse" ("B"). Such a division is by no means unique in romantic poetry, but to an unusual degree Wordsworth finds the two combined ambiguously in given scenes. The central questions that they pose in terms of pastoral contrasts and transformation are these: what happens stylistically when one is imposed upon the other? In what forms and modes can they be combined? Can Wordsworth's mixture of elevated joy and elegiac sorrow be defined as an outgrowth of the two? How is memory of a former, golden time affected by them? How does Wordsworthian narrative and description progress from one to the other, or toward a reconciling perspective? What happens to traditional pastoral under the impact of their tension?

Since Wordsworth himself speaks more or less explicitly to the last of these questions in book eight of *The Prelude* and totally redefines the nature of the *locus amoenus* in doing so, we can bypass it for now in favor of the others. To the young wanderer who finds nature primarily a cause for spiritual joy and a symbol of a spiritual presence beyond itself—either actually in nature or projected into nature by the mind—art at its best (not the "mimic art" that Wordsworth condemns in *The Prelude*) is congruent with rather than opposed to nature. Nature requires no shaping or enclosure or artificial adornment. Merely an enumeration of a scene's concrete elements will prepare for our perception of its revelatory symbols. Poetry's function is not so much to interpret those symbols as to celebrate them in appropriate hymnal modes. Thus in "Tintern Abbey," the dynamics of nature's material presence and

its vital spirit are reflected primarily in the energy of the verse
rather than its precise definitions. Spirit "interfuses" all things;
it is manifest in "the light of setting suns," and as it rolls actively through nature and draws the mind to it, it paradoxically nudges both mind and scene toward an infinite inaction
—toward the stillness and grandeur of the "All" that only an
expansive style can express:

> I have felt
> A presence that disturbs me with the joy
> Of elevated thoughts; a sense sublime
> Of something far more deeply interfused
> Whose dwelling is the light of setting suns
> And the round ocean and the living air,
> And the blue sky, and the mind of man;
> A motion and a spirit, that impels
> All thinking things, all objects of all thought,
> And rolls through all things.

Likewise in *The Prelude* both "wind" and "words" reveal a
glory that raises the beholder above imprisonment in specific
forms. Wordsworth often in fact progresses from descriptive
canvassing and action to an emblematic stillness that freezes
vitality, from a pastoral of sensuous observance to a pastoral
of immanent glory (reminiscent of Eden and celestial paradise
respectively). The interesting moment is the transition from
one to the other and the hovering vision that includes them
both simultaneously:

> Visionary Power
> Attends upon the motions of the winds
> Embodied in the mystery of words.
> There darkness makes abode, and all the host
> Of shadowy things do work their changes there,
> As in a mansion like their proper home;
> Even forms and substances are circumfused
> By that transparent veil with light divine;
> And through the turnings intricate of Verse,
> Present themselves as objects recognis'd,
> In flashes, and with a glory scarce their own.
> [*The Prelude,* 5.619–629] [1]

[1] Quotations from *The Prelude* are from the 1805 text unless
stated otherwise, ed. Ernest de Selincourt (London: Oxford University Press, 1933).

In theory at least, Wordsworth came eventually to stress the compatibility of the two natures less than their differences and the strain they place upon language. As the "Essay Supplementary to the Preface of 1815" explains, language necessarily refers to the specific forms of nature (A) and therefore always to matter in motion, to discrete objects. Poetry's capacity to deal with mysteries is highly questionable since the poet must assume an attitude of reverence without being able actually to present the objects of reverence:

The concerns of religion refer to indefinite objects, and are too weighty for the mind to support them without relieving itself by resting a greater part of the burthen upon words and symbols. The commerce between Man and his Maker cannot be carried on but by a process where much is represented in little, and the Infinite Being accommodates himself to finite capacity. In all this may be perceived the affinity between religion and poetry; between religion—making up the deficiencies of reason by faith; and poetry—passionate for the instruction of reason; between religion—whose element is infinitude . . . submitting herself to circumscription, and reconciled to substitutions; and poetry—ethereal and transcendent, yet incapable to sustain her existence without sensuous incarnation.

This discrepancy between poetry's ethereal and transcendent subject and its sensuous incarnation is especially troublesome in Wordsworth's narrative verse when the speaker begins as a teller of personal anecdotes and translates incidents and images from his past into ethereal symbols. We often feel that Wordsworth makes this shift in scenic description without sufficient awareness of the paradoxes and spiritual trials involved in his doing so. Timeless and stillness, for instance, are manifest in moving torrents and decay in the Simplon Pass passage (*The Prelude*, 6.556–572), as stationary blasts (oxymoronic frozen violence) and a dialectic of light and dark, raving tumult and peace, decay and renewal give way to a mystic unity of "one mind." In terms of the observer's perception and psychology, the scene is transformed from a group of measurable and sensuously discernible properties first to recurrent and abstract qualities and then to an intuition of disembodied mind (basically from nature A to B). The self-division and

the philosophic antinomies of such a transition are not part of
the speaker's own conscious problem. Perhaps they should not
be, at least not in all such passages in Wordsworth; but part
of the impression of vagueness that these passages give derives
from the rapidity of the shift from tangible scenes, precisely
located in time and place, to monumental symbols. Again in
a slightly different way when Wordsworth translates regional
shepherds into models of natural form in book eight, we feel
that he has eliminated all tangible character, realistic, traditional, artificial, or otherwise, in order to create symbols to
which infinite being might accommodate itself more easily.

In addition to the kind of sacred emblems that Simplon Pass
and other concrete places provide for him, Wordsworth also
relies frequently upon abstract nouns to bridge the gap between the two natures.[2] In "Influence of Natural Objects,"
words like "form," "things," "spirit," "universe," "passions,"
"life," "nature," "elements," and "thought" permit a meeting
of the finite and the infinite (or at least the universal), and
thus a stylistic progression from an anecdotal to a philosophic
treatment of childhood:

> Wisdom and Spirit of the Universe!
> Thou Soul, that art the Eternity of thought!
> And giv'st to forms and images a breadth
> And everlasting motion! not in vain,
> By day or star-light, thus from my first dawn
> Of childhood didst thou intertwine for me

[2] In "Essay Supplementary to the Preface of 1815" Wordsworth
castigates eighteenth-century pastoral for lack of precise imagery,
which may seem inconsistent with his own frequent preference for
abstraction. The difference, however, between his use and eighteenth-century generality is pronounced: it lies primarily in the
anecdotal beginning of the movement toward the sublime. Emerson's concept of the *sublime commonplace* is closer to Wordsworth's, though less inclined to dissolve the paradox and leave the
commonplace object behind: "I embrace the common, I explore
and sit at the feet of the familiar, the low . . . show me the
sublime presence of the highest spiritual cause lurking, as always
it does lurk, in these suburbs and extremities of nature [i.e., the
meal in the firkin, the form and gait of the body]; let me see

>The passions that build up our human Soul;
>Not with the mean and vulgar works of Man,
>But with high objects, with enduring things,
>With life and nature, purifying thus
>The elements of feeling and of thought.
>
>   [*The Prelude,* 1.428–438]

The abstract noun reinforced by certain elements of epic style spans much of the distance between ordinary and "high" experience. The alteration of normal syntax, the ceremonial form of address, the extension of the sentence into a verse paragraph, the climaxing summary of a final three lines ("sanctifying / . . . pain and fear—until we recognize / A grandeur in the beatings of the heart") help spring the influence of natural objects loose from concretion, yet make that influence seem real by impassioned, direct address. The immediacy lies in the I-Thou relation rather than in particularities of imagery, the grandeur in distance from definite objects rather than in the shape and form of named emblems. The high narrative mode presupposes but does not demonstrate the immanence of the grand in the humble, which is given a "glory scarce its own"; it passes from anecdote to high vision as Wordsworth elsewhere passes from real shepherds to symbolic models of dignity without carrying either details of English shepherdom or pastoral conventions with him.

Wordsworth's reliance on "types and symbols of eternity"

---

every trifle bristling with the polarity that ranges it instantly on an eternal law; and the shop, the plough, and the ledger referred to the like cause by which light undulates and poets sing;—and the world lies no longer a dull miscellany and lumber-room, but has form and order; there is no trifle, there is no puzzle, but one design unites and animates the farthest pinnacle and the lowest trench" ("The American Scholar").
David Ferry in *The Limits of Mortality: An Essay on Wordsworth's Major Poems* (Middletown, Conn.: Wesleyan University Press, 1959), also stresses the two levels of Wordsworth's diction and two natures, with emphasis on the conflict between nature's "sacramental" function as a source of symbols and mystical experience that requires no intermediary symbols at all. See especially the excellent analysis of the benedictional-elegiac mode of the Intimations Ode, pp. 44–50.

and on abstract nouns derives in part from what the *Preface to the Lyrical Ballads* describes as an act of throwing over common events and ordinary things a "coloring" that makes us aware of "the primary laws of our nature." Those laws are usually manifest in particular experiences, and Wordsworth is perhaps most convincing when he focuses upon the act of perceiving them. If we repeat the question "what happens stylistically when one nature imposes on another" in the context of a poem like "My Heart Leaps Up," we get a quite different answer than the Simplon Pass episode affords us:

> My heart leaps up when I behold
> A rainbow in the sky:
> So was it when my life began;
> So is it now I am a man;
> So be it when I shall grow old,
>   Or let me die!
> The Child is father of the Man;
> And I could wish my days to be
> Bound each to each by natural piety.

Personal experience is here raised to venerable law, the proper reaction to which is a natural piety that one could easily imagine in a pastoral figure of a certain kind—simple, direct, capable of philosophic reflection and compression, freed of all obvious artifice. This reaction is the distinction of the Wordsworthian natural man when he is fully engrossed in the *locus amoenus;* he is stimulated by it to an act of moral imagination that places him well above the traditional lovelorn, indolent shepherd. Childhood, middle age, and old age are bound together by an old but newly realized law triggered by a phenomenon rare enough to remind the poet of both particular events in the past and of the continuing strange and awesome side of nature. The stylistic effects are not those of descriptive sensuousness but those of ritual recurrence and proverbial observation based in personal reaction. The clauses are short, and the rhythm suggests the excitement of the nursery rhyme but transmutes it into calm dignity, justly resting on an effective abstractness—justly because the response itself transcends all specific occasions; it comes consistently whenever the stimulus is there. The wonder of the child and the wisdom of maturity thus meet in a simple but exalted language.

The example is nonetheless of limited value in defining Wordsworth's unique pastoral contrasts and transformations because it does not encompass nature's extremes, its particularities and its apocalyptic note, and it avoids the issue of rusticity. When Wordsworth insists upon seeking in humble life for evidence of human dignity and exaltation, he encounters much more stubborn resistance in the details of rustic life. Why does he in fact look to pastoral situations for the best incarnations of "primary law"? In both early and late poems he finds "law" and "elementary feeling" virtually the same, and the section of the *Preface to the Lyrical Ballads* which describes "humble and rustic life" bases its pastoral manifesto on that identification:

> The principal object, then, proposed in these Poems, was to choose incidents and situations from common life, and to relate or describe them throughout . . . in a selection of language really used by men. . . . Humble and rustic life was generally chosen, because in that condition the essential passions of the heart find a better soil in which they can attain their maturity, are less under restraint, and speak a plainer and more emphatic language; because in that condition of life our elementary feelings co-exist in a state of greater simplicity; . . . because the manners of rural life germinate from those elementary feelings, and from the necessary character of rural occupations, are more easily comprehended, and are more durable; and, lastly, because in that condition the passions of men are incorporated with the beautiful and permanent forms of nature.

Wordsworth's preference for rusticity, then, rests upon its "beautiful" and "more permanent forms" and unfortunately upon the vagueness of "incorporate with" and "the language really used by men." As Coleridge observed, Wordsworth here assumes that the passions of Shakespeare's kings or noble Romans or of the urban laborers of Wordsworth's own day are less "essential," less elementary than those of shepherds and hence would have to be more dramatically altered to become poetic:

Assuredly the omissions and changes to be made in the language of rustics before it could be transferred to any species of poem, except the drama or other professed imitation, are at least as numerous and weighty as would be required in adapting to the same purpose the ordinary language of tradesmen and manufacturers. Not to mention that the language so highly extolled by Mr. Wordsworth varies in every county, nay, in every village, according to the accidental character of the clergyman, the existence or nonexistence of schools; or even, perhaps, as the exciseman, publican, or barber happen to be, or not to be, zealous politicians and readers of the weekly newspaper. [*Biographia Literaria,* chap. 17]

Wordsworth intends the comparison of his pastoral diction and proper poetic language to be with eighteenth-century "literary" style; but even so, when we regard other examples of colloquial pastoral, the limits of the Wordsworthian revolution become clear. Taking a shepherd as an index of human dignity, the poet must maintain a respectful distance from him; the style silently makes the human animal conform to a preexistent idea of his "grace and honour, power and worthiness" quite as unlike him as the conventional portrait:

> Thus was man
> Ennobled outwardly before mine eyes,
> And thus my heart was early introduc'd
> To an unconscious love and reverence
> Of human Nature; hence the human form
> To me became an index of delight,
> Of grace and honour, power and worthiness.
> [*The Prelude,* 8.409–415]

We are struck both by the intangibility of the diction and by the harmony of the portrait as a model of combined medium and high styles. On the basis of enduring forms and examples of primary law that appear before him, Wordsworth weds the shepherd's mind to the "goodly universe" as though there were no difference between the poetic intelligence remaking nature in the orderly, enclosed forms of symbolic narrative and the sensations of common men; easy passage from nature A to B allows him to put aside, he believes, the fiction of pastoral:

> Paradise, and groves
> Elysian, Fortunate fields—like those of old
> Sought on the Atlantic Main—why should they be
> A history only of departed things,
> Or a mere fiction of what never was?
> For the discerning intellect of Man,
> When wedded to this goodly universe
> In love and holy passion, shall find these
> The simple produce of the common day.
>
> [*The Recluse,* 800–808]

DEADENING PARTICULARITY

I have rehearsed these familiar aspects of Wordsworthian style in order to suggest an inverted ratio between the two natures in their dialectical clashes and in Wordsworth's transformations of one into the other within given ambiguous scenes. If we begin with the proposition that Wordsworth's celebration of nature B requires a withdrawal from nature A rather than an exacting observation of "objects" or realistic portraits of rustics, we will be better prepared to understand the resources of his language and the difficulty that particularized description sometimes caused him. Locality and place are often most meaningful as a resistance that a speaker must overcome in his desire to recapture transcendental experience; he cannot maintain both levels of pastoral simultaneously, the natural and the supernatural. Moreover, as several poems on rustics illustrate, pathetic rural victims are often prevented from having any significant commerce with the primary laws of nature on either level, except with basic laws of nutrition and economy. In "The Last of the Flock," for instance, the owner of the flock is forced to sell lambs to feed children, and the loss unmans him. Because society leaves her too slim a margin, Alice Fell represents not the "love and holy passion" of the "common day," merely poverty: new coat in hand, she becomes a proud creature once more, but her pride will probably fray with the coat.

More important for Wordsworth's lyrics and ballads, the speaker himself is sometimes imprisoned in nature and realizes that nature must erase worthwhile human distinctions if it is

to "universalize" those whom it "adopts." The problem of
language then becomes, quite properly, the problem of human
response to real things, usually to the speaker's close friend or
beloved, who becomes as much a victim as a fortunate child
of nature. To the extent that one creates nature B, one must
kill nature A; and the "mode" becomes not a celebrational
conversion of one into the other through abstraction and em-
blem-making but a modified elegy lamenting the loss of particularity. The irony of "A Slumber Did My Spirit Seal," for
instance, stems from the speaker's sorrow at Lucy's incapacity
to escape oneness with rocks, stones, and trees:

> A slumber did my spirit seal;
>   I had no human fears:
> She seemed a thing that could not feel
>   The touch of earthly years.
>
> No motion has she now, no force;
>   She neither hears nor sees;
> Rolled round in earth's diurnal course,
>   With rocks, and stones, and trees.

The main irony lies in the "touch" of things that now over-
whelm a "thing" that once seemed untouchable. Linguistically,
this irony represents a collapse of what would normally be
vital universality in Wordsworth into dead generality. For
ordinarily, the spirit that finds in things that which cannot
feel the touch of years is not sealed in slumber but raised to a
high range of spiritual perception; the bounded self is preserved even as the circumference of vision expands. Here
"Lucy" is either herself or nothing. (The logic of the little
girl in "We Are Seven" is more typically Wordsworthian: five
alive and two dead equal seven because the dead are still
present in their way, still numerical entities. Unless we read
into "A Slumber" the ideas of other poems, it does not seem
to have the ambiguity of the girl's position or of pastoral elegies
that define death as communion between the self and a pan-
theistic whole.) [3] The catalog "rocks, and stones, and trees"
is an enumeration of inert, general masses.

[3] Those interpretations of the poem that put "live universality"
or some form of pantheism back into the concluding lines would

In "Strange Fits of Passion Have I Known" the lover is led to associate the fall of the moon with Lucy's ceasing to be—which causes his heart to "leap up" in a different sense—in this case at the perception of earth's diurnal turning as a death-giving mechanism. Again in "Three Years She Grew in Sun and Shower," the poet discovers that nature may preempt human relations in converting its children from one level of existence to another. Nature's "law and impulse" kindle and restrain the girl; but the power of restraint, on second glance, proves the stronger. Though nature grooms its victim with "vital feelings of delight" and though we may suppose that if a beauty passes from murmuring waters "into her face" she in turn may pass into nature spiritually, her loss to the speaker is finally all that is certain: the rest remains speculation. Nature's silence and calm thus take on terrifying aspects, not merely complementing but cancelling Lucy's wild sportiveness:

> "She shall be sportive as the fawn
> That wild with glee across the lawn,
> Or up the mountain springs;
> And hers shall be the breathing balm,
> And hers the silence and the calm
> Of mute insensate things."

As force, motion, and the concrete activities of seeing and hearing are lost to the past, emotion and tranquillity are saturated with elegiac feeling:

> She died, and left to me
> This heath, this calm, and quiet scene;
> The memory of what has been,
> And never more will be.

Stylistically Wordsworth might be said to discover here a sensitive interaction of live particularity and deadening generality. Elements of nursery rhyme similar to those of "My Heart Leaps Up" work a crushing finality as the normal life of Wordsworth's basic verbs of being (what was, is, and will be)

seem to be stretching the language beyond limits, canceling one mood with another. The stress on lifelessness in "no motion" and "neither hears nor sees" closes off that range of ambiguity.

yields to negatives (never more will be). The energy collected
into "springs" is first quieted in imageless calm and silence
and then extinguished in the lifelessness of "mute-insensate"
and the inanimate abstraction of "things."

If one must consume nature A to produce nature B or ab-
stain from one to participate in the other, the healthy animalism of a life among nature's particular scenes and occasions
can seldom coexist with the sublimity of the universal spirit
that Wordsworth intuits in nature. To the extent that he is
absorbed in nature, the Danish boy is unavailable to the particular occasion: "for calm and gentle is his mien; / Like a
dead boy he is serene." In "Lucy Gray" the case remains open:
did the snowstorm consume Lucy, or did it bring her to a different kind of fulfillment by liberating her into nature's spiritual totality? Should the speaker grieve over, or stare in wonder at, the point of her disappearance?

> They followed from the snowy bank
> Those footmarks, one by one,
> Into the middle of the plank;
> And further there were none!
>
> —Yet some maintain that to this day
> She is a living child;
> That you may see sweet Lucy Gray
> Upon the lonesome wild.
>
> O'er rough and smooth she trips along,
> And never looks behind;
> And sings a solitary song
> That whistles in the wind.

As in pastoral elegies that release the spirit of the dead into
nature, the question of whether or not Lucy lives another
kind of life may seem problematic since a specter so fleeting
could be no more than a shadow of the former singing girl.
Though the speaker suggests that in some manner the singing
ghost figure transcends the former Lucy, "lonesome wilds"
do not suggest unqualified joy, and if Lucy has in fact passed
into a spirit world, the poet cannot follow. He goes only to the

middle of the bridge, and there words, too, like Lucy's transformed intangibility, must become elusive and suggestive. The final function of concrete language is to point at the tracks left behind.

The Matthew poems as well are concerned with the discovery of nature's sinister aspect and the returns of memory and spiritual presences. In "Matthew" nature has selected Matthew as her "favourite child," and all that remains of him is a "little wreck of fame, / Cipher and syllable," "two words of glittering gold." Such chosen favorites may indeed be the "soul of God's best earthly mould," but they nonetheless end mute, "silent as a standing pool":

> Thou soul of God's best earthly mould!
> Thou happy Soul! and can it be
> That these two words of glittering gold
> Are all that must remain of thee?

The astonishment of the question suggests that despite the uncommon bliss that nature gives, some part of the soul's destiny remains inexplicable and is capable of raising terror. The further question, "is death an evaporation into nothingness or an expansion into all nature?" is again posed implicitly in the ambiguities of the passage. Is "best" ironic or straightforward? ("You were the best God produces, and we can be thankful for it"; or "even the best comes to nothing.") The irony of "mould" ("form giving paradigm" and "funereal decay") and the mere "glittering" of Matthew's name are characteristic of Wordsworth's most compressed language, the eulogistic and the sinister jostling each other without detracting from the uncommon sympathy the speaker feels for the subject. The quiet of the poem depends not upon a romantic conversion of nature into something it is not but upon the equilibrium and tactfulness with which questions are raised in the context of nature's ambiguity.

This equilibrium stems from the inverted ratio between the two natures, in which gains and losses are balanced so exactly. Exploring the balance is the function of the older Matthew in reciting his past to a younger man and, of course, of Wordsworth's own habitual recollections in tranquillity, which often seek a partial return of nature B or a just estimate of the present life from which it has escaped. Remembering joyful youth and visionary moments diminishes the present and reminds the poet of the shrinkage of age, but at the same time, by re-creating the past, it also lifts the present, infusing it with a secondary echo of former times. Similarly, seasoned by the expense that nature A exacts from aging men, the older Matthew of "The Fountain" is aware both of nature's deadening power and of the reverberations of his own recollections. A joyful past can make age seem all the heavier when one is reminded by it of the little that is left:

> "My eyes are dim with childish tears,
> My heart is idly stirred,
> For the same sound is in my ears
> Which in those days I heard.
>
> "Thus fares it still in our decay:
> And yet the wiser mind
> Mourns less for what age takes away
> Than what it leaves behind.
>
> "The blackbird amid leafy trees,
> The lark above the hill,
> Let loose their carols when they please,
> Are quiet when they will.
>
> "With Nature never do *they* wage
> A foolish strife; they see
> A happy youth, and their old age
> Is beautiful and free:
>
> "But we are pressed by heavy laws;
> And often, glad no more,
> We wear a face of joy, because
> We have been glad of yore."

"Nature" in this case is neither decay nor spiritual transcendence separately but each superimposed upon the other in the remembering and reflective mind. Wordsworth's sense of their interaction means that no moment or experience can be uncon-

ditional or unreflective. Though in their spontaneity, blackbirds and larks (or daffodils, cuckoos, and butterflies elsewhere) feel no tension between their moment-by-moment existence and visionary joys, memory forces the aging man to
acknowledge the continuously dialectical nature of his experience.

Formally, "The Fountain" is a combination of lyric and
ballad which Wordsworth and Coleridge invented for such
purposes as the crossing of common everyday occurrences with
something "ghostly." The folk narrative in this case offers
gnomic wisdom and songlike stanzas. The eclogue discussion
of youth and age heightens the conflict between them and yet
eventually encourages a compromise. The first outcome of
their conversation is Matthew's rejection of the youth, and
implicitly, the possibility of restoring losses:

> "I'll be a son to thee!"
> At this he grasped my hand, and said,
> "Alas! that cannot be."

But a second response follows this. As they walk together
through a landscape nearly neutralized by their opposing views
of nature, Matthew sings the songs his friend originally asked
for. It is both a concession to their friendship and an example
of Wordsworth's amiability in the presence of irreconcilable
opposites:

> And, ere we came to Leonard's rock,
> He sang those witty rhymes
> About the crazy old church-clock,
> And the bewildered chimes.

The song represents not a shrugging off of nature's heavy laws
in the manner of larks and blackbirds who "loose their carols
when they will" but a recapitulation of the dialogue. Such
"witty rhymes" as the old man sings sound less like simple
nursery rhymes than symbolist lyrics with an uncanny ballad
quality. The friendship of the two maintains something of the
spirit of youth but is also qualified by the shadow of Matthew's
recollection.

Perhaps more effective in imposing Matthew's multiple vision of the past upon the young wanderer's single-minded view of nature is "The Two April Mornings," which like "The Fountain" is a fruitful combination of traditional ballad, pastoral, and lyric forms. The reaction of the youthful enthusiast is the "outer" subject, the lyric beginning and ending of the poem:

> We walked along, while bright and red
> Uprose the morning sun;
> And Matthew stopped, he looked, and said,
> "The will of God be done!"
>
> . . . .
>
> Matthew is in his grave, yet now,
> Methinks, I see him stand,
> As at that moment, with a bough
> Of wilding in his hand.

Spiraling down into the past from that initial arrested moment, Wordsworth makes effective use of the ballad's interceptions of surface life by the preternatural, the effect of which is much like the startling intrusions of death in Arcadia only more richly inlaid with reminders of a personal past. The seeming recurrence of the original April morning is jarring enough that even Matthew, though experienced in mortality, is led into corners of awareness he has successfully buried. The interruption of their outing begins the education of the youth, who discovers in an eclogue "challenge" that it is Matthew's fate to see the interaction of the past and present, the absent and the incarnate, life and death.

The two April mornings bring a confrontation in the present similar to Matthew's startling encounter thirty years earlier with a girl near the grave of his daughter:

> "A blooming Girl, whose hair was wet
> With points of morning dew.
>
> "A basket on her head she bare;
> Her brow was smooth and white:
> To see a child so very fair,
> It was a pure delight!

> "No fountain from its rocky cave
> E'er tripped with foot so free;
> She seemed as happy as a wave
> That dances on the sea."

Farther back is Emma, the daughter, our glimpse of whom is distanced by the speaker's narrative of the second April morning and by Matthew's of the first. The plunge into the past brings the second girl to mind in such fresh detail that one assumes the memory of Emma to have been equally vivid when Matthew first saw Emma's apparition. Her blooming, the points of dew, the smooth brow, and the sea-wave gracefulness—soon dissolved into the "sea," the source and grave of its momentary "dancers"—are all double, like the two April mornings, beautiful and immediate but perishable. Memory in this case obviously does not produce an exciting "primary law": the act of seeing is first an unreflective recognition of the beauty of the scene and the girl, then a perception of death's signature on them, so that Matthew sees ghosts, not Spirit, behind them. As Emma is brought back from the dead, then, the live girl is consigned prematurely to her grave. Matthew's rejection of her is a rejection of the double vision itself, of the ghostly recurrence of "Emma" in memory, which merely redoubles her original loss:

> "There came from me a sigh of pain
> Which I could ill confine;
> I looked at her, and looked again:
> And did not wish her mine!"

The ballad repetition "looked at her, and looked again" echoes the poem's structure of ghostly seeing and double recitation that results in Matthew's initial gesture of self-protection.

The last stanza offers a final example of the return of a "particular" ghost to haunt the memory—memory that ideally ought to revive in tranquillity the transcendental experience of the past. As the young friend sees his own apparition of Matthew holding "a bough / Of wilding in his hand," Matthew's double vision passes to him, and through him to the reader. For as the speaker's reaction to Matthew's story moves forward as the dominating lyric framework of the ballad, we, too, find our images doubling: the young man and his specter stand emblem-like before us.

Before proceeding further, let us recapitulate these possibilities for the reciprocity between natures A and B and recall that we are considering it as Wordsworth's central variation on pastoral contrasts, especially contrasts of level. Loss of visionary powers to natural decay and material fact makes nature (A) a prison house and leaves the poet vulnerable to the deadening mass of rocks, stones, and trees. Correspondingly, the liberation of material being into spirit loses particularity, which sometimes means a friend or loved one, as well as the concreteness of occasions and places. Emblems of high grandeur such as Simplon Pass maintain a qualified material presence, but only because abstract language allows some sense of place and time to coexist with types of eternity. The poet may also beckon us to the "middle of the bridge" where something has left earth and bid us listen to its haunting song still in the wind, so that we are both sorrowful at the loss and entranced by its new possibilities. The seeing of ghosts behind surfaces and the sensing of invisible presences are Wordsworth's special powers, and they allow him to make effective use of a double language of concretion and spiritual suggestiveness.

Wordsworth is perhaps most effective, however, in mixing elegiac and lyric or benedictional modes of pastoral. He evokes a sense of loss in what remains behind in the *locus amoenus* and yet also of presences no less part of the speaker's experience for their intangibility. With skillful modulation and control, he blends the joys of visionary experience with the sorrow of the reflective mind.

Joy dominates whenever a supernatural presence rises from within the scene and carries the observer "From earth to Heaven, from human to divine." It is usually discovered in quiet scenes because "deathly" stillness, as we have seen, releases awareness of a dynamic if somewhat ghostly force in nature. Thus in "It Is a Beauteous Evening," the girl appears all the more alive for her absorption into the calm of the evening. The first two quatrains balance quiet and breathlessness with remarkable suggestiveness. As Reuben Brower remarks, the language has a "subtle imprecision" that Wordsworth manages with great tact: [4]

> It is a beauteous evening, calm and free,
> The holy time is quiet as a nun
> Breathless with adoration.

"Adoration" gathers breathlessness and holiness into a kind of ceremonial excitement, as it collects them musically (the "r" from one and the "o" from the other). The initial quiet lets one hear the great roar and perceive the motion hinted in the slow setting of the sun. The sound is "like" thunder but also different, because it lasts forever and comes from the entire planet. The girl herself appears to have nature's totality within and so is not lost to it as Lucy is. To the extent, however, that either is absorbed in the quiet outside him, he cannot talk with the other. Both the poet and the girl are necessarily withdrawn, "abstracted," and again we perceive a certain regret behind the poem's ostensible exaltation.

As the Intimations Ode also reveals, the tone of Wordsworthian benediction moves imperceptibly into sad solemnity at its most exalted moments. In the Intimations Ode, rather than converting personal anecdote into high benediction, Wordsworth converts personal loss into elegiac hymn. The poem is structured as a series of contrasts between youthful enthusiasm and the philosophic calm of an aging speaker, the child's nature B having again developed into nature A by the natural processes of aging and rational reflection. But the poem is not merely an account of that deterioration; it is also a dramatic response to it that explores possible compensations for it in those "intimations" of immortality that nature's emblems still reveal. The first section stages an imbalance between exaltation

---

[4] Reuben A. Brower, *The Poetry of Robert Frost* (New York, 1963), p. 45.

and lamentation, and these moods continue to alternate until Wordsworth fuses them in the poem's final "beautiful sorrow" or "sad elevation." The first voice of the poem is equivalent to Matthew's in mourning the loss of youth. The second is a rejuvenated voice, as the speaker answers cataracts "blowing their trumpets from the steep." But the second mood proves to be forced and the apostrophe strained ("Shout round me, let me hear thy shouts, thou happy / Shepherd-boy!"). The simple joys of shepherd and children are neither visionary like those that the speaker has lost nor philosophical like those he will achieve. Hence a radical turn follows the benediction and leads to the questions posed by the philosophic mind, "Wither is fled the visionary gleam? / Where is it now, the glory and the dream?" Having established this succession of "listlessness" and "mad endeavor," Wordsworth proceeds to the deliberative style of the experienced man concerned with uniting "man and boy," past and present, spiritual transcendence and common reality.

The perpetual benediction that issues from that meditation is the final subject of the poem (stanzas ix–xi). The mood is a purposeful, stoic joy. The speaker knows his bounds and why he cannot soar too high:

> Though nothing can bring back the hour
> Of splendor in the grass, of glory in the flower;
>   We will grieve not, rather find
>   Strength in what remains behind;
>   In primal sympathy
>   Which having been must ever be;
>   In soothing thoughts that spring
> Out of human suffering;
>   In faith that looks through death,
> In years that bring the philosophic mind.

Imagistically, common day modulates into clouds "that gather round the setting sun" as a kind of screen between the observer and the "mighty Being" of beauteous evenings, and again a subtle imprecision assists the fusion: what remains behind besides memories, the content of soothing thoughts, and exactly how such thoughts are to "spring" out of "human suffering," Wordsworth leaves unexamined. But "the thought of our past years" nonetheless breeds "perpetual benediction"; the "shadowy recollection" of memory is the "fountain light of all our seeing." Recollection hovers ghostlike over the materiality of the aging man and his prison house: the immediate splendor and glory are not so much in the grass and flowers as coexistent with them in the "sober coloring" of the mind's reflection. Thus sifted through long experience, the two natures find a philosophic compromise and urge the mixed style of the ode.

That style is the later Wordsworth's most characteristic handling of pastoral contrasts. A visionary ideality that might once have been associated with a transcendent paradise, and temporal processes that might once have been associated with a pagan nature of growth and decay, Wordsworth translates into "soothing thought" and awareness of "human suffering." Other later variations of the two natures are less impressively managed, partly because of Wordsworth's increasing substitution of religious and national institutions for nature's revelations. Wordsworth fosters what Kenneth Burke calls with respect to Carlyle social and ecclesiastical surrogates for God (as in Carlyle's philosophy of clothes, "vestments" become "modes of preternatural manifestation" and "mystery" is equated with "class distinctions").[5] In "The Happy Warrior," for instance, Wordsworth is pleased to find the boyhood wanderer's "natural instinct" engaged in the "high endeavor" of disposing of enemies—which makes a bizarre union of pastoral and heroic themes. The warrior is said to be commanded not by political purposes but by heaven itself:

> if he be called upon to face
> Some awful moment to which Heaven has joined
> Great issues, good or bad for human kind,

he is

> happy as a Lover; and attired
> With sudden brightness, like a Man inspired;

[5] Kenneth Burke, *A Rhetoric of Motives* (Cleveland and New York: Meridian Books, 1962), p. 646.

And, through the heat of conflict, keeps the law
In calmness made, and sees what he foresaw.

Thus in Carlyle's portrait of the god-man Odin, the rude
nobleness of the hero in communion with "the divineness of
Nature" will provide a mysterious foundation for a *hero*archy:

Wonder, hope; infinite radiance of hope and wonder, as of
a young child's thoughts, in the hearts of these strong men!
Strong sons of Nature; and here was not only a wild Captain
and Fighter; discerning with his wild flashing eyes what to do
. . . but a Poet too. . . . I feel that these old Northmen were
looking into Nature with open eye and soul: most earnest,
honest; childlike, and yet manlike; with a great-hearted simplicity and depth and freshness. [*On Heroes, Hero-Worship
and the Heroic in History*]

The portrait is a faintly recognizable distortion of Wordsworth's pastoral-heroic figure.

But these retrenchments are not essential Wordsworth; they
represent accidental dangers in his difficult transition in the
later period from nature figures to men of duty. It is a more
cogent criticism that Wordsworthian elevation does not always
carry with it a recognition of the improvements it makes on
nature, that the eye sees what the mind wants it to, and that
the mind desires mythopoeic emblems rather than transactions
with people and real places. Even so, at their best Wordsworth's lyrics unite spiritual elevation with anecdotes of time,
place, and common experience in a new way that reconceives
their relationship and radically reconceives pastoral. The
golden past and the pleasant place become a personal time and
a personal landscape and yet retain the equivalent of mythic
dimensions. "Paradise, and groves / Elysian, Fortunate fields"
need no longer be sought in ancient, fictional localities; they
are "the simple produce of the common day." It was probably
Wordsworth more than any other single poet who disentangled
the spirit of pastoral from conventional description, the formal
devices of pastoral, and the traditional figure of the shepherd.
Together with Keats, he helped to free that spirit for its modern transmigrations among the American transcendentalists,

Frost, and Wallace Stevens. At the same time, he contributed
to the separating of visionary experience from Christian tele-
ology by locating the poet's paradisal fulfillment immanently
in the personal experience of nature, not forecast at the completion of linear history or projected backward to an un-
precedented genesis. (*The Prelude* in this respect is to the
romantic poet's relationship to a conceivable ideal what *Paradise Lost* and *Paradise Regained* are to Christian pastoral.)
In its more promising moments, the poet's development from
a personal, childhood golden age to maturity reconciles spiritual needs with temporal growth and decay. In lesser moments, it at least encourages the poet to lament his losses with
philosophic dignity.

ELEVEN

Keats's Pastoral Alchemy
as Therapy

Wherein lies happiness? In that which becks
Our ready minds to fellowship divine,
A fellowship with essence; till we shine,
Full alchemiz'd, and free of space.

—"ENDYMION"

I am certain of nothing but of the holiness of the
Heart's affections and the truth of Imagination—What
the imagination seizes as Beauty must be truth—
whether it existed before or not—for I have the same
Idea of all our Passions as of Love: they are all in
their sublime, creative of essential Beauty. . . . The
Imagination may be compared to Adam's dream—he
awoke and found it truth. . . . Adam's dream . . .
seems to be a conviction that Imagination and its
empyreal reflection is the same as human Life and its
Spiritual repetition.

—LETTER TO BENJAMIN BAILEY, *November 22, 1817*

The two epigraphs tell much of the story of Keats's pastoral
transformations, in which poetry and dream succeed in making truth conform to them and prefigure an actual "empyreal"
existence of essential beauty comparable to the old dream of
paradise. For Keats, Adam's dream begins in nature, in the
realm of Pan, carries the imagination into the realm of tran-
cendent being, and returns Adam to the waking world to discover an altered reality comparable to the dream. Unlike the
dream of Milton's Adam to which Keats alludes, his dreamers
do not rely upon a divine power of transformation—the creator

of Eden and Eve for Adam—and many of his dreamers, less fortunate than Adam, awaken to find the world just as it was before. Keats sometimes borrows the myths of Elizabethan and seventeenth-century poetry but not their explanations of how paradises come to be realized. Hence, thrown back upon the purely human power of the imagination, the poet finds his magic failing; it cannot really make truth out of dreams without assistance. As William Empson points out, some earlier pastoral, too, situates the power of transformation outside orthodoxy and sometimes outside discernible causes altogether. Moreover, as in Keats's less fortunate dreamers, the delight of passing into the realm of the subnatural and supernatural is often counterbalanced by guilt and by a fear of being divorced from humankind. The alignment of the "power of beauty" and the "power of magic," as Empson writes of Greene's *Friar Bacon and Friar Bungay,* is "individualistic, dangerous, and outside the social order."[1] Thus for Keats's romantic pastoralism, a central difficulty is to reconcile the desire for individual transcendence, through poetic alchemy and dreams, to a social sympathy that does not allow the poet to ignore the suffering of his fellow men— not all of whom can be expected to dream new truths into existence even if the poet can.

The prior problem, however, is to discover a sense in which the imagination can be said to produce a legitimate transformation of reality to begin with. Traditionally, explanations of spiritualizing transformations of the kind Keats describes in the letter to Bailey—transformations from what reality seems to be to what it ought to be and in essence is—derive from the Neoplatonists, who maintain that by extracting the soul's quintessence from its various historical activities, one purifies it. In Sir John Davies's account of the soul's spiritual transformation, the soul turns

> Bodies to spirit by sublimation strange,
> As fire converts to fire the things it burns,

[1] William Empson, *Some Versions of Pastoral* (London: Chatto and Windus, 1935), p. 33.

As we our food into our nature change.
From their gross matter she abstracts their forms,
And draws a kind of quintessence from things;
Which to her proper nature she transforms
To bear them light on her celestial wings.

In seventeenth-century Puritan-Platonism, such purification is usually rescued from the realm of magic and sublimation and assigned to the intellective faculties. Swift in *Tale of a Tub* and *The Mechanical Operation of the Spirit* unceremoniously shrinks its stature and implies that when certain Neoplatonist wizards and other Enthusiasts among modern "projectors" resort to "sublimation strange," they are confusing insides and outsides, the realm of mind and the realm of bodies. They mystify one with a vague spiritualism while they mutilate the other with their science.[2]

The romantics typically think of imagination rather than magic or the intellective faculties as the controlling force of transformation. In referring to the passage from Sir John Davies, Coleridge equates "poetic imagination" with Davies's "soul" as the means of "extraction" whereby material nature becomes spiritual illumination in symbolic dress. By manifesting the divine mind to us, imagination raises the poet's crea-

[2] To Swift, as to Jonson in *The Alchemist*, this confusion of spiritual and material motives is a lucrative strategy. It forecasts in some respects the analogy that Norman O. Brown discovers in Marx between money and alchemy: "gold is the quintessential symbol of the human endeavor to sublimate— 'the world's soul' (Jonson). The sublimation of base matter into gold is the folly of alchemy and the folly of alchemy's pseudosecular heir modern capitalism. The profoundest things in *Capital* are Marx's shadowy poetical presentiments of the alchemical mystery of money and the 'mystical,' 'fetishistic' character of commodities. . . . Commodities are 'thrown into the alchemistical retort of circulation' to 'come out again in the shape of money.' 'Circulation is the great social retort into which everything is thrown, to come out again as gold-crystal.'" See *Life Against Death* (New York: Random House, 1959), pp. 258–259. From this viewpoint all users of magic have one thing in common: they would produce gold quickly. Magic becomes the power by which leaden realities are transformed instantly into things of high value.

tive power to godlike proportions. It is his discovery of that power that then enables him to turn about from his lone journey to benefit society, serving as its stimulus to renewal. Thus Alick West is quite right to speculate in *Crisis and Criticism* that Coleridge intends to achieve communion not merely with a divine power through the imagination but with the total body politic. Likewise, in Shelley's version of the transformative power of the imagination, what the west wind and the skylark offer to the poet reaches society through him.

Certainly Keats, too, intended poety to be a means of political and social reform by its offering of realizable dreams. His express purpose in writing "Endymion" was to discover cures for society that an apothecary's medicines could not effect. Hence we are not misreading his poetry if we treat it as an attempt at pastoral transformations that seek paradise— Heaven's bourne in Keats's terms—through verbal magic and dreams. Keats wished to find out if he could work therapy by the special means open to poets. Beginning in the realm of Pan to establish his visions in the sensuous realm of nature's forms, the poet works like a gatherer of secret herbs and tries to penetrate each form of life to the core. Establishing rapport with nature—finding "fellowship with essence"—is his first task. Then, rising to a discovery of nature's higher essences, he leaves the daily world behind him and becomes godlike through perceptions beyond ordinary learning:

> At Morn, at Noon, at Eve, and Middle Night,
>   He passes forth into the charmed air,
>   With talisman to call up spirits rare
> From plant, cave, rock, and fountain.—To his sight
>
> The hush of natural objects opens quite
>   To the core; and every secret essence there
>   Reveals the elements of good and fair;
> Making him see, where Learning hath no light.
>
> Sometimes, above the gross and palpable things
>   Of this diurnal ball, his spirit flies
>   On awful wing; and with its destin'd skies
> Holds premature and mystic communings:

> Till such unearthly intercourses shed
> A visible halo round his mortal head.
>
> ["The Poet"]

Such "unearthly intercourses" substitute metaphysical for physical possession, which suggests a residue of Neoplatonism in the poet's night-wandering.

Sensuous or "palpable things" are as important as the "talisman" to the initial stages of the formula. In the poet's transactions with "plant, cave, rock, and fountain," there is a tangible sensuousness to complement his panspiritualism and to be held in tension against it, much as Wordsworth's two natures react against each other or Herbert's nature and grace wage their recurrent struggle. Keats's natural scenes also serve as background for a central courtship, like Endymion's, Lycius's, or Porphyro's and graft conventional courtly plots of achievement and social-sexual rewards onto the poet's quest for transcendence. The ambiguity between these two motives, the advance to Heaven's bourne and the courtship of a lady, can be resolved only if the material "Indian maiden" fades into "Cynthia." As "Sleep and Poetry" suggests,

> a bowery nook
> Will be elysium—an eternal book
> Whence I may copy many a lovely saying
> About the leaves, and flowers—about the playing
> Of nymphs in woods, and fountains; and the shade
> Keeping a silence round a sleeping maid;
> And many a verse from so strange influence
> That we must ever wonder how, and whence
> It came.
>
> [63-71]

In such surroundings, the transformation of the poet from mortal to immortal occurs as though through the power of the forest itself. The processes of vision and metamorphosis begin with a fever that signifies a state of high receptiveness and bodily weakness demanding therapy; fever is then followed by deep sleep as the poet is "Calm'd to life"; and sleep is followed by an awakening in which the dreamer is confronted by frozen, statuary beauty. As the world is transformed and the fever cured, he hears a singing that seems to transfer into art the intoxication of dream—as the vision of Madeline in "The Eve of St. Agnes" materializes in the magic and music of the circumambient evening. We are by then deep in the enchantment of a restored paradise, where Eve and Eden together fulfill the poet's adamic dream.

The hero may also have to brave certain enemies, as the shepherd Endymion does, or descend into nether regions. But his enemies cannot disturb the dream itself, which prepares for alchemization by bringing down "shapes of beauty" from above like "An endless fountain of immortal drink, / Pouring unto us from the heaven's brink" ("Endymion" 1.23–24). In Keats's mythological terms, this is equivalent to the dissolving of the Indian maiden into Cynthia, as eroticism spiritualized:

> into her face there came
> Light, as reflected from a silver flame:
> Her long black hair swell'd ampler, in display
> Full golden; in her eyes a brighter day
> Dawn'd blue and full of love. Aye, he beheld
> Phoebe, his passion!
>
> [4.982–987]

But even in granting Endymion success, Keats obviously only half believes in the formula. The desire not to divorce poetry from more tangible means of social therapy is as strong as the desire to make "guesses at Heaven" come true. "Sleep and Poetry" suggests that the poet can change the world only by taking into account eventually the "agonies, the strife / Of human hearts." For

> we've had
> Strange thunders from the potency of song;
> Mingled indeed with what is sweet and strong;
> From majesty: but in clear truth the themes
> Are ugly clubs, the Poets Polyphemes
> Disturbing the grand sea. A drainless shower
> Of light is poesy; 'tis the supreme of power.
>
> [230–236]

The poet's development actually falls into two stages and results in two different kinds of poetry not altogether compatible, magical transformation and real therapy, one the product of dreamers and the other of what Keats thinks of as genuine prophets. In "The Fall of Hyperion," the one is sealed off from suffering, but the other sees the wreckage of transient life and is struck with sorrow over it. The wan goddess Moneta, "sole priestess" of Saturn's desolation, explains the difference in these terms:

> "Are there not thousands in the world," said I . . .
> "Who love their fellows even to the death? . . ."
> "Those whom thou spak'st of are no visionaries,"
> Rejoin'd that voice,—"they are no dreamers weak;
> They seek no wonder but the human face,
> No music but a happy-noted voice—
> They come not here, they have no thought to come—
> And thou art here, for thou art less than they.
> What benefit canst thou do, or all thy tribe,
> To the great world? Thou art a dreaming thing,
> A fever of thy self—think of the earth."

Likewise, though the lovers of "The Eve of St. Agnes" vanish into the intangible kingdom of fairies, we see behind them a palace strewn with mortals—frozen, drunk, or dead—who will awaken to another kind of reality.

Supposing, then, that the power to make real transformations in the waking world lies beyond the power of the visionary: what kind of reality does the poet's dream have? In "Ode to Psyche" Keats considers the possibility that it belongs solely to the inner mind in isolation from an extrinsic world. Except for Psyche the hierarchy of Olympus is faded, and even Psyche appears only in a dreamlike vision: "Surely I dreamt to-day, or did I see / The winged Psyche with awaken'd eyes?" The poet must therefore see and sing by his "own eyes inspir'd" and build his fane in some untrodden region of the mind, where "branched thoughts, new grown with pleasant pain, / Instead of pines shall murmur in the wind." The gardener is not a real alchemical power, merely "Fancy," and the realm of Pan shrinks to "branched" thoughts.

The imaginative mind and its poems have then become the only pastoral enclosure and are sealed off from communication and therefore from any possibility of curing social ills at large.[3]

Linguistically, this change from magic and mythology to psychology means that Keats must reconsider the concept of metaphor and correspondence as well as the poet's social function: are analogies between men and nature the mind's own invention? Or are there real correspondences of the kind that magic assumes, that enable the poet to understand nature's essences as his ready mind penetrates to the core? And where does the power of word-magic register—on those who need therapy in society or only on the poet himself? In the Nightingale ode, the bird's song invites its hearer through "magic casements" into another world where he may liberate himself from thoughts of mortality by identifying with "essence." But the poet's own sounds are unmagical phonetics and lead nowhere: the "very word forlorn" is "like a bell / To toll me back from thee to my sole self!" Perhaps, then, if "fancy cannot cheat so well / As she is fam'd to do," rather than trying to create inner bowers or discovering an "empyreal reflection" of temporal life in dreams, the poet should rid himself of all transformational ambitions. Perhaps he should station himself outside both art and dream-visions and engage them dramatically or dialectically, as pure "subjunctives" outside reality.

The "Ode on a Grecian Urn" moves the speaker to just such a position, in alienation from an artifact that stands above feverish, time-ridden mortals. The speaker cannot "waken into" it or find a rite that will apply its pattern to mortal ailments. His relationship to the urn and the urn's to nature

[3] As Mario L. D'Avanzo suggests in *Keats's Metaphors for the Poetic Imagination* (Durham, N.C.: Duke University Press, 1967), Keats stresses the privacy of poetic processes, which are analogous to dreams, sleep, flight, the riding of steeds, the moon, woman, fine frenzy, manna, flower dew, labyrinth, bower, and other figures for the subterranean depths of the unconscious. Imaginative frenzy opens up an unfathomable world, a sanctuary of poetry, and when the poet returns to the exterior world the imagination wanes, leaving him in fever (p. 201).

are both problematic. Unlike the woven trellis of "Ode to Psyche," the pastoral scene on the urn appears to exist outside the mind of the perceiver, but it may be merely someone else's invented image: it may imitate a real scene and speak the truth about it, or it may be the artist's own "branched thoughts" imprinted on the artifact. Does the urn lead the observer into timeless essence beyond itself or does it create its own "reality"? Does its prefigure truth, like Adam's dream, or merely describe an unreachable condition?

The fourth stanza is critical in any weighing of the poem's mythological and psychological elements because it mixes the pretextual subject of the urn with the urn's art until it is impossible to say whether the speaker addresses the town as part of a real history or suggests that it lacks history, that it is merely an artist's image of a town:

> What little town by river or sea shore,
>   Or mountain-built with peaceful citadel,
>   Is emptied of this folk, this pious morn?
>   And, little town, thy streets for evermore
>   Will silent be; and not a soul to tell
>   Why thou art desolate, can e'er return.

A full paraphrase, I think, would have to reveal the possibility of both disillusionment and an uncritical Endymion-like fellowship with the scene. For if the entire scene is fabrication rather than reality immortalized, the streets (or images of streets) will indeed be silent forever: they never existed to begin with except as cold, silent art, were never emptied of folk, and cannot now "speak" to the observer. Certainly no one will return to the town since all life in art is frozen beyond process. But if art does indeed beckon

> Our ready mind to fellowship divine,
> A fellowship with essence; till we shine,
> Full alchemiz'd, and free of space,

the speaker may be so completely absorbed in the scene that he forgets the distinction between it and art. He talks to it as one might call out to an actor about to strangle Desdemona.

Whatever the truth of the urn's scene—whether pure invention or the expression of nature's timeless essence—the
scene's desolation suggests that paradisal bliss is not possible in
a life of process and change. Only a summary act can be fully
satisfying, and by definition there can be but one summation,
one elongated moment, in the highest idyllic fulfillment. All
movement toward it (as toward a future golden age) must
be thought of as anxious and fretted and all movement away
permeated by a sense of loss. If beauty and truth are to be
equated, time must be suspended. But here the town is frozen
in a state of desolation rather than fulfillment. Whatever "fellowship" one has with it must be elegiac.

In the final stanza, while reporting the urn's declaration that
beauty and truth are identical, the poet steps back from the
urn and considers it as an artifact, its men and women mere
marble decorated with forest branches. We are left with two
kinds of statement, objective reporting about the urn and the
urn's own transcendentalist pronouncement about life; we
have no conclusive proof about the speaker's position regarding them. The range of meanings in the urn's statement alone
is bewildering. It includes not only Kenneth Burke's translation of truth and beauty into science and poetry but also, implicitly, a translation of body into soul, pain into pleasure, time
into eternity. All life must become art if it is to be beautiful.
Or so it is if the urn does not mean to say the opposite: "if
this pain is all there is to beauty, then there really is none;
what we thought was beauty is only truth at last," to which
statement of resignation we would add an "alas!" to make it
consistent with the tone of the fourth stanza. The difficulty
is that to exhaust the full range of the formula's ambiguity is to
find in it all degrees of transformation of truth into beauty or
of beauty into truth. For the strategy of a linguistic equation
of this kind is to substitute one term for two; and if we have,
say, two colors, blue and green, one offensive and the other
attractive, and then decide for various reasons to call them
blue-green, cannot any range of blends be thought essentially
the true substance of the combination? Or if we call body and
soul, soul-body, could not gluttony be its primary quality as

well as spiritual cleanliness? Each word potentially becomes all or part of the other, the only requirement being that the two sides of the equation balance. Since Keats's formula does not specify the contents of each side—as say 30 percent idyllic content in truth and 70 percent sorrow in beauty—a full paraphrase of possibilities would have to reflect its openness: "this (undefined) condition is the way things are; resign yourself to it or rejoice over it. The only beauty you'll ever see (alas) is what you now have, or all this beauty you now see is yours forever!"

But it seems reasonably safe to assume that the urn, at least, means to say that truth is 100 percent transformable into beauty: "from the highest perspective, my permanence as the foster-child of slow time and my beauty indicate what timeless paradisal summation is." Its word "truth" is still perplexing, but it probably means something like "real objective existence," which enables us to translate the formula in this way: "beauty inheres in real historical objects; it is not merely the product of chimerical dreams." Or more simply, "all dreams will come true like Adam's and Endymion's; the beauty that one desires will not turn out to have been the illusion of a Lamia or Belle Dame sans Merci. In sum, beauty is satisfyingly strong despite appearances to the contrary in a world of apparent flux and sickly deterioration. Poetry reveals this to us in the nature of its created artifacts." Still, since it is the urn that says so and we cannot know what kind of reality it has, even this reading of the statement could be intended (by Keats) as either an accurate description of life and art or a great hoax. We end up with something like "ambiguity squared with irony."

The ambiguity of the "Ode on a Grecian Urn" is resolved in "Lamia," however, by the clear collapse of beauty into truth as magical power fails and hostile critics crash into the bower. Since Lycius's romantic temperament demands all or nothing, the disillusionment is severe. Lycius's guests in fact are much like the critics to whose dissecting reason Keats had exposed the fragile visions of "Endymion":

> The herd approach'd; each guest, with busy brain,
> Arriving at the portal, gaz'd amain,

And enter'd marveling: for they knew the street,
Remember'd it from childhood all complete
Without a gap, yet ne'er before had seen
That royal porch, that high-build fair demesne;
So in they hurried all, maz'd, curious and keen.

                                    ["Lamia," 2.150–156]

Their desecration of the bower is at Lycius's own invitation,
however, and Apollonius says nothing about Lamia that
Keats has not already hinted in his own ironic view of her.
Her wooing of Lycius is a tissue of coyness and feminine
strategies that in a sense trivialize the mystical delay of Cynthia in "Endymion":

"Alas! poor youth
What taste of purer air hast thou to soothe
My essence? What serener palaces,
Where I may all my many senses please,
And by mysterious sleights a hundred thirsts appease?
It cannot be—Adieu!" So said, she rose
Tiptoe with white arms spread.

                                    [1.281–287]

We already know that this spirit of poetry does not plan to
fly away, which makes her teasing semicomic and in retrospect
casts doubt on the Keatsian magic words in the passage, "essence," "serener palaces," "purer air," "mysterious sleights,"
sleep and awakening, and the "tiptoe" image that normally
symbolizes moments when the poet is poised for visionary
flight. Like the singing voices that come to Endymion upon
awakening, she sings "a song of love, too sweet for earthly
lyres" (1.299), but in her case the song is false enticement; and
though "Real are the dreams of God," who do not grow pale
"as mortal lovers do" (1.127, 145), Lycius' dream cannot be
realized. Hence, though he is cajoled and flattered by fairyland
love, even before Lamia withers away his passion has grown
"fierce." Only haunting music supports the "fairy-roof," which
suggests that only the pretty sounds of poetry, divorced from
meaning, keep us entranced. The "forest" is mere decoration,
set out for pleasing effects (like the lush revels of "Endymion")
in an orgy that offers something for every palate:

Soon was God Bacchus at meridian height;
Flush'd were their cheeks, and bright eyes double bright:
Garlands of every green, and every scent
From vales deflower'd, or forest-trees branch-rent,
In baskets of bright osier'd gold were brought
High as the handles heap'd, to suit the thought
Of every guest; that each, as he did please,
Might fancy-fit his brows, silk-pillow'd at his ease.

[2.213–220]

The wedding party—Lycius's first venture into the publication of his dreams—brings together critical reason and fantasy, magic and an audience. The recognition scene results in a clear realization of the fragility of poetic feigning. With the exposure of Lamia,

the loud revelry
Grew hush; the stately music no more breathes;
The myrtle sicken'd in a thousand wreaths.
By faint degrees, voice, lute, and pleasure ceased.

[2.261–265]

Understandably, all is now "blight" to Lycius. As befits the illusion without substance that Burton's *Anatomy of Melancholy* had made her and the foul creature Lycius has discovered her to be, Lamia vanishes.

Beyond this discrediting of poetic powers lies the autumn ode and a new elegiac mood. The myths are gone but poetry remains in the improvised responses the poet feels for unmetamorphosed and perishing things. The spirit of autumn, Keats's last goddess figure, is more naturalistic, than mythic. Under her influence all singing creatures prepare gracefully for their journeys:

Where are the songs of Spring? Ay, where are they?
    Think not of them, thou hast thy music too,—
While barred clouds bloom the soft-dying day,
    And touch the stubble-plains with rosy hue;
Then in a wailful choir the small gnats mourn
    Among the river sallows, borne aloft
        Or sinking as the light wind lives or dies;
And full-grown lambs loud bleat from hilly bourn;

> Hedge-crickets sing; and now with treble soft
> The red-breast whistles from a garden-croft;
>   And gathering swallows twitter in the skies.

The music of the creatures is both sweet and dissonant, a music of pure process and change, as nature nudges them toward fruition and simultaneously toward death. The poet who celebrates their passage is not one who flies with "awful wing" above "the gross and palpable things / Of this diurnal ball"; rather, exploring form and substance homeward to their untranscendent essences, he finds them a choir of mournful gnats on the wind, their music a mimetic representation of their temporal processes.

TWELVE

Hardy's Novels of
Scene and Manners

Before Thomas Hardy, the natural scenery of the novel is not usually related dynamically to human motive and action. Robinson Crusoe's island offers some resistance to its colonizer but requires no personal cajoling and has no primitive curse (though perhaps some malignancy). Its function is primarily to produce, when skill and industry are applied to it; Crusoe puts so much in and gets so much out. Though its god resides far off, he is a good provider, committed to rewarding labor not merely with sufficiency but with an excess that can later be invested. Because it falls so largely under social control eventually, it fits conveniently into plots of social-economic gain with which Defoe replaces, in the bourgeois novel, the schedules of military and feudal honor in older romances and allegories. To Richardson, Fielding, and Austen, the scene is even less an influence on the central action. *Joseph Andrews* and *Pride and Prejudice* begin not with settings, of course, but with social maxims that provide the governing laws of the work, or at least sets of rules that the hero confronts and may ironically invert:

> It is a trite but true observation that examples work more forcibly on the mind than precepts: and if this be just in what is odious and blameable, it is more strongly so in what is amiable and praiseworthy. . . . A good man therefore is a standing lesson to all his acquaintances, and of far greater use in that narrow circle than a good book. [*Joseph Andrews*]

Beginning with a common sense axiom, Fielding proceeds syllogistically—and with tongue-in-cheek—to the proposition that this kind of history is the best account of human affairs.

The main tension is between individual vitality, associated with the lower classes, and social law, mostly hypocritical or impotent. Fielding harmonizes these eventually by having the robust hero discover an upper-middle-class parentage that adds respectability to his native vitality.

The shift of emphasis to forest, rural, provincial, and urban scenes in nineteenth-century novels, particularly in Hardy, Eliot, and Dickens, presupposes a shift in the concept of nature that makes it a contributing element of plot. As Dorothy Van Ghent suggests in *The English Novel* with respect to *Tess,* the dilemma of Hardy's protagonists is essentially that to sink into oneness with nature as an undomesticated force is to sacrifice both morality and social distinction; yet either to assert independence from it or to hold dominion over it as property is to become alienated from one's only stable source of identity.

As it falls under the influence of the scene's mysterious omnipresence and becomes partly magical, the social hierarchy also undergoes a change. The individuating drive of the protagonist (Clym Yeobright, Giles Winterbourne, Jude, Tess, Henchard) is thwarted from two sides, by the society he tries to enter and by the land whose influence he tries to divert or escape. On one hand, judged by position and manners, society ranges from uncultured and often amoral rustics to those who are moralistic, wealthy, and conversant with books. With respect to agreement with nature, on the other hand, society ranges from those who are tainted, alienated, impotent, and pretentious, like the Clare family in *Tess,* to those who are pure, simple, and sometimes (but not often) happy. The vitality of the new rustic in the second category offers an alternative to the hero's social ambition, especially in Hardy's early novels, in which the provincial community is relatively close and merry, and nature has not yet revealed a maliciousness of its own. In all the novels, the hero must define his relationship with nature and society and sort out the ambiguities of each, crossing conventional courtship, the goal of which is a favorable contractual match, with scenic romance. His experience with nature usually proves to be primary and also partly obscure. Provincial life is situated within a pervasive natural

force that in later novels ruins his chances, as though it re-
sponded enigmatically to his attempt to rise socially: the
hidden strand of nature's plot provides a system of checks and
balances founded in hubris and guilt and bringing retaliation
for every social advance.

The Return of the Native illustrates perhaps Hardy's simplest set of reciprocal responses between nature and society.
The heath is in a sense the chief antagonist to the central marriage: it drives Eustacia to despair, assists in the killing of
both her and Mrs. Yeobright, presides over the drowning of
Wildeve, and defeats Yeobright's plans for an educated bucolic
community. In each of these acts, it resists all graduated steps
by which society ordinarily might be expected to move toward
a higher culture. "Mysterious in its swarthy monotony," the
untameable "Ismaelitish thing that Egdon now was it always
had been. Civilisation was its enemy; and ever since the beginning of vegetation its soil had worn the same antique
brown dress." [1] Escape from it is virtually impossible: only
two people, Diggory Venn and Thomasin, succeed in establishing themselves outside it, on its edge, and it is predictable
that Venn will do so because, of all those caught in the heath,
he alone is adept at keeping afloat. He does so, however, only
by staying within its laws and refusing to assert himself "hero-
ically." Though he clearly has the better of his competitor
Wildeve, a conventional "weak" romantic figure, his victory
cannot be considered a successful fusion of pastoral and social
romance. While Wildeve plunges impulsively into Shadwater
pool (into which much of the viciousness of Egdon is fun-
neled), Venn judges the movement of the water and instinc-
tively adjusts to it. But his influence is not decisive: he cannot
save any of those whom the heath dooms, and he asserts his
own modest claims in courtship only after other contenders
have destroyed themselves.

At the opposite extreme from Venn, Mrs. Yeobright distinguishes herself from the rustics and struggles stubbornly
against the heath by sending Clym into the world. Her self-

[1] Thomas Hardy, *The Return of the Native* (New York: Random House, n.d.), p. 7.

destructive journey to visit Clym is an ill-timed, incautious gesture that provokes a reaction from the scene, with which she finds her son much too closely associated. He seems in fact little higher than the insects breeding there:

The silent being who thus occupied himself seemed to be of no more account in life than an insect. He appeared as a mere parasite of the heath, fretting its surface in his daily labour as a moth frets a garment, entirely engrossed with its products, having no knowledge of anything in the world but fern, furze, heath, lichens, and moss. [P. 343]

As the heath's lurid moments reveal, Mrs. Yeobright is pitted against something more than accident but something less than definable and meaningful hostility:

The trees beneath which she sat were singularly battered, rude, and wild, and for a few minutes Mrs. Yeobright dismissed thoughts of her own storm-broken and exhausted state to contemplate theirs. Not a bough in the nine trees which composed the group but was splintered, lopped, and distorted by the fierce weather that there held them at its mercy whenever it prevailed. [P. 344]

Clym Yeobright is less foolhardy in resisting the heath and more aware of its poetry, but he is nonetheless baffled by it. Though "permeated with its scenes, with its substance, and with its odours" (p. 213), he runs counter to its primitivism. Whereas Venn handles it practically, he attacks it intellectually. He violates the leveling pressure implicit in its resistance to civilization quite as much as Eustacia's taste for trivial finery does. He is overpowered by "the dead flat of the scenery,"

though he was fully alive to the beauty of that untarnished early summer green which was worn for the nonce by the poorest blade. There was something in its oppressive horizontality which too much reminded him of the arena of life; it gave him a sense of bare equality with, and no superiority to, a single living thing under the sun. [P. 256]

There is perhaps also some inconsistency between Clym's intellectual ambition and his ready acquiescence in that leveling:

his impulse to rise is countered by an equal impulse for self-humiliation—as, symbolically, reading leads directly to blindness. In a sense, then, he desires what fate imposes on him: "the monotony of his occupation soothed him, and was in itself a pleasure. A forced limitation of effort offered a justification of homely courses to an unambitious man, whose conscience would hardly have allowed him to remain in such obscurity while his powers were unimpeded" (p. 312). Though he finds "horizontality" oppressive, he answers Eustacia's disappointment over his acceptance of the worker's life by conceding, "the more I see of life the more do I perceive that there is nothing particularly great in its greatest walks, and therefore nothing particularly small in mind of furze-cutting" (p. 315).

Yeobright's compromise with the heath is perhaps what saves him from a worse fate, since ambition is punished mysteriously in Hardy, like hubris by Greek fates. But passive acquiescence does not guarantee that nature will not destroy those who are implicated in it. Tess, for instance, is not assertive, but she cannot avoid its curse. The more her animalism allows natural appetite its unreflective freedom, the more vulnerable she is. At the same time, guilt and conscience also contribute to her ruin, which is conceived ironically against the conventional pattern of the heroine whose sin destroys and repentance redeems: her most natural moment in the forest-seduction, according to the Christian idea of sin and its consequences that dominates the Clare family, should have cost her paradise but leads instead to the idyll at Crick's dairy; her repentant confession to Angel, which should then have redeemed her, leads to the purgatory of Flintcomb-Ash.

This inversion obviously reflects unfavorably upon Christian morality as well as upon the cosmic injustice that Hardy eventually impugns. Yet nature in itself offers no alternative to the set of moral laws and conventions by which character is defined. As Crick's dairy reveals, when nature is pleasant, society may gear itself to a kind of practical Arcadian economy and circumvent its usual difficulties with class: "Dairyman Crick's household of maids and men lived on comfortably, placidly,

even merrily. Their position was perhaps the happiest of all
positions in the social scale, being . . . below the line at which
the *convenances* begin to cramp natural feeling, and the
stress of thread-bare modishness makes too little of enough." [2]
But Crick's dairy remains merely that—a place where cows are
milked and butter churned. Despite its influence on Clare, who
escapes the domination of moral prescriptiveness there, it
cannot be taken as a model compromise. And here as elsewhere, as Dorothy Van Ghent points out, nature is not always
romantic. It coincides with society's idea of distinction no better than Giles Winterborne's elaborate dinner and the slug that
turns up in Grace Melbury's salad: well boiled, Robert Creedle
hastens to tell Giles, and " 'twas his native home come to that."
But nonetheless, "there my gentleman was."

Tess's difficulty in integrating nature and society from her
relatively low place in the hierarchy is reversed in Angel
Clare's attempt to "naturalize" himself from above. In a sense,
Clare has only to put aside the meddling intellect to become
an instinctive creature; "with more animalism he would have
been the nobler man," Hardy remarks (p. 213). But to do so
would require an act of mind and will so alien to the instinctive man as to completely remake him. Delightful as he finds
the dairy, it no more prepares for such a change than Sir
Calidore's sojourn with Pastorella prepares for the queen's
service. It is not surprising that his change of heart proves
temporary when Tess confesses her fault to him. (His subsequent reform in Brazil is an unanalyzed necessity of the
plot.) To the bucolic community, he can never be more than a
friendly outsider.

The dilemma of Clare and Tess can be seen even more
clearly in the chief lovers of *The Woodlanders* where the
hierarchy is broken into rustic and conventional romance pairs:
corresponding to Tess and Clare are Grace Melbury and Fitzpiers, with Mrs. Charmond pulling Fitzpiers upward and
Marty South and Giles providing a lower, unconventional

[2] Hardy, *Tess of the D'Urbervilles* (New York: Harper, 1920),
p. 165.

pair eventually relinquished to the woodland. At one time or another, each of the following five "visits" each of the others and establishes grounds for "pastoral" negotiation:

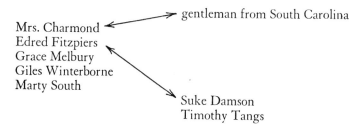

The two men are situated just inside each extreme and Grace Melbury between them, to be drawn in opposite directions by them. Outside liaisons between Fitzpiers and Suke Damson and between Mrs. Charmond and the exiled Southerner do not essentially complicate the arrangement. (The peripheral crude or rustic lovers of both *Tess* and *The Woodlanders* fare little better than the others. Like Arabella's victimizing of Jude, their success in dragging down those above them only proves that no one is invulnerable to crude nature.) Marty South, in allowing Mrs. Charmond to appropriate her hair for a wig, takes herself out of running in the social romance, as Mrs. Charmond, by appropriating it, takes herself farther out of "nature." That the five lovers compose an odd number guarantees that one will always be left out and provides numerous opportunities for pastoral laments over unrequited love as well as some higher level demonstrations of "romantic" abstinence (one case of which brings about Giles's death). Generally speaking, differences are heightened in the context of the village economy and lessened by the democratic timelessness of the forest. Grace and Mrs. Charmond fall into each other's arms in the forest, and Fitzpiers, under the mutual influence of spring and the trees, is led to abandon his plans for advancement in order to court Grace.

What this hierarchy demonstrates more clearly than that of Tess's society is that each is doomed because he is stationed, and because the only real alternative to conventional courtship is the biological, rudimentary life of the provincial community and the forest. The question for Grace Melbury is whether to distinguish herself from the hamlet (and thus become as bored and lifeless as Mrs. Charmond) or to lapse into the background by marrying Winterborne—resigning herself to red hands and a bounding walk like the "regular Hintock shale-and-wamble."

It is true that the hamlet of *The Woodlanders*, like some rare aspects of nature in *Tess*, is also poetic and romantic in its own right, its poetry deriving from its long association with the woodland. But nature does not allow one to transcend local politics and economy; and only for a few is the scene satisfying without the added interest of social position and contractual marriage:

Winter in a solitary house in the country, without society, is tolerable, nay, even enjoyable and delightful, given certain conditions; but these are not conditions which attach to the life of a professional man who drops down into such a place by mere accident. They were present to the lives of Winterborne, Melbury, and Grace; but not to the doctor's. They are old association—an almost exhaustive biographical or historical acquaintance with every object, animate and inanimate within the observer's horizon. He must know all about those invisible ones of the days gone by, whose feet have traversed the fields which look so grey from his windows; recall whose creaking plough has turned those sods from time to time; whose hands planted the trees that form a crest to the opposite hill; whose horses and hounds have torn through that underwood; what birds affect that particular brake. . . . The spot may have beauty, grandeur, salubrity, convenience; but if it lack memories it will ultimately pall upon him who settles there.[3]

Only the natives of Hintock have such memories, and only rustics are really natives. Even for them, the other side of nature is far less attractive. The scene that the woodlanders rise to greet each morning does not encourage fine manners: "Owls that had been catching mice in the outhouses, rabbits that had been eating the winter-greens in the garden, and stoats that had been sucking the blood of rabbits, discerning that their

[3] Hardy, *The Woodlanders* (London: St. Martin's, 1958), pp. 128–129.

human neighbours were on the move, discreetly withdrew from publicity, and were seen and heard no more till nightfall" (p. 26). Nature's deformities are as pronounced as society's:

On older trees . . . huge lobes of fungi grew like lungs. Here, as everywhere, the Unfulfilled Intention, which makes life what it is, was as obvious as it could be among the depraved crowds of a city slum. The leaf was deformed, the curve was crippled, the taper was interrupted; the lichen ate the vigour of the stalk, and the ivy slowly strangled to death the promising sapling. [P. 56]

The chief similarity between nature and society is their mutual rapacity. Squires and landlords trap poachers with machines, and their machines have jaws like wild boars, wolves, and bears—beginning with the toothless kinds used by soft-hearted trappers, progressing through a middling sort with "two inches of mercy, two inches of cruelty," and climaxed in "the bruisers, which did not lacerate the flesh, but only crushed the bone" (p. 362).

It is not surprising, therefore, that Robert Creedle, serving as historian, finds no grounds either in the past or in the common cruelty of nature and poacher-trapping landlords for a happy integration of nature and society. He and his fellow rustics offer instead a free commentary on the vanity of position:

"O yes. Ancient days, when there was battles, and famines, and hang-fairs and other pomps, seem to me as yesterday. Ah, many's the patriarch I've seed come and go in this parish! There, he's calling for more plates. Lord, why can't 'em turn their plates bottom upward for pudding, as we bucks used to do in former days!" [P. 79]

Such commentary is not merely a clownish view of social pretensions but a "Shakespearean" countercheck, from a variety of subplot character, to love's main plot. The same voluble chorus says of Mrs. Charmond:

"My brother-in-law told me, and I have no reason to doubt it," said Creedle, "that she'll sit down to her dinner with a gown hardly higher than her elbows. 'O, you wicked woman!' he said to hisself when he first see her, 'you go to the Table o' Sundays, and kneel, as if your knee-jints were greased with very saint's anointment, and tell off your hear-us-good-Lords as pat as a business-man counting money; and yet you can eat your victuals a-script to such a wanton figure as that!' " [P. 29]

Christians, money-counters, and dress styles come and go, but Creedle, his brother-in-law, and the slug who lives in the lettuce endure like nature itself.

Hence, inevitably, the ending of the novel dissolves the commerce between the upper and lower ranks of the hierarchy. While Grace Melbury forgets Winterborne and leaves Hintock with Fitzpiers, Marty South remains at graveside. The novel begins with her sacrifice to Mrs. Charmond and ends with her repossession—for Giles, after all, is her lover and one who has nothing else may at least claim elegiac consolations. In taking this consolation, she illustrates both the lowest rank among the novel's lovers and the highest surviving communion with nature. She alone "had approximated to Winterborne's level of intelligent intercourse with nature" (p. 340), and only that intercourse creates the enduring meeting of minds that transcends ordinary social contracts:

she had formed his true complement in the other sex, had lived as his counterpart, had subjoined her thoughts to his as a corollary. . . . They had been possessed of [nature's] finer mysteries as of commonplace knowledge; had been able to read its hieroglyphs as ordinary writing; to them the sights and sounds of night, winter, wind, storm, amid those dense boughs, which had to Grace a touch of the uncanny, and even of the supernatural, were simple occurrences whose origin, continuance, and laws they foreknew. They had planted together, and together they had felled; together they had, with the run of the years, mentally collected those remoter signs and symbols which seen in few were of runic obscurity, but all together made an alphabet. [Pp. 340–341]

Theirs is the kind of bond that creates both Arcadian friendship and the elegiac dignity of Arcadian death, which Hardy can allow without improving on nature since it does not demand a strong idyllic element: nature dignifies here by destroying and by associating the dead with the long chronicles of woodland history.

But the elegy would be a legitimate solution to the separation of social distinction and natural dignity only if the novel were willing to surrender one to the other; and both this novel and Hardy's other scenic romances stress instead the ironic reciprocity of nature and society. Consequently, Hardy's final perspective on Marty South implicitly "looks down" upon her. She has obviously paid a high price for her escape from the complications of the social plot, not merely transcending society in "the loftier quality of abstract humanism" but also wearing herself down by poverty and toil. She accepts a life of solitude outside the normal human processes of marriage, reproduction, and social organization:

As this solitary and silent girl stood there in the moonlight, a straight slim figure, clothed in a plaitless gown, the contours of womanhood so undeveloped as to be scarcely perceptible in her, the marks of poverty and toil effaced by the misty hour, she touched sublimity at points, and looked almost like a being who had rejected with indifference the attribute of sex for the loftier quality of abstract humanism. [P. 379]

While Grace leaves the woodland, then, Marty leaves the realm of the living for the woodland's unreclaimable dead. In a sense, the heroic images shatter: Giles abandons common sense to become a chivalric lover in his protection of Grace; Marty draws further and further into the solitary depths of nature; Grace tends to become the conventional heroine; and Fitzpiers moves a little toward the natural man, but not enough. Neither Grace nor Fitzpiers is quite able finally to suggest a fruitful rebirth of their "slain" doubles.

Though it might seem logical to consider Marty's tribute Hardy's version of a final tragic chorus, her rustic dialect suggests a mode somewhat closer to the Theocritean elegy than tragedy:

"Now, my own, own love," she whispered, "you are mine, and only mine; for she has forgot 'ee at last, although for her you died! But I—whenever I get up I'll think of 'ee, and whenever I lie down I'll think of 'ee again. Whenever I plant the young larches I'll think that none can plant as you planted; and whenever I split a gad, and whenever I turn the cider wring, I'll say none could do it like you. If ever I forget your name let me forget home and heaven! . . . But no, no, my love, I never can forget 'ee; for you was a good man, and did good things!" [P. 380]

Both the elegy and tragedy universalize those who by their inescapable endings might appear to have proved local and particular: their individual careers are ended by primary forces of nature. But the pastoral elegy differs from tragedy in the measurement of worth that it assumes. The tragic hero is remembered primarily by social tributes, and his death often brings about a purification that makes possible a public rite free in conscience. The result is frequently a restitution of social order after he has paid for whatever faults he has had; members of his society, by implication in his fate, have vicariously paid for their flaws, too.

The pastoral elegy, however, dignifies its subject by association with the natural seasons and their recurrence, which Marty will measure by the rustic tasks she performs in their proper times. Her apostrophe thus remains close to the spirit of the pastoral lament in combining an expansive association between nature and the fallen rustic with certain constrictions inherent in her own obscurity, loneliness, and inarticulateness. Though the gloom of the churchyard hides the marks of her poverty and gives her a moment of near sublimity, her ways of recalling Giles are, at the same time, reductively simple— and no doubt even Giles would like to be remembered as more than a planter of larches and a cider man. She ritualizes death and her own losses in ceremonially balanced and eloquent syntax, the *whenever* clauses of which represent in serial form the temporal continuity and recurrence she promises; but that dignity is undercut by such phrases as "cider wring," "split a gad," and "you was" and again by the redundancy of the last sentence.

When we consider this generic mixture of pastoral elegy and the novel's documentary manner, the final direction that

Tess takes, too, becomes somewhat clearer. For like *The Woodlanders, Tess* concludes with what we might call a novelistic elegy that fuses two main areas of concern, social standing and nature's hidden strand. As we have seen, Tess misses connections on both planes: the worst of each is evident in the "starve-acre" farm at Flintcomb Ash, where Tess is subdued both by the land—the chalk formations, the stony soil, the "white vacuity" of the sky—and by economic and moral elements that reduce her to a transient laborer. Their influence on her is not limited to Flintcomb Ash, of course, nor is Tess alone in her ruin. Other dairymaids from Crick's dairy are dispossessed with her, and longtime residents of her old community are uprooted and their very names stolen. Those more fortunate either do not understand the longevity and un-bounded scope of the land or are too busy maintaining their titles to think about it—like Mrs. Brooks, the last householder of the novel, who owns "handsome furniture" but is "too deeply materialized, poor woman, by her long and enforced bondage to that arithmetical demon Profit and Loss" to "re-tain much curiosity for its own sake, and apart from possible lodgers' pockets" (p. 485).

This combination of social and natural enemies requires a novelistic-pastoral final statement of some kind, and it is just such a statement that Stonehenge makes possible. It is a last attempt to transform Tess's defeat into a meaningful and dignified victimage. Whereas Marty South mourns alone in the language of a provincial, Tess's sorrow implicitly becomes that of all those who have helped ruin her, and it suffers no ironic diminishing. For one thing, the distinction between classes (one of which speaks Tess's regional dialect and the other the standard speech of novels of manners) is finally transcended. Though Tess's own people were once shepherds there ("Now I am at home," she remarks), her sacrifice is a "fulfillment" of another kind than the Durbeyfields would have expected. Since Angel Clare has joined her, the conven-tions of the social romance are also brought into the scene and deepened. Stonehenge is thus a culmination that summarizes Tess's itinerary and condenses the novel's other settings; it adds to all of these things Tess's own willing participation. She becomes one with the god of the rising sun and the spirit of the plain which fuses the benediction and malediction of other scenes.

The success of the scene is due in part to Hardy's flexible point of view, which extricates us from Tess's entanglement and sets aside clashes of social values in the interests of the sacrificial rite itself. Since Stonehenge transcends both the pursued and the pursuers, both parties can surrender to its sense of elegiac rightness. Initially, the point of view is Clare's, which gives us a close association with Tess. But the sense of nature's encompassing participation in the rite is more Hardy's than Clare's:

> In a minute or two her breathing became more regular, her clasp of his hand relaxed, and she fell asleep. The band of silver paleness along the east horizon made even the distant parts of the Great Plain appear dark and near; and the whole enormous landscape bore that impress of reserve, taciturnity, and hesitation which is usual just before day. The eastward pillars and their architraves stood up blackly against the light, and the great flame-shaped Sun-stone beyond them; and the Stone of Sacrifice midway. Presently the night wind died out, and the quivering little pools in the cup-like hollows of the stones lay still. At the same time something seemed to move on the verge of the dip eastward—a mere dot. It was the head of a man approaching them from the hollow beyond the Sun-stone. Clare wished they had gone onward, but in the circumstances decided to remain quiet. The figure came straight towards the circle of pillars in which they were. [P. 504]

As the dawn continues to brighten, Clare discovers other pursuers among the stone columns. His glances from the center outward toward the horizon and back give the scene enough "far awayness" to associate the ritual act with nature, yet enough proximity to Tess to allow us to sense the closing in of her destiny.

If Marty South's elegy fuses the poetic strategies of the pastoral elegy with the novel's matter-of-factness, here the combination of styles is even richer. It includes tragedy's combination of elevation and catastrophe, the elegy's combination of the natural and the human, and the documentary novel's concern with manners and social justice. These are naturally not clean distinctions, yet we can sift out some of their separate components. (Note, for instance, the sudden quiet of the quivering pools in the hollows of the stones. The image puts a "novelistic" tension in a pastoral image that is basically peaceful.) As representatives of social justice materialize out of the dark, they too are made to seem as inevitable and right as the sun that shines upon them, as though the ennobling qualities of nature could be transferred to them; and, perhaps, in turn, a sense of their purpose is invested in nature. The seasonal turning that has been measured here since the Druids thus appears to bring around the catastrophe of the plot. The requirements of the novel and of elegiac pastoral are momentarily the same.

Since Tess is no longer a laborer or dairy nymph but a tragic victim seeking atonement, both the capture and the hanging can subsequently be seen as ceremonially right—as part of the inevitable sacrifice. Though we are not shown Tess's final moments, her resolve suggests what they are like: obeying the spirit of Stonehenge, she finds at last a role that she can play willingly. Though sleep has been a prelude to disaster previously, this time she arises and goes forward willingly.

After Stonehenge has cleared the air, Hardy resumes the novelist's role as epic-historian and remains far enough from the new romance between Clare and Tess's sister to round the work out quietly. The last view that we have of nature is a panoramic survey that places Tess's hanging within a larger scene and again suggests a coincidence between the sacrificial demand of justice and the compliance of nature. If Stonehenge makes use of the dignity of the deep past, the final panorama makes use of the dignity of high spatial sweep:

The prospect from this summit was almost unlimited. In the valley beneath lay the city they had just left, its more prominent buildings showing as in an isometric drawing—among them the broad cathedral tower, with its Norman windows and immense length of aisle and nave, the spires of St. Thomas's . . . the tower and gables of the ancient hospice, where . . . the pilgrim may receive his dole of bread and ale. Behind the city swept the rotund upland of St. Catherine's Hill; further off, landscape beyond landscape, till the horizon was lost in the radiance of the sun hanging above it. [P. 507]

Under the influence of this spatial distance, the victim Tess is almost apotheosized by hanging while the new "Tess" is freed of her sister's guilt and may receive the blessings of the sun and the "high" view of things.

But Hardy does not allow us to fade thus operatically and poetically entirely out of the novel, which still has its historical and didactic responsibilities. First, perhaps by accident, a momentary awkwardness creeps into the description, which inconsistently takes us inside the cathedral to observe its long aisle; and the historian that sees over the shoulder of the two gazers is aware that at least one social problem continues "to this day." Following this, the final paragraphs turn in another direction. In fact, they may seem to shatter altogether Hardy's careful tonal control in assigning a kind of natural rightness to Tess's capture:

"Justice" was done, and the President of the Immortals, in Aeschylean phrase, had ended his sport with Tess. And the d'Urberville knights and dames slept on in their tombs unknowing. The two speechless gazers bent themselves down to the earth, as if in prayer, and remained thus a long time, absolutely motionless: the flag continued to wave silently. As soon as they had strength they arose, joined hands again, and went on. [P. 508]

Why does Hardy complicate the closing in this way? Perhaps a sufficient answer is that the novel generally and Hardy especially have another commitment, to a close-up focus on society, to its language, and to the localized points of view of those inextricably caught in its web. *Tess,* after all, like *The Woodlanders,* is only secondarily tragic and elegiac; it is primarily documentary fiction, to which prisons and hangmen are more native than rites of druidic priests and pastoral lamentation.

Though we have been encouraged to think of Tess's death

partly "in the name of" the seasons, this commitment to social documentation resists the direction that both Stonehenge and the visual panorama carry us. From the high view, Hardy passes to "a large red-brick building" in front of the others in town, "with level grey roofs, and rows of short barred windows bespeaking captivity" (p. 507). "From the middle of the building" (he continues), "an ugly flat-topped octagonal tower ascended against the east horizon"—which is to say, ascended against the sunrise, like a modern debased substitute for Stonehenge. And it is with this symbol of human desecration, "this blot," and not "with the beauty, that the two gazers were concerned" (pp. 507–508). Its prominence in the foreground of the panorama suggests that the sun shines indifferently on beauty and on the crude, stark instruments of social injustice; and this suggestion reflects ironically upon the entire Stonehenge scene.

But so rapidly does Hardy progress through possible relations between the elevated perspective and the novel's encircling realism, that he controls this irony with what would seem to be an effective and (for Hardy) rare combination of styles. The final effect is to allow the elegiac mood and the historical moralist to coexist. We are obviously not meant to be entirely at ease with Tess's fate, but at the same time we are sufficiently reconciled to it to take solace in the new life salvaged from it. The worlds of Tess and her sister necessarily divide under the pressure of time and circumstance, and Hardy stands between them: the living and the dead are parted with something less than ceremonial dignity, yet in triumph over the injustice and the ironies of fate, the two gazers remember; they ceremonialize; they pay tribute to. We are manipulated into accepting the quiet dignity of their frozen posture. (The flag is a ceremonial substitute for a direct account of the hanging, and that stylistic discretion assists their detached pantomime.) Even though neither Tess nor any other addressee is listening (and so their gesture, if it were intended as communication, would be futile), they need the ceremony of the saying itself. Perhaps the final irony of the passage is that their gesture can be a sufficient center of the novel's final commitment to form: it is a creation of a dignified social manner such as no one up to now has achieved. That they can make it without defiance of the social order or the mysterious fates conditions the bitterness of the narrator and prevents him from being drawn too far into the close-up. Though they are as surely exiled from paradise as Milton's famous pair that Hardy recalls here, they suggest also the same forward-looking, hopeful-elegiac ambivalence.

I would not maintain that their long view removes all the bitterness left by the sport of gods, who take human "justice" for their temporal instrument, or that it removes the sting of Hardy's irony with respect to the indifferent d'Urberville knights and dames. But the rhythm of the concluding sentence is effectively peaceful in its way, as when mourning shepherds move on at the end of pastoral elegies. It is appropriate that Hardy keep the perspective aloof enough to generalize 'Liza Lu and Clare into silhouettes so as not to predict a specific future—and therefore specific new kinks in their lives at the instigation of fate: they belong now merely to the general order of nature, relatively free of a society that twists nature with its laws, its classes, its speech, manners, wealth, marriage.

In *The Mayor of Casterbridge,* Henchard's dissatisfaction with what fate imposes on him is much stronger, partly because the cycle of his rise and fall is dissociated from the rhythm of the seasons and natural life, or so mysteriously related to these that no rites can establish the connection. Except for Abel Whittle, Henchard ends alone, denied both ceremony and witnesses. Rather than taking part in a public sacrifice that assumes a natural validation of social acts, he writes a futile "will," in isolation, denying implicitly any overseeing law of nature and explicitly any contact with society. Neither he nor other members of the Casterbridge marketplace are close to nature; "nature" in the small town economy of the novel means primarily crops and sellable produce, and even so vagaries of weather and an uncanny bad luck defeat his attempts to use nature as market strategy.

Henchard's twofold alienation, from his own natural sympathies and from the social order, begins when he sells his wife Susan. In committing themselves to that contract, both Henchard and Susan implicitly assume that all things are subject to the laws of barter and exchange, and they initiate what is to be come a wholesale trading of partners around the circle —Susan to Newsome (leaving Henchard free to acquire Lucetta later), Lucetta to Farfrae, and eventually Farfrae to Elizabeth, who has left Henchard. Though Susan is simple enough to believe implicitly in official-looking transactions despite their unnaturalness, Henchard realizes that he has misused contractual forms and does not feel easy about it until he has confessed to his accuser, the furmity woman. Logically, his tragic *anagnorisis,* if there is to be one, should be a recognition of a "kinship" above economic negotiations that would cement all bonds (as it does in Arcadian societies). It would reintegrate him with the bonds of the natural family and the seasons, one softening the fate that inevitably grows out of the other. Instead, his recognition of his mistake is marred first by his treatment of the reunion with Susan as a business deal ("He said nothing about the enclosure of five guineas. The amount was significant; it may tacitly have said to her that he bought her back again"),[4] and then by his failure to find proper terms for his will.

From the trade in Vanity Fair onward, Henchard's advancement is founded almost exclusively upon contracts that bind him to property, yet deny him true "ownership." That he achieves a seat at the head of the council table at the "King's Arm" suggests that the business establishment of Casterbridge is a surviving baronial skeleton; yet the central bonds of the king's arm are gone and in their place are various stations of financial success, continually changeable and negotiable. In pinning his faith to them, Henchard has indeed "quitted the ways of vulgar men, without light to guide him on a better way" (p. 148). In trying to unearth proof in black and white of his claim on Elizabeth, for instance, he finds that because

[4] Hardy, *The Mayor of Casterbridge* (New York: Random House, n.d.), p. 90.

of the original violation of the marital bargain with Susan he has ceased to understand his wife, who now offers documentary evidence against him. And calling Elizabeth to witness Lucetta's promise to him only alienates both of them. It is an excess of passion that leads him into these mistakes, rather than greed, just as his craving for "some human object for pouring out his heart upon" moves him to hire Farfrae on impulse despite a tentative agreement with Jopp for the same position. Thus in a sense, he finds no adequate forms for the social expression of natural impulses, and an incongruity between social form and impulse results in guilt and a disproportionate self-punishment. (In Arcadian societies, of course, social form arises spontaneously from desire and no one need contend for what he wants: both friendship and love ideally find ceremonial expression that marries true minds without further negotiation.)

In contrast with Henchard, Farfrae is "lucky" in these respects. He redeems bad contracts with a magical touch, as in restoring wholesomeness to Henchard's spoiled wheat, and he separates clearly the realms of romance and market dealings. Though he talks only profit and loss and it is soon obvious to Lucetta that "the curious double strands in Farfrae's thread of life—the commercial and the romantic"—are "very distinct" (p. 207), the cleavage works for rather than against him. His first understanding with Henchard, pressed on him fervently by Henchard and merely accepted with detachment on his part, is a mixture of business and friendship. Whereas Henchard's business manner, like his ledgers, is "like a bramble-wood," Farfrae handles business entirely "by ciphering and measuring": letters and ledgers, legal contracts and their accompanying accounting system, take "the place of 'I'll do it,' and 'you shall hae't'" (p. 116). Having made the division between these two elements so decisive, he is free of the guilt that arises from trying to see one in terms of the other. He would never be guilty of selling affection or loving money, because money is money; love, love. Yet at the same time, his division implies a complete severance of the natural and the social orders as well, and inevitably the balance between them is upset. His romantic side diminishes as he grows in public stature: "engrossed with affairs and ambitions," he loses "in the eyes of the poorer inhabitants something of that wondrous charm which he had had for them as a light-hearted, penniless young man who sang ditties as readily as the birds in the trees" (p. 346). This severance means politically a class structure without conscience and it means morally a lack of articulate values that can organize the total life of the community.

In the novel's double chart, Henchard's fall and Farfrae's rise, then, every discrepancy between affairs of heart and pocket which brings bad luck to one brings good luck to the other; but neither Henchard nor Farfrae manages successfully to solve the dilemma he poses. Henchard is destroyed by self-denunciation, and Farfrae's compromise with ledgers and contracts eventually squeezes him dry.

The dilemma is readily recognizable as similar to that of *The Woodlanders* and *Tess* translated into a small-town setting, and it might seem that as in these novels one way of handling it would be to transcend it in the manner of the Stonehenge scene or Marty South's elegy. The difficulty in *The Mayor* is that "nature," even for the rustics, is more a compulsive set of needs than association with the long chronicles of the dead and the dignity of the elegy. In Maister Billy Wills's words,

we be brukle folk here—the best o' us hardly honest sometimes, what with hard winters, and so many mouths to fill, and God a'mighty sending his little taties so terrible small to fill 'em with. We don't think about flowers and fair faces, now we—except in the shape o' cauliflowers and pigs' chaps. [P. 68]

In fact, one must enter the complexities of trade and work to protect himself and is forced to forget flowers when the stomach calls for cauliflowers. Struggle for betterment exacts a price in guilt and isolation even among the tavern group, which responds with its own viciousness to the troubles of the hierarchy above them. As choral speakers, they take relish in predicting the downfall of those whom they have cause to distrust. "She'll wish her cake dough afore she's done by him" Nancy Mockridge predicts of Susan: "There's a bluebeardy look about 'em; and 'twill out in time." Portents of disaster make Christopher Coney "as clammy as a cocklesnail." The criticism grows caustic and embittered in the roar of sarcastic laughter and the rude music of the skimmity-ride parody of Lucetta. These prophets of social collapse offer reinforcement of Henchard's final version of the "contract" in the will.

The futility and moral decay that Billy describes pervade all levels of the novel from the failing businesses of the opening scene to Henchard's final cottage. Indeed, when Henchard and Susan first appear still members of the peasant class, they are not only half defeated but already committed to competitive bidding as a way of life. Susan plods passively beside him as one "who deems anything possible at the hands of Time and Chance, except, perhaps, fair play" (p. 5), and when Henchard sells her she realizes that rather than violating the order of things he is really subscribing to it. After he has fallen destitute again and rejoined the "bruckle folk," Henchard retreats to a place of ruin worn by "years of rain-washing to a lumpy crumbling surface" (p. 428) in which he joins long ages of ruin and obscurity. This cottage retreat brings into full statement the implicit context of the hero's "will" that has hovered around the action throughout, just as the various scenes of *Tess* converge into the symbolic setting of the Stonehenge sacrifice. (The ruins outside Casterbridge have offered a silent commentary on the market, for instance: after gliding through them, thistledown tumbles through the market and settles in shop doorways.)

Seemingly Abel Whittle offers a chance to translate that pervasive ruin into a new sense of human dignity since he represents Henchard's one bond outside the contractual order. Because he cannot be scheduled, his worth is *unrated* and he stands ready to provoke Henchard out of his customary standards:

"There is sommit wrong in my make, your worshipful!" said Abel, "especially in the inside, whereas my poor dumb brain gets as dead as a clot afore I've said my few scrags of prayers. Yes—it came on as a stripling, just afore I'd got man's wages, whereas I never enjoy my bed at all, for no sooner do I lie down than I be asleep, and afore I be awake I be up. I've fretted my gizzard green about it, maister, but what can I do? Now last night, afore I went to bed, I only had a scantling o' cheese and—"

"I don't want to hear it!" roared Henchard. "Tomorrow the waggons must start at four, and if you're not here, stand clear. I'll mortify thy flesh for thee!" [P. 126]

Whittle's language is that of a simple underling and Henchard's a combination of the King's Arm dispenser and a modern boss. But because Whittle is so far outside that this level of their relationship fails to register with him, he can later respond to Henchard less as a "worshipful maister" than as one "kind-like to Mother when she were here below."

Yet despite Whittle's compassionate alliance, Henchard's final renunciation of bonds is not softened; it is not so much the gesture of a tragic hero who has profited from the company of the fool (like Lear) as an act of disgruntled failure. His will is an inarticulate refusal to claim anything for his own and recalls his overzealous self-denunciation at the furmity woman's trial:

> Michael Henchard's Will.
> That Elizabeth-Jane Farfrae be not told of my death, or made to grieve on account of me.
> & that I be not bury'd in consecrated ground.
> & that no sexton be asked to toll the bell.
> & that nobody is wished to see my dead body.
> & that no murners walk behind me at my funeral.
> & that no flours be planted on my grave.
> & that no man remember me.
> To this I put my name. [P. 430]

Its formality ("to this I put my name" and the series of parallel clauses) is meaningful only if Henchard intends it to be at last a public document, a substitute for the rites it denies, which suggests that it is partly a staged repudiation. In any case, it is a contradiction in terms because the authority it assumes as a quasi-legal document it negates by its content. For no social contract is valid unless its signers bargain in good-will with those named in it. Henchard, while signing his name as though the legal rite still existed, wills an end to precisely the honoring of the name that commands authority. It negates familial bonds, burial rites, memorials, and flower tributes. His last document, then, implicitly assumes not only the impossibility of commemoration and the kind of elegiac relief represented by Marty South's speech and by Stonehenge but also a severe limitation in the instrumenting of one's own will and testament.

But Henchard's negation does not reflect the position of the novel, which seems much closer in sympathy to Elizabeth's more partial renunciation. The cost of her education is eventually a certain shrinkage in feeling in which joy dims in anticipation of disaster. Earlier, overlooking the marketplace with Lucetta from High Place Hall, she observes, calculates, and reaches "understandings" without committing herself either to contracts or to other vows. While Lucetta speaks a dialect of social French, she learns Latin, the language of those who lie buried under the town. Though she realizes that " 'Take, have, and keep, are pleasant words' " (p. 112), she anticipates the ruin of all contracts and possessions and knows that "to keep in the rear of opportunity in matters of indulgence is as valuable a habit as to keep abreast of opportunity in matters of enterprise" (p. 113). Expanding "tight economy" into universal terms, she will not be gay because providence is a quixotic account-keeper that makes and unmakes people indecipherably. Like A. A. Milne's Eeyore, minus Eeyore's irony, "she had learnt the lesson of renunciation, and was as familiar with the wreck of each day's wishes as with the diurnal setting of the sun" (p. 231).

Every mistaken contract to which Henchard commits himself thus teaches her the value of stoic reserve: "It was an odd sequence that out of all this wronging of social law came that flower of Nature, Elizabeth" (p. 412). The gifts she receives are measured to last a lifetime, which is the limit of one's foreseeable need. For one is doomed ultimately to the indignity of ransacking, either by human hand or nature. As Mother Cuxsom remarks concerning the violation of Susan's grave for a few pennies, final negations of ceremony and of the economy of the self are anything but polite: "Well, poor soul; she's helpless to hinder . . . anything now. . . . And all her shining keys will be took from her, and her cupboards opened; and little things a' didn't wish seen, anybody will see; and her wishes and ways will all be as nothing!" In view of this disregard of one's dreams and private property, the only defense is not to care too deeply: one must chasten the will, taking a little now and then when the world seems to have its back turned. Social ambition and the uncalculating, expansive life of Hardy's earlier pastoral communities find a diminished compromise indeed in the marriage of this caution to the conservative minstrel.

In cramping the novel into the spirit of Henchard's will and the stoic reserve of Elizabeth, Hardy sacrifices, for a monotone pessimism, the resonant overtones that he gains in *Tess* from the strategies of the elegy. The difference is essentially the same as that between poems like "Hap" and "Neutral Tones," which ring few changes on the theme of gray ruin, and poems like "The Ruined Maid," "The Oxen," and "During Wind and Rain," the latter a song form that pivots from the joy of family ceremonies and rites to elegiac sorrow without settling into a determined bitterness. I quote it as a final, instructive example of Hardy's skill in combining attitudes and gaining from their reciprocation.

> They sing their dearest songs—
> He, she, all of them—yea,
> Treble and tenor and bass,
>   And one to play;
> With the candles mooning each face. . . .
>   Ah, no; the years O!
> How the sick leaves reel down in throngs!
>
> They clear the creeping moss—
> Elders and juniors—aye,
> Making the pathways neat
>   And the garden gay;

And they build a shady seat. . . .
   Ah, no; the years, the years;
See, the white storm-birds wing across!

They are blithely breakfasting all—
Men and maidens—yea,
Under the summer tree,
   With a glimpse of the bay,
While pet fowl come to the knee. . . .
   Ah, no; the years O!

And the rotten rose is ript from the wall.
   They change to a high new house,
   He, she, all of them—aye,
Clocks and carpets and chairs
   On the lawn all day,
And brightest things that are theirs. . . .
   Ah, no; the years, the years;
Down their carved names the rain-drop ploughs.

In each stanza the ceremonies of first a simple and then a relatively sophisticated society are reversed by nature, whose countermovements appears almost to imitate the family's own innocent forms. But the leaves do not in fact quite "dance" to the music: they "reel" in their own way. In each stanza, what ruins the family is itself impressive in power and beauty —the leaves, the storm-birds, the rose (now rotten but not always so), and the rain-drop stronger than the chisel that carves gravestones. The difference between this ruin and the ghostly wanness of Elizabeth's pessimism is apparent in the exuberant rhythm of the five first lines of each stanza and the reversal of the last two, which allows full scope to the songlike impulse of joy and then to the reconsiderations of the philosophic mind. That the last two lines are also songlike in their way indicates that perhaps what Marty South and Tess have sought is not so much the dignity of the elegy as rhythmic expression, by way of catharsis. It is not beyond speculation that one reason for Hardy's decision to abandon the novel for the lyric was that the diffuse and unrhythmic form of prose fiction prevented him from transforming novelistic realism into poetic ceremony in this way. In any case, Farfrae's original tunefulness and Elizabeth's realism are combined in the poem without canceling each other, and the later Hardy clearly desired at times something like *Under the Greenwood Tree* rewritten as elegy.

THIRTEEN

Stevens's Supreme Fiction
and Its Printed Fragments

I

The archangel of evening, the expounder of the text of evening in Wallace Stevens's "One of the Inhabitants of the West," testifies that

> Our divinations,
> Mechanism of angelic thought,
> The means of prophecy,
>
> Alert us most
> At evening's one star
> And its pastoral text,[1]

and warns that included in the text are "horrid figures of Medusa," Lamia-like snakes, so much guilt is in autumnal innocence. Just so, Stevens defines one state of mind by its opposite and finds in nature both glimmers of paradise and disorder. These elements are comparatively consistent throughout his poetry despite significant changes in texture and style; nature offers a submusic, subspeech, incipient poetry at some remove from the observer, yet corresponding to his state of mind—not romantic superspeech. The divinations and the mechanism suggest that, though "angelic," the pastoral text is a diminished affair—a reduction of old myths. As the mechanism of the text is a "means of prophecy," so in his own assembled parts of the Ultimate Poem, the poet confects,

---

[1] Quotations are from *Collected Poems of Wallace Stevens* (New York: Alfred A. Knopf, 1954) and *Opus Posthumous* (New York: Alfred A. Knopf, 1957).

tabulates, cites real things in shadowy words, and arranges lines of verse for the typesetter. If I may play with a couple of Stevens' metaphors, the function of words marching in unison toward their poem is like that of the worms at heaven's gate which carry fragments of Barroulbadour from her grave to whatever unifying power has the unenviable job of reassembling her ("The Worms at Heaven's Gate"), or that of the finical bearers of Rosenbloom ("Cortège for Rosenbloom") taking him in rhymed pomp "to a jumble of words / Of the intense poem" into the sky, where they plan to enshrine him. While reality and imagination belong to inevitably separate realms, when each imposes itself on the other the medium of their transaction is words. Together with perception—usually a unifying composition of things around a central point—words are Steven's means of rearranging reality, and perhaps no one else has been so consistently aware of the rearranging they do in all acts of the mind.

In sum: taking the disintegrated Badroulbadour as an ultimate fragmentation of the kind that nominalism finds in the exterior world and "heaven" to be the unifying term-of-terms in the imagination (where all moments and fragments of reality find their fulfillment), a pastoralist who would create a world answerable to our desire for aesthetic order is left with the difficult task of "carrying" one to the other. The relationship between them is fluent and dynamic, but neither can be totally transformed into the other. Put together, they create a kind of triangle, thus:

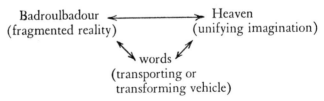

The disentanglement of these begins afresh with each perception and each poem because each is in flux—the thing itself, the imagination, and the language. Broken free from controlling myths of the past (usually based in some manner on religious or philosophical universals), the mind finds itself free to create innumerable poems, each proving its validity and demonstrating the mind's own compositional powers. Each point of the triangle resembles the other two. For what is "heaven" without the corporeal graces of a Badroulbadour, correctly reassembled? And are words not miracles of compression also, in which the mind and reality meet, naming exterior things and at the same time giving them relation, subordination, conjunction, and association? The vehicles are actively at work, forming a train to convey "Badroulbadour" to her salvation.

But they are also quite helpless by comparison to that single Word that commands resurrection in a flash and reconstructs according to ideal imagination a reality gone awry. What is missing obviously is an ultimate poem of reality, created by the Word breathing life into scattered particles of clay. The modern poet's words each handle merely a "mouthful." Lacking such a divine "composer," Stevens suggests in "Two or Three Ideas" and *The Necessary Angel,* a merely human imagination cannot fix a permanent center: the star of evening is on the move, though situated in place and time long enough to compose part of a daily or a seasonal cycle. The poems that poets actually write, unlike an ultimate poem or supreme fiction, are invaded by disarrangement or lead to a multiplicity of arrangements—to thirteen ways of looking at a blackbird or a sea surface full of clouds. They sometimes have too much abstraction, sometimes too much concretion, or the right amounts of each but in disarray. Nonetheless words are hope, and Stevens finds encouragement too in the flexibility of the imagination, which recomposes what has been decomposed, re-creates what has been "de-created."

Some exterior star must always be there to aid the mind's composition because the mind requires a locus, a defining center. Stevens frequently explores the range of composition between exotic abundance, in which sheer physical presence overwhelms the mind's desire for concentric composition, and a stringent order, in which the mind imposes an aesthetic pattern, oftentimes sterile, on its materials.

Even natural abundance, however, proliferates as much from

the imagination as from the fertile earth in Stevens and takes shape in a varied and exotic diction. It comes from the tropics and the zoo rather than the farm belt and so assists the mind's "divinations" of meaning by suggesting startling resemblances between the human and the natural. Stevens jostles the imagination with peacocks, kildeer, blue and white pigeons, turkeycocks, radishes, seaweed, warty squashes and weeping burghers, nincompated pedagogues, rasberry tanagers, yuccas, fat guzzly fruit, toucans, a dish of peaches in Russia, and just plain bananas (a representative but highly selective list). These creatures and plants consort with words like prinks, palankeens, femes, spiss, caracoles, ki-ki-ri-ki, rou-cou-cou, and nic-a-nic, until we are almost surprised to hear a straightforward statement like "Marx has ruined nature." Though frequently the nostalgic distance between ordinary nature and Stevens's nature resembles the distance between us and a conventional golden age, we have clearly come a long way from the traditional inventory of the *locus amoenus*. The vocabulary consorts with the creatures like grace notes playing around heavy melodies, punctuating their substantives with adverbial qualities or pinning odd adjectival colors to them.

Though we have the impression at times that these creatures offer us a child's view of the zoo, they are not merely exotic. The mind has obviously been at work on them, more in the later Stevens than in *Harmonium,* where the boundary between imagination and reality is not always clear. Except for a few creatures like the Prince of Peacocks and the blue baboon, they never quite drop far enough out of native habitat for the dream permutations of French symbolism: they remain at the edge of the world of fact, even when the imagination puts them in its "red weather," with the tigers that the drunken sailor of "Disillusionment of Ten O'Clock" hunts in his dreams. The bristling firecat of "Earthy Anecdote," for instance, we seem to remember having seen somewhere if not exactly in the *World Book Encyclopedia,* and the bucks who swerve around him help to make him material. His dance, in turn, presses them into patterns, like the mind encountering facts or fact composing scattered thoughts. Nor is it mood by which Stevens links nature and poet. He knows the atmospheric qualities of Georgian poetry as well as the techniques of romantic idealizing, and though he uses them both occasionally, he totally remakes them. Finally, though the transcendentalizing impluse is sometimes strong in Stevens, the self that observes the permutations of tree and cloud does not try to obliterate the line between it and them: the self does not expand outward as in Whitman or assume the scene to be merely a veil before a primarily spiritual reality.

Because poems move to the mind's working and at the same time imitate nature, every poem tries implicitly or explicitly to reconcile antinomies. The poet writes in the context of disarray and knows that as he composes he must know what lies beyond composition. He may witness "during the long period of his life, a general transition to reality," Stevens writes in *The Necessary Angel,* but "his own measure as a poet . . . is the measure of his power to abstract himself, and to withdraw with him into his abstraction the reality on which the lovers of truth insist." Thus the beasts and the vegetables are drawn into the lair of his working mind where the poetic vehicle, the printed text-to-be, takes their measure in its unisoned, composed words.

In Stevens's early poems, the mode of adjustment between the phenomenal world and the working imagination is often what "The Weeping Burgher" describes as a "belle design / Of foppish line," an outrageous proliferation of poetic adornment to cover the world's grayness. But Stevens usually invents such bell designs with tongue in cheek, mocking the poet as a comedian busily "contriving."[2] Adornment sometimes fails to cover reality; but more often something happens in the act of composing to change reality itself. Ordinary women rise from poverty and flit through palace walls to the sound of guitars. They trade monotony and disease for articulate coiffures, civil fans, moonlight, and puissant speech, their passage being roughly equivalent to the singer's filigreeing of reality. Or if nature's bombardment of the consciousness

[2] See Samuel French Morse, "Wallace Stevens, Bergson, Pater," *ELH,* 31 (1964), 1–34.

proves too fierce, the poet, fearing its assault, may be tempted
to impose too rigid an order on it. In keeping with a "foppish" aesthetic, imagination is associated with "emperors" who
combine adornment and love of art with dictatorial power,
like Oscar Wilde made king. At the same time, in keeping
with the ironic view that Stevens takes of it, such a constrictive imagination usually proves stifling and barren. Hence the
emperors are by no means unambiguously noble. The famous
jar in Tennessee sterilizes the "slovenly" wilderness as it takes
dominion over it. The wilderness is forced to rise up to it as
it stands "tall and of a port in air" but its reform is futile:
birds and bushes remain alive as it shapes itself elegantly
around nothing, a figuration enclosing a vacuum. The emperor of ice-cream superimposes the rites of a wake on the
tawdry, stale reality of a dead lady's room, in which she has
herself once made "embroidered fantails." Less imperial than
the Tennessee jar, he spans more of the middle ground between art's elegance and nature's physical abundance and slovenliness. Though an emperor's rituals might be thought to
offer relief from the daily round of tasks, the speaker commands the lady's guests to come as they are, to roll their accustomed cigars, and to continue dawdling in everyday dress.
As the artist of the revels, he commands simply that the lamp
"affix its beam" on reality (on the horny, protruding feet of
the lady, who suggests a cold, prehistoric, and now extinct
nature). Instead of a ceremonial muskrose or a well-attired
woodbine, his flowers will be wrapped in newspapers a month
old—perhaps a symbol of what the dead matter of unpoetic
print does to live flowers.

Given this insistence of reality on its own implacable nature,
the chant "the only emperor is the emperor of ice-cream" can
be taken either as the democrat's cry of relief—the tyrannical
hold of art over natural inclination is broken—or the aristo-
crat's lament for lost form. Though the emperor's culture has
destroyed the dignity of dying by its failure to find a balance
of ceremony and human slovenliness, Stevens seems to relish
the possibility of not choosing between the alternatives. The
dead one gets her celebration, such as it is, and if the emperor's rites last no longer than his perishable ice-cream, it

will scarcely matter that the mind's lamp reveals only how
cold and dead things are.

The chill of the emperor's domain is at least partly delec-
table; that of the "Snow Man" on the other hand is a metaphysical, absolute chill at the extreme opposite of Stevens's natural abundance. The snowman thinks neither of "misery in
the sound of the wind" nor of beauty; his imagination adds
"nothing that is not there" and beholds "the nothing that is."
Clearly a perceiver must be more alive than he if he is also
to see the something that is there. Yet even a severe dehuman-
izing of this kind may prove to be a kind of purification out
of which the capacity to see more clearly may grow, a preliminary step to a discovery of reality's irreducible strangeness and
thus a discovery of poetry. The snowman belongs to the family
of the subman of "somber Figuration" (*Opus Posthumous*),
"the man below the man below the man," and of Canon Aspirin in "Notes toward a Supreme Fiction," who explores
nothingness as a prelude to harmonious creation. As "Stars
at Tallapoosa" suggests, such darkness enables the mind to
find pleasure "all bright-edged and cold," for "the mind
herein attains simplicity." In darkness one makes "recoveries
of young nakedness / And the lost vehemence the midnights
hold." This freshness counteracts with new divinations the
deadliness of abstraction and the mechanical set of the "text."
We are most alert when there is just one star: something surrounded by a broad nothingness.

The discipline of the snowman naturally reduces the adornment of art as well as the abundance of nature. In contrast,
the elegance-seeking yokel Crispin of "The Comedian as the
Letter C," neglecting discipline, finds his path leading not to
seraphic declarations of nature's higher implication but merely
to "the malady of the quotidian." Too much abundance spoils
the poet's voice, and though he may expect to find therapy in
a stringent reduction of nature to bare elements, he must wait
passively for his cure:

> Perhaps, if winter once could penetrate
> Through all its purposes to the final slate,
> Persisting bleakly in an icy haze,
> One might in turn become less diffident,

> Out of such mildew plucking neater mould
> And spouting new orations of the cold.
>
> One might. One might. But time will not relent.
> ["The Man Whose Pharynx Was Bad"]

As the comedian also illustrates, the collision of the foppish line and primitivism may produce humor as well as lassitude, jarring the poem into ironic adjustments, as in the American wilderness, the tall story, plain living, and rough-hewn humor were often juxtaposed with imported elegance. The Chieftain Iffucan of Azcan in "Bantams in Pine-Woods," for instance, is a universal cock who commands the sun to be a blackamoor to bear his "blazing tail." But as a "ten-foot poet among inchlings" strutting in the midst of bristling pines, he also suffers comic buffeting from them, like a poet on an American main street splashed by horses and mocked by onlookers. His song is a barbaric "hoo" and his body "Fat! Fat! Fat!" as well as tall. The perspective of the poem is partly that of the inchlings, the proletarians below looking up, which makes him appear a bantam pretender, a chieftain of "as-can," the inchlings taunt, only "if-you-can." But even while he suggests that all attempts to beautify the wilderness are vain, he nonetheless approaches the "universal." He is, after all, one of the emperors aware of his dignity. He does not answer the charges against him but continues to be a fop of belle design. The quixotic language of the poem sets both extremes, the pretentious poet and his detractors, loosely together in whimsicality.

In his middle period, Stevens tends to replace the emperor with men "on the dump" and sorts through the refuse of modern civilization searching for poetry. His own comments on the disappearance of the gods in "Two or Three Ideas" (Opus Posthumous) explain the shift. He observes that "a time of disbelief is precisely a time in which the frequency of detached styles [that is, styles ineffective, arbitrary, "literary"] is greatest" (p. 212). "In the presence of the gods, or of their images, we are in the presence of perfection in created beings," which makes the Ultimate Poem seem possible. But the poet moves inevitably from gods to emperors and, entering political matters, on down the ladder until his images become not those of the gods but tramps in Central Park: "Since men made the world, the inevitable god is the beggar" (Adagia, *Opus Posthumous,* p. 171). The poet cannot say even of emperors— as Stevens says of the gods—that "the exhilaration of their existence, their freedom of fate, their access to station, their liberty to command fix them in an atmosphere which thrills us as we share it. . . . What matters is their manner, their style" (p. 212), their art of living. The poet cannot expect to mix elegance with the truths of the terrified and miserable whom he benefits by sharing his imagination with them. Rather than deriving the style of poetry from the style of noble gods, an artist derives "the style of the gods from men," at least in part from the style of common asphalt men. In many of the poems of Stevens's middle period, the winter scene and an accompanying concern for poverty penetrate the "purples" of the foppish line and the zoological abundance, as a kind of preliminary "barbarism." A change of emphasis in this direction is hinted in *Ideas of Order.*

In "Evening without Angels" and "Botanist on Alp (No. 1)," Stevens gives the imagination humbler metaphors than the emperor cluster. The evening is not only without angels but also without the voluptuous items of the emperor's closet, the coiffure of haloes and the jewels. The poet's tune is modulated to a "seething minor" because "bare night is best. Bare earth is best. Bare, bare, / Except for our own houses, huddled low." From that proletarian humbleness, the poet can rise "Beneath the rhapsodies of fire and fire, / Where the voice that is in us makes a true response," Whitman-like, abandoning his role as *chef d'orchestre* with seraphim for lutanists. The air of "Evening without Angels" is merely air; its "vacancy glitters round us everywhere. / Its sounds are not angelic syllables." The poet in these bad times must look directly upon "the hovels of those that live in this land" ("Dry Loaf").

The process of reduction to a fecund minimum (or "green barbarism turning paradigm") can function in several ways, stripping aside the fancy embroidery of false aestheticism and

revealing the plainness of what lies beneath ("Ach, Mutter, /
This old, black dress, / I have been embroidering / French
flowers on it"), or establishing a new sense of liberation. As
the latest freed man discovers one morning, escaping the
white collar and stripping life to its primitive essentials may
put one at the center of reality, like Adam first awakening in
Eden:

> It was how the sun came shining into his room:
> To be without a description of to be,
> For a moment on rising, at the edge of the bed, to be,
> To have the ant of the self changed to an ox
> With its organic boomings, to be changed
> From a doctor into an ox, before standing up,
> To know that the change and that the ox-like struggle
> Come from the strength that is the strength of the sun.

In one of the most remarkable of Stevens's poems, "The
Man on the Dump," the reduction of exotic abundance makes
the poet a kind of trash collector:

> Day creeps down. The moon is creeping up.
> The sun is a corbeil of flowers the moon Blanche
> Places there, a bouquet. Ho-ho . . . The dump is full
> Of images. Days pass like papers from a press.
> The bouquets come here in the papers. So the sun,
> And so the moon, both come, and the janitor's poems
> Of every day, the wrapper on the can of pears,
> The cat in the paper-bag, the corset, the box
> From Esthonia: the tiger chest, for tea.

The dump contains not only the residue of past culture and
poetic traditions (images and icons of reality no longer of any
use because the world is in process—day creeps down, the
moon creeps up continuously) but also part of Stevens's own
metaphoric collection. Juxtaposing the natural and the artificial
in a kind of tired, ironic monotone that on occasion rises to an
unexpected lyric intensity, the speaker "reads off" previous
connections among the items he finds and what they were designed to represent. The items of Belinda's Augustan boudoir
end up here, as do the myths of the romantics and the emperor

of ice-cream, all papier-mâché creations of the imagination that have failed to move with the flux. In a sense, life is long but artifice quickly dead: "The freshness of night has been fresh a long time."

Paradoxically, though discarded and broken apart, separated from their times and original syntax, these used icons, too, can be seen freshly. Stevens manages to make a new poem out of them even while mocking the inadequacy of words and reading them ironically; he recovers lost images in raking through the trash, rejuvenating, reassembling:

> The freshness of morning, the blowing of day, one says
> That it puffs as Cornelius Nepos reads, it puffs
> More than, less than or it puffs like this or that.
> The green smacks in the eye, the dew in the green
> Smacks like fresh water in a can, like the sea
> On a cocoanut—how many men have copied dew
> For buttons, how many women have covered themselves
> With dew, dew dresses, stones and chains of dew, heads
> Of the floweriest flowers dewed with the dewiest dew.
> One grows to hate these things except on the dump.

The paradox is compressed into the last line: one hates imitative images except on the dump; there "in the time of spring" one "feels the purifying change." For change is what kills and what renews, altering continuously our views of the creeping day and moon and the artifices of the past so inadequate to the reality of green that smacks in the eye:

> That's the moment when the moon creeps up
> To the bubbling of bassoons. That's the time
> One looks at the elephant-colorings of tires.
> Everything is shed; and the moon comes up as the moon
> (All its images are in the dump) and you see
> As a man (not like an image of a man),
> You see the moon rise in the empty sky.

Having begun with the junkiness of manmade products, Stevens can allow the survival of lyric moments. The tired cadence tightens and we are surprised to discover that even castoff tires can remind us of elephants because the mechanisms of which they were once part have been dismantled and their special texture and color reannounces itself. Seemingly merely miscellaneous trash, the dump proves to be a fund of startling metaphors. It offers a new and largely ironic inventory for the *locus amoenus*. Stevens suggests that as the ear learns to solace itself on the cries of peevish birds, so the imagination can "sit among mattresses of the dead, / Bottles, pots, shoes and grass and murmur *aptest eve*." We hear "the blatter of grackles and say / *Invisible priest*," not cynically but as if we heard some genuine if ironic resemblance.

II

These poems make it clear that one need not choose an elegant life in defiance of one's crude surroundings as the Chieftain of Azcan does. But they also reduce the scope of poetry and alienate the poet from much of nature, whereas to realize himself fully, "Holiday in Reality" says, the poet has to find his own attractive earth and sky. To lose poetry is to become worse than merely destitute:

> To lose sensibility, to see what one sees,
> As if sight had not its own miraculous thrift,
> To hear only what one hears, one meaning alone,
> As if the paradise of meaning ceased
> To be paradise, it is this to be destitute.
>   ["Esthétique du Mal," ix]

While a poet sees both pain and beauty in a well-made scene, the man of bitter experience feels only the pain of the moment. A political-minded Konstantinov, walking beside Lake Geneva and thinking only of revolution, is not aware of what to the poet is a well-confected scene:

> He would be the lunatic of one idea
> In a world of ideas, who would have all the people
> Live, work, suffer and die in that idea
> In a world of ideas.
>   ["Esthétique du Mal," xiv]

Such is the difficulty with merely economic adventurers in humanity, those who are unaware "of the clouds, / Lighting the martyrs of logic with white fire." Paradise becomes too much a matter of logical materialization—of programmatic Marxism whereas for the unparalyzed mind and imagination it should be quite otherwise:

> out of what one sees and hears and out
> Of what one feels, who could have thought to make
> So many selves, so many sensuous worlds,
> As if the air, the mid-day air, was swarming
> With the metaphysical changes that occur,
> Merely in living as and where we live.
> ["Esthétique du Mal," xv]

The most comprehensive treatment of these themes is "Notes toward a Supreme Fiction," whose first aim, like that of "Credences of Summer," is to "trace the gold sun about the whitened sky / Without evasion by a single metaphor," which is to say, without embroidered language or Wordsworthian benediction: "Look at it in its essential barrenness / And say this, this is the centre that I seek." Stevens again begins with "pure" ignorance, then, in keeping with the American break with the past: the mythic sun is dead and so the sun can now be itself. But such a reduction paradoxically causes the air to swarm with metaphysical changes, and the strangeness of the true sun again catches the imagination and prepares for a fresh sense of the *locus amoenus*. We perceive a proliferation of voices and harmonies in nature. The hoobla-hoo of the wood dove and the "grossest iridescence of ocean" are a nonsense that pierces us with "strange relation." (The voices of divination enliven images before the text composes them.) In this relation is the birth of both meaning and metaphor, the first murmurs of poetry in nature; it reveals connections among objects that, when fully arranged, compose entire scenes, setting each peacock and turkeycock, toucan and banana in its place and generating the new orders and arrangements of words. Could we but see them thus "washed in the remotest cleanliness of a heaven / That has expelled us and our images," we should not mind the disappearance of the gods from the scene.

If, however, "poetry" is indeed implicit in the real, untransformed scene before us, does not the poet's art then become an insignificant series of "pips" among nature's "abysmal instruments"? Stevens explores that possibility candidly, realizing that he may be either destroying the occupation of poets or—what amounts to the same thing—creating poets on all sides without words at their command, only poetic perceptions. The lion that roars at the enraging desert is so impressive as a maker of song that the poet may seek only to curb it, to lash the lion and teach bears to juggle.

Hence, in part, the importance of abstraction, which prevents the poet's enslavement to natural fact. "The idea of man" is his major abstraction, the form beyond the form of a single mind. We are subdivided not by class but according to what majesty the mind perceives before it. But the question remains, can abstraction be poetic, or does it remain merely a retraction from reality? Isn't it basically out of keeping with a concept of the good place? Stevens seems to intend it as a supplement to what the imagination discovers in the freshness of the tanagers and warty squashes, and in this respect it does not transcend them, as Ideas in the Neoplatonic garden do. Together with the primitive perception of things, abstraction forms a part of aesthetic perception, uniting intellect and imagination. Yet even so Stevens's major man is less sensuous than, say, the speaker of Marvell's "The Garden," whose act of intellectual transcendence is paired with the body's involvement in a physical garden. As part of the "commonal," major man "is more fecund as principle than particle, / Happy fecundity, flor-abundant force."

The last section of "Notes" restores something of the hedonist pleasure of all pastoral places by stressing the pleasure of art and proposing a new harmonium principle based on what men of imagination may actually see in nature. Annihilation like the snowman's, which reduces nature to nothingness, results from a failure to discover the interworkings of imagination, words, and reality. Canon Aspirin chooses not one extreme or another—lushness or severe discipline, imperial imagination or imagination run riot—but "the whole, / The complicate, the amassing harmony." Presumably the whole does not subvert its parts but reorders them. He finds order emerging on its own from crude compoundings (vii); then angels return to the pastoral scene, as order and beauty are imagined to "descend" from above in a gliding visitation from "abysmal glory." If such a vision is possible for one hour, he finds, it can become a permanent part of one's noble self-definition: if

> There is a month, a year, there is a time
> In which majesty is a mirror of the self:
> I have not but I am and as I am, I am.
>
> [viii]

The fat girl terrestrial of the last poem provides a final test of the combination of change, abstraction, and beauty. The poet is constrained to name her flatly and waste no words since she has obviously not glided down from angelic heights and cannot be reduced to slim grace. Yet plebeian as she is, bent over work, she becomes for him a "soft-footed phantom," a kind of modern nymph, and a symbol for the working imagination. The seemingly ugly fact of her appearance is absorbed, with help from irony, into a "fiction that results from feeling." The empress is dead, long live the fat fluent mundo. With a glance at the philosophers, Stevens is satisfied that that finishes it: "They will get it straight one day at the Sorbonne." Thus "flicked by feeling" in a gildered street, he will call her by name, and so named by the artist the fat girl will revolve in the crystal of his art, in the invented mechanism of the poem.

When one glances backward from "Notes" both to Stevens's previous gropings toward a supreme fiction and to other concepts of an ultimate poetic place, it becomes evident that he has more theorized about than realized such a fiction. We do not leave the poem with a sense of how the imagination is actually to seize reality and discover in it, or create out of it, either a present sense of harmony diffused through nature or a sense of teleological direction that will eventually carry us to some new realization of adamic simplicity and heightened perception. Historically speaking, the poem does not solve the problems of the imaginative man in the American new Eden, gathering his abundance and constructing his new order—the problems left by Thoreau, Whitman, and others. We have only to juxtapose the poem with "Sunday Morning," "The Idea of Order at Key West," "The Man on the Dump," or later poems like "An Ordinary Evening in New Haven," "Angel Surrounded by Paysans," "The Rock," "Of Mere Being," and "Not Ideas about the Thing but the Thing Itself" to see how much it leaves out or makes more cerebral than poetic. Though Stevens perhaps does as much as any poet since the romantics to create modern equivalents to traditional harmonies of mind and place, he does not do so merely in theory, or perhaps not finally in theory at all; he does so primarily as a poet of fresh, working perceptions and mythologizing capacities. But he does not do so in "Notes."

The poems of *The Auroras of Autumn, The Rock,* and *Opus Posthumous* (in its later sections) are by no means consistent in maintaining the optimism of "Notes," nor are they uniformly impressive as glimpses of a possible supreme fiction. The emphasis in *The Rock* falls increasingly on the diminution of nature's power to evoke even fragments of poetry:

> Weaker and weaker, the sunlight falls
> In the afternoon. The proud and the strong
> Have departed.

> Those that are left are the unaccomplished,
> The finally human,
> Natives of a dwindled sphere.
>   ["Lebensweisheitspielerei"]

Nor does reduction to bare elements necessarily reveal anything new:

> Little by little, the poverty
> Of autumnal space becomes
> A look, a few words spoken.

> Each person completely touches us
> With what he is and as he is,
> In the stale grandeur of annihilation.

But if Stevens laments the incapacity always to achieve a fruitful interaction of imagination and reality (in "Saint John and the Back-Ache," "In a Bad Time," and "World without Peculiarity"), he continues to probe for their boundaries in "A Primitive Like an Orb," "Not Ideas about the Thing but the Thing Itself," and "The Auroras of Autumn"). The first sounds that grow out of darkness as though made of "ice" itself ("A trinkling in the parentage of the north, / The cricket of summer forming itself out of ice") are available to human conception: they make the sprawling winter stand clear in the mind, which journeys upward and catches glimpses of an ultimate order behind the fragments:

> We shall have gone behind the symbols
> To that which they symbolized, away
> From the rumors of the speech-full domes,
> To the chatter that is then the true legend,
> Like glitter ascended into fire.
>
> ["The Sail of Ulysses," v]

Thus the highest creator (Whitmanesque in this dimension) is a sailor-journeyman, a Ulysses, representing all men and traveling with eyes and ears responsive to a wide range of "glitter" and "chatter."

The Ulysses-major man figure is Stevens's final variation of heroic-pastoral which begins with a radical equality of all people before nature and suggests that each must make himself large by poetic perception. The idea is similar to one unintentionally parodied by Hans Christian Andersen's parable of the "bell" (the distillation of nature's beauty into sound). Despite the pursuit of separate paths, a prince and a rag boy meet on equal terms before This Beautiful World:

And the prince stretched his arms toward the sky, towards the sea and the woods—and at that very moment, along the right-hand path, came the poor boy with the short sleeves and the

clogs. He had arrived there just as quickly; arrived by his own
way. And they ran forward to meet each other, and clasped
each other by the hand in the great temple of Nature and poetry; and over their heads pealed the invisible holy bell, while
blessed spirits danced airily around them to the sound of a
jubilant hallelujah.[3]

Unlike Andersen, Stevens is aware that much must be annihi-
lated to get "down" (or "up") to a common ground; but that
minds work more or less alike in composing harmony is valid
metaphysically. The "poetic" mind climbs mountains, in motion upward in a world of constant becoming, seeking the
fire of the All and finding occasional hints of it:

> We live in a constellation
> Of patches and of pitches,
> Not in a single world,
> In things said well in music,
> On the piano, and in speech
> As in a page of poetry—
> Thinkers without final thoughts
> In an always incipient cosmos,
> The way, when we climb a mountain,
> Vermont throws itself together.
>
> ["July Mountain"]

Such seeking means the end of the "pastoral text" in the
sense of the protected enclosure or the fixed crystal of conventional art. The frozen moment into which the pastoralist
locks change, abstraction, and harmonic pattern is dissolved in
the ardent climbing of mountains, in an always merely incipient cosmos.[4] But the mythic search is also a matter of

[3] Hans Christian Andersen, *Fairy Tales and Stories,* trans.
Reginald Spink (London: J. M. Dent, 1960), p. 260.

[4] Cf. Frank Doggett's comment in "Wallace Stevens' River that
Flows Nowhere," *Chicago Review,* 15 (1962), 71: "The paradox
of meeting doom and genesis in each moment is one of several
related paradoxes . . . [that Stevens] presents of the character of
process." See also Sister M. Bernetta Quinn, *The Metamorphic
Tradition in Modern Poetry* (New Brunswick, N.J.: Rutgers University Press, 1955); "Metamorphosis in Wallace Stevens," also
in *Sewanee Review,* 70 (1952), 230–252.

idyllic perception as well as an action, and nature comes to
meet us halfway: "The Great Omnium *descends* on us / As a
free race. We know it, one / By one, in the right of all." Thus
the necessary angel of reality-transcribed-into-poetry suggests
to "paysans" that the insights of poetry enable them to transcend the unwieldy stuff of earth and the unwieldy stiffness
of printed language. It speaks directly if fleetingly to them;
they must be alert indeed to catch divinations of angelic
thought:

> I am the angel of reality,
> Seen for a moment standing in the door.
>
> I have neither ashen wing nor wear of ore
> And live without a tepid aureole. . . .
>
> I am one of you and being one of you
> Is being and knowing what I am and know.
>
> Yet I am the necessary angel of earth,
> Since, in my sight, you see the earth again,
>
> Cleared of its stiff and stubborn, man-locked set,
> And, in my hearing, you hear its tragic drone
>
> Rise liquidly in liquid lingerings,
> Like watery words awash; like meanings said
>
> By repetitions of half-meanings. Am I not,
> Myself, only half of a figure of a sort,
>
> A figure half seen, or seen for a moment, a man
> Of the mind, an apparition . . . ?
>   ["Angel Surrounded by Paysans"]

So saying, the angel—not one from the pages of Aquinas but
an agent of imaginative annunciation—turns and "quickly, too
quickly" is gone. The peasants remain peasants (and "there
must be something of the peasant in every poet," Stevens
writes in the adagia); but the perceptive modern, like the first
man, has heard it say distinctly "I am one of you." The peasants' gain in poetic perception is balanced by its fleeting qual-

ity, so inseparable from "the thing itself" and therefore so difficult to place as part of any grander poem.

Connecting their kind of perception with a sense of the greater harmony of the supreme fiction is nonetheless the renewed task of the later Stevens, and one of his more complex treatments of an intuition of a more encompassing poem is "Not Ideas about the Thing but the Thing Itself." The abundance of the early Stevens is here reduced to the weakest of bird's songs, devoid of "organic boomings":

> At the earliest ending of winter,
> In March, a scrawny cry from outside
> Seemed like a sound in his mind.
>
> He knew that he heard it,
> A bird's cry, at daylight or before,
> In the early March wind.

The speaker's awakening is like a new birth after winter when only the faintest hint of the full reality of summer is perceivable in the bird's weak cry. The cry seems part of his own mind because it is not strong enough to impinge upon him with full-bodied force. He knows for certain only that he has heard it, and he fumbles to place it in the daily and yearly turning of a cosmos whose cyclical recurrences give the poet a sense of aesthetic rhyme and structure in the nature of things:

> The sun was rising at six,
> No longer a battered panache above snow . . .
> It would have been outside.
>
> It was not from the vast ventriloquism
> Of sleep's faded papier-mâché . . .
> The sun was coming from outside.

That it would have been outside is explored tentatively, as though a proposition about reality that the mind must examine. Reflection does not contribute ideas about the thing however; it reinforces the senses and the presence of the thing itself. The speaker is reassured by that augmented presence because it proves sufficiently to him that he is not dreaming a world. Inside and outside are not to be confused; their relation presupposes their distinct separation.

As reality is strengthened by reflection, the mind, too, discovers its special powers and the mode of its operation and swells with the incipient sense of a cosmos extending beyond the bird. It prophecies from the one note a larger sound to come:

> That scrawny cry—it was
> A chorister whose c preceded the choir.
> It was part of the colossal sun,
>
> Surrounded by its choral rings,
> Still far away. It was like
> A new knowledge of reality.

The fully awakened speaker interprets the bird's cry as part of the sun surrounded by choral rings he cannot see. But in linking one season with another and comparing what is present with what is far away, the mind also anticipates more than the senses now offer it. The full choir is a thing of the imagination in this season. The cry itself is very small, "like" a new knowledge of reality. Out of a perfect equilibrium of sparseness and amplified power, the small and the grand, the working of the mind and the gift of reality, the poem is composed. It imitates in its movement the steady unfolding of a world in change, but from the gift of abstract words ("Knowledge" and "reality" especially), it also arrives at a finished and definitive statement. It encompasses a segment of experience, breaking it off from the continuum of the hours and the course of the sun in which it is first located. The bird's cry is itself a kind of language that tells of things beyond it still to come, yet distinct and bounded in itself as an event to be contemplated. Hence it points toward the kind of thing a poem, too, should be: the bird's cry is to the full choir as the individual poem is to the ultimate poem "still far away" in its colossal grandeur. Both are tentative instruments of intuition, not satisfying in a final degree but hinting at a fuller satisfaction. If paradise is only incipient in such signs as the bird's cry and the angel's brief appearance to the paysans, poems are always in the making. They must appear to flow with reality itself, to dissolve or grow as the perceptions of the moment demand. Nor can an inventory of the good place be settled once and for all. A sense of pastoral harmony may develop from "a man skating, a woman dancing, a woman / Combing" ("Of Modern Poetry"). The poet himself is an impromptu actor twanging

> An instrument, twanging a wiry string that gives
> Sounds passing through sudden rightnesses, wholly
> Containing the mind, below which it cannot descend,
> Beyond which it has no will to rise.
>
> ["Of Modern Poetry"]

It is in such contentment, in momentary and yet perfect matchings of the mind and its sufficing physical circumstances, that Stevens locates his remodeling of the old myths of perfection.

FOURTEEN

Bellow's Idyll of the Tribe

Why so sad and so earthy? Now you are a lion. Mentally, conceive of the environment. The sky, the sun, and creatures of the bush. You are related to all. The very gnats are your cousins. The sky is your thoughts. The leaves are your insurance, and you need no other. There is no interruption all night to the speech of the stars.

> —Dahfu in *Henderson the Rain King*

You will remember that my Hans is really a simple-minded hero, the young scion of good Hamburg society, and an indifferent engineer. But in the hermetic, feverish atmosphere of the enchanted mountain, the ordinary stuff of which he is made undergoes a heightening process that makes him capable of adventures in sensual, moral, intellectual spheres he would never have dreamed of in the "flatland." His story is the story of a heightening process, but also as a narrative it is the heightening process itself.

> —Thomas Mann, "The Making of *The Magic Mountain*," appended to the novel

Hallett Smith observes concerning renaissance pastoral that "the central meaning of the pastoral is the rejection of the aspiring mind" and that in order to respond to otium Elizabethans had to feel the force of ambition. Both the arduous routes that ambition takes and the idyllic locality of otium have naturally changed considerably since that version of the pastoral contrast, but the psychology of retreat remains similar. Pleasure and labor, fraternal feeling and hierarchical edginess, daydream and the discipline of reason, contemplative ideals and competition, eroticism and "standoffishness" are several aspects of pastoral's typical psychological dualism. Two of its traditional literary extensions are laments for the loss of the idyllic life and lyric responses to the release from social tensions, in rediscoveries of animistic correspondences between man and nature.

It may seem a muscular leap from the tradition of otium in Elizabethan pastorals and such texts as Marvell's "The Garden" to Saul Bellow's *Henderson the Rain King,* but when we remember the recurrence of "soft" pastoral throughout the tradition and especially in the American dream of retreat, we can see some logic in the association. Complementing the georgic Adam, who colonizes and cultivates the new Eden he has entered, is an easygoing Adam who seeks for something quite different from a tilled garden. Occasionally, the two are combined in the same figure, as in the Walden experiment in which Thoreau seeks to combine work and play, practicing a celestial economy and collecting transcendental symbols among his rows of cultivated beans. The gods of fertile productivity and of peace reign alternately over the garden. Not to feel the contrast between otium and ambition in such a place would be to miss the delights of a lazy but heightened sensibility, the attractiveness of which increases in proportion to the prominence, outside the retreat, of economic competition, urban life, and perhaps a strict Protestant work ethic.

Henderson shares with the traditional shepherds and knights of Spenser and Sidney the psychology of their dispraise of social life and the philosophical and spiritual susceptibility that replaces other pursuits. But Bellow's version of the pastoral retreat is also a quest story and has affinities with romance as well as with pastoral. To combine the two is to strengthen the contrasts between otium and ambition, which alternate in Henderson with extravagant humor. From another direction, Henderson shares with Mann's protagonist in *The Magic Mountain* the search for a cure of his sickness in a place of "heightening" possessed of an underlying magic. The difficulty of his quest is to become deeply involved in such a place and still return. In his sanitarium, Hans Castorp is exposed to broad, basic contrasts between life and death, sickness and health, ambition and its suspension in a state of inactivity; yet his highest dreams are of quite ordinary life, as though the magic dimension that he discovers on the mountain has all the while been inherent in his bourgeois sensibility and the life of the flatlands. He returns to life below the same as he was in substance but with an increased awareness of the underside of his experience. Typical of his new awareness is the storm episode, in which the "good place" unfolds new paradisal dimensions:

A rainbow flung its arc slanting across the scene, most bright and perfect, a sheer delight, all its rich glossy, banded colours moistly shimmering down into the thick, lustrous green. It was like music, like the sounds of harps commingled with flutes and violins. The blue and the violet were transcendent. And they descended and magically blended, were transmuted and re-unfolded more lovely than before. Once, some years earlier, our young Hans Castorp had been privileged to hear a world-famous Italian tenor, from whose throat had gushed a glorious stream to witch the world with gracious art. The singer took a high note, exquisitely; then held it, while the passionate harmony swelled, unfolded, glowed from moment to moment with new radiance. . . . So now with the scene before him, constantly transformed and transfigured as it was before his eyes.[1]

Paradoxically, Castorp grasps the significance of the landscape the better for his preparation in the arts of civilization; the music of the good place is that of opera rather than the simple shepherd song. And his paradox is duplicated by that of the novel, which brings him to an ultimate, dissolving appreciation of basic nature through a finely structured, tension-filled treatment of numerous leitmotif repetitions and a full documentary treatment of society itself.[2]

[1] Thomas Mann, *The Magic Mountain*, trans. H. T. Lowe-Porter (New York: Alfred A. Knopf, 1953), p. 490.

[2] As Mann suggests, art is to the novel as the magic mountain is to its hero, a form of rest cure that restores what has been tarnished by life in the flatlands. *The Magic Mountain* grew out of his not staying at the Davos sanatorium: "If I had followed his (i.e., the head doctor's) advice, who knows, I might still be there! I wrote *The Magic Mountain* instead," [p. 721].

Henderson's fresh start, his break with the institutions of his own flatland, his treatment for spiritual disease, and the isolation of Africa are similar not only to Castorp's retreat to the mountain top but also to the recurrent American escape from social complexity in the homesteading novel, the Western, and the child cult. Rather than applying the lessons of the journey to civilization, however, American romance more often divorces the two: the hero turns his back on civilization like Huck Finn; or like Steinbeck's Pepe (in "The Flight"), he is forced to grow up too quickly and fails. Or he may also discover that society is bent upon spoiling the wilderness and will not allow a Leatherstocking or an Ike McCaslin to dwell in leisure in it. Always an alien because he has no order with which he wants to be identified, the outcast hero is lost in the wilderness or the desert, condemned to perpetual adventure. No power can absolve whatever guilt he may have accumulated, because there are no wise elders, no Setembrini-humanists, to unlock the riddles of the universe and apply them to industry, the household, or the town.

However seriously we are meant to take Dahfu's notion of imitation and transformation in Henderson—the "utterly dynamic" influence of which Henderson finds overwhelming—there can be little doubt that under Dahfu's guidance Henderson changes for the better and sheds part of the burden of wrath that his highly competitive life has heaped upon him. He can make his return partly because the tribal society's belief in magic and its wisdom are translatable into the life of the modern doctor that Henderson plans to become. Moreover, the journey brings to light some of the origins of his own society. He discovers the dynamic laws of his former life in the ancient, bold outlines of Africa, especially in the fusion of action and otium in Dahfu himself. Thus Henderson discovers his old troubles condensed, epitomized, and displaced enough to be dealt with in Africa. He finds new modes of appeal to the hidden powers of nature, modes both cryptic and farcical, in a kind of "riotous imprecation" by which the clown-saint can approach the sacred through the bizarre and grotesque. He finds mythic dimensions in the turmoil and indignities of

tribal life, interwoven with those more or less recognizable
social institutions and psychological eccentricities that are the
main novelistic aspects of his quest.

Henderson's therapy is based not only upon the discovery of
a proper style of imprecation but also upon the adaptability of
the "prince of organisms." He creates or "rediscovers" identity
with a number of totemistic animals with whom he seeks to
make peace: "The grass should be my cousins," he discovers,
projecting familial relations into nature. Part clown and part
child, he seeks to deepen these components of his character
by transposing them into the kind of simplicity he remembers
once owning:

It is very early in life, and I am out in the grass. The sun
flames and swells; the heat it emits is its love, too. I have this
self-same vividness in my heart. There are dandelions. I try to
gather up this green. I put my love-swollen cheek to the yellow of the dandelions. I try to enter into the green.[3]

From this discovery of kinship comes a redirection of psychic
energy and physical exuberance that leads eventually to effective action. In Dahfu's words,

All human accomplishment has this same origin, identically.
Imagination is a force of nature. Is this not enough to make
a person full of ecstasy? Imagination, imagination, imagination! It converts to actual. It sustains, it alters, it redeems! . . .
What homo sapiens imagines, he may slowly convert himself
to! [P. 240]

Both sacred parody and imagination help alleviate Henderson's terror and moneyed isolation. Though he lashes himself
verbally and feels at times that something intangible is against
him, his travels are not an endless self-punitive nightmare;
their catharsis is as though the mere expression of riot and
imprecation together, in the context of imaginative kinship
with nature, were a sufficient straightening-out of Henderson's
many crossed wires. If he regresses to the squeals and roars of

[3] Saul Bellow, *Henderson the Rain King* (New York: Popular
Library, 1960), p. 250.

childhood, he does so only to control them. The counsel of his "father" Dahfu helps him use the style of the pantomime and the comic blitz as a way of breaking down the barriers between himself and the things imitated and "prayed to."

His success, however, apparently depends as much on "luck" as upon either imagination or lessons in philosophic self-control. After the Arnewi episode lucky and unlucky appear indefinable except in magical terms: one either is or is not going to step on the banana peel, as one tribe always loses and the other always wins. But the moving of Mummah (Mommy?) that calls down the blessing of the rain is also a cause of sorts, as is the destruction of the Arnewi cistern. Since Henderson is responsible for both events, what appears to be luck is due in part to the kind of correspondence between the inner man and nature that both magic and dreams assume.

Jung's *Psychology and Alchemy* provides perhaps the best explanations for that correspondence. In assuming a machinery of the mind slightly different from Freud's theory of dream-condensation and displacement, Jung suggests that the radical descent of reason and *anima* figures into the defiling, grotesque element of the passions reintegrates them. To oversimplify a little, we can say that the bizarre rituals of the rain king reflect a similar process: they require Henderson to leave behind the values of a culture dominated by the male principle and expressing itself in military oppugnancy rather than a proper form of sacred parody—a culture that has driven underground and distorted chthonian femininity and love (as represented by the large, untidy Lily), whose only real rituals are New Year's Eve orgies and world wars. "When I think of my condition at the age of fifty-five when I bought the ticket, all is grief," Henderson laments. "The facts begin to crowd me and soon I get a pressure in the chest. A disorderly rush begins—my parents, my wives, my girls, my children. . . . They belong to me. They are mine. And they pile into me from all sides. It turns into chaos" (p. 5). Then as an alchemist releases the Cybele-Attis type from imprisonment by "marrying Apollo" to it, Henderson in Africa is relinquished comically to another variety of disturbance by a king who dares, himself, to submit to ultimate states of self-denial in the lioness Atti and his own death. He embraces Mummah, an image of *prima materia* or a kind of fecund earthwomb, and his initiation sorts out the tangle of his American experience, which has heretofore assumed no clear direction or pattern. Like Lewis Moon in the jungles of Peter Matthiessen's *At Play in the Fields of the Lord,* he participates in the primeval clash of male and female, king and mob, reason and passion, spirit and body, light and dark, love and hate, earth and rain. (Later, in another image of the same polarity, the "sun," drowned in the lion, as in Jung's archetype of the lion swallowing the sun, emerges through the animal's skin as an incandescent power, like reason returning from its descent.)

The wild mob ruled by the king, insulting its gods as it reverences them—indeed reverencing them through insult—is typical of the novel's method, which disrepectfully disrobes its truths in wild eccentricity:

At this moment came furious or quarrelsome shouts, and I thought "Ha, the light part of the ceremony is over." Several men in black plumes, like beggarly bird men—the rusty feathers hung to their shoulders—began to lift the covers from the gods. Disrespectfully, they pulled them away. This irreverence was no accident, if you get what I mean. . . . Just the same they [the gods] had dignity—mystery; they were after all the gods, and they made the awards of fate. They ruled the air, the mountains, fire, plants, cattle, luck, sickness, clouds, birth, death. . . . The attitude of the tribe seemed to be that it was necessary to come to the gods with their vices on display, as nothing could be concealed from them anyway by ephemeral men. [Pp. 160–161]

Stylistically this means that the "noumenal department" must be approached not in romantic imprecation but through absurdity, the most therapeutic way being the way of wit and satire.

For this reason the genre of the novel may seem closer to an "anatomy" than to either romance or pastoral. But the three are combinable, as Theocritus demonstrates in the approach of the Alexandrian housewives to the sacred presence of the gods

(fifteenth Idyll), and again in the fishermen who try to connect the dream world of Poseidon to the lives of semicomic
poverty and hard labor.[4] In any case Henderson's deep-chested
growls as an imitator of lions prepare him for a reintegration
of spirit and body, conscious ego and the subconscious. He
learns to release energies that have been bottled up or turned
to destructive uses in the society he has left.

Though Africa repeats the confusion of his civilized life, it
does so in what proves to be a meaningful, purgative way.
Henderson's simple ancestral past emerges there with fewer
distortions. "I believed that there was something between the
stones and me. The mountains were naked and often snake-
like in their forms, without trees, and you could see the clouds
being born on the slopes" (p. 42). If in his former life "rude
begets rude, and blows, blows" until the clash warms toward a
nuclear explosion, here he recovers a basic synchronization of
impulse and natural rhythm, which in its broadest human
scope is the rhythm of dying and rebirth, no less violent than
the life of blows but less chaotic. Living with the cycles of rain
and drought, the election and strangling of kings, descent into
the lion's den and return, is practice in seeing and accepting
one's own controlling patterns. Insofar as initiations require the
death of an old self before rebirth into a new order, they pre-
suppose a willingness to relinquish much of what one stands
for. "Entering into the green" has as its final implication
descent into the grave, and a "satiric" stripping and humiliation are preparatory dying. That this is political as well as
individual therapy is due to the analogy between political and
individual organisms so strong in the village, where such an
analogy can be clearly seen in family transfers of power. The
son must be devoted to his ancestral order before the tribal
order will work, and in turn the father must practice "relin-
quishing" or his dignity will stiffen into mere authority.

[4] Perhaps the closest parallel to Henderson's experience in this
phase in traditional pastoral modes is not the romance journey but
the masque, in which the kingly dignity of royal masquers is be-
sieged by the riot of an antimasque.

Henderson's adolescence has been prolonged because he could not, before, become either a true inheritor or a true father.

Unlike Hans Castorp, however, he does not return to a social order that he can accept outright. The bizarre kinship between ennobling and defiling elements will apparently continue among countless ways to go wrong, and it must be enacted not only in the pleasant context of sun and water but also before hostile onlookers. The final image of the new Henderson running, leaping, pounding, and tingling (his "son" in his arms), before the dark faces of those inside the plane returning him to America, implies that he still is an outsider. The cold of "almost eternal winter" attacks him, albeit as part of the remedy, the applied medicine—which suggests another image of incongruous brotherhood-before-the-crowd that has lain in the back of Henderson's mind, though he did not have the wit to summon it:

> We're two of a kind. Smolak was cast off and I am an Ismael, too. . . . So before pigs ever came on my horizon, I received a deep impression from a bear. So if corporeal things are an image of the spiritual and visible objects are renderings of invisible ones, and if Smolak and I were outcasts together, two humorists before the crowd, but brothers in our souls—I enbeared by him, and he probably humanized by me—I didn't come to the pigs as a tabula rasa. . . .
> Whatever gains I ever made were always due to love and nothing else. And as Smolak (mossy like a forest elm) and I rode together, and as he cried out at the top [of the roller coaster], beginning the bottomless rush over those skimpy yellow supports, and up once more against eternity's blue . . . we hugged each other, the bear and I, with something greater than terror and flew in those gilded cars. [P. 299]

In sum: Henderson dabbles in philosophy, magic, psychology, and politics in order to carry part of Africa back with him. He begins with a realistic awareness of personal and social sickness in a body politic given to aggression. It all began, he confesses, when "my ancestors stole the land from the Indians. They got more from the government and cheated other settlers too, so I became heir of a great estate" (p. 21). Substituting competitive for cooperative motives, he has himself somehow become a representative of warlike eccentricity, aggravated by wealth. Thus he sets out to find peace but by warlike means at first, the only means he knows, and is lost to wrath, given over to stalking, blowing up, threatening, and punching, until truth itself seems to come in blows—and "that's a military idea if there ever was one" (p. 22). The critical stage in his reform is a scene of great violence, but this time staged as purgative ritual and comic "theater," according to Jung's prescription for soul-therapy. Eventually a philosophy of "pastoral" cousin-ship with bears and grass translates the magic of the tribal rites into rational terms. (One hopes he will be able to find a patch of grass near his medical school to remind him of that.)

A socialist as opposed to tribal idyll at this point might have made Henderson submerge his individualism in some joint enterprise, perhaps a symbolic suicide or a dream of better times to come, or had him surrender his wealth. But Hender-son holds Sir Wilfred Grenfell and Albert Schweitzer rather than social revolutionaries for models. His moving of the statue results from a desire to help society personally. When the land and the soul need rain, one calls upon the deities, not upon the Commissar of Moisture. Conversely, pure individualism without social considerations would only cause him to suffer more intensely. He burns for self-fulfillment, but self-fulfill-ment as social service. Hence, rather than taking either ex-treme, he maintains his independence as a capitalist but be-comes a humanitarian. Unlike incurable pastoralists, he seeks relief in action, in a continued testing of his personal harmony against social confusion.

To make the conversion of the old to the new Henderson possible, Bellow must assume that his sickness is not too seri-ous—not tragic but comic—and that there is still time. But Henderson is a capitalist of the mid-twentieth century, well along in middle age and therefore dangerously close to the point of no return. Clearly he would have had little chance without a profound shaking up, and as it is, we cannot be sure that the cure will take. The novel ends on a mixed note: on the family level, a marriage full of commotion will apparently go more smoothly, and on the social level Henderson may find his new outlet for charity satisfactory. But in both cases, his story is not finished with a rediscovery of America (the newfound land): he merely starts again, with less innocence but more wisdom than those who first invaded the continent.

FIFTEEN

Frost's Enclosures and Clearings

Few poets have elaborated images and metaphors more insistently than Robert Frost or mixed them so judiciously at
times with controlling axioms and guiding philosophic commentary. My intent here is to explore several of these metaphors—the road, the boundary line and clearing, the woods, the
spring pools, and the streams—and to examine ways in which
they convert the landscape of New England into the symbolic
materials of poetry. Without attempting to explicate each of
them thoroughly, I hope first to sketch their range of meanings
and then to suggest the concerted statement they make on the
ancient tension between art and nature and between pastoral
and georgic modes. Ultimately, the context of any single image
in Frost is not merely the poem in which it occurs but the
special language that develops throughout the collected poems.
Taken as a related set of symbols, these elements of Frost's
habitual landscape form a particularly comprehensive view of
many of the pastoral themes in the tradition that we have
observed and allow us to realize their modern potential in perhaps the only way it can be fully realized—in the densely com-
pacted medium of the lyric. Frost's insights into the nature of
pastoral can thus be of valuable help to us in understanding
those aspects of pastoral that have managed to survive and get
translated into modern terms.[1] They have an additional value
in that, like Stevens, Frost is very conscious of the nature of
the poem in its fusion of the imagination and reality and its
creation of an order pleasing to the mind in the midst of
potential confusion and chaos. Thus "poetic" and "pastoral"

[1] Cf. John Lynen, *The Pastoral Art of Robert Frost* (New
Haven: Yale University Press, 1960).

are again identified in him, as so often in the tradition, and a theory of one is immediately relevant to the other.

ROADS AND BOUNDARIES

One of Frost's simplest metaphors is the road, the traveling of which commits one to essentially his own individual, form-giving direction. Roads not taken are useful as imaginative alternatives by which one talks about roads taken and as an indication of what has become unreachable by virtue of one's prior choices. Such roads belong in the realm of the contrary-to-fact and hence to a fictive pastoral landscape, which Frost entertains with whimsy and sometimes with nostalgia: they are outside time while determined fatality and time are the essence of roads taken—along which no potential or dream is ever entirely fulfilled—if for no other reason than because all moments are sequential. Along time's sequential roads (the ones we have in fact pursued) everything brought to fruition is eventually left behind, and other things are missed or still in the future. Thus in the poem "The Road Not Taken" the traveler's other potential selves become impossible once he has chosen his particular direction, and since there can be no avoidance of choice he can never be all he might have been. Time and direction—the laying of an irreversible purpose across random possibility—thus defeat the full realization of the traveler's dreams, and imagination yields to contingency and fact. At the same time, his choice defines all that he has become and makes "all the difference."

To this anecdote of lost possibility, with its twinge of Arcadian regret and longed-for ideality, Frost adds an obstacle in "On a Tree Fallen Across the Road":

> The tree the tempest with a crash of wood
> Throws down in front of us is not to bar
> Our passage to our journey's end for good,
> But just to ask who we think we are
>
> Insisting always on our own way so.
> She likes to halt us in our runner tracks,

And make us get down in a foot of snow
Debating what to do without an ax.

And yet she knows obstruction is in vain:
We will not be put off the final goal
We have it hidden in us to attain,
Not though we have to seize earth by the pole

And, tired of aimless circling in one place,
Steer straight off after something into space.

Because this road leads somewhere in particular, the focus is
less on the nature of time and process or upon potential roads
not taken than upon future goals and resisted purpose. The
obstacle is not a source of serious anguish, merely of annoy-
ance, and the philosophical question that it raises—who we
are if not nature's favorites—is "reduced" by the colloquial
banter and the brassy confidence. The romantic flight away
from the road is also qualified by the Yankee manner. The very
exaggeration of our common heroic strength and high destiny
helps Frost slip by the question of how one gets a sleigh aloft
and what the "something" is, the reaching of which will
define us. Thus the imagined flight from reality becomes something of a road not taken, too, though a future possibility is
obviously quite different in this respect from a past now beyond reach.

The contrast in both road poems is essentially between one's
present reality and the imaginary life that we desire but are
also quite content not to define too closely—caught as we are
among real contingencies and exiled from the landscape of
dreams. What might have become elegiac regret for some better landscape—where one could take all roads and where trees
do not fall across any of them—Frost diverts into a hopeful
statement about the uses of adversity in forcing us to make the
best of what we have.

If we can speak more schematically without losing sight of
the symbol in its particular contexts, Frost's roads might be
said to complement his clearings. In these, typically, rather
than moving toward some end taken for granted or making
an irreversible choice that carries the traveler out of reach of
former possibilities, the speaker is defined by what he has

"encompassed" or by the clearing he enters. By comparison to the road image, whose essence is the evolving of a self in time, the clearing is an image of stability and resistance to several kinds of encroachment: the erosion of time, the inevitable losses of linear travel, the confusing mass of midwood. The poet works in clearings and to make clearings or "clarifications," and in this task he is allied with the farmer, as we will see in a moment.

The clearing for Frost has foremost certain epistemological implications that "All Revelation" explores. In this brief but very crucial poem, Frost suggests that the act of seeing is itself a dynamic building out of reality as the mind thrusts into a self-contained, encompassed piece of reality.[2] The meaning discovered in the ghostly mind's encounter of the geode (a crystal clearing like a cave) is empirical in the sense that, unlike roads not taken or flight toward the stars, it actually exists. It is by nature bounded, given, and irreducible and has something of the relative permanence of an artifact about it. Both the mind and the object it enters are mysteries except in their mutual encounter in the defining act, during which they create a poetic correspondence between ideal place and mind. The geode is a miniature landscape worthy of Marvell; it allows self and object to unite in a single dynamic life much like that of a poem in its organic integrity and inherent meaning. The speaker cannot say where mind is before or after it thrusts in, or what it is that it thrusts into except at the time of its entrance. But it ponders these questions in the realm of the abstract imagination for only a moment, delighted with the order and beauty the mind has discovered; it asks and is gone.

Customary Frostean clearings are like the geode in that revelation frequently occurs in them. Yet they also resemble the road image at times in that they reflect the randomness of temporal movement that may reassert its ancient rights over the clearing at any time. Though each clearing and act of

[2] As Reuben Brower points out, "Ge-ode" (a "nodule of stone having a cavity lined with crystals or mineral matter") means "earth-like," *The Poetry of Robert Frost* (New York: Oxford University Press, 1963), p. 140.

clarification is different in its context, one is especially central and further explains the peculiar effectiveness of the geode figure, the clearing in the poem "Beech." Here the self is not so much created as protected, and its act is less an imaginative act of seeing than an assertion of its boundaries and possession of its haven:

> Where my imaginary line
> Bends square in woods, an iron spine
> And pile of real rocks have been founded.
> And off this corner in the wild,
> Where these are driven in and piled,
> One tree, by being deeply wounded,
> Has been impressed as Witness Tree
> And made commit to memory
> My proof of being not unbounded.
> Thus truth's established and borne out,
> Though circumstanced with dark and doubt—
> Though by a world of doubt surrounded.

We should note first that Frost's controlled, bounded area assumes the compatibility of private ownership, selfhood, and nature, and in fact fuses them. Presumably some of what is wild falls inside the boundary, though unlike the romantic, Frost does not plunge into it. No wood spirits or mythological creatures are expected to come calling. Nor is the wounding of the tree an affront to nature as it would be if deities had declared it sacred and inviolable. Whereas for Faulkner's Ike McCaslin the wilderness is a final refuge of the romantic visionary and is "constantly and punily gnawed at by men with plows and axes who fear" it, in Frost nature's dimensionlessness is unavailable to the mind. It must be fenced: as in the choice of a road, one cannot elect not to establish himself because the alternative is chaos. And the boundaries must be real, not idealistic or imaginary: the piled rocks and the tree farther out in the wild give manifest tangibility to the imaginary line (the equivalent to which in poetic would be pinning ideas to such images as these very concrete ones). They suggest that without the physical wounding of the tree and the pile of rocks, one would not be memorialized. The marked place bears witness to the poet's character.

The important themes in this version of the bounded place

are indicated by three word groups, the stance group (established, circumstanced, founded, and bounded); the manifestation group (proof, borne out) and their opposites (doubt, dark); and the imprisoning, wounding group (impressed, circumstanced, and wounded). These are summed up in the witness tree as a thing both seen and, like the sycamore that Zaccheus did climb "Our Lord to see," a thing to see from. As an interrelated group, they indicate clearly that one must be established to be seen and must mark off and wound nature to be established. What the farmer does to nature in making his claim is closely parallel to what the poet does to the random possibilities of nature in reducing it to poetic enclosure and imposing his stylistic mark upon it. A landscape poem draws upon nature for its symbols and at the same time defines as out of bounds what it cannot use. (Actually, more than unbounded nature is excluded from the privileged place: the speaker who comes into express being in the poem and invites an audience to bear witness to him also leaves interior areas of doubt outside the compass of his making, in the circumstancing doubt and dark.) [3] His act of declaration bespeaks a public recording

[3] Though any diagram risks being overly schematic, we might see some of the implications of Frost's associations between design and clearing, poetry and enclosure more clearly by experimenting with one:

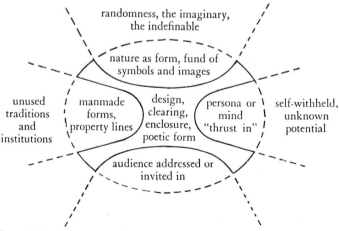

Dotted lines indicate the tenuousness with which Frost draws an aesthetic circle around a subject and the necessity of looking beyond the boundary at areas left unformalized.

and assumes a proper way of registering claims. Hence as the farmer draws upon legal conventions in regards to property, the poet employs linguistic conventions in regards to expressive choices, summoning from all possible elements in the confusion of language the vocal pattern, the sound-shape of the poem, until he is thoroughly committed to its "terms" (from *terminus,* boundary). The finished product says in effect, "I, Robert Frost, am here established in these words, which all may experience who enter this enclosure." But the poem is not quite a "complete Frost" as it may seem to claim, for reasons that we will examine in a moment.

CREATIVE LABOR AND NATURE'S FORMLESSNESS

This need to fence private places that both close off an outside chaos and express the boundaries of the self gives Frost a ready defense of industry. We must pause upon that defense long enough to see that among the many pastoral themes that Frost recasts in modern terms is the ancient tension between the life of creative play and the life of industrial effort and work. These correspond roughly to dream and fact at times, and at other times to poetry and farming, imagination and reality, and pastoral and georgic. Like Stevens, who maintains equilibrium among similar opposites, Frost refuses to sacrifice one to the other without a struggle. Characteristically, he seeks to fuse them and to deny that they have irreconcilable difficulties. But he cannot always locate a logical ground for their identification and just as characteristically forces us to be aware of their separate claims.

One traditional way to handle the interplay of the order of play and the order of work in pastoral is to isolate a moment of escape from duty and to return at the conclusion of the poem to the demands of real shepherdom, as when Theocritean shepherds take leave of their sheep-tending for song-contests and then return to work. At times in the tradition, when pastoral and georgic collide more forcefully, harvest labor or economic need intrudes conspicuously into the ceremonial rites of Arcadia. In realists such as Crabbe, the artifice of the singing shepherds is destroyed by the pressing demands of economy. Frost's version of this traditional tension revolves around the landscape and the poet-farmer figure. The symbol-seeking poet requires "clarifications" from nature; the farmer must scratch out a meager living from a modest acreage. Their differences underscore not only the tension between aesthetic and pragmatic uses of landscape but also the boundary between the imaginative life of the mind and the existential facts upon which realists insist. The laboring farmer must deal with things as things and commit himself to actual "roads taken"; the poet is free to fictionalize, dream, reorder, and convert raw materials into expressive symbols. Then in seeking reconciliation, the farmer must try to discover potential poems in labor; the poet must seek meaning and productiveness in poetic dreams.

How satisfying to the potential Arcadian is labor in Frost? We find a wide range of answers. In cooperative as opposed to individual forms, industry has numerous ways to go wrong. By itself, without sufficient checks, the working social order is likely to impose unnecessary limitations on choice, limitations that, as a conservative seeking to preserve his own particular "clearings" and property lines, Frost resists wholeheartedly. He often associates labor not with the establishing of a necessary order within the encroaching woods but with the power of the machine, which endangers those involved with it and tyrannizes over the mind while mangling the body. After being injured by the machine, as "The Self-Seeker" reveals, one cannot escape to a quiet, restorative place but becomes still more deeply entangled in the system that requires the machine and hence in self-seeking competition and bargaining. The self-seeker's wound deepens his isolation and causes him to sacrifice his flowerland (his one poetic diversion) and even personal relationships to "get settled." Despite its injury of him, however, the machine is essential to the village economy, and the self-seeker does not condemn it:

> "You can hear the small buzz saws whine, the big saw
> Caterwaul to the hills around the village

As they both bite the wood. It's all our music.
One ought as a good villager to like it.
No doubt it has a sort of prosperous sound,
And it's our life."
    "Yes, when it's not our death."
"You make that sound as if it wasn't so
With everything. What we live by we die by."

We have only to remember, however, the sweeter sounds of scythes and poems to see how disappointing the "music" of the buzz saw is. The social organization that derives from modern technology is not entirely inimical in Frost's eyes despite its indifference to "flowers," but if nature is driven completely underground and smothered, the social organism grows sick. To draw upon a metaphor that we will examine later, the brook, in "A Brook in the City," Frost suggests that not so much trade and machine labor as the entire social organization is the cause of modern estrangement from nature and self-strangulation. A prehistoric "immortal force" like the brook cannot wear a number, and to "staunch it at its source" with loads of cinders would be distasteful, if not impossible. Society's impulse is collectively most unpoetic; rather than sample the force and life of the brook, it channels it into the sewer, where it runs troubled. Presumably, the city stifles the naturalness of its citizens as well in making them good villagers attuned to the caterwaul of its necessary buzz saws. Of the main components that we might specify for an ideal configuration in Frost—energy, order, communication, and beauty—the city's grid of addresses has only one: order.

But it is no secret that Frost's pastoral speakers feel free to turn their backs on the machine and the city whenever they want and to seek elsewhere for a fusion of work and creative play, especially in the acts of labor that the farmer-poet performs in isolation from others—often on the edge between poetic aspiration and grinding monotony. In "The Tuft of Flowers," the speaker begins in that isolation, working well behind the mower who has cut the hay he turns and who is also alone in his task. They form a very independent production line. As the speaker discovers a tuft of flowers spared by the mower, their common field becomes a place not merely of productivity but also of expressiveness. The landscape changes instantly from georgic to pastoral because, as a gratuitous and unnecessary act, the sparing of flowers enables the two workers to become fellow appreciators of beauty for its own sake. The startling "tongue of bloom" stands forth from the scene as both a humanizing symbol and as a token of nature's cooperation with our aesthetic sense. The incident suggests that a kind of poetry resides both in and apart from the georgic realm of productivity and therefore that the farmer and the poet are compatible though distinct. In fact they seem to require each other as companionable contrasts. The flowers did not stand forth so visibly before the mower cleared the hay from around them, and as Frost indicates elsewhere, flowers survive best in clearings that have been tamed. The civilizing effort of the laborer makes possible the survival of poetry. Nor did the brook, which now contributes to the total composition of the scene, reveal itself so clearly before the scythe had performed its work.

When we consider all the elements that have gone into making the flowers announce themselves in just this way for the speaker—as a focal point of an act of communication and aesthetic perception—the implication is clearly that a previous unpreparedness in the worker and in the scene is also necessary for the surprise of the flowers, which triggers a series of speculations about the dreams of the mower and the common humanity that links laborers, not as laborers as a Marxist would wish, but as poets who happen to labor in the same vicinity. It is the flowers that enable two isolated men to join in "dream" atop their necessary economic functions. The distinction between beauty and work remains sharp; poetry is more than a communal accompaniment to harvest (as Christopher Caudwell treats it). The flowers are a stylistic transcendence or symbolism that carries the mind beyond its georgic tasks. But at the same time the context of the hayfield is vital to the meaning of the symbol and neither occupation makes sense without the other.

Ideally the poet-farmer seeks to fuse them more closely than this, rather than abandoning one to seek the other (as Frost does in "After Apple Picking," the most complex and perhaps the most impressive of all the poems concerned with this theme) or going back and forth between them or making one the context of the other. In "Mowing," Frost suggests that such a fusion is possible and that, therefore, the making of hay is virtually identical with the writing of the poem itself. Ultimately pastoral seems to want to identify aesthetic dream and the activities of the Arcadian landscape; Frost here merely goes one step farther by drawing what would ordinarily be a georgic activity into the world of animated sensibility, in which the physical landscape composes itself into a "real" poem and the messages that scythes whisper to their users are the same as the messages that poems whisper to those who listen closely:

There was never a sound beside the wood but one,
And that was my long scythe whispering to the ground.
What was it it whispered? I knew not well myself;
Perhaps it was something about the heat of the sun,
Something, perhaps about the lack of sound—
And that was why it whispered and did not speak.
It was no dream of the gift of idle hours,
Or easy gold at the hand of fay or elf:
Anything more than the truth would have seemed too weak
To the earnest love that laid the swale in rows,
Not without feeble-pointed spikes of flowers
(Pale orchises), and scared a bright green snake.
The fact is the sweetest dream that labor knows.
My long scythe whispered and left the hay to make.

The equation of fact to dream is a general equation that includes specific representatives of each, such as the labor of the farmer and the dream of the poet. The scythe's earnest love is to whisper poems, and the poem's aim is to fulfill itself in imitations of pure scythe-sound or "fact" and therefore to say nothing more or less than the truth, to romanticize nothing. Actually, the speaker's rational statement about the scythe's whispering and speculation as to its meaning are somewhat dissociative; rather than experiencing the identification of fact and dream, Frost explores the possibility of their fusion as if in "fact" the scythe were animate and intelligent. It takes an act of imagination to attribute to it the qualities the poet needs it to have in order to write the sonnet about it. And despite the scythe's inarticulate whispering, the poem itself is neither inarticulate nor whispering; it speaks forcefully to the issue, especially in the penultimate line. If the scythe-sound is beyond the reach of intelligence, the axiom of the philosophical observer is equally beyond the "statements" that scythes make. Still, fields of "feeble-pointed spikes of flowers" are basically poems, beflowered with images laid in rows for the poet to harvest. Both the enigma of the scythe's message and the field are still "making" in our minds after the rhythmic sweep of the poem's strokes is finished. Despite the differences between the poem and the landscape, they are magnificent mirrors of each other, in which we see much more than we could in either apart. Georgic is transformed by pastoral perspectives and pastoral is made "honest" by the farmer's commitment to the world of labor and "truth." Having discarded the animation and pretended correspondences between shepherd and nature in the old pastoral conventions, Frost transfers the feeling of that correspondence to the muscular activity of the laborer. Like Marvell's mower before his fall, the mind of Frost's mower is the "true survey"

> Of all these meadows fresh and gay;
> And in the greenness of the grass

sees his "hopes as in a glass."

When labor interferes with the psychic freedom of the worker and the aesthetic composition of the landscape, this fusion obviously becomes impossible, and, like the "lone striker," Frost is pulled between the factory and nature. The lone striker does not reject the factory outright because it represents a craftsmanship that no one who values human effort and skill can avoid admiring. But useful as man's ingenuity and the deftness of quick-working fingers might be, he finds them "easy to resist." He escapes to nature where he can think and act with freedom. To grant the need for

industry and its potential as one of the components of our partial victories over confusion is thus not to grant it high priority—unless, as seems unlikely, industry is doomed without the
poet-farmer, in which case they may "come get him." The key
to his truancy lies in the word "lone." Frost's fusion of georgic,
or industrial activity, and pastoral occurs almost exclusively
during moments of solitude or in dialogues between two people. Society is a distraction, and a planned, mass economy is
destructive to the concentrated act of mind that extracts from
the landscape and from labor itself the focal symbols that compose it as an aesthetic experience.

Consequently, in other encounters with labor and planned
economy, Frost risks randomness and wildness rather than im-
prison himself in a system. In several poems he suggests that
one must be able to escape even from his own self-constructed
enclosures. In "Unharvested," for instance, the "road" the
speaker has taken is a limiting commitment that he is luckily
able to transcend, at least momentarily, and it is an untamed
aspect of nature that entices him to do so:

> A scent of ripeness from over a wall.
> And come to leave the routine road
> And look for what had made me stall,
> There sure enough was an apple tree
> That had eased itself of its summer load,
> And of all but its trivial foliage free,
> Now breathed as light as a lady's fan.
> For there there had been an apple fall
> As complete as the apple had given man.
> The ground was one circle of solid red.
>
> May something go always unharvested!
> May much stay out of our stated plan,
> Apples or something forgotten and left,
> So smelling their sweetness would be no theft.

His escape is from usefulness and rationality to intuition and
myth, across the line where poetry may thrive without paying
duty to conscious purpose. The discovery of such surprises,
Frost suggests, is worth the loss of Eden, and in fact one

apple "fall" is like another. Routine and discipline thereby become equatable with the original plan for Eden shattered when Adam and Eve, too, crossed the line and discovered surprise and wonder—at the expense of waste and eventually decay. Chance underlies all discoveries, especially those that come about in the making of poems, as Frost indicates in a number of places. A poem does not emerge from a preconceived idea or a rigorous plan but from the free play of intuition. A scythe that spoke too forthrightly or a tuft of flowers left as a definite message would not have the immense suggestiveness Frost is able to give them. Much as it is to be feared, wildness is as necessary to the poet's ungeorgic "harvest" as nature's abundant fertility. Or to remember the road figure here again, the traveler's escape from purpose frees him from sequential progress: he stalls and is able to accept the moment for its own rewards, forgetful of the decay that follows sweetness. He accepts the defining radius of the apples and the gracefulness of the fanlike tree as a shape made by nature rather than imposed by his own encompassing acts of definition. The harvest that georgic rites are designed to bring forth is squandered for an aesthetic moment totally outside the world of labor and efficiency.

"Plan" for Frost means not only the apple farmer's economy, of course, but also the aims and ambitions of the poet. He thought frequently of the parallels between the two and was aware that poems are written for "consumption." One who goes to market with overly programmed regularity endangers the fertility of poetry's productive ground. Shepherd Tityrus in "Build Soil—A Political Pastoral" suggests that though "To market 'tis our destiny to go," we should refuse to take everything there: "I will go to my run-out social mind / And be as unsocial with it as I can." Poems are created in solitude and cannot be commissioned by czars of culture or booksellers: "We're too unseparate out among each other— / With goods to sell and notions to impart." There are also areas of the self that should not be put onto the market at all but left outside the realm of communication. As Pike remarks in the eclogue "From Plane to Plane,"

> A man has got to keep his extrication.
> The important thing is not to get bogged down
> In what he has to do to earn a living.

The result is not a denial of the public as in the elite cult of obscure and unpopular poets but a fruitful alternation of private and public moments, productivity and creativity. Rather than hoeing both ways, up one row and down another, one hoes one way and walks back in leisure, in a rhythm of routine and escape.

To abandon public order, plan, and meaningful production altogether, however, would be to fall prey ultimately to randomness and therefore to destroy both the social order and art. Not far beyond the unharvested tree and the witness tree in the wild is the chaos of undifferentiated woods. Again, in defining the reciprocity of work and poetry, the road and the clearing images help us considerably. In "The Wood-Pile," for instance, we discover among other concerns both a road and a clearing. In this case, the landscape is not promising for the pastoralist and writer of georgics seeking a compromise between vocation and avocation. The speaker has moved so far into midwood that no order, either economic or poetic, has much chance to survive. Everything is at sixes and sevens: he does not know where he is and where he should go. The snow breaks through underfoot and the poet's meter breaks down as though in imitation. Part of the difficulty is that the bond between the lonely individual and society is broken. Except for a stray bird, the speaker has no one to posture before. No one has left a mark to follow.

In pressing on, however, the speaker discovers a woodpile wrapped about with clematis like a string binding a bundle—the product of a clearing operation. It obviously does not speak the message of the tuft of flowers, nor is it, like the unharvested apple tree, a signal of nature's abundance. It is a very ill-placed effort at productive work gradually being absorbed into the formlessness of the swamp in "the slow smokeless burning of decay." Clearly, in creating his perfectly measured and stacked product, the craftsman has spent himself to no one's benefit when by "going to market" he might at least have helped to warm a household. Yet Frost does not condemn him, at least not explicitly, because it was within his right to keep busy as he saw fit. Given the extent of the world that needs warming, no human effort was likely to have altered it significantly, and to work for pure pleasure is a kind of heroic defiance. The use-lessness of the effort is precisely what proves the spirit of the man and the aesthetic satisfaction of the task. In a succession of possible readings of his product, we see first its extravagance, then its disregard of necessity, as play, and finally the all-encompassing victory of nature. Despite all anyone does as either poet or worker, nature's laws cannot be circumvented. The discovery of the woodpile is the speaker's end of the "road" and the woodpile itself is all the "clearing."

THE LANGUAGES OF POETRY AND NATURE

Though taken together, Frost's statements about the fusion of work and play reveal a basic satisfaction with those moments when the poet-farmer manages to make his creative efforts mo-mentary "stays against confusion," "The Wood-Pile" stands out as an especially central and less optimistic recognition of the temporary nature of the stay. Elsewhere, Frost notices that an artifact rescued from an ancient civilization no longer de-livers its original message because it is scarred and obscure; and again in poems such as "The Last Mowing" and "West-Running Brook" he seems ready to reconsider the position of earlier poems like "The Tuft of Flowers" and "Mowing." Nature still provides objects in which the poet sees the pos-sibility for transcendent aesthetic moments, but flux is on the march. The moralizing of the speaker of "The Wood-Pile" is entirely different from the assurance of "The Tuft of Flow-ers" that "Men work together . . . whether they work to-gether or apart" because the original builder of the woodpile is much further from him and they share no "brotherly speech." The difficulty is that neither work nor imagination can make anything of the swamp that it does not basically want to be. The context of the act of labor, which turns by accident into communication, encroaches on the meaning of the message. The special writ inscribed by decay, superimposed on the intention of the artisan, demands to be read as part of the symbol's total significance.

Such creations of personal order—clearings, piles of wood, poems—are more often than not performed against nature's indifference or active resistance. Occasionally Frost cannot resist seeking for design in nature to confirm the poet's need for order and purpose, and the rare perceptions of meaning in nature that he discovers then become a signal for an expansive lyric feeling like that of "Unharvested." But these are immediately checked by reminders of the swamp or midwood condition that "The Wood-Pile" makes so prominently, the all-encompassing condition of the journey and the discovery. Frost balances lyric crescendo with the countering mood of the shrewd Yankee in such poems—so delicately at times that they fuse into a single complex talk-song, flexible enough to sing about what there is to sing about and yet also to talk realistically about the rest. Consider "The Most of It":

> He thought he kept the universe alone;
> For all the voice in answer he could wake
> Was but the mocking echo of his own
> From some tree-hidden cliff across the lake.
> Some morning from the boulder-broken beach
> He would cry out on life, that what it wants
> Is not its own love back in copy speech,
> But counter-love, original response.
> And nothing ever came of what he cried
> Unless it was the embodiment that crashed
> In the cliff's talus on the other side,
> And then in the far-distant water splashed,
> But after a time allowed for it to swim,
> Instead of proving human when it neared
> And someone else additional to him,
> As a great buck it powerfully appeared,
> Pushing the crumpled water up ahead,
> And landed pouring like a waterfall,
> And stumbled through the rocks with horny tread,
> And forced the underbrush—and that was all.

The concern with purpose that Frost sometimes makes too explicit is here shortened and made part of the drama between the speaker and the scene, which reveals something to him quite different from what he asked for (was it Eve he wished?). Like Herbert's "Heaven," the poem suggests the echo-poem tradition in which an oracle of some sort sends back an enigmatic answer to a shepherd's call. In Herbert's variation on the theme, the oracle speaks for mankind and renders for it a vision of paradise that corresponds to the fullest dream, beyond the usual nymph that the shepherd desires. But Frost's nature, though it frequently offers suggestions of personified forces, is without spirits and demons. The adamic figure remains alone in a boulder-strewn terrain thick with underbrush, too rough, dense, and obscure for him to penetrate—either to make a road through or a clearing in if he wanted to. The creature that crashes forward is indeed an "embodiment" of an answer—not a member of the sign family sent as counter-response but a member of the thing family, a beast that wills his own progress and will not be translated by the symbol-seeking mind. Though a representative of the natural context (his horny hoofs are as tough as the rocks), he remains a singular, impenetrable object. But something like a poetic response to him is nonetheless possible because he does correspond to something in us. Though the discrepancy between expectation and discovery is ironic, the speaker does not disparage the gift he has received. The mind merely has to adjust; it remains disengaged enough to define its engagement with the "embodiment"—and perhaps to guard against future expansive moments.

To define its engagement and disengagement, to winnow the grain of rationality from the chaff of meaningless objects in the landscape, is in effect the mind's special "georgic" labor. For Frost, pastoral is an easier set of correspondences that come about in scenes where wonder and beauty thrust themselves forward, like the tuft of flowers, without need of arduous probing. One simply crosses a fence and discovers an abundance he has not expected. In contrast, georgic requires a muscular effort against a resistant terrain, and Frost's poetry frequently works hard at creating its rational, axiom-filled order in a universe at odds with it. "The Most of It" is an impressive balance of these two impulses because the laboring poet has not forced himself to encapsulate the grain in axioms: he merely brings the central revelation far enough forward for us to wonder at it with him as the poem remains arrested between plunging in and witholding. The concluding phrase suggests the well-defined doubt of "For Once, Then, Something" but with less pause in the voice, with an emergent conclusiveness in "all" as a climaxing ambiguity. That ambiguity might be paraphrased several ways: "that was all the creature did, stumble, crash through the brush and disappear, not what he expected, perhaps not even distinguishable from the nothing that came of his other calls"; "that was all the disturbance, following which—rest and thought"; "there was no more, that was all, but even this much was magnificent, though not what he in his foolishness expected and demanded."

The revelations of the clearing stand opposed both to such chance and partial revelations of the underbrush and to the strictly useful economy of the hayfield. It is in the meaning created by enclosures that Frost is able frequently to find a common ground for the poet and the farmer: "truth" depends upon one's having offered meaningful expressions of himself in his clearings, as "Beech" indicates. Even then it is difficult to determine whether the meanings one imagines are added to things or discovered in them. Is the "embodiment" that comes forward from nature possessed of a value or does the special need of the observer ascribe value to him? A manmade clearing with nature's flowers in it, set off and heightened by the prepared consciousness of the poetic mind "thrust into" it, comes close to a Frostean ideal, but can any such clearing remain stable? Besides the chaos that one may walk into and get lost in, in midwood, is a chaos that moves aggressively into the clearing of its own accord and seems to destroy the possibility of meaning. The edges of symbolic objects melt until the disintegrated woodpile will speak to no one and offer no special mark in the undifferentiated swamp.

In desperation for counterspeech and original response, the

poet may be tempted to seek moments of transcendence or romantic boundlessness, and though he usually resists that impulse, Frost does make occasional gestures toward the infinite—not so much as the only possible location of pastoral repose as simply a way of putting the finite and the temporal in perspective. In "A Boundless Moment," he quickly returns to earth after such a moment outside time, and in "Birches" he suggests that ideally one climbs "Toward heaven" and then returns to earth ("the right place for love") in a rhythm of aspiration and realism. It is necessary to get away from earth when "life is too much like a pathless wood" but equally necessary to come back. By comparison to "The Most of It," "The Wood-Pile," and "Beech," "A Boundless Moment" is an especially instructive attempt to define the boundary between the miraculous and the commonplace. The poet's initial surprise over a beech tree's apparently unusual behavior conditions us for his return to common fact:

> "Oh, that's the Paradise-in-bloom," I said;
> And truly it was fair enough for flowers
> Had we but in us to assume in March
> Such white luxuriance of May for ours.

> We stood a moment so, in a strange world,
> Myself as one his own pretence deceives;
> And then I said the truth (and we moved on).
> A young beech clinging to its last year's leaves.

Thus a startling May paradise becomes an elegiac wilderness that reminds us of time and the laws of nature. The shrunken truth has a remnant of romantic faith in the clinging of the beech to its leaves, but it is merely a leftover piece of diction, not a genuinely strange phenomenon. The poet notices the truth and moves on, presumably down one of those roads or paths that indicate his previous commitments. Boundlessness is once again a form of the subjunctive, a strangeness in a nonexistent world that circumstances ordinary bounded life. The recognizable laws of trees make it possible for the poet to offer satisfactory names for them, which is some linguistic repayment for missing a grandeur that would have escaped definition. The discovery of the phrase "A young beech clinging to its last year's leaves" in a sense lays to rest the uneasy feeling raised by wild (and false) conjecture and by the misleading title "Paradise in Bloom."

But implicit in the diminishing of the tree is a problem that neither the Witness Tree nor this beech allows Frost to explore: what is bounded must be stable enough to be named in substantive words, yet the flux of nature is sometimes too dramatic to allow verbal fixation. Suppose, for instance, that one's clearing or area of nameable certainty becomes a spring pool: how is it then to be recorded or bounded? The transience of properties may well become an uncertainty in one's own circumstance. Thus in "Spring Pools" what was "snow" yesterday is a "pool" today and will be "dark foliage" tomorrow:

> These pools that, though in forests, still reflect
> The total sky almost without defect,
> And like the flowers beside them, chill and shiver,
> Will like the flowers beside them soon be gone,
> And yet not out by any brook or river,
> But up by roots to bring dark foliage on.
>
> The trees that have it in their pent-up buds
> To darken nature and be summer woods—
> Let them think twice before they use their powers
> To blot out and drink up and sweep away
> These flowery waters and these watery flowers
> From snow that melted only yesterday.

Do we not have here a symbol that undermines the confidence of "Beech"? A wilderness that merely circumstances the boundary keeps its place: its very act of surrounding the property gives it its place (*circum*-stance), though circumstancing also retains something of its usual randomness as chance incident or occurrence. One's encounter with the static wilderness establishes an edge between the order within and the vast extent of the "world of doubt" outside.

But spring pools, though equally defined for a moment, are continuously melting at the edges and so may well prove to be more accurate symbols for both the changing self and nature's flux. The difference between words of "establishment" and "being" and words of the flux family is that one names a stable Form and the others are basically paradoxical: "Spring Pools" in fact is a misleading title because while the words stay the same the phenomenon changes. And if the poet cannot bear witness to things, he himself cannot be permanently defined by his place among them. He offers gestures of resistance and imperatives ("stay," "let it not be too soon"), but nature blots, drinks, sweeps away as pent-up buds have their own purposes to fulfill. One form devours another until all forms "add up" to confusion and draw the poet once more into mid-wood chaos.

In each of these images—the road, the unharvested area, the swamp and the woodpile, the witness tree, and spring pools— Frost explores the basic metaphysical reasons that nature cannot be idyllic and that, by implication, the poet cannot compose himself in final acts or pure poems as he might like. Another way of putting it is to say that neither the design nor the language of poetry can derive from a realm of Ideas abstractable from nature's forms but must try to be reflections of real things in passage in a local geography obviously quite unlike the permanent landscape of an Eden or Arcadia. Even the kind of songs that nature offers (like the ovenbird's) are a guide to the poet's songs and symbols for them; they are clearly not those of the romantic cuckoo, skylark, or nightingale, who bear little resemblance to the real songsters that pass under those names.

Though the poet's lyric response is often to things in flux, however, it may at the same time issue in aphorisms that define recurrent attitudes, as in the concluding formula of "Hyla Brook":

> By June our brook's run out of song and speed.
> Sought for much after that, it will be found
> Either to have gone groping underground
> (And taken with it all the Hyla breed
> That shouted in the mist a month ago,
> Like ghost of sleigh-bells in a ghost of snow)—
> Or flourished and come up in jewelweed,

Weak foliage that is blown upon and bent,
Even against the way its waters went.
Its bed is left a faded paper sheet
Of dead leaves stuck together by the heat—
A brook to none but who remember long.
This as it will be seen is other far
Than with brooks taken otherwhere in song.
We love the things we love for what they are.

The shutting off of the brook's song and the shout of the "Hyla breed" is curiously like the quieting of the noisy world in an enclosed garden. But rather than finding evidence of universals behind the quieted object, Frost discovers purely material change. The difference, in terms of poetic imagery, is clear if we compare "ghost of sleigh-bells in a ghost of snow" to Marvell's "green thought in a green shade." Both annihilate the physical world to what the mind contains, but Marvell's annihilation allows the mind to re-create in essence what exists only imperfectly in the physical garden. The mind contains all the "kinds" within itself and beyond that, by transcending them, escapes them and creates other worlds. Yet it is still harbored within green shade and is itself green-tinged, with suggestions of renewal and growth. Though the substantives thought and shade are opposed, shade is the least tangible thing in the garden and might be said to "lean toward" ghostly thought, and so the two things, thought and shade, are strangely alike; they are interwoven in the brotherly green, and by assuming that nature can be essentially present in the mind even though physically separate, Marvell claims the best of both worlds. The gardener, too, imitates God in measuring intangible pattern into the forms of his creation; his dial of flowers and herbs is a green image of the zodiac. Though the particular components of his measure change, the divine form is an abiding presence to be re-created again and again: all poems seek the patterns that are both embedded in nature and transcend nature.

In contrast, to Frost the fading of material things leaves only ghosts of memory; the flourishing of new life is the destruction of the old forms. The present offers three inadequate substitutes for the original Hyla Brook: memory, jewel-weed, and "dead leaves stuck together by the heat." That other poets take brooks otherwhere suggests that they violently draw the phenomenal world into poetry and give it a linguistic ride, rather than bringing poetry to reality without romantic or idealistic avoidance. The contrast in method is inherent in the difference between "taken" and "are," Frost's brook refusing to transcend what nature makes it, and the poet in turn refusing to be disillusioned by it: he "establishes" not a safe enclosure but an attitude against the flux.

A metaphor that can reconcile the various possibilities of the road, the witness tree, melting pools, and disappearing streams would obviously be of some importance to Frost, whose thought is so committed to symbols. Putting them together, we get something like "flow resisted by defining act," or "momentary stay against confusion," which seems closer to a complete Frost than the terms and property lines of "Beech."

What we have in fact is something very like "West-Running Brook," which collects several Frostean themes and develops them as part of a communications problem between a husband and wife.[4] After his wife has attempted to personalize the brook by inviting it into the human spectrum almost as a third partner in their marriage, "Fred" opposes her with a counterreading:

> "Speaking of contraries, see how the brook
> In that white wave runs counter to itself.
> It is from that in water we were from
> Long, long before we were from any creature.
> Here we, in our impatience of the steps,
> Get back to the beginning of beginnings,
> The stream of everything that runs away.
> Some say existence like a Pirouot
> And Pirouette, forever in one place,
> Stands still and dances, but it runs away,

[4] Cf. Brower's exploration of the man-wife dialogues in "Dialogue of One or Two," pp. 152–179, and Lynen's useful commentary on this and other aspects of Frost's pastoralism, especially "The Yankee Manner" and "Pastoralism and the Dramatic," pp. 80–139.

It seriously, sadly, runs away
To fill the abyss's void with emptiness."

While all things rush toward the void, the self is a dance on the surface, a purpose in action, not statistically bounded. Far from making the two of them three—man and wife and nature, all destined for union in heaven—the brook threatens to isolate them. "It flows between us / To separate us for a panic moment"; and worse, it flows "over us, and with us." The difference is obviously critical: the poem's "point of view" is not from inside an enclosure or beside a changing mass but both in and out of the flux, part of the water but also a defining resistance to its flow. As part of it, we, too, are "substance lapsing unsubstantial," in danger of losing not merely our relations with natural objects and those we think we know but our "selves." But we can will consistency, or "throw back" toward the source: we are

"Not just a swerving, but a throwing back,
As if regret were in it and were sacred. . . .
It is from this in nature we are from.
It is most us."

And so, too, by willing their own union, the two of them can form a social unit, a marriage of two minds resisting the flow in the same way. In fact, the marital contract is defined by their give and take over the stream, whose reflection of their way of being helps them discuss what they themselves are. Their contract is sealed ceremonially, by the signature they have put on the ideas they have each offered. As different as thesis and antithesis, they arrive at their agreement in the saying itself, in their resisting acts:

"Today will be the day
You said so."
"No, today will be the day
You said the brook was called West-Running Brook."
"Today will be the day of what we both said."

First the definition of the thing-in-motion, then themselves, and then the social bond. The "eclogue" is a record of their discovery of harmony, not in Arcadian nature, of course, but in their endurance and in their capacity to speak to the issue.

Such acts of communication are central to Frost's poetry, which survives between the flux of the wilderness and the order that people choose to enact, in the difficulty of living on the "edge." For the place the poet most seeks to establish form is the boundary between himself and the Alien, where form is negotiation rather than an artifice of eternity.

Typical of these places of discovery, and perhaps an appropriate one to cite as a summing up of the pastoral aspects of Frost's clearing operations, is "Far-away Meadow" in "The Last Mowing":

> There's a place called Faraway Meadow
> We never shall mow in again,
> Or such is the talk at the farmhouse:
> The meadow is finished with men.
> Then now is the chance for the flowers
> That can't stand mowers and ploughers.
> It must be now, though, in the season
> Before the not mowing brings trees on,
> Before trees, seeing the opening,
> March into a shadowy claim.
> The trees are all I'm afraid of,
> That flowers can't bloom in the shade of;
> It's no more men I'm afraid of;
> The meadow is done with the tame.
> The place for the moment is ours
> For you, O tumultuous flowers,
> To go to waste and go wild in,
> All shapes and colors of flowers,
> I needn't call you by name.

Though echoes of romanticism are strong plangencies here, Frost's meadow compromises between them and the world of necessary mowing and plowing. Unlike mythological scenes, Far-away Meadow is a real place (or could be), and unlike the infinitude that lies beyond boundaries for the romantic, the distance beyond it is unknowable and inhospitable: one does not want to go farther, and the trees will soon erase all human marks even there.

Now, then, at this point in the disappearance of the clearing, is the chance for flowers. Though awareness of past and future condition the moment, it is the present that counts. The poet must take leave momentarily of farmhouse gossip, but he talks about the clearing so that those in the farmhouse, unless lost to poetry, might understand it. It is a grammar of exclamatory praise for the tumultuous flowers (yet wry enough to risk a galloping rhythm and the rhyming of *season* with *trees on* and *afraid of* twice with *shade of*); of imperative moods that ask us to come to the poet's harvest; of declarative citations of shapes and colors but not a naming of either them or the things that we know well enough already; of familiar apostrophes but not thees and thous; and of elegiac awareness that the season for pastoral eulogy is short and that the clearings that men have made will soon return to indefiniteness. Rather than force an identity between farming and the poet's harvest of flowers, Frost acknowledges their separation implicitly, but this is a concession to realism that pastoral has sometimes made willingly. (Nature's flux is not more terrifying to Frost than to shepherds who listen apprehensively in Theocritus and Virgil for the dread sound of Pan ranging through the woods around them.)

In all these images that we have examined and in the last clearing especially, Frost places the age-old concerns of pastoral in a new context. Like the main poets of the tradition, he seeks for ways to transform into the harbored order of poetry the momentary perfection that he glimpses in the landscape of New England. But these moments exist for him only perilously between social disturbances of one kind or another and the shadowy claims of an impenetrable nature. At times they exist only in the poet's verbal enclosures, which like woodpiles are not permanent but are more long-lived than most things. Thus poems are momentary havens from the confusion that presses insistently into the life of the real Frost, the struggling farmer and poet. Not only his success as a poet but his peace of mind depended upon his reconstituting of pastoral and discovery of forms to withstand those dark powers that "blot out and drink up and sweep away."

Pastoral Romance

METAMORPHOSES

The joining of pastoral and romance may appear a strange and even ill-fated union, since the emphasis in one falls on active exploits and adventurous travel and in the other on a quiet life of songs and games. The shepherd who converts passion into elegies and complaints is seemingly incompatible with the knight who hurls himself constantly into action. The combination may result, however, in a meaningful reciprocity if the pastoral sojourn of the romance wayfarer helps define his goals and if the pastoral place calls upon all its resources to influence him. To some extent, these resources—especially in renaissance pastorals that expose a courtly society to the green world—derive from Ovid as well as from Theocritus and Virgil, and they work their spell not merely as part of the languid peacefulness of the shepherd's life but also as part of nature's capacity to rearrange identities, trick the eye with magical transformations, and release subterranean forces that have heretofore remained invisible.

One aspect of Ovidian transformation is the radical displacement of normal ambition under the combined influence of nature and art. The spirit of Pan presides over the games of the forest and meadow, which include the identity-changing of masks and revels as well as shepherd songs. Behind the haunting melodies to which his fauns and nymphs dance, Pan is as elusive as Proteus. His better side is reflected in figures like Ariel and Puck; his demonic aspect, in lust-filled satyrs and tempers such as Comus. Classical pastoral, however, keeps him at a distance characteristically, as an ungraspable god, talked about but seldom seen. His influence is mellowed by the Arcadian atmosphere and distilled into the music of the shepherds. In Marvell's partly Ovidian poem "The Garden," Pan himself is quieted by the sacred garden and by the metamorphosis of Syrinx into potential material for a musical instrument. Where haunting changes of shape and melodic voices beckon to weary men of ambition, all the pursuits of the outside world are set aside as they enter a world of pure playfulness, music, and innocent eroticism:

> The *Gods,* that mortal Beauty chase,
> Still in a Tree did end their race.
> *Apollo* hunted *Daphne* so,
> Only that She might Laurel grow.
> And *Pan* did after *Syrinx* speed,
> Not as a Nymph, but for a Reed.

Ariel's song in *The Tempest* reveals similar idyllic effects that Ovidian art has in translating life into something more permanent and beautiful than it was:

> Full fathom five thy father lies;
>   Of his bones are coral made;
> Those are pearls that were his eyes:
>   Nothing of him that doth fade
> But doth suffer a sea-change
>   Into something rich and strange.

Ovid's *Metamorphoses* was perhaps suggested to Marvell and to Shakespeare because the result of Ovid's transformations is often the calming of strife in the harmony of art and melody. When the carnage of the battle between Perseus and Phineus (*Met.* 5) metamorphoses into marble statuary, the work of art has the effect of Marvell's hushed enclosure. When the arts of medicine fail to save Hyacinthus, Apollo converts him into a purple lily inscribed with the letters of lamentation, AI, both a symbol of grief and a thing of beauty (*Met.* 10). Unable to bear the grief of his human nature, Glaucus plunges into the sea:

The sea-divinities received me, deeming me worthy of a place with them, and called on Oceanus and Tethys to purge my mortal nature all away. And then they purged me, first with magic song nine times repeated to wash all evil from me, and next they bade me bathe my body in a hundred streams. [*Met.* 13] [1]

Insisting on hunting wild boar, Adonis brings disaster to himself; but as part of nature he is transformed into a flower. Yearly laments for him make his transfiguration a symbol of the rebirth of all things that perish, which "pastoralizes" the disruptions of time in cyclically recurrent rites. Similar purgations and use of music and dance in the rites of cleansing are evident in Spenser, Sidney, Shakespeare, Jonson's pastoral masques, and Milton's "Comus" and "Arcades." They suggest a special collaboration between art and nature in infusing the harmony of the landscape and its guardian spirits into those who come under their power.

Unfortunately, metamorphosis can also work against the heroic figure who suddenly finds himself in the realm of Pan and the fairies, when a cursed magic brings forward a nightmarish potential formerly hidden from him. Again Ovid initiates the tradition. Expecting to make a paradise out of vast sums of gold, Midas finds instead that the idyllic life is the very thing that gold destroys: stones, clods, wheat, fruit—the gifts of Ceres—are converted into mere money until, "wretched, he seeks to flee his wealth." Only by cleansing himself in a Lydian stream is Midas able to purge himself and live as a worshiper of Pan, whose rude notes on "rustic pipes" charm him beyond the power of wealth and position (*Met.* 11). Others experience equally trying sequences of change. As Oberon and Puck illustrate in *A Midsummer Night's Dream,* the power to work metamorphoses can misfire and further entangle, in the confusion of the forest, the original confusion of the court. In Milton, Comus has a power of transformation temporarily strong enough to defeat all rivals.

These aspects of shape-changing indicate a kinship between people and animals and serves as a kind of metaphor for man's "wolfishness" or other aspects of his beastliness. Romance, pastoral, and myth overlap in imaging such kinships

[1] Ovid, *Metamorphoses,* trans. Frank J. Miller (London: Loeb ed., 1916). All references are to this edition.

as anamorphosis, metempsychosis, dream-displacement, transmigration, and pseudomorphosis, all of which illustrate a general pliancy in man's nature but not necessarily a capacity to change for the better. The shape-changes of Proteus, for instance, are neither good nor bad: they are simply changes of the kind that the sea and the land undergo in their daily and seasonal cycles and that men undergo in their inventive games. Anthropophagy, theriomorphic and therianthropic shapes, and nightmarish shape-changing like lycanthropy indicate basic biological and spiritual identities that one may assume, usually temporarily. By making characters and objects radically changeable, all these forms of metamorphosis are potentially idyllic: as long as the hero's identity remains unfixed and magically dissolvable, the permanent identity he seeks may be just around the corner of the next adventure—whatever confusion he may be in at the moment. In most of the pastorals that make use of Ovidian resources, "beastly" change is merely one stage in a rebirth that eventually restores harmony between the hero and nature. Shakespeare's fairies prove governable by good intent or by the discipline of a Prospero; and Milton's Comus, though impressively equipped to torment those who get lost in his forest, is forced to yield to Sabrina.

Akin to these themes of magical social and psychological metamorphosis is a species of fairy tale that submits the court to the influence of a simpleton shepherd. "The Goatherd and the King's Daughter" is typical: rather than sending a knight into the forest to prove his worth or be influenced by a landscape foreign to him, the king attracts a goatherd to court to take part in a contest for his daughter. Thanks not to heroism but to wit and the magic of a flute, the lowborn hero controls a hundred loose rabbits in an open field (no easy accomplishment under the pressure of the daughter's constant badgering), summons ants to separate peas from lentils for him, and calls mice to eat a roomful of bread. His mastery of the creatures and insects—and his instinct for exploiting the king's snobbery—enable him to pass each test. Such archetypal heroes able in some magical way to turn the tables on their betters—shepherds with a thousand faces—turn up in many fairy tales

("Swan, Stick!" "The Repentant Thief," "The Greedy Couple and the Golden Birds," "The Shepherd's Dream," and "The Enchanted Princess"). They suggest that nature is in need of corrective exposure to the world of creaturely simplicity and transformative magic.

Pan himself shares in both the magic of the forest and the strange ambiguity of lowly figures capable of greatness. Though only at a late stage does he become the horned devil of the Christians and a symbol of illicit power over nature, from the first he is part goat-footed buffoon, frightening nymphs from behind bushes and behaving in a crude and boastful manner. At the same time, he is also nature's "all" and the most skillful of pipers. Shepherds do not see him directly or try to imitate him, but their art is practiced in his domain. Together with Venus and Cupid, he presides over heroic-pastoral combinations, and knights who ride forth from castles must come to terms with him before they can return. When they do return, his influence (like that of Shakespeare's fairies) may be extended to the drawing room and bridal chamber where, as a symbol of nature standing behind the elemental themes of love, death, and generation, he is a common denominator in all marriages and births.

PASTORAL SATIRE

Only if the romantic hero is extremely fortunate does he discover an Arcadia with which he feels completely attuned, however. His journey is more likely to be a return to a primitive state, followed by a series of new insights into his former motives, and a return to them. The knight-errant does not end his search with a discovery of shepherdom because it lies outside his status system. Some visitors to Arcadia become dissatisfied itinerants, like Jaques in the Forest of Arden, all the more aware of the barbarity of civilized life and the crudeness of rusticity for exposure to both. The hero may then refuse to return to society, as Gulliver, after visiting the land of rational horses and yahoos, rejects the wretched island of animals which England has become in his mind, and the land discovered on the journey is useful mainly for the satiric perspective it provides on normal society. But the desire to locate an ideal place apart from accustomed societies may itself be subjected to ridicule for its naïveté, as the contrast between sophisticated and simple lives works a mutual criticism. A pastoral element frequently turns up in mock-heroic modes to exploit that possibility. John Barth's Ebenezer Cooke, for instance, would have it that epic heroes have wrought wonderful changes in the wilderness of Maryland, and he plans an "epic to out-epic epics" in praise of the "heroic founding" of that province. Its subject will be "the courage and perseverance of her settlers in battling barb'rous nature and fearsome salvage to wrest a territory from the wild and transform it to an earthly paradise!" [2] But, unfortunately, to put such gentle heroes addressed to such high-minded purposes into his poem requires a preliminary doctoring of the actual settlers:

Lo, the crook'd nose grows straight, the lean shank fleshes out, French pox becomes a bedsore, shady deeds shed their tarnish, bright grow brighter; and the whole is musicked into tuneful rhyme, arresting conceit, and stirring meter, so's to stick in the head like *Greensleeves* and move the heart like Scripture! [P. 86]

Though the poet is quite prepared to improve his materials in this way if they seem to require it, the combination of wilderness pioneering and idyllic yearning disintegrates in the handling. Innocence leaves a hero helpless and action corrupts him. The wilderness is indeed transformed, but from a barbaric to a civilized den of vice.

The combination of adamic naïveté and disillusioning experience that *The Sot-Weed Factor, Gulliver's Travels, Don Quixote, Candide,* and other romance satires illustrate overturns the marriage of the heroic and the pastoral. In *Don Quixote,* for instance, the mixture of pastoral and romance parodies the normal feudal relationship between shepherds and knights and uses one genre to ridicule the other. As a questing knight, Quixote actively seeks adventure in a pro-

[2] John Barth, *The Sot-Weed Factor* (New York: Universal Library, 1964), p. 87.

gram of heroic name-making and trophy-winning; as a guest of shepherds, he substitutes passive lamentation for the kind of militant self-injury that results from tilting against windmills. In both spheres, the intractableness of the physical world interferes with the assumed styles of the modes that he has learned from books: horses refuse to be the decorative beasts of knights and perform like the animals they are in life; rather than languishing in long periodic sentences, nymphs use the language of shrews against him, and goatherds refuse to speak Virgilian lines.

In the main pastoral episode, Quixote, in defiance of the strict hierarchy of knight errantry, invites Sancho to sit beside him as his equal and bask in the warmth of a new democratic feeling:

"So that you may see, Sancho, the virtue there is in knight errantry, and how speedily those who perform any function in it may attain the honour and estimation of the world, I wish you to sit here beside me in these good people's company, and be on terms of equality with me, who am your master and natural lord. Eat from my plate and drink from the vessel I drink from; for it can be said of knight errantry as of love: that it puts all things on the same level." [3]

Quixote feels free to convert the class feeling of the feudal order into brotherly goodwill because in the company of the goatherds good friends are outside the normal codes. So it was in that "ancient time," Quixote points out, when people "did not know those two words *thine* and *mine*"; in "that blessed age all things were held in common." Sancho, however, whom we might expect to be eager to exchange feudal for pastoral "courtship" and allow the spirit of social metamorphosis to prevail, remains more hungry realist than instinctive democrat. He refuses to set "mine" and "thine" aside because each man's stomach is, after all, his own:

"I thank you," said Sancho, "But I must confess to your worship that so long as I have plenty to eat, I can eat it as well,

[3] Cervantes, *Don Quixote,* trans. J. M. Cohen (London: Penguin Books, 1950), p. 84.

and better, standing by myself, as seated beside an Emperor. And, to tell you the truth, even if it's only bread and onion that I eat in my corner without bothering about table manners and ceremonies, it tastes to me a great deal better than turkey at other tables where I have to chew slowly, drink little, and wipe my mouth often, and where I can't sneeze and cough when I want to." [P. 85]

Hoarding his store, he challenges Quixote's idealism with a doglike protectiveness that reaches one step further back than Quixote's "blessed age" when all things were held in common: beyond the manners of arcadian courtship is a primitivism that is after all more "natural" than communal sharing. For him the Golden Age would ideally be populated with well-cared-for servants, each in his own corner. Ironically, Sancho reaffirms the hierarchy but strips aside the elaborate manners and codes that civilize it, exposing the barbarity that hovers on the periphery of most renaissance Arcadias awaiting the breakdown of propriety and ceremony.

Quixote never realizes how thoroughly his quest has been bound up in the hierarchy and codes of chivalry and how much each episode follows the same pattern of broken decorum, as the various social fictions that he has taken from books are shattered. In place of scenes of courtship and mutual recognition of worth, his adventures are made up of accidental buffetings, mistaken identities, and twisted ceremonies in which everyone plays by different rules. Quixote himself contributes to the confusion by assuming that he is Sancho's master and "natural" lord and yet that they may choose to play other roles as they please: " 'You must sit down all the same, for whosoever humbleth himself, God doth exalt.' And seizing him by the arm, Don Quixote compelled Sancho to sit beside him" (p. 85). Sancho's ravaging hunger and Quixote's social graces find a strange union that leaves the real goatherds puzzled; never having heard either of knightly codes or of Virgil, the latter understand nothing of "this gibberish about squires and knights errant," watching in silence as their guests, with good grace and appetite, cram down "lumps as big as their fists" (p. 85). Though the size of the bites indicates that hunger is the stronger partner in this union of grace and appetite, Quixote continues to yearn for the graces of nobility and the ideal brotherhood of the Golden Age.

Though Quixote fails to transform or even impress Dulcinea, his chivalric code and the conventions of shepherdom are something more than merely grist for the satirist's mill. His illusions have an appeal even for Sancho, who begs his master not to abandon his dreams:

"Oh, don't die, dear master!" answered Sancho in tears. "Take my advice and live many years. For the maddest thing a man can do in this life is to let himself die just like that, without anybody killing him, but just finished off by his own melancholy. Don't be lazy, look you, but get out of bed, and let's go out into the fields dressed as shepherds. . . . Perhaps we shall find the lady Dulcinea behind some hedge, disenchanted and as pretty as a picture." [P. 937]

What comes of these multiple refractions of conventional romance and pastoral is a deep-seated social criticism from the vantage point of the idyllic life, a criticism of the hocus-pocus of idealistic forms and conventional modes of social courtship in romance, in pastoral and, presumably, in life; and a profound regret that somehow the best of everything cannot be worked out.

Whenever the pastoral element is substantial, pastoral satire has a way of deepening its nostalgia for lost ideals and balancing criticism with lyric or elegiac moods in this way. At the same time, the stilted artifice of pastoral is vulnerable to parody, and the satirist usually finds it necessary to rid himself of them—as Rosalind rids Arden of stagey distortions of courtship in order to discover behind them the genuine harmony between social classes and lovers that the forest encourages.

Idylls, Eclogues, and Masques

Eclogues and idylls often submit the disturbances of Arcadia to a kind of soft focus and artificial stylizing that is in itself satisfying enough to make other means of dealing with them unnecessary. Theocritus's first idyll is typical in converting shepherd-bartering into the negotiations of Arcadian friendship, and unrequited love into ceremony. The polite greeting of the shepherd and the goatherd sets apart within the bucolic scene a society neither intimate nor cold but companionable enough to encourage goodwill:

Thrysis. Something sweet is the whisper of the pine that makes her music by yonder springs, and sweet no less, master Goatherd, the melody of your pipe. Pan only shall take place and prize afore you; . . . and if a she be for him, why, you shall have her kid; and kid's meat's good eating till your kids be milch-goats.[1]

The respectful deference of the speech is in keeping with nature's own politeness, as harmony spreads in rings from the rustic negotiators to Pan's universe. Yet the idealizing imagination also has to contend with very practical considerations and bits of rustic advice concerning kids and goats; it is tethered to details of husbandry. Thus the herdsmen are touched by two quite different orders, Arcadian economy and Arcadian ceremony.

Before they agree to entertain each other, they look closely at an engraved bowl that portrays a stronger kind of contention than their mild bargaining, between two men who love

[1] *The Greek Bucolic Poets,* trans. J. M. Edmonds (London: Loeb ed., 1912).

the same woman. As a desire for personal possession, basically for property, love poses a greater threat to the simplicity of Arcadian friendship than an ordinary exchange of goods. But the suggestion is that, because this second image of negotiation is at one remove from the primary characters of the dialogue, the strength of the contention can be increased without undermining the basic harmony of Arcadia. That ratio between aesthetic distance and strength of disturbance is further illustrated by another image carved on the bowl, of a fisherman in the midst of his labors:

Besides these there's an old fisher wrought on't and a rugged rock, and there stands gaffer gathering up his great net for a cast with a right good will like one that toils might and main. You would say that man went about his fishing with all the strength o's limbs, so stands every sinew in his neck, for all his grey hairs, puffed and swollen; for his strength is the strength of youth.

The muscular world of animal economy is stronger here than in the shepherd's initial and concluding involvement in the creaturely matters of milch-goats and kids. While the lovers in their stylized love contest merely become wasted and hollow-eyed, the fisherman gains sustenance and youth from his labor.

A third portrait complements the first two and restates the tension between ornamental art fixed timelessly on the bowl, the dreamy Arcadian atmosphere, and the realities of the animal economy. A boy weaves a locust cage in the midst of a lush vineyard while one of two foxes is busy plundering and the second plots to rob him, vowing that "he will not let him be till he have set him breaking his fast with but poor victuals to his drink." An exemplary escapist weaving to his heart's content, lost in the fond dream of his pet, the boy cares nothing for either adult labor or the vain strivings of lovers. But after all, he is merely a boy: Theocritus from his higher perspective on the three pastoral "poses" sees the foxes as clearly as he sees the strain of the fisherman and the futility of the lovers. The bowl presents a harmony of discords fixed in a typical Theocritean tableau—harmonious as art but realistic as implied ironic commentary. Theocritus tellingly juxtaposes the frozen world of the artifact and a moving, temporal, economic and biological life. Like the songs of the herdsmen, art is a moment aside, surrounded by the necessities of a living nature, into which the moment aside melts finally—after it has represented that nature in its symbolic forms.

Before returning to the original framework of the idyll, Theocritus has Thrysis sing an elegy on the death of Daphnis, who in turn—as song is enclosed within song—has previously lamented an unreciprocated love. The death of the shepherd and his anguish are thoroughly distanced by the stylization of the song and by Thrysis's own commentary on Daphnis's foolish magnifying of his misfortunes when, with a little common sense, he might have cured them. (Thus the singer offers a critique of what will eventually become a conventional pastoral lament.) The idyll then returns explicitly to its more solid rusticity, and we are led to interpret all the secondary or "interior" examples of art and song as a kind of truancy from labor.

The dignity of Theocritus's rustics lies in their ironic awareness of practical matters and their ready shifts among attitudes ranging from a realistic acknowledgment of economic necessities to sentimental indulgence in Arcadian emotion. Perhaps the final irony of the first idyll is that for all Daphnis's absurdity, his was finally a "pretty" death that a practical-minded goatherd will pay to hear about. Dreamy noontime songs and art are not without value in the world of barter and exchange.

The twenty-first idyll, the fisherman idyll, employs similar tactics but pushes them a step farther and inverts some of them. It begins with a portrait of stringent poverty rather than an idyllic setting:

One night against the leafy wall of a wattled cabin there lay together upon a bed of dry tangle two old catchers of fish. Besides them were laid the instruments of their calling: their creels, their rods, their hooks, their weedy nets and lines, their weels and rush-woven lobster-pots, some net-ropes. . . . This was all the means and all the riches of these poor fishermen.

Key, door, watchdog, had they none; all such things were ill-store to the likes of them, seeing in that house kept Poverty watch and ward; neither dwelt there any neighbour at their gates, but the very cabinwalls were hemmed by the soft and delicate upflowing of the sea.

Along with the litter of their "means," Asphalion, the dreamer and skillful fisherman, and his experienced older friend are distinctly etched (much as Giovanni Verga might have done it). The range of actual transformations open to them is limited since poverty will obviously remain their watch and ward, the "one stirrer-up of the crafts." It now disturbs slumber, jars quietude, and reminds them of the incongruity between what they desire and dream about, and what they have. But the contrast between the affluence of those who have key, door, and watchdog and their poverty is only one aspect of a more basic contrast, again, between the dreamlike atmosphere of Arcadia and the life of work. Though the fishermen are below city dwellers on one scale, they are beyond them on another: the sea suffuses Asphalion's dream with a beauty and peacefulness absent from the jealous watchfulness of those with property to guard.

The dialogue method is again functional in the general movement toward a reconciliation of these opposites. The act of telling and interpreting the dream is one way to handle the discrepancy between dream and reality: "Aye, we share our catch, and e'en let's share all our dreams. . . . Come, thy dream; for a friend, look you, is always told a man's dreams." The dream of "kinging" it away from the sea in luxury, while seemingly incompatible with their eating early to "give bellies short commons," suggests that in his skill as a craftsman, Asphalion lovingly performs a daily kind of dream-toil. The realism of his friend's answer does not destroy the dream; it merely questions the validity of the oath that derives from it, which would cause Asphalion to abandon his craft. Presumably if dreams can be so realistic that Asphalion catches the fish of gold bleeding at the mouth as though it were of flesh, in return he may also catch real fish as though they were of gold, or at least touched by the mystery of the sea: the "delicate up-flowing" of the sea that pervades the dream may become an aspect of daytime reality. Rather than absorbing a hostile intrusion into a pastoral scene and disposing of it, Theocritus (or an imitator) in this case allows the dream to permeate the life of labor and soften its harshness. Asphalion is too realistic to utter the cry of Caliban upon awakening:

> And then, in dreaming,
> The clouds methought would open, and show riches
> Ready to drop upon me, that when I waked
> I cried to dream again.
>
> [*The Tempest*, 3.2.149–152]

The twenty-first idyll is typical of Theocritus and his imitators in combining contrastive but reconcilable orders in the alembic of irony and humor. In the fourth idyll, Bucaeus and Milon foreshadow Sancho Panza and Don Quixote and Gay's cloddish rustics in *The Shepherd's Week* in parodying pastoral ceremonies—Bucaeus unintentionally, with a charming song of "Bombyca," and Milon with a harvest song that answers him by exploding the poses of pastoral love with hardheaded frankness: "That's the stuff for men that work in the sun to sing. And as for your starveling love, Bucaeus—tell it [to] your mother when she stirs in bed of a morning."

A similar clash works to different effect in the fifteenth idyll, in which the gossip and everyday trials of two Alexandrian housewives are eventually transcended by the noble celebration of Adonis. If the tactics of the first and twenty-first idylls might be described as the discovery of symbolic dimensions in real life through art and dreams, in the fifteenth idyll, the new dimensions discovered in art are only a holiday matter. Forcing their way through a crowd resentful of their pushiness, they pass through a form of ordeal on their way to a poetic ceremony. The rituals in a sense translate all daily trials into the general sorrow of the dying god and the beauty of the dying god reborn. But this "idyllic" translation, though it brings "some sweet thing for all," cannot quite dispel the irritation of a pressing crowd and a pressing life. The idyll ends with a return to work and the more practical palliative of wit:

O Praxinoa! what clever things we women are! I do envy her knowing all that! and still more having such a lovely voice. But I must be getting back. It's Diocleidas' dinner-time, and that man's all pepper; I wouldn't advise anyone to come near him even, when he's kept waiting for his food. Good-bye, Adonis darling; and I only trust you may find us all thriving when you come next year.

As the fifteenth idyll illustrates, Theocritus tends to interject larger amounts of humiliation into the lives of his simple characters than other pastoralists. The Virgilian eclogue, however, often does similar things more quietly, retaining the structure of contrasts and condensing them into a mellow Arcadian mood. As Erwin Panofsky remarks, Virgil's Arcadia is "sufficiently remote from Roman everyday life to defy realistic interpretation" and yet is "saturated with visual concreteness." [2] The distancing is "aesthetic" in the sense that half shadows, which create a dreamlike reverie, encroach upon the foreground action:

human suffering and superhumanly perfect surroundings create a dissonance. This dissonance, once felt, had to be resolved, and it was resolved in that . . . mixture of sadness and tranquillity which is perhaps Virgil's most personal contribution to poetry. With only slight exaggeration one might say that he "discovered" the evening. [Pp. 299–300]

In the ninth eclogue, for instance, Menalcas yearns for a harmony already past, but the mood of the eclogue is ambivalently poised between light and darkness, and Moeris suspends his judgment of the recent disruptive events that have threatened Menalcas. If and when Menalcas finds reason to rejoice, he will sing, but not yet. (His skepticism contrasts with the optimism of Lycidas, who has heard and wishes to believe pleasanter stories of the eviction which suggest that Menalcas has saved his "fortune with a song.") That poetry and hard times do not mix is Moeris's final point—but then again, one never knows, a "friend at court" might set things straight.

[2] Erwin Panofsky, *"Et in Arcadia Ego:* Poussin and the Elegiac Tradition," in *Meaning in the Visual Arts* (New York: Doubleday, 1957), p. 300.

Thus the contrasts soften into a complex Virgilian nostalgia
and are further distanced by a general philosophic realization
that, inevitably, "time bears all away," and by Moeris's nostalgic recollection, "I remember in my boyhood how I would
sing all the long summer's day." Also Phoebus, one of the
friends of the pastoral order, has protected Menalcas and
Moeris from the grim Captain; and despite the change that
"untunes" those newly exposed to wolves, the shepherds even
now sing pieces of old songs as they travel.

As opposed to pastoral-heroic figures who seek a place of
momentary rest, we have here shepherds-made-errant but still
clinging to the comforting ceremonies of Arcadian quiet. The
implication of the entwining of poetry and politics is that
nature's richness and beauty, the proper subject of idyllic
poetry, could be free for everyone—and would be, were there
the right kind of civil order. The final balance of hope and
despair is therefore an implicit rhetorical appeal to predatory
leaders as well as a passive adjustment to the fact of dispossession, half dissolved as it already is in the depths of time
and decay. This mood is clinched by the shepherds' arrival at
the tomb of Bianor, where artisan laborers have erected a
memorial to the ancient founder of Mantua. The scene embodies an intangible atmosphere of regret, beauty, resignation,
and nostalgia for the past.

For such functions as Virgil here reserves for them, shepherds need no longer be rustic, nor Arcadia a real place. The
atmosphere itself is capable of absorbing virtually any subject
into its general solvent. If combinations of fantasy and pointed
realism make Theocritean idylls into parables, Virgil's encounters, situated on the edge of confusion, resemble dramatic in-
terludes; they convert the symbolic content of the parable into
a form of stylized social drama. (A simple turn in eighteenth-
century imitations makes the eclogue into a medium for social
eulogy. Virgil's melancholy becomes the languishing humbleness of the poet, who adopts rusticity as a convenient mask
and sets about thanking a patron for help in salvaging the
arts.) The opening exchange between Meliboeus and Tityrus,
in the first eclogue, is typical:

MELIBOEUS

Tityrus, thou where thou liest under the covert of spreading beach, broodest on thy slim pipe over the Muse of the woodland: we leave our native borders and pleasant fields; we fly our native land, while thou, Tityrus, at ease in the shade teachest the woods to echo fair Amaryllis.

TITYRUS

O Meliboeus, a god brought us this peace: for a god ever will he be to me: his altar a tender lamb from our sheepfolds shall often stain.[3]

While the peace-minded Tityrus eulogizes the powers that have given him the plenty he enjoys, Meliboeus talks of political victimizing. One remains apparently above time while the other is engulfed in mutability (the reverse side of pastoral transformation). The key to Virgilian pastoral effects is the poise itself, which offers momentary stays against confusion while it measures blessings against deprivation. Again the dialogue form of the eclogue proves useful in establishing the equipoise, one flying, the other sitting still, each representing one part of the spectrum of pastoral opposites. They are tenor and bass to each other, opposites harmoniously negotiating, which, on second glance, prove to be not so distinctly different as they first seem: Meliboeus is without envy, and Tityrus is in fact not above time but growing old. Meliboeus hymns his friend's good luck while Tityrus, brooding on his pipe, in turn eases the suffering of his friend: "here for tonight thou mightst rest with me on green boughs: we have mellow apples and soft chestnuts." Then operalike they fade into evening as "shadows fall larger from the high hills."

Frost supplies us with modern equivalents to many of these variants of idyll and eclogue form and demonstrates even more convincingly the inappropriateness of standard critical terms for them, which stress the idyllic escapism of pastoral rather

[3] *Virgil's Works,* trans. J. W. Mackail (New York: Random House, 1950). Subsequent quotations are from this translation.

than its typical contrasts. He credited Virgil's eclogues for revealing to him the possibilities of the speaking voice, a crucial matter for his own versions of pastoral. Though Theocritus might have done equally well, the connection is by no means strained. The beginning of the dialogue between Lycidas and Moeris, for instance, could easily have suggested the kind of dramatic encounter and speech cadence that Frost, distrustful of Tennysonian "music," had not yet found a way to handle. The poem is situated precariously on the threshold of anxiety, both by the slight surprise of the speaker and by the symbolic implications of the unusual trip to town by the dispossessed shepherd: "Quo te, Moeri, pedes? an, quo via ducit, in urbem?" ("Where are you headed, Moeris? Does your way lead to town?"). Likewise, the eagerness of Lycidas (at Bianor's tomb) to return to song is subtly reinforced by a stepping up of the pace, a ceremonial repetition of "hic," and the gesture to help carry the load if only they can sing as they go:

> hic, ubi densas
> Agricolae stringunt frondes, hic, Moeri, canamus;
> Hic haedos depone, tamen veniemus in urbem.
> Aut si nox pluviam ne colligat ante veremur,
> Cantantes licet usque (nimus via laedit) eamus;
> Cantantes ut eamus, ego hoc te fasce levabo.

(Here, where rustics strip the thick-leaved sprays, here, Moeris, let us sing; here set down thy kids; for all that, we shall reach the town. Or if we fear lest night ere then gather to rain, we may go singing all the way; so the road wearies the less: that we may go singing, I will lighten thee of this bundle.)

Given such situations and the techniques of dialogue, Frost had only to look closely at the local dramas of his own place and time and symbolic eclogues emerged everywhere. In such "modern Georgics" (as Pound called them, confusing Virgil's two distinct forms) as "The Death of the Hired Man," "A Servant to Servants," "The Housekeeper," "The Self-Seeker," and "The Code" in *North of Boston,* what might have been becomes a distant echo in the tangle of what is, the deficiencies of which concern an unhealthy farm economy or a domestic relation gone sour or a natural disaster. In Frost's most effective dramatic poems, parabolic implications arise naturally out of such dialogue exchanges.[4]

"A Masque of Reason" illustrates both that dramatic technique and its expansion into the more ambitious form of the masque, which off and on in the tradition stands between the pastoral eclogue and full-fledged drama. The setting is an idyllic spot surrounded by waste, a "fair oasis in the purest desert," roughly equivalent to the traditional *locus amoenus,* and it is invaded, ironically, not by death or another of the traditional enemies of Arcadia but by God. The Devil "stands in for" rationality in place of the usual mediator and founder of paradise in the desert, Christ. In keeping with this mythological heightening of Frost's normal domestic contests, the wife is given a keen edge and Job suggests Milton's Adam more than an ordinary Frostean bucolic figure. But the outbreaks of Job and his wife in the blunt idiom of simple people cross the eloquence we might normally have expected from an adamic encounter with God. The masque is in part a contrast of styles, as traditionally the pastoral masque normally is with its alternating scenes of wild rout and musical, sacred order. In this case, the collision between colloquial speech and expected decorum reflects the discrepancy between the absolute "high singular" and poetic design that the artist in Job seeks and the little "arrangement" they eventually settle for under his wife's realistic guidance. Corresponding to the artifice of traditional masques and eclogues is the wife's fixing of their antagonism in a snapshot and her admonition to God, Job, and the Devil to smile. Turning on gold-enameled-artificial-birds for Yeatsian sound effects and lighting the Mosaic bush, she is ready for a representation of them, a photographic likeness, slightly doctored by the arrangement. The contest between

[4] Cf. the discussion of Frost's eclogue forms in Reuben A. Brower, *The Poetry of Robert Frost* (New York: Oxford University Press, 1963), pp. 152–179, and John F. Lynen, *The Pastoral Art of Robert Frost* (New Haven: Yale University Press, 1960), pp. 108–139. Quotations are from *Complete Poems* (London: Jonathan Cape, 1951).

them finishes in a static, symmetrical pose, as they are locked in a pleasant-appearing improvement of their normal relationship.

Unlike the shepherds of most eclogues, characters in pastoral masques normally participate in a spirit of make-believe like this, often (in court masques) behind transparent disguises. Thus courtiers and gods masquerade as shepherds, women as men, and recognizable personages as various allegorical figures. This make-believe allows different levels to consort together—the divine with the human, the mythological with the political, the artificial with the natural. It allows combinations of myth and wit suitable to the devilish spirit of Pan, who is both god and imp, real and elusive. When conscious of its own devices, the masque technique provides a way of mirroring the artifice of social masks and styles and of reflecting upon art itself—especially upon possible ways to make the ceremonies, costumes, and music of the masque answerable to those tutelary spirits responsible for the harmony and the riot of nature (Pan, Astrea, Jove and Comus, and in Frost's version, God and his necessary adversary). Jonson's gods and goddesses, Milton's Sabrina and the Countess Dowager of Derby, and Frost's humble wife of Job all become poet's helpers in staging visible principles of order in the symbolic devices of masque pageantry. At the same time, the masque's awareness that it is a show maintains an appropriate distance between the things it represents and the photo copy. Hence, the metamorphoses that narrative and lyric passages describe in Ovidian pastoral, the masque puts before us as changes of scene and costume, in an atmosphere of music and symbolic pageantry.

Selected Secondary Bibliography

This list contains primarily theoretical items or works either marginal or not mentioned in footnotes that might tend to be overlooked. It does not include the bulk of practical criticism on major figures.

Arthos, John. *The Language of Natural Description in Eighteenth-century Poetry*. Ann Arbor: University of Michigan Press, 1949.

Aubin, Robert Arnold. *Topographical Poetry in Eighteenth-century England*. New York: Modern Language Association, 1936.

Beach, Joseph Warren. *The Concept of Nature in Nineteenth-century English Poetry*. New York, 1936.

Blair, Hugh. *Lectures on Rhetoric and Belles Lettres*. Lecture no. 39, "Pastoral Poetry—Lyric Poetry." London, 1801.

Blunden, Edmund. *Nature in English Poetry*. London, 1929.

Booth, Edward Townsend. *God Made the Country*. New York, 1946.

Broughton, Leslie Nathan. *The Theocritean Element in the Works of William Wordsworth*. Halle, 1920.

Bryan, J. Ingram. *The Feeling for Nature in English Pastoral Poetry*. Tokyo, 1908.

Calderwood, James L., and Harold E. Toliver. "Introduction to Pastoral." In *Forms of Poetry*. Englewood Cliffs, N.J.: Prentice-Hall, 1968.

Carrara, Enrico. *La Poesia Pastorale*. Milano, 1909.

Chambers, E. K. *English Pastorals*. London, n.d.

Congleton, J. E. *Theories of Pastoral Poetry in England, 1684–1798*. Gainesville: University of Florida Press, 1952.

Danby, John F. *Poets on Fortune's Hill: Studies in Sidney, Shakespeare, Beaumont and Fletcher*. London: Faber and Faber, 1952.

Deane, C. V. *Aspects of Eighteenth-century Nature Poetry*. London: Oxford University Press, 1935.

Dike, Donald. "The Difficult Innocence: Blake's Songs and Pastoral," *ELH*, 28 (1961), 353–375.

Durling, Dwight L. *Georgic Tradition in English Poetry*. New York, 1935.

Empson, William. *Some Versions of Pastoral*. London: Chatto and Windus, 1935.

Fairchild, Hoxie Neale. *The Noble Savage: A Study in Romantic Naturalism*. New York, 1928.

Fontenelle. "Discours sur la nature de l'églogue," *Oeuvres*. Vol. 3. Paris, 1818.

Frye, Northrop. "Blake's Treatment of the Archetype," *English Institute Essays* (1950), pp. 170–196.

——. *Fearful Symmetry: A Study of William Blake*. Princeton: Princeton University Press, 1947.

Giamatti, A. Bartlett. *The Earthly Paradise and the Renaissance Epic*. Princeton: Princeton University Press, 1966.

Grant, W. Leonard. "Later Neo-Latin Pastoral: I," *SP*, 53 (1956), 429–451.

Graves, Robert. "The Pastoral." In *The Common Asphodel*. London, 1949.

Greg, Walter W. *Pastoral Poetry and Pastoral Drama*. London, 1906.

Haddakin, Lilian. *The Poetry of Crabbe*. London: Chatto and Windus, 1955.

Herrick, Marvin T. "Pastoral Tragicomedy." In *Tragicomedy*. Urbana: University of Illinois Press, 1955.

Johnson, Samuel. *Rambler* 36, 37 (July, 1750).

Johnstone, Paul H. "The Rural Socrates," *JHI*, 5 (1944), 151–175.

Jones, Richard F. "Eclogue Types in English Poetry of the Eighteenth Century," *JEGP*, 24 (1925), 33–60.

Kermode, Frank, ed. *English Pastoral Poetry from the Beginnings to Marvell*. London, 1952.

——. Introduction to *The Tempest*. London: Methuen and Co., 1954.

Laidler, Josephine. "A History of Pastoral Drama in England until 1700," *Englische Studien*, 35 (1905), 191–259.

Lewis, R. W. B. *The American Adam*. Chicago: University of Chicago Press, 1955.

Lievsay, John Leon. "Italian *Favole Boscarecce* and Jacobean Stage Pastoralism." In *Essays on Shakespeare and Elizabethan Drama*. Ed. Richard Hosley. Columbia: University of Missouri Press, 1962.

Lilly, Marie Loretto. *The Georgic*. Baltimore, 1917.

Lovejoy, Arthur O. " 'Nature' as Aesthetic Form," *MLN*, 42 (1927), 444–450.

Lynen, John. *The Pastoral Art of Robert Frost*. New Haven: Yale University Press, 1960.

MacLean, Kenneth. *Agrarian Age: A Background for Wordsworth*. New Haven: Yale University Press, 1950.

Magowan, Robin. "Fromentin and Jewett: Pastoral Narrative in the Nineteenth Century," *CL*, 16 (1964), 331–337.

Mantz, Harold Elmer. "Non-dramatic Pastoral in the Eighteenth Century," *PMLA,* 31 (1916), 421–447.

Marks, Jeannette. *English Pastoral Drama from the Restoration to the Date of . . . the 'Lyrical Ballads.'* London, 1908.

Marx, Leo. *The Machine in the Garden.* New York: Oxford University Press, 1964.

Moorman, Frederic W. *William Browne: His Britannia's Pastorals and the Pastoral Poetry of the Elizabethan Age.* Strassburg, 1897.

Panofsky, Erwin. "Et in Arcadia Ego," in *Meaning in the Visual Arts.* New York: Doubleday, 1957.

Poggioli, Renato. "Naboth's Vineyard or the Pastoral View of the Social Order," *JHI,* 24 (1963), 3–24.

———. "The Oaten Flute," *Harvard Library Bulletin,* 11 (1957), 147–184.

———. "The Pastoral of the Self," *Daedalus,* 88 (1959), 686–699.

Purney, Thomas. *A Full Enquiry into the True Nature of Pastoral.* Augustan Reprint Society no. 4, 1948.

Puttenham, George. *The Arte of English Poesie.* Bk. I, chap. 18. Ed. Gladys D. Willcock and Alice Walker. Cambridge, 1936.

Reynolds, Myra. *The Treatment of Nature in English Poetry between Pope and Wordsworth.* New York: Gordian Press, 1966. (First published in 1909.)

Røstvig, Maren-Sofie. *The Happy Man.* Oslo, 1954.

Sewell, Elizabeth. *The Orphic Voice: Poetry and Natural History.* New Haven: Yale University Press, 1960.

Smith, Hallett. "Pastoral Poetry." In *Elizabethan Poetry: A Study in Conventions, Meaning and Expression.* Cambridge, Mass.: Harvard University Press, 1952.

Snell, Bruno. "Arcadia: The Discovery of a Spiritual Landscape." In *The Discovery of Mind.* Trans. T. G. Rosenmeyer. Oxford: Blackwell, 1953.

Stewart, Stanley. *The Enclosed Garden.* Madison: University of Wisconsin Press, 1966.

Tayler, Edward William. *Nature and Art in Renaissance Literature.* New York: Columbia University Press, 1964.

Tickell, Thomas [?]. *The Guardian.* Nos. 22, 23, 28, 30, 32. London: April, 1740.

Trowbridge, Hoyt. "Pope, Gay, and *The Shepherd's Week,*" *MLQ* 5 (1944), 79–88.

Truesdale, Calvin William. "English Pastoral Verse from Spenser to Marvel." Ph.D. dissertation, University of Washington, 1956.

Unwin, Rayner. *The Rural Muse: Studies in Peasant Poetry of England.* London: George Allen and Unwin, 1954.

Walker, Roy. *The Golden Feast.* London, 1952.

White, H. O. "Thomas Purney: A Forgotten Poet and Critic of the Eighteenth Century," *Essays and Studies,* 15 (1929), 67–97.

Wicksteed, Joseph H. *Blake's Innocence and Experience.* London, 1928.

Willey, Basil. *The Religion of Nature.* London, 1957.

Wilson, Harold S. "Meanings of 'Nature' in Renaissance Literature," *JHI,* 2 (1941), 430–448.

Wind, Edgar. "Pan and Proteus." In *Pagan Mysteries in the Renaissance.* New Haven: Yale University Press, 1958.

Winn, Norman Field. "The Treatment of Humble Life in the Poetry of George Crabbe and William Wordsworth." Ph.D. dissertation, University of Washington, 1955.

Wolff, Samuel Lee. *The Greek Romances in Elizabethan Prose Fiction.* New York: Burt Franklin, 1961. (First published in 1912.)

Index